Access™
INSIDER

THE WILEY INSIDER SERIES

If you think this book is just another computer book, stop right there. I am proud to tell you that this book is part of a stunning new series created by the Coriolis Group and published by John Wiley & Sons. What you're holding is a "tour-de-force" of Access insider tips, secrets, undocumented features, shortcuts, and technical advice that has never been available in a book format like this.

Margaret Levine Young, long-time Access expert and author, has gathered together her best tips and techniques based on her many years of experience to create this sixth book in the INSIDER series. The book is jam-packed with innovative ideas for using and customizing Access in ways you never thought possible. But the real kicker is that the unique format of this book will help you understand and use the tips and techniques presented as if a friendly expert were at your side, ready to answer any question you might have.

In creating the new INSIDER series, we wanted to break with tradition and develop books that go way beyond the typical "documentation approach" of most computer books. In each INSIDER book, we'll show you how to customize your software, put new features to work right away, work smarter and faster, and solve difficult problems.

What you're holding represents an innovative and highly practical guide that was developed by some of the best minds in computer book publishing. We hope you enjoy each and every INSIDER guide.

—Keith Weiskamp
INSIDER Series Editor

Access™ INSIDER

Margaret Levine Young

Keith Weiskamp, Series Editor

John Wiley & Sons, Inc.

New York • Chichester • Brisbane • Toronto • Singapore

Library of Congress Cataloging-in-Publication Data

Young, Margaret Levine.
    Access insider / Margaret Levine Young.
        p.   cm.
    "Coriolis Group book."
    Includes index
    ISBN 0-471-30430-1 (paper)
    1. Data base management. 2. Microsoft Access. I. Title.
  Qa76.9.D3Y68 1993
  005.75'65--dc20   93-28663
                             CIP

Printed in the United States of America

10 9 8 7 6 5 4 3 2 1

This book is dedicated to my sisters, Ruth DiAngelo and Audrey Wynne, their husbands, Ted and Donald, and to their children, Dana, Teddy, Sean, and Kyle—part of our next computer generation.

Contents

Part 2 Forms and Datasheet Shortcuts   101

Chapter 4 Data Entry Shortcuts   103

Chapter 8   Making Dynamic Forms

Chapter 10   Summarizing Data with Total and Crosstab Queries   261

Chapter 13 Printing Subtotals, Totals, and Other Calculations 349

Chapter 14 Sample Report Formats 379

Chapter 17 An Introduction to Access Basic   487

Introduction

When Microsoft released Access at the end of 1992, users welcomed it as the first major relational database for Windows. Access combined the power of relational database management programs like Paradox and dBASE IV with the ease-of-use and elegance of the Windows interface. Microsoft had been working on the program for years, had beta-tested it extensively, and hundreds of thousands of users flocked to buy it.

Access was designed from the ground up to be a graphical, mouse-driven program, and takes full advantage of the mouse for designing and using all the objects in a database. It is fun to use, because you can create impressive-looking applications very quickly, including beautifully formatted forms and reports.

However, Access is also a complicated program. It has an incredibly rich set of features, including two complete programming languages. Although it's easy to get started with Access, it is also easy to miss many shortcuts and useful features. After learning a basic set of commands, many Access users never advance beyond that stage, and continue to perform tasks that Access could streamline or completely automate—if only they knew how.

The purpose of the book is to help you make Access work for you, minimizing repetitive commands and data entry whenever possible. This book contains shortcuts, tricks, handy macros, and Access Basic procedures for making your Access databases smarter. The topics cover both mouse and keyboard techniques and suggest ways to use them. Some techniques are completely undocumented, some are described only in the Access online Help system, and some are incompletely described in the Access documentation. You can use this book to make your Access databases easier to use and to make Access more fun.

How the Book Is Organized

Access Insider is divided into five parts, which contain related chapters based on the types of tasks you want to perform. Each part begins with a brief description of the chapters it contains, so you can quickly find the information you need.

Part 1, *Designing and Creating Databases*, describes how to design a database as efficiently as possible, how to move a database application from another database program to Access, and how to maintain your databases.

Part 2, *Forms and Datasheet Shortcuts*, discusses ways to view data on-screen. This portion of the book starts with general tips that apply to both datasheets and forms, then progresses into the details of form design, including using macros to make "smart" forms.

Part 3, *Query Techniques*, reveals tips for selecting, relating, summarizing, and cross-tabulating information in your tables using queries.

Part 4, *Designing Effective Reports*, contains techniques for designing and printing reports and forms, including step-by-step procedures for creating commonly used report formats like mailing labels, envelopes, columnar reports, and invoices.

Finally, Part 5, *Customizing Access*, shows how you can configure Access' default settings, how to use macros and Access Basic procedures to automate tasks, and how to create your own functions using Access Basic.

Conventions

This book uses typographical conventions to make it easier for you to distinguish Access commands, properties, and keystrokes from descriptive text. When I define a new term, it appears in *italics* in the text. Names of menus, commands, dialog boxes, and properties appear with Initial Capital Letters. Properties are spelled as they appear on the screen, with spaces between words. Keys that you press appear in **bold type**. Text that you type appears on a separate line like this:

```
msaccess.ini
```

The Goals of This Book

Because Access is a complex, feature-rich program, no book can contain all the information about it. Many introductory books lead you through the basics of creating tables, queries, forms, and reports. *Access Insider* is a more practical, hands-on book—I assume that you are already using Access, that you have already created a database or two, and that you want to know how to use Access more effectively. It is not a programming book—Access Basic is a complete programming language that merits a book all its own—but the tips and techniques in this book are useful for beginners and programmers alike.

Access comes with hundreds of pages of documentation, and the last thing you need is the same information again. In writing this book, I followed the guidelines characteristic of the *Insider* series:

1. *If the documentation covers a topic well, I don't.* For example, the Access *Introduction to Programming* contains an excellent guide to debugging and testing Access Basic procedures, so this book doesn't repeat this information. Instead, I include sample procedures you can use in your databases, as well as general information on how to write useful functions.

2. *If the documentation only hints at a feature, I tell you more about how to use it.* The Microsoft Access *User's Guide* frequently refers you to the online Help, or completely omits important topics. These are the topics you'll find in this book. For example, the documentation doesn't say much about configuring Access, so I devote a chapter to it.

3. *I organize the information the way you use it.* Rather than grouping topics by feature, I group them by tasks you want to do. For example, if you are planning to print mailing labels and envelopes, you may consider using either the Mailing Label ReportWizard or exporting the information as a merge file for use with Word for Windows. Rather than including one topic under "Reports" and the other under "Exporting," they appear together so that you can easily decide between the two approaches.

4. *I include information that is not in the documentation.* The Access documentation is clearly written and contains a wealth of information. However, it doesn't cover everything, so this book picks up where the manuals leave off. For example, I couldn't find any information in the Access *User's Guide* about entering international characters into Text fields, so I included a topic with two ways to do it. I also cover Windows features that are useful for Access, such as creating a program item in the Windows Program Manager for your frequently used databases.

Features of This Book

This book is not designed to be read cover to cover. Instead, its modular design helps you find the topic that interests you and get the answers you need quickly. Each chapter is divided into major sections, like *Using Command-Line Options* and *Customizing the Toolbar*. Each section contains a general introduction, and is then divided into topics, such as *Making an Icon for a Database* or *Speeding Up Access*. Each topic begins with a scenario that describes a problem you may encounter and the remainder of the topic shows you the solution.

HOT TIP

Sprinkled throughout this book you will find *Hot Tips*, such as *Temporarily Suspend Snap to Grid* and *Give a Button an Access Key*, which reveal little-known techniques or ways to use Access features that you may not have considered.

Companion Disk

Access comes with several excellent sample databases, and it is well worth your time to explore them. However, Access can be used for many other types of databases, which are not included in these samples. As a result, I created an optional companion disk for *Access Insider*, which includes:

- *Sample Access Databases* that illustrate many of the techniques covered in this book, including all the tables, queries, forms, reports, macros, and Access Basic procedures that I describe.

- *Microsoft Access Knowledge Base*, an online Help file that contains many additional tips and bug reports about Access. Microsoft created this file and updates it every few months.

Another terrific source of sample databases and utilities is the CompuServe MSACCESS forum. The forum contains many databases created either by Access users or by the Microsoft Product Support Staff. To see a complete list of the files available, go to section 1 of the MSACCESS forum and download the file CATLOG.ZIP. For the latest version of the Microsoft Knowledge Base for Access, download the file ACC-KB.ZIP from section 1—but be warned that it is huge (around 1Mb). Throughout this book, I mention utilities and Wizards that have been created by Microsoft and are available for downloading from the MSACCESS forum. For information on CompuServe, call 800-848-8990 (or 0800 289458 in the U.K.).

Because many files on the MSACCESS forum are large, they have been compressed using the PKZIP utility. You will need the PKUNZIP utility to "unzip" these compressed files. You can download PKUNZIP from section 10 of the PCVENC forum on CompuServe, or you can order it from PKWare, Inc. at 414-354-8699.

Acknowledgments

Writing any book requires lots of help, including editing, proofing, and general encouragement. A book like this one, which is full of tips and tricks, requires additional technical help from other users and support personnel as I figure out how to use undocumented features and try out different approaches to problems.

I'd like to thank Christine Rivera for starting me on the path toward this book, as well as Matt Wagner, Bill Gladstone, Paul Farrell, and Allison Roarty for help to make it happen. Keith Weiskamp, the *Insider* series editor, provided tremendous support, technical expertise, and wisdom in the ways of authors. Many thanks are also due to Jenni Aloi-Wolfson, Robin Watkins, Pat Vincent, Brad Grannis, Rob Mauhar, and Erica Schrimsher for their careful help.

Much of the information in this book was gleaned from the questions and answers on the MSACCESS forum on CompuServe. Both the Microsoft Product Support Services staff and interested Access users do a great job of answering questions, and I especially appreciate the help I received from Kim Abercrombie, Scott Austin, Neil Black, Brian Blackman, MariEsther Burnham, Jim Ferguson, Don Funk, Ken Getz, Ryan LaBrie, Jim Hance, Kim Hightower, Joe Howard, Tim Leidig, Dan Madoni, Tim O'Brien, and W. Craig Trader, as well as everyone on the MSACCESS forum who asked such good questions.

I appreciate the willingness of Ross Hunter, Microsoft Access Product Manager, to allow me to include the Microsoft Access Knowledge Base on the Companion Diskette for this book.

And finally, most of all I thank Jordan, who even took our two-year-old on vacation when I fell behind schedule!

Access™

INSIDER

Part Overview

1 Good Database Design 5

You will find out how to create an efficient, well-designed database, avoiding redundancy and un-needed fields.

2 Migrating from Other Programs 39

In this chapter, you will learn strategies for moving your information from another database program—or a spreadsheet or text file—into Access.

3 Maintaining Access Databases 71

Learn how to document your databases so that new users can easily get up to speed using them and more advanced users can maintain them. You will also find out how and when to back up, repair, and compact databases.

PART 1

Designing and Creating Databases

The chapters in this first part of the book concentrate on smart ways to implement new databases. By designing a new database carefully, you can save hours or even days of work when you create and use it. And because many Access databases start with information stored in other files, you can save time by importing your information into your Access tables.

Chapter 1 demonstrates how to design a database from scratch, determining what tables to create, how to relate the tables, and what fields to include in each table. Chapter 2 helps you move data from any existing database, spreadsheet, word-processing, or text file into Access, as well as how to work directly with information in other formats by attaching to external tables. Chapter 3 discusses database maintenance—how to keep your database running smoothly, including how to make backups in an efficient and safe manner.

CHAPTER 1

Good Database Design

Creating a database in Access, as with all other database programs, takes a good deal of planning. How easy it is later to create useful queries, forms, and reports depends on how your database is designed. A good database design can streamline your work in Access.

In this chapter, you'll find pointers for designing tables for an Access database, using the right fields and field types for the job. First, you'll see how to determine how many tables to create, and which fields belong in each. Then, you'll find tips for choosing field types, lengths, and other characteristics that make your Access database easy to use. You'll see several examples of database design, including a membership database for a non-profit organization like a club, church, or synagogue.

Designing a Multi-Table Database

Access allows you to create as many tables as you need for your application. The tables in a database are usually related, so that you can combine data from several tables in queries, forms, and reports. Tables can be related to each other in several types of relationships: one-to-many, one-to-one, or many-to-many.

Designing One-to-Many Relationships

Use two tables with a one-to-many relationship if there are different numbers of values for different fields.

The *one-to-many relationship* is the most common way to relate two tables. A one-to-many relationship is one in which a single record in a table corresponds to no record, one record, or many records in another table. For example, an application for a non-profit organization that tracks both the groups members and their donations would include a listing of each member and that member's donation(s). One member can make no, one, or many donations.

One way to tell whether your application will require multiple tables is if your initial design indicates that there are different numbers of values for different fields. Let's say your organization has 500 members and receives approximately 1,200 donations a year. You have 500 different member names, addresses, and phone numbers, while you have 1,200 different donation dates and amounts. Because it is likely that some members may have made multiple donations, while others have made none, you should store the information in at least two different tables—a Members table with 500 records and a Donations table with 1,200 records. By using two tables, the data will be stored more efficiently, and sorting and searching will be faster.

The Members table would contain the member information—the member's name, address, and phone number. The Donations table would contain the donation information—the date, amount, and name of the member who made it, as shown in Figure 1.1. In this figure (and other figures showing a one-to-many relationship between tables), there is a small black dot at the "one" end of each arrow showing the relationship to the "many," in this case, a member who makes multiple donations.

You could store this information in a single table, adding the member information to the Donations table and entering the member name, address, and phone over and over for each donation. But this approach is not only a waste of time and disk space, it makes the data harder to maintain. Here are some problems you encounter by using one table when you should use two:

- If a member moves, you have to change the address in every donation. If you store member information only in the Members table, you change the address in just one place.
- Until a member makes a donation, there is no record in the Donations table in which to store the member's name and address.
- When a member leaves, there is no good way to indicate this. You can't erase all the donations the member made, because your financial records would then be wrong.

The table with the fewest records, in this case the Members table, is frequently called the *master table* or *primary table*. The table with most records, in this case the Donations table, is called the *detail table* or *related table*. There is a one-to-many relationship between the Members

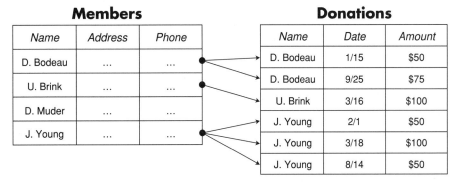

Figure 1.1 A one-to-many relationship between the Members and Donations tables.

and Donations tables. This term is misleading because it is quite possible that a member has not made any donations and is in no way related to the Donations table. However, there should be only one record in the master table for each record in the detail table. Each donation is made by one member.

Designing One-to-One Relationships

Use two tables with a one-to-one relationship if you are storing two different, independent types of information.

You may also use relational lookups to connect two tables where there is a *one-to-one relationship* between the records. For example, if you want to store a great deal of information about each employee in your company, you may want to divide it into several tables. You can put the confidential information in a separate table from the non-confidential information. But at times, you want to print out all the information about each person.

You could create two tables: an Employees tables containing non-confidential information, and a Salaries table containing salary and other confidential information These tables are shown in Figure 1.2. Both tables would include an Employee Number field, which would link the tables together by indicating which record in the Employees table corresponds to which record in the Salaries table. In this case, there should always be one record in Employees for each record in Salaries, and vice versa.

Another reason to use a one-to-one relationship is if some information is needed for only a small subset of the records in the table. For example, if some of the employees sign up to work on the annual charity auction, there is no point storing information about what job they have volunteered for in the Employees table. For most employees, the field would be blank. Instead, you should create a new table for the charity auction information, and relate it to the Employees table by including the Employee Number field, as shown in Figure 1.3. With a one-to-one relationship, there can be only one record (or no record) in one table for each record in the other table.

Employees

Emp. No.	Name	Address
1001	B. Bryant	...
1002	D. Kay	...
1003	F. Weeks	...

Salaries

Emp. No.	Annual Salary
1001	$42,500
1002	$27,000
1003	$35,000

Figure 1.2 A one-to-one relationship between the Employees and Salaries tables.

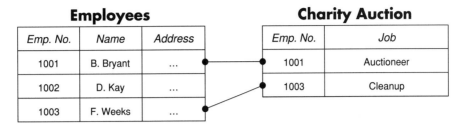

Figure 1.3   A one-to-one relationship between the Employees and Charity Auction tables.

Designing Many-to-Many Relationships

Use an intermediate table to turn a many-to-many relationship into two one-to-many relationships.

Sometimes in a multi-table application there can be many records in one table that relate to many records in the other table. For example, suppose your non-profit organization is subdivided into several committees, and you want to store information about who is on what committee. In this situation, you could add a table for Committees, with information about each committee—its name, its budget, and its type (standing or ad hoc). The relationship between the Members table and the Committees table is many-to-many—one member can be on many committees, and one committee can have many members, as shown in Figure 1.4.

Access cannot store many-to-many relationships directly. Neither can any other relational database program, because many-to-many relationships are not part of the relational model (the way relational databases work). To store this information, you must turn the many-to-many relationship into two one-to-many relationships, by adding a new table.

For example, to store who is on what committee, you can make a new table called Committee Assignments, shown in Figure 1.5. The Committee

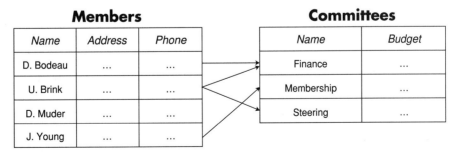

Figure 1.4   A many-to-many relationship between the Members and Committees tables.

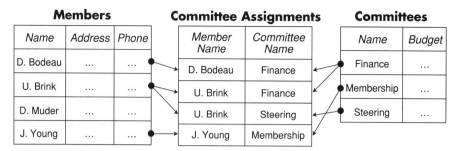

Figure 1.5   Creating a new table to store a many-to-many relationship.

Assignments table contains just two fields: the member's name (or other identifying information, like a membership number) and the committee name. For each member, there can be no, one, or many records in the Committee Assignments table, depending on whether the member is on no, one, or many committees. For each committee, there can be no, one, or many records, indicating that there are no, one, or many members on it. This new table stores the many-to-many relationship information between the Members and Committees tables.

Enforcing Referential Integrity

Use referential integrity to ensure that there is one record in the master table that relates to each record in the detail table.

Once you have determined that two tables are related, you can decide whether to enforce referential integrity between them. *Enforcing referential integrity* means that entries are not allowed in the related (detail) table unless there is already a corresponding entry in the primary (master) table. For example, you might decide to enforce referential integrity for the relationship between the Members and Donations tables, where the Members table is the primary table and the Donations table is the related table. Access would then prevent you from entering donations from a member if there is no record in the Members table for that member. This is an extremely valuable type of validation, and Access can do this automatically, with no programming.

There are also cases in which you may not want to enforce referential integrity. For example, you may accept donations from outside sources, so there are donations that do not come from members. In this case, it is still a good idea to set up a relationship between the Members and Donations tables so that for donations from members, you can look up information about the members. But you should not enforce referential integrity, so you can enter records in the Donations table that don't relate to any record in the Members table.

Steps for Designing Your Database

Efficient databases are the result of good database design and planning. Choose carefully when deciding what tables to create and what fields to include. If you include extra fields that you never use, you waste disk space and make processing slower. If you choose the wrong fields, you can make querying and reporting much more complicated. Luckily, Access makes it easy to fix your mistakes by changing table design even after you have entered data.

The following topics outline the most efficient procedure to determine how many tables you need, what fields should be in each table, what the primary key fields should be, and which fields relate the tables.

Stating the Problem

Know the purpose of your database, so you can include the information you will need.

State what kind of information you want to handle and what output you want to be able to produce. For example, if you are creating a system for a non-profit organization to track its membership, pledges, donations, and committees, the statement might be, "Keep a mailing list of members, so we can print mailing labels for all members and for committee members. Track pledges and donations so we can collect donations better."

To get a good idea of what the problem is, determine what kinds of reports you want to be able to get out of the database. Make "mockups" of the reports you need—examples of what the reports would look like, using real data.

Identifying the Possible Fields

List the fields the database might contain.

Find out what information is available, who maintains it, what it looks like, and how it is used. Then, make a list of the possible fields. For example, for a membership database you might end up with the list of the following fields:

```
First Name
Last Name
Address
City
State
ZIP Code
Phone Number
Male/Female
Birth Date
Age
Board Member?
Years of Membership
Annual Pledge
Amount Paid
Payee
Date Paid
Balance Due on Pledge
Date Joined
Committee Name
Committee Budget
Committee Type
Committee Members
Committee Chairs
```

Eliminating Unnecessary Fields

Get rid of fields that store information twice, or that can be calculated.

Look over the fields that you have identified to make sure that all are needed for your application. Remove any that are redundant or that aren't needed to produce the output you want.

For example, in the membership database, you might be able to leave out whether the person is male or female, because it doesn't appear on any report and is never used.

If you can calculate one field from another field, store only one. For example, you might eliminate storing the number of years each person has been a member, because you (and Access) can calculate this from the date the person joined. Also, delete the Balance Due on Pledge field, which can be recalculated every time a member makes a donation. There's no need to store both birth dates and ages, since you (and Access) can calculate ages from birth dates. Decide which piece of information you want to enter, and have Access figure out the other one as a calculated field.

You can create calculated fields in forms (see Chapter 8), queries (see Chapter 9), or reports (see Chapter 13). If you create a calculated field in a query, you can display it in a form, sort records by it, and include it in a report, just as if it were stored in a table.

Organizing the Fields into Tables

Look at the information to see if it falls into groups with one-to-one, one-to-many, or many-to-many relationships.

Next, look at the list of fields and determine if there should be one table or several related tables.

If there are different numbers of values for different fields, put them in different tables. For example, in the membership database, you might initially set up these three tables:

```
Members
First Name
Last Name
Address
City
State
ZIP Code
Phone Number
Birth Date
Date Joined
Board Member?
Annual Pledge

Donations
Payee
Amount Paid
Date Paid

Committees
Committee Name
Committee Budget
Committee Type
Committee Members
Committee Chair
```

However, the Committees table still isn't right, because for one value of Committee Name there can be lots of values of Committee Members. You could use one long Text field to contain a list of members' names, but this would prevent you from easily looking up committee members' addresses and phone numbers for a committee phone list. It is better if each member's name is in a separate field.

Instead, add a new Committee Assignments table to your design to store information about which person is on which committee. In this table, you can also include a Job field that indicates whether the person is the chair of the committee or has another specific committee job. The following list shows the revised Committee and Committee Assignments tables.

```
Committees
Committee Name
Committee Budget
Committee Type

Committee Assignments
Committee Name
Member Name
Job
```

Choosing a Primary Key for Each Table

Choose a field that is unique for each record in the table.

For most of the tables in your database, you will need a *primary key* field, which uniquely identifies the record. Any table on the "one" side of a one-to-one or one-to-many relationship will need a primary key for the relationship to work. For other tables, a primary key field can be useful. If a table has a primary key, Access displays its records sorted into order by the primary key. Also, searching by primary key is fast because Access creates an index for the field.

If there is already a unique ID code in the table, use it as the primary key. For example, if your non-profit organization issues membership numbers that are unique for each member, this would be the perfect field for the primary key of the Members table. If not, look for a field, or a combination of fields, that is unique for each record. For lists of people's names, you may be able to use a combination of first and last name, but this often fails once the list gets big. You may be able to use the telephone number field unless you will include more than one person from the same family. For lists of companies, a combination of company name and ZIP code may work (company name alone is usually not enough).

If no field or combination of fields is unique for each record, add a Counter field to the table. Access will assign a unique number to each record automatically as records are added.

For the membership database, there is no field or combination of fields that is unique for each person. We can add a Counter field, named

Membership Number, to the Members table. This will be the table's primary key.

In the Donations table, the Payee field can contain the member's Membership Number to indicate who made the donation. Assuming that members make at most one donation per day, a combination of the Payee and Date Paid fields uniquely identifies each donation.

For the Committees table, each committee has a different name, so the existing Committee Name field can serve as the primary key field. For the Committee Assignments table, there is a record for each person on each committee, so each committee name appears many times and each member's name may appear many times. Neither field by itself is unique. But the two fields together are unique—each person is on a committee only once.

The following list shows the updated design of the membership database, with primary key fields indicated by asterisks.

```
Members
* Membership Number (Counter)
First Name
Last Name
Address
City
State
ZIP Code
Phone Number
Birth Date
Date Joined
Board Member?
Annual Pledge

Donations
* Payee
* Date Paid
Amount Paid

Committees
* Committee Name
Committee Budget
Committee Type

Committee Assignments
* Committee Name
* Member Name
Job
```

How Counter Fields Work

When you add records to a table that contains a Counter field, Access automatically fills in the field with the next available integer, starting with one for the first record. If you want to number your records starting with another number, see *Starting a Counter at a Number Other Than One* later in this chapter.

You can't modify the contents of a Counter. When you delete a record, Access does not reuse the value of its Counter field.

Choosing Key Fields to Relate the Tables

Use fields with the same type and size.

For two tables to be related there must be one field (or a group of fields) in one table that relates to one field (or a group) in the other table. In at least one of the tables, the field must be the primary key. How this works depends on the type of relationship between the tables: one-to-many, one-to-one, or many-to-many.

In one-to-many relationships, include a field in the detail table (the "many" side of the relationship) to relate to the primary key field from the master table (the "one" side of the relationship). The field in the detail table is called a *foreign key,* indicating that it relates to the primary key field in some other table. For example, to relate the Members and Donations tables, include a field in the Donations table that relates to the primary key field from the Members table, Membership Number. It can be the Payee field, since it identifies who made the donation.

In one-to-one relationships, the related fields are the primary key fields in both tables. For example, in a personnel database with an Employees table and a Salaries table, each table contains a primary key field that uniquely identifies the employee each record describes. It is usually an employee number. When you are designing your database, use these primary key fields to relate the Employee table to the Salaries table.

In many-to-many relationships, you must create an intermediary table that contains the primary key fields of the two tables you want to relate. Each of the tables is related to the new table by its primary key. The new table contains two foreign key fields. In our example, we have already created this table (Committee Assignments) to store the many-to-many relationship between the Members and Committees tables. The Committee Assignments table contains a field that relates to the primary key field in Committees (Committee Name). We can change the other field in Committee Assignments from Member Name to Membership Number, so it relates to the primary key field in Members (Membership Number).

In all of these relationships, you can use one field to relate the tables, or you can use a group of fields. For example, if the master table's primary key consists of two fields, the detail table contains two corresponding related fields.

Choosing Names, Types, and Sizes for Fields

Keep table and field names short, descriptive, and readable. Use the same field types for related fields, except for Counter fields.

You will use table and field names often in Access as you design forms, reports, and macros. Give your tables and fields clear, concise names so that you can remember what's what later on.

Some people like to use capital letters for table names and mixed case for field names so it is immediately obvious which is which. For example, your membership database might be called MEMBERS, containing tables named Members, Donations, and Committees. In this book, as in the Microsoft Access documentation, you'll see both table and field names displayed with initial capital letters.

Choose field types and sizes based on what fields will contain. For sizes, consider where the information will appear on forms and reports, and how much space they will have. There's no point allowing space for 50-character street addresses if only 35 characters fit across your mailing labels. You'll find tips for choosing field types in the next section of this chapter.

For related fields, be sure to use the same type and size in both tables. For example, if the Committee Name field in the Committees table is a 20-character Text field, the Committee Name field in the Committee Assignments table should also be a 20-character Text field.

HOT TIP

Relate a Counter Field to a Long Integer Number Field

If you use a Counter field as the primary key field in one table, you cannot use a Counter as the foreign key field in the other table. Access will not allow a foreign key to be a Counter field. Instead, use a Number field with size Long Integer as the foreign key field. (Counters are essentially Long Integer numbers, that is, integers that can be as long as approximately 2 billion.)

When choosing a name for a foreign key, you do not have to use the name of the primary key field in the related database. For example, the primary key field in the Members table is called Membership Number, but the related foreign key field in the Donations table could be called Payee. However, it is usually less confusing if you use the same names for related fields, so that you don't have to remember which name appears in which table.

How to Name Your Tables for Export

If you plan to export a table to another database program, such as dBASE or Paradox, the table name will be truncated to eight letters on export. Limit the table name to eight characters, or make sure that the first eight characters of the name will be a meaningful filename.

Creating the Tables in Access

Indicate the primary key for each table.

Now that you have designed your database, it's time to create the tables in Access. For each table, you must designate the primary key field or fields.

You can assign a primary key to the table using one of the two following methods:

- Select the row that contains the field, then click on the Key button from the toolbar.
- Enter the name of the field in the Primary Key property for the table, using the proper sheet in Design views.

Create Multiple-Field Primary Keys

There are two ways to indicate a multiple-field primary key (for example, the combination of the Payee and Date Paid fields for the Donations table). If the two fields are adjacent in the list of fields, click on one of the fields, **Shift**-click on the other field, and click on the Key button from the toolbar. You can also enter the field names in the Primary Key property for the table, separated by semicolons.

Creating the Relationships in Access

Use the Relationships dialog box to create relationships between tables.

Once you have created the tables, follow these steps to create the relationships between them.

1. In Table view, choose Edit Relationships from the menu to display the Relationships dialog box, shown in Figure 1.6.

2. Choose the name of the primary (master) table (for example, to create the relationship between the Members and Donations tables, choose Members). Access displays the table's primary key field (Membership Number).

3. Choose the type of relationship for the tables, usually many (one-to-many).

4. In the Related Table text box, choose the name of the related (detail) table (Donations).

5. In the Select Matching fields text box, choose the name of the foreign key field (in this example, the Payee field in the Donations table).

6. Click on the Enforce Referential Integrity box to tell Access not to allow values in the related table that don't exist in the primary table. Click on Add to create the new relationship, then click on Close to exit the Relationships dialog box.

Using Access, you can create only one relationship between two tables. If you create a second relationship between the same two tables, Access will delete the first relationship.

The MEMBERS Database

Tables 1.1 through 1.4 show the final design for each table in the membership database. The MEMBERS database is on the optional Access Insider companion disk. You'll find descriptions of the validation rules later in this chapter.

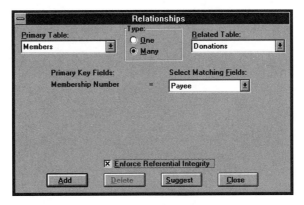

Figure 1.6 Relating two tables in the Relationships dialog box.

HOT TIP

Get Rid of Unused Relationships

If you create the wrong relationship between two tables, you can delete it. In Table view, choose Edit Relationships from the menu. Choose the name of the primary table to display its primary key. Choose the name of the related table to display the related field. Click on Delete to delete the existing relationship, then click on Close to exit the Relationships dialog box.

Table 1.1   Members Table

Field Name	Field Type	Field Size	Key?	Contents	Validation
Membership Number	Counter	Long Integer	Primary Key	Unique number for each member	None
First Name	Text	15		First name	None
Last Name	Text	20		Last name	None
Address	Text	35		Street address or P.O. box	None
City	Text	20		City or town	Is Not Null
State	Text	2		State or province code	None
ZIP Code	Text	5		Five digit ZIP code	([ZIP] Like "[0-9][0-9][0-9][0-9][0-9]")
Phone Number	Text	12		Phone numbers in the format 123-456-7890	None
Birth Date	Date			Birth date (optional)	None
Date Joined	Date			Date became member	None
Board Member?	Yes/No			Member of the board (default is No)	None
Annual Pledge	Currency			Amount of annual pledge	None

Table 1.2 Donations Table

Field Name	Field Type	Field Size	Key?	Contents	Validation
Payee	Number	Long Integer	Primary key, with Date paid	Membership Number of person who made donation	Related to Membership Number in Members table with referential integrity enforced
Date Paid	Date		Primary key, with Payee	Date donation received	None
Amount Paid	Currency			Amount of donation	None

Table 1.3 Committees Table

Field Name	Field Type	Field Size	Key?	Contents	Validation
Committee Name	Text	20	Primary key	Name of committee	None
Committee Budget	Currency			Annual budget for committee	None
Committee Type	Text	10		Standing or Ad Hoc	="Standing" Or "Ad Hoc"

Table 1.4 Committee Assignments Table

Field Name	Field Type	Field Size	Key?	Contents	Validation
Committee Name	Text	20	Primary key, with Member Number	Name of committee	Related to Committee Name in Committees table with referential integrity enforced
Member Number	Number	Long Integer	Primary key, with Committee Name	Membership Number of person on committee	Related to Membership Number in Members table with referential integrity enforced
Job	Text	10		Job on the committee, e.g., Chair or Secretary	None

Choosing the Right Field Types and Sizes

Here are some pointers for choosing the right Access field type for each field in your tables.

Choosing between Text and Yes/No Fields

Use a Yes/No field if a field will contain only Yes, No, True, False, On, or Off.

You can store yes/no information (also called *logical* or *Boolean* values) in a one-letter Text field that contains either *Y* or *N*. But if you use a Yes/No field, Access can display the information in the form of a check box, option button, or toggle button on forms, and as a check box or option button on reports. You can also easily switch between displaying the field as *Yes* and *No*, *True* and *False*, or *On* and *Off*, by changing the format property for the field. (Access actually stores Yes/No fields as –1 for *Yes, On,* or *True* and 0 for *No, Off,* or *False.*) A Yes/No field also takes less storage than a Text field.

Using a custom format, you can choose any two text values to display instead of *Yes* and *No*. For example, you can display the values *Member* and *Nonmember.* See Chapter 5 to learn how to use custom formats.

Choosing between Text and Memo Fields

Use a Memo field for notes or descriptions that may be longer than 255 characters.

When should you use a Text field and when should you use a Memo field?

Text fields are limited to 255 characters, so if you need more than that, use a Memo field. Access Memo fields can contain up to 32,000 characters of textual information. Although they can contain large amounts of text, don't store unnecessary information because it slows processing and wastes disk space.

You cannot index a Memo field, so if you plan to sort on the field or search for information in the field, you will find a Text field to be more efficient. Also, Memo fields cannot be primary keys or foreign keys. If you want to relate the table to another table based on the value of the field, use a Text field.

HOT TIP

Set the Maximum Size of Text Fields

When you enter a number for the Field Size property for a Text field, you're telling Access the *maximum number* of characters to store for that field. However, Access actually stores only the characters you enter. Access doesn't waste space storing spaces for fields with short or no entries, so don't scrimp on Text field sizes!

Choosing between Text and Number (or Currency) Fields

Use Number or Currency fields only for values that might involve mathematical calculations. Use Text fields for numeric codes.

Access displays and sorts Number and Currency fields differently from Text fields in the following ways:

- Access can calculate totals, subtotals, and averages for Number and Currency fields, as well as other calculations.

- When displaying a number, Access drops leading zeros (06 becomes 6).

- Number and Currency fields can be formatted in many ways, giving you control over the number of decimal places and use of currency symbols. When printing reports, Access can vertically align both Number and Currency fields on the decimal points.

- When sorting a Number or Currency field into ascending order, values sort from smallest to largest. But when you sort a Text field, values are sorted alphabetically from left to right. This means that in a Text field, Access sorts 55 before 6, because the "5" character comes before the "6" character. For example, Figure 1.7 shows how Access sorts the same list of numbers in Number and Text fields.

Number Sort	Text Sort
1	1
2	11
6	15
11	2
15	21
21	55
55	6

Figure 1.7 Sorting values stored in Number fields and in Text fields.

Use Number fields for all numbers except those that are numeric codes, like ZIP codes or phone numbers. Any number you might want to total up must be stored in a Number (or Currency) field.

Choosing between Number and Currency Fields

Use Currency fields for storing monetary amounts.

For most applications, you can use either Number or Currency fields to store amounts of money. However, if you perform calculations on large amounts of money, use a Currency field to ensure that Access will not round off the amount incorrectly.

Design Tips

You can tell Access how to format field values, what validation rules entries must follow, and what default values to enter if the user doesn't enter one. Here are ideas for formatting and validating the fields in your tables.

Letting Access Enter Data for You

Enter default values for fields in your tables.

For many fields, you may want to define a *default* value, that is, a value for Access to use if you don't tell it otherwise. If most of your members live in New York State, let Access enter "NY" automatically for the State field. You can change it for the few members who live out of state.

To enter a default value for a field, choose the table, then choose Design. Highlight the row for the field. Enter the default in the Default Value property. Now, whenever you create a new record in the table, the field displays the default value. You can enter a different value for the field when necessary.

Copy Field Properties

If you have several fields with the same or similar properties, you can copy the properties from one field to the next instead of typing them over and over. Once you have entered a property for one field, press **Ctrl+C** to copy the data to the Clipboard. To enter the same property for another field, press **Ctrl+V** to paste the text from the Clipboard.

Formatting Fields for All Forms and Reports

Enter a format for each Number, Currency, and Date field.

Formats can enhance the way information displays in a report or on a form. Formats *do not* affect the way information is stored in a field, just how it is displayed. You can set the format for a field when you design the table, so that you don't have to set it in each form and report you create. Access uses the format to display the data in the datasheet. For example, if a Number field will contain the discounts each customer receives (for a sales database), the number should always be formatted as a percentage. Rather than setting the format in each form and report, set it in the table.

To choose a format for a Number, Currency, or Date field, enter your selection in the Format property for the field. For example, choose Percent as the format for a customer discount field. Choose the format you expect to use most often. You can override it in reports and forms if you sometimes want to see the field in a different format. For example, you might choose Short Date for the format of the Date Paid field in the Donations table to display dates in MM/DD/YY format (e.g., 12/25/94). You might enter a different format in a report that prints form letters to members.

In addition to using the formats that Access provides, you can create your own custom formats. Like other formats, custom formats do not affect the way information is stored in a field, just how it is displayed. See Chapter 5 for information on creating your own custom formats.

Preventing "Garbage In, Garbage Out"

Enter validation expressions for fields, and an informative error message that will display if you enter the wrong thing.

If you enter erroneous data in your database, your reports will be wrong, too. It is very easy for wrong data to creep into your database. The bigger the database gets, the harder it is to keep it up to date and correct.

To help you enter the correct data, you can enter a *validation rule*, which tells Access what kind of entries to allow in the field. You can enter one or more legal values for the field, or you can enter an expression that must be true for values. For example, you can instruct Access to accept only numbers greater that zero for a Number field, or only dates within 30 days of today for a Date field.

For Text fields, you can enter validation rules using the wildcard characters listed in Table 1.5. When entering your validation require-

Table 1.5   Wildcard Characters in Validation Rules for Text Fields

Wildcards	Meaning
*	Matches any number of any characters
?	One of any character
#	One digit (0 through 9)
[A-Z]	One of the range of characters inside the square brackets (e.g., one capital letter from A to Z)
[!qxz]	One character, but not one that is inside the square brackets (e.g., one character that is not q, x, or z). The exclamation point indicates that the rest of the characters should be excluded.

ments for Text fields containing phone numbers, invoice numbers, credit card numbers, purchase order numbers, and other codes, you must decide whether to use all capitals where codes can include letters, and whether to include or omit dashes and spaces. For example, if you ask Access to search for the credit card number 9999–1234–5678, and the card number was entered as 999912345678, Access will not find the record.

For Number fields, the validation rule can use comparison operators like < (less than) and > (greater than) to specify the range of numbers that are allowed.

For Date fields, be sure to type a # before and after specific dates in the validation rule. The pound signs tell Access that you are entering a date rather than a text value. You can also use comparison operators to enter a range of dates that are allowed.

If you enter a validation rule, you should also enter a message for Access to display if the wrong data is entered. This should contain a description of what a valid entry should look like, to remind you or other users what is acceptable.

To enter a validation rule and error message, choose the table, then choose Design. Highlight the row for the field and enter the rule in the Validation Rule property and the error message in the Validation Text property. Table 1.6 shows some useful validation rules with corresponding error messages.

Some types of data clean-up cannot be done using validation rules. For example, a validation rule can require that input be in all capital letters, but it cannot capitalize the letters for you. Instead, you can use a macro on a form to do this type of automatic data clean-up (see Chapter 8).

Table 1.6   Examples of Validation Rules and Validation Text

Field Type	Validation Rule	Validation Text
Number	>0	Enter a number greater than zero.
Number	Between 0 And 100	Enter a number from 0 to 100.
Text	In ("US", "Canada", "Mexico")	Enter US, Canada, or Mexico
Text	Like "###-###-####"	Enter the phone number in the form 123-456-7890.
Text	Like "[A-Z]#[A-Z] #[A-Z]#"	Enter Canadian post code in the form A1B 2C3.
Date	>=Date()	The date can't be before today.
Date	Between #1/1/90# And #12/31/99#	Enter a date between Jan. 1, 1990, and Dec. 31, 1999.
Date	Between Date() and Date()+30	Enter a date within the next 30 days.

Avoid Empty Fields

Access doesn't always handle null (empty) values in fields the way you might like. For example, when doing calculations with Number fields, if the field is null, the answer is null, unless you use special functions to avoid this. To avoid nulls in a field, use the validation rule

```
Is Not Null
```

to force the user to enter a value in the field. Also enter a default value for the field. If there is no default value, the user can omit entering a value for the field despite its validation rule.

Validating a Field Against a List of Values

Use Access's referential integrity checking to check values automatically.

In our database, the Members table contains a State field for the two-letter state or province code of each member. To validate this State field, we can add another table (States) that contains the two-letter codes and the full names of the states and provinces. The relationship between these two tables is a one-to-many relationship because there can be many members from one state, but each member lives in only one state. In this type of situation, when you have two related tables, you can ensure that values entered in a field in one table appear in a field in the other table, by enforcing *referential integrity*. Referential integrity tells Access not to allow values in the related (Members) table that don't exist in the primary (States) table.

To ensure that only valid state abbreviations are entered in the State field of the Members table, *don't* use a validation rule. Instead, you should define a relation between the two tables and then tell Access to enforce it.

First create the primary table (States) or input it from the MAILLIST database on the optional companion disk. It can have two fields, as shown in Table 1.7, but the second field is optional—include it only if you foresee wanting full state and province names to appear on reports or form letters.

Next, make sure that the primary table has a primary key field, and that this field is the code you want to validate (in this case, the State field in States table is the primary key field for the table). To define the membership:

1. In Table view, choose Edit Relationships from the menu.

2. Choose the name of the primary table (States), then choose the name of the related table (Members).

3. Choose the name of the field in the related table that should contain only values that exist in the primary table (in this example, the States field in the Members table).

4. Click on the Enforce Referential Integrity box to tell Access not to allow values in the related table that don't exist in the primary table.

5. Click on Add to create the new relationship, then click on Close to exit the dialog box.

Now whenever you add or edit values in the related table (Members), Access validates them against the primary table (States). If you enter a value that isn't in the primary table, Access displays the message, "Can't add or change record. Referential integrity rules require a related record in table," followed by the name of the primary table.

Table 1.7   States Table

Field Name	Field Type	Field Size	Key?	Contents	Validation
State	Text	2	Primary Key	Two-letter standard code for states and provinces	None
State Name	Text	20		Full name of state or province	Is Not Null

Avoiding Duplicate Values in a Field

Index the field with a No Duplicates index.

If you want to ensure that there are no two records in the database with the same value in a field, you can use a No Duplicates index. Primary key fields automatically have No Duplicates indexes, since the purpose of a primary key is to uniquely identify each record. But there may be other fields that should contain unique values as well. For example, if the membership database were used for a health club, the Members table might include a field for Locker Number. If each member gets his or her own locker, no two records in the Members table should have the same value for the Locker Number field.

To index a field with a No Duplicates index, open the table in Design view and select the field. In the Indexed property, choose Yes (No Duplicates).

Creating Tables without Primary Keys

Choose No when Access asks if you want to create a primary key.

If you design a table that has no primary key, when you save the table Access says, "There is no primary key defined. Create one?" You can choose No to create a table with no primary key. (If you choose Yes, Access adds a Counter field to the table.)

Tables with no primary keys have a few drawbacks:

- In the datasheet, the records are displayed in the order in which they are entered, rather than sorted by any field.
- You can't create relationships using Edit Relationships. However, you can relate the table to other tables when you create queries.

Using a Table from Another Access Database

You can attach any table in another database to the current database if the two databases need the same data.

If you create more than one Access database, you may want to include the same table in more than one database. For example, you may want the States table (containing the standard abbreviations for states and provinces) in several databases that contain address lists.

Just as Access lets you attach to external tables maintained by dBASE or Paradox, you can attach to a table in another Access database:

1.   Open the database that does not contain the table and choose File Attach Table from the menu.

2.   In the Attach dialog box, select Microsoft Access as the data source and click on OK.

3.   Choose the Access database that contains the table you want to include in the current database and click on OK.

4.   In the Attach Tables dialog box, shown in Figure 1.8, choose the table from the list of tables Access displays and click on Attach. Access confirms that it successfully attaches the table.

5.   When you have attached all the tables you need, click on Close.

Access doesn't make a copy of the table, it simply creates a link to the table in the other database. Any changes made to the table in either database appear in both databases. You cannot change its design, but you can enter and edit records. To change the design, you must change the table in the database containing the table. You can't create relationships to other tables, although you can create join lines in queries.

Importing a Table from Another Access Database

Import the file from the other database if you want to use similar, but not identical, information in two databases.

If you attach a table from another Access database, any changes you make to its records are reflected in both databases. But what if you want to start with a table from another Access database and adapt it for use in a new database?

Access allows you to import a table using the File Import command. Importing *does not* create a link between database tables. Instead, it

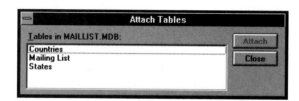

Figure 1.8   Attaching a table from another Access database.

copies the table, which allows you to freely edit the data and structure of the imported table. To import a table:

1. Choose File Import from the menu.
2. In the Import dialog box, select Microsoft Access as the data source and click on OK.
3. Choose the Access database that contains the table you want to include in the current database and click on OK.
4. In the Import Objects dialog box, shown in Figure 1.9, choose Table as the type of object to import, and then choose the table from the list of table names.
5. Click on Import. Access confirms that it has successfully imported the table.
6. When you have imported all the tables you need from the database, click on Close.

Access makes a copy of the table in the current database, allowing you to modify the structure of the table as well as its data.

Copy a Table's Structure

If you are creating a new table and there is a similar table in another database, you can tell Access to import just the table's structure. Then you can modify the structure rather than starting from scratch.

To import just the table's structure, choose the Structure Only option in the Import Objects dialog box (Figure 1.9). Access imports the table with no records.

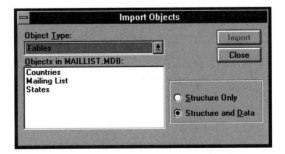

Figure 1.9 Importing a table from another Access database using the Import Object dialog box.

Starting a Counter at a Number Other Than One

To set a starting value for a Counter field, create a temporary table and append a new starting value for the counter.

Access automatically fills in Counter fields as you enter records. Normally, Counter fields start with number 1. However, you can start a Counter with another numeric value.

For example, if you want the Membership Number field in the Members table to begin with the number 1000, complete the following steps *before* entering any records in the Members table:

1. Create a temporary table containing just one field and name the field with the same name as the Counter field you want to change.

2. Use field type Number with size Long Integer.

For example, to change the starting number of the Membership Number field in the Members database, create a new table with one field called Membership Number. Save the table with a name like Temp. When Access asks to create a primary key, click on No.

3. Enter a record in the temporary table. For the Number field, enter a number that is one less than the number at which you want your Counter field to start. For Membership Number to start at 1000, enter 999 in the temporary table, as shown in Figure 1.10.

Next, you need to create an append query to append the record from the temporary table to the table whose Counter you want to change. To do this, follow these steps:

1. Make a query based on the temporary table, and drag the single field name onto the query grid.

2. Choose Query Append from the menu to change the query from a select to an append query.

3. In the Query Properties dialog box, set the Append To Table Name option to the table whose Counter field you want to reset (for example, the Members table).

4. Click on OK.

   The append query is ready to run.

5. Click on the ! button from the toolbar (or choose Query Run from the menu). Access tells you that one row will be appended. Click on OK. Then close the query—there is no need to save it.

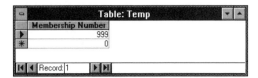

Figure 1.10 Temporary table used for setting the starting value for a Counter field.

When you open the original table, you will see a new record—the one you just appended— at the end of the table. The Counter field (Membership Number in the Members table) contains the value you entered in the temporary file (999, in this example). When you enter a record in the table, Access resumes numbering with the next number—1000.

After you have entered at least one record, you can delete the temporary record you imported.

Note: Don't compact the database between when you import the temporary record and when you enter another record in the table, or Access will reset the Counter back to 1.

Tips for Creating Commonly Used Fields

Almost everyone creates fields for ZIP codes or phone numbers in at least one database. Here are pointers for choosing the right field type, size, format, and validation for some commonly used fields.

Creating ZIP Code Fields

Use a Text field for ZIP codes, and leave space for foreign postal codes.

Store ZIP codes in Text fields, not Number fields, even though ZIP codes in the United States consist only of numbers. ZIP codes aren't numbers with which you want to do arithmetic. If you store them as numbers, Access drops any leading zeros. For example, the ZIP code for Princeton, New Jersey, which is 08540, would be stored and displayed as 8540 if stored in a Number field.

If you expect to have any Canadian or other foreign addresses in an address list, make the ZIP code field at least six characters long (enough for Canadian post codes) or even eight characters long (to contain British post codes). Be sure to include a field for the country name, too.

If you ever expect to do large-scale mailings, you may want to leave space for nine-digit ZIP codes. Unless you mail to hundreds of thousands of people, though, this is strictly optional.

It's not a bad idea to have a ZIP code directory on hand when entering addresses, since mail without ZIP codes can be delayed.

Make Sure ZIP Codes Are Valid

If you plan to enter only five-digit U.S. ZIP codes, enter the following condition as the Validation Rule property for your ZIP code field:

```
Like "#####"
```

This rule is true if the ZIP code is five characters long and all digits. Otherwise, it is false and Access doesn't allow the ZIP code to be entered. Be sure to enter an error message about ZIP codes in the Validation Text property.

If you want to enter five-digit or nine-digit ZIP codes, use this validation rule:

```
Like "#####" Or Like "#####-####"
```

If you plan to allow U.S. or Canadian postal codes (in the format A1B 2C3), use a validation rule like this:

```
Like "#####" Or Like "#####-####" Or Like "[A-Z]#[A-Z] #[A-Z]#"
```

If you plan to allow Mexican postal codes, they use the same format as U.S. five-digit ZIP codes.

Storing Phone Numbers

Use a Text field for phone numbers, leaving space for extensions and international numbers.

Store phone numbers in Text fields. Like ZIP codes, they are not numbers with which you do arithmetic. Choose a standard format for entering all the numbers, such as:

```
123-456-7890
```

or

```
(123)456-7890
```

or

```
123/456-7890
```

Don't bother storing the *1* for each long-distance number.

Using a standard format makes it easier to search for a phone number later, and makes your reports look neater. Decide if you want to leave room for extensions or foreign phone numbers. If you will enter extensions, decide on a standard way to do so, like this:

```
123-456-7890x333
```

Standardize Phone Number Formats

For phone number fields, you can use a validation rule like this:

```
Like "###-###-####*"
```

The asterisk wildcard at the end allows you to optionally enter an extension.

Storing People's Names

Use separate fields for first and last names, as well as for middle names, salutations, and suffixes.

To store people's names, use several fields rather than one long Text field. Use separate fields for the first and last names so that you can alphabetize records by last name. You may also want to provide fields for middle initials or names, salutations like "Mr." and "Ms.," or suffixes like "Jr." and "III."

To decide how many fields to use for names, consider the reports you plan to generate, especially address lists and form letters, to see how you will want names to appear.

Creating Percentage Fields

Use a Number field formatted to display percentages.

To store a percentage, such as a discount, create a Number field with field size Single, and enter numbers between zero and one (inclusive). Format the field as Percent. When you enter a value, you can type "10%" and Access will convert the value to 0.10.

To ensure that percentages are entered as fractions, rather than as 10 for 10 percent, enter this validation rule:

```
Between 0 And 1
```

Enter validation text that reminds the user to enter a number between zero and one, or to enter a number from 0 to 100 with a percent sign.

Designing a Mailing List

Create separate fields for each part of the address.

One of the most common database applications is a list of names and addresses, as a mailing list, membership list, or customer list. The information can be stored in a single table. For example, a typical mailing list usually contains the fields in Table 1.8, plus application-specific code fields.

Table 1.8   Standard Design for Mailing List Table

Field Name	Field Type	Field Size	Key?	Contents	Validation
ID Number	Counter	Long Integer	Primary Key	Unique number for each person	None
Salutation	Text	3		Mr., Ms., Dr., etc.	None
First Name	Text	12*		First name	Is Not Null
Middle Initial	Text	1		Initial, without period	None
Last Name	Text	20*		Last name	Is Not Null
Suffix	Text	3		Jr., Sr., III, etc.	None
Title	Text	45*		Title in organization (for business adresses only)	None
Organization	Text	45*		Company or organization name	None (for business mailing lists, use "Is Not Null" to require org. name)
Street Address	Text	45*		Street address or P.O. Box	None
Second Address Line	Text	45*		Continuation line for street address, useful for company divisions or mail routing codes	None
City	Text	25*		City or town	Is Not Null
State	Text	2		State or province code	Related to table of state/province codes, with referential integrity
ZIP	Text	10		Five-digit ZIP code, nine-digit ZIP code, or postal code for international addresses	Like "#####" Or Like "#####-####" Or Like "[A-Z]#[A-Z]#[A-Z]
Country	Text	15		For international mailing lists only	Related to tables of country names, with referential integrity

Table 1.8 Standard Design for Mailing List Table (Continued)

Field Name	Field Type	Field Size	Key?	Contents	Validation
Phone	Text	15 or more		Phone numbers in a standard format, with space for extensions. Optionally, use separate fields for home phone, business phone, and fax number.	Like "###-###-####*"

Choose Field Lengths for Mailing Labels

If you plan to print mailing labels of a particular size, check to see how many characters fit across one label. Make sure that the combined fields for salutation, first name, middle initial, last name, and suffix (or whichever fields you plan to print) fit on the label. In Table 1.8, the field sizes marked with asterisks are based on using mailing labels that fix a maximum of 45 characters across.

The MAILLIST Database

The Mailing List table, along with the Countries and States tables used to validate it, is in the MAILLIST database on the optional *Access Insider* companion disk.

Migrating from Other Programs

If you have been using computers for a while, you may have information stored in other formats (application programs) that you now want to move into Access. The information may be in another database program, like dBASE or Paradox, or it may be in the form of a spreadsheet or a word-processing document. You may even want to convert a complete application that now runs in another database program.

Luckily, Access can read files in many formats. You can move your information into Access by importing it, or Access can *attach* to files in other formats, reading from and writing to them while leaving them in their original formats.

This chapter describes how to move information from a variety of different programs into Access. Once you have imported the data, you'll find out how to change the fields to their proper Access field types, split up tables that contain unnormalized, related information, and validate the imported data.

Migration Strategies

If you have existing applications in other database programs, spreadsheets, text files, or word-processing documents, there are many ways to *migrate* the applications, or switch them over, to Access. You may want to revamp the database design at the same time you move to Access. (See Chapter 1 for techniques for designing a database, creating tables, choosing fields types, and setting up defaults, formats, and validations.)

Here are strategies for moving to Access quickly and easily.

Migrating from a Database Application

Attach to the existing tables, create Access forms and reports, and import the tables when you are ready to switch to Access.

If you have a complete application running in dBASE, Paradox, FoxPro, Btrieve, Microsoft SQL Server, or another database program that stores its data in a compatible format (such as Alpha or PC-File), you can migrate to Access in stages by *attaching* the existing files. Access can work with data in other types of files by attaching them as tables in an Access database. Then, when you are ready, you can import the files into Access. Here is the general procedure:

1. Make a new Access database and attach the tables in the existing non-Access database. Rename the tables if the original names are cryptic.

To attach a table from another database application, use the File Attach Table command. Once the table is attached, you can rename it using the File Rename command.

2. Set formats, defaults, and validations for the fields in each table.

3. Look at the layout of the tables, and determine if you want to use the same set of tables and relationships. If needed, create additional tables for validating codes (for example, a table of state codes).

At this point, you can't change the table designs, because Access cannot modify the design of attached tables. Instead, you may be able to create queries that approximate the tables you want. (See *Working with Attached Tables* later in this chapter.)

4. Create forms to replace the data entry screens in your existing application. You may need to create queries as the record sources for the forms, especially when forms display data from multiple tables.

5. Create reports to replace those in the existing application. Again, you may need to create queries as the record sources for the reports.

6. If the system from which you are migrating contains customized menus, you may want to create custom menus in Access. Using forms, you can create menus that correspond to existing menus, to open forms and print reports. You can also create a macro named AutoExec to open a form with a main menu. (See Chapter 16 for how to do these tasks.)

7. Where the existing application contains additional processing capabilities, you may need to write macros and Access Basic modules to replace them. (See Chapters 16 and 17 for information on writing macros and Access Basic modules.)

Up to this point, you can continue to use your existing application or the new Access database interchangeably because Access is updating attached tables from the original application. When the new Access database contains enough capabilities that you no longer need the old database application, complete the procedure with these steps:

8. Import all the tables you previously attached. See *Importing Text Files* later in this chapter for details. If possible, move the old database program and data files onto backup diskettes or tape, so that no one will update them. Make all new updates to the Access database.

9. Create primary key fields and indexes for each table. Where appropriate, change field types and sizes.

10. You may want to rename fields that have confusing field names. Be sure to change the names everywhere they occur in queries, forms, reports, macros, and modules.

11. Now you can make structural improvements to the database design that you couldn't do while the tables were attached. You can delete unnecessary fields, split up tables that contain redundant information, and define relationships between tables. Again, be sure to update all your queries, forms, reports, macros, and modules to match.

12. Update any written instructions about the application.

Sharing Data with Other Applications

Attach to external databases, or export data from Access on a regular schedule.

If other applications need to share data with your Access application, you have two options:

- Let the other applications maintain the shared data in their own files, and let Access attach to the files.

- Import the information into Access. Then, on a regular basis (perhaps at the end of every day), export information from Access in a format the other applications can read.

The advantages to attaching are:

- Other applications can read the files directly, so that the information in them is always up to date (changes are "live").

- Information in the Access table isn't duplicated in other databases so disk space isn't wasted.

The advantages of importing and exporting are:

- Viewing and editing data is faster with the data stored in Access than with storing information in attached tables.

- You can change the table design, field types, and field sizes, and set primary keys and indexes in Access. (Access can't do any of these actions with attached tables.)

- You can create relationships with the Relationships dialog box. (Access can't store relationships between attached tables, although you can relate them when you create queries.)

Working with Attached Tables

When possible, import rather than attach tables.

When you are attaching a table rather than importing the table data into Access, you will find that there are a number of limitations to the things you can do with the attached table:

- Structural changes to attached tables are not permitted in Access. For example, if you want to create new fields or change field types, you cannot make the changes in Access. If you open an attached table in Design mode, Access warns you that you cannot make many changes. Instead, make the changes in the native database—they will be reflected automatically in Access. If the attached table is part of a shared database, you will need to consult the owner of the database in order to make the changes.
- You can't relate attached tables in the Relationships dialog box. However, you can relate attached tables when you create queries.
- Attached Paradox tables must have primary keys. Otherwise, Access can't write to them.

Note: If you make changes to the structure of an attached table using its native application, delete and reattach the table in Access to update its structure.

Rename Attached Tables

You can change the name of an attached table. However, the table name is only valid in Access; the name doesn't change in the native database. You'll probably find renaming tables useful when using attached dBASE or Paradox tables with cryptic names like CUSTORD and EMPSAL2.

To rename a table in Access, simply highlight the table name in the list of tables in the Database window and choose File Rename from the menu. It's much easier to rename a table before you create queries, forms, reports, and macros that refer to it by its old name.

Migrating from a Spreadsheet

Import data from spreadsheets into Access tables, clean it up, and create forms and reports.

It is possible to store a table of information in a spreadsheet, though spreadsheets are not well suited to maintain them. For example, spreadsheets don't provide a convenient way to store address lists. Printing labels, membership rosters, and personalized form letters requires extensive macro programming. No multi-table application, like the membership database we have been designing, works well in a spreadsheet—spreadsheet programs have limited facilities for relational lookups and validation.

If you have information stored in a Lotus 1-2-3, Microsoft Excel, or compatible spreadsheet, you can import it into Access; Access cannot attach to a spreadsheet.

To migrate a spreadsheet file into Access:

1. Look at the spreadsheet file(s) to determine what fields each table contains, and in what order. Make sure that the information in the spreadsheet(s) is in the right format (one record per row, one field per column). Note the cell ranges that contain the table(s) you want to import. Also note which columns contain data and which contain formulas. (You will delete the columns that contain formulas from the Access table into which they are imported, to be replaced by calculated fields in queries.)

2. In a new Access database, create new, empty tables to import the spreadsheet data into. Create one table for each spreadsheet range to be imported, with fields in the same order as they appear in the spreadsheet and with appropriate field types. Use Number or Currency fields for columns containing numbers, Text fields for columns containing labels, and Date fields for columns containing values formatted as dates. Create the tables without primary keys or indexes, so that importing will be faster. By creating the tables first, you are able to control the field types and sizes—otherwise, Access guesses based on the data in the first row of spreadsheet data.

3. Import the data from the spreadsheet file(s) using the File Import command and selecting the type of spreadsheet file. Append each range to the existing tables you just created. For each spreadsheet, Access displays the Import Spreadsheet Options dialog box, shown in Figure 2.1. Rather than importing the whole spreadsheet, enter the range that contains the data. Import each spreadsheet range into a separate table.

Now you can clean up the data in the table, using the remaining steps as a guide.

4. Where appropriate, change field names, types, and sizes. For example, convert fields that contain only *Yes* and *No* to Yes/No fields.

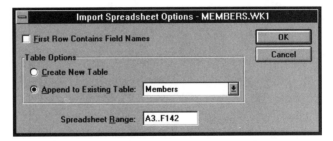

Figure 2.1 Importing a spreadsheet file.

Delete fields that contain the results of calculations (you can create new calculated fields in queries). Adjust the lengths of Text fields.

5. Add formats, defaults, and validations for each field in the tables. Add primary keys and indexes to each table.

6. Create relationships between the tables in the Relationships dialog box.

7. Create queries that create the calculated fields you need (to replace those you deleted in step 4). To find out what expressions to use, load the spreadsheet and look at the formulas in the calculated cells.

8. Create forms for data entry. You may need to create queries as the record sources for the forms.

9. Create reports. Again, you may need to create queries as the record sources for the reports.

10. If the spreadsheet used macros to present menus, you can make forms to display menus that open forms and print reports. Create a macro named AutoExec to open a form with a main menu. (See Chapter 16 for details.)

11. Where the spreadsheet contained additional macro-based capabilities, write macros and Access Basic modules to replace them. (See Chapters 16 and 17 for more information.)

12. Update any written instructions about the application.

Import a Named Range from Excel

If you plan to import data regularly from an Excel spreadsheet, you can simplify importing by using a named range. In Excel, name the range that contains the data as *Database*, including the first row of field names. In Access, type **Database** in the Spreadsheet Range text box on the Import Spreadsheet Options dialog box.. This is the only range name Access will import.

Migrating from Text Files or Word-Processing Documents

Determine the file format, import the data, and create forms and reports.

Many users frequently use text files or word-processing documents to store address lists and other tables of information. You may also use word-processing macros for prompted data entry or other processing.
   To migrate a text file or word-processing document into Access:

1. Look at the file to determine what format it is in, and, if necessary, what format it can be converted to that Access can read. You will find descriptions of the formats Access can read and tips for making files that match these formats later in this chapter.

2. Clean up the file, eliminating information that is not to be included in the imported data. Delete headers and footers, comments, and any text that doesn't belong in the table.

3. For word-processing documents, eliminate formatting codes, then save the document as an ASCII file. For example, if you use Word for Windows, choose File Save As from the menu, then choose Text Only w/line breaks (*.TXT) from the Save File as Type list box.

4. In a text editor (like the Windows Notepad), look at the file and note the names, sizes, and types of the fields in the order in which they appear. If there are fields that you will not want once the table has been imported, you can either delete them now, or import them into Access and delete them then. It is usually easier to delete unneeded fields in Access rather than manually deleting the values in the ASCII file.

5. In a new Access database, create a new, empty table for the imported data. Create one table for each file, with fields in the same order as they appear in the file. Use number or Currency fields for numeric values, Date fields for dates, and Text fields for all other information. Create the tables without primary keys or indexes, so that importing will be faster. By creating the tables first, you are able to control the field types and sizes—otherwise, Access guesses based on the data in the first record in the file.

6. Import the file. Append it to the existing tables you just created. Import each file into a separate table. (See *Importing Files* later in this chapter for exactly how to import each type of text file.)

Now you can clean up the data in the table, using the remaining steps as a guide.

7. Where appropriate, change field names, types, and sizes. For example, convert fields that contain only *Yes* and *No* to Yes/No fields. Delete fields that you don't need for the application.

8. Add formats, defaults, and validations for each field in the table. Add primary keys and indexes to each table.

9. Create relationships between tables in the Relationships dialog box.

10. Create forms for data entry. You may need to create queries as the record sources for the forms.

11. Create reports. Again, you may need to create queries as the record sources for the reports.

12. If the application used programs or word-processing macros to present menus, you can make forms to display menus that open forms and print reports. Create a macro named AutoExec to open a form with a main menu. (See Chapter 16 for how to do this.)

13. Where the application contained additional macro-based capabilities, write macros and Access Basic modules to replace them. (See Chapters 16 and 17 for information about macros and modules.)

14. Update any written instructions about the application.

Determining the Format of a Text File or Word Processing Document

Determine if the file is delimited, fixed-width, or another format.

Text files or word-processing documents can contain information in many different formats. Data formats for text files differ in how they arrange the data in the file, how they separate one record from the next, how they separate one field from the next, how they indicate the beginning and end of each text field, and the formats of date fields. Access can import data in one of three ways:

- as a *delimited* text file
- as a *fixed-width* text file
- in another format (this requires writing Access Basic code to import)

Regardless of which of the three formats you choose, the file must contain only text—no formatting codes. If your data is in a word-processing document, save it as an ASCII text file (see step 3 in the previous topic).

Many data formats use *delimiters* or *separators* to perform these functions. Access lets you define the following types of delimiters:

- The *field separator* character (usually a comma) separates one field from the next.

- The *text delimiter* character (usually a quotation mark) surrounds text values.

- The *date delimiter* character (usually a slash) separates the parts of dates (for example, month/day/year).

- The *time delimiter* character (usually a colon) separates the hours from the minutes in time values.

- The *decimal separator* character (usually a period) separates the integer parts of numbers from the decimal parts.

- The *record separator* character, which separates one record from the next, is *always* a carriage return. Access will not let you change this delimiter.

Some formats use a record delimiter but no field delimiter; some use both. Some use text delimiters, some don't. For example, one format might use commas to separate fields, while another format might not use any character to separate one field from the next within each record or to show where text fields begin and end.

If no carriage return separates one record from the next (that is, if there is no record separator, or if it is not a carriage return), Access can't read the file as a delimited or fixed-width file. You must insert carriage returns at the end of each record before Access can import the file.

A *delimited* text file uses record, field, and text delimiters. The most commonly used delimited format is called *comma delimited* (also *comma separated values* or *MailMerge format*). It uses commas as the field delimiter, carriage returns as the record delimiter, and quotation marks as the text delimiter. That is, there is one record per line with commas between the fields and quotes around text fields. Usually, all fields except numeric fields are enclosed in quotation marks and the extra spaces at the ends of text fields are left out. In a comma-delimited file, records are not all the same length, because character fields are not padded out with spaces. Figure 2.2 shows sample data for a membership list in comma delimited format.

```
"Bodeau, D.", "9/1/92", 150
"Brink, U.", "6/24/56", 250
"Muder, D. J.", "3/18/84", 1000
"Young, J.", "12/4/90", 400
```

Figure 2.2 Membership data in delimited text format.

Delimited text files frequently have the file extension .TXT or .PRN. (See *Importing a Delimited File* later in this chapter.)

A *fixed-width* text file (also known as *standard data format, SDF,* or *fixed-length record* file) doesn't use field or text delimiters. Instead, the fields in each record are listed with no separators between them, and each field is padded out to its full length with spaces. The only way for a program to tell where the fields start and end is to know the lengths of the fields and to keep count of the characters.

For example, Figure 2.3 shows the same data as Figure 2.2, but in fixed-width format.

The length of the first field (Member Name) is 15, so five spaces follow the first value, "Bodeau, D." The second field (Date Joined) starts at character 16, and continues for eight characters. The third field (Pledge) starts at character 24 and is four characters long. Every record is *fixed* at a particular number of characters (hence the name).

This format is widely used on PCs, minicomputers, and large mainframe computers. COBOL programs almost always write fixed-length record files. The file extension for a fixed-width file is usually .TXT, .FXD, or .SDF. (See *Importing a Fixed Width* File later in this chapter.)

Importing Text Files

Now that you have decided on your migration strategy, you are ready to import files. Importing database or spreadsheet files is straightforward, because Access can read them with no additional information from you.

```
Bodeau, D.     09/01/92 150
Brink, U.      06/24/56 250
Muder, D. J.   03/18/84 1000
Young, J.      12/04/90 400
```

Figure 2.3 Membership data in fixed-width text format.

But to import text files, you must describe the format before Access can read it. In some cases, Access cannot read every field correctly, and you will have to clean up the results.

The next several topics include tips for importing text files into Access.

Importing a Delimited File

Create a table with the same fields as the delimited file and import the file into it.

For a delimited file to import correctly into Access, the following must be true:

- Every record in the file must have the same fields in the same order.
- Every delimiter and separator character must be in place.
- Every record must end with a carriage return. Only one record can be stored on each line.
- Numbers cannot contain commas (assuming you use periods as decimal separators).

To import a delimited file:

1. Open the delimited file in the Windows Notepad or another text editor. For each field, note its name and data type. For text fields, note (or estimate) the length of the longest value of the field. Note the text delimiter, the field separator, and the format of any dates and times.

2. In Access, create a new, empty table with the same fields as the file you are importing. Create each field with the same data type as in the delimited file. Set the size of Text fields to *at least* the length of the longest entry. Don't give the table any indexes and don't create a primary key (these just slow down the importing). You are now ready to import the file.

3. Choose File Import from the menu, and then choose Text (Delimited) as the Data Source. Click on OK.

4. Select the name of the delimited text file from the Select File Dialog box and click on Import. Access displays the Import Text Options dialog box (Figure 2.4).

5. Choose the Append to Existing Table option, and choose the name of the table you just created.

6. Click on Options to display the rest of the import options.

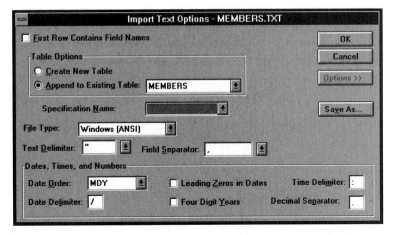

Figure 2.4 Changing the delimiters in the Import Text Options dialog box.

7. Enter the text delimiter, the field separator, and the date and time formats.

8. Click on OK to import the file. If Access finds any records it can't read, it creates a table called "Import Errors - *User Name*," where *User Name* is your name. (See *Handling Importing Errors* later in this chapter for information on this table.) Access confirms that the data has been imported, and tells you how many records it contained. Click on OK.

9. Access displays the Select File dialog box again, so you can choose another file to import. When you are done importing, click on Close.

10. Open the table containing the imported data and make sure the information is in the right fields and that all the records were imported. If not, you can delete all the records and try again. Now, you can make changes to the design of the table, including defining a primary key field and indexes.

Save the Format of a Delimited File

If you plan to import the same delimited file many times, or many delimited files with the same delimiters, separators, and date formats, save the formatting information as an import/export specification. While an import/export specification is not required for importing delimited files, it can be convenient if you find yourself entering the same format again and again.

To make an import/export specification, choose File Imp/Exp Setup from the menu. Import/export specifications are described further in the next topic.

Importing a Fixed-Width File

Create an import/export specification with the same fields as the
fixed-width file, and import the file using it.

For Access to import a fixed-width file correctly, the following must be true:

- Every line in the file must contain the same number of characters. Open the text file in a text editor and set the margins wide enough that lines do not wrap; check the right margin for irregularities. (The last field of each record can be short or missing, but all other fields must be the same width in all records.)

- Numbers cannot contain commas (assuming you use periods as decimal separators).

- Dates must be a standard format, preferably *MM/DD/YY.*

To import a fixed-width file:

1. As you view the file to check the field lengths, note each field name, field type, and starting character position on the line.

2. In Access, create an import/export specification that defines the position of each field. Choose the File Imp/Exp Setup command to display the Import/Export Setup dialog box, shown in Figure 2.5.

3. In the Field Information table, enter the definition of each field.

4. If the data includes dates or times, enter the date and time format in the Dates, Times, and Numbers section of the dialog box.

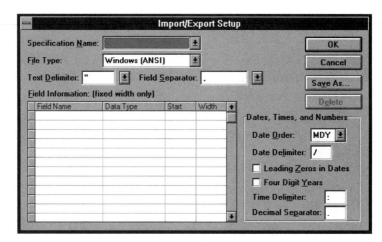

Figure 2.5   Defining a fixed-width format using the Import/Export Setup dialog box.

5. Click on Save As to save and name the import/export specification.

6. Import the file by choosing File Import, and then choosing Text (Fixed Width) as the Data Source. Click on OK. Access displays the Select File dialog box.

7. Select the file to import. Click on Import to display the Import Text Options dialog box, shown in Figure 2.4.

8. In the Specification Name list box, choose the import/export specification you just created.

9. Click on OK to import the file.

10. If Access finds any records it couldn't read, it creates a table called "Import Errors - *User Name*," where *User Name* is your name. (See *Handling Importing Errors*, later in the chapter for information on this table.) Access confirms that the data has been imported, and tells you how many records it contained.

11. Access displays the Select File dialog box again, so you can choose another file to import. When you are done importing, click on Close.

12. Open the table containing the imported data and make sure the information is in the right fields and that all the records were imported. If not, delete all the records, fix the import/export specification, and import the file again. Now, you can make changes to the design of the table, including defining a primary key field and indexes.

HOT TIP

End the Fixed-Width File with a Carriage Return

If the last line of the fixed-width file doesn't end with a carriage return, Access will not import it correctly. On the other hand, if there are two carriage returns at the end of the file, Access may import the last record twice. Using the Windows Notepad or another text editor, open the file and make sure that there is one, and only one, carriage return at the end of the last record of the file.

Importing Text Files That Aren't Delimited or Fixed-Width

When you want to import a file that is neither fixed-width nor delimited, you can either edit the text file into a delimited or fixed-width format, use another program to do the conversion for you, or write an Access Basic module to read the file.

If you find yourself in this situation, don't give up! There are several possible approaches.

- If another program can read the data, capture a report from the other program in a file (see the next *Hot Tip*).

- If possible, edit the file into a delimited or fixed-width format. If the information is stored in a word-processing document, you may be able to use the word processor's find-and-replace feature to insert delimiters. If the word processor has a macro language, investigate writing a macro to do the reformatting.

- If the format is fairly standard, there may be some other program that can read the information in its current format and write it in a format that Access can read. For example, PC-File is an inexpensive shareware database program from ButtonWare. It can read and write a large number of formats, including dBASE III, DIF, fixed-width, fixed-width with no carriage returns between records, comma delimited, line delimited (one field per line), and WordPerfect secondary merge files. If your data is in one of these formats, you can use PC-File to read your existing data file and write it in dBASE format, which Access can then import.

- You can write an Access Basic module to read the data file, find each field in each record, and copy the information into one or more tables. You might find that writing Access Basic modules is also a good method for importing a file in which data from two or more tables is mixed together. Chapter 18 provides an introduction to Access Basic programming.

Create a Fixed-Width File from Another Program

Sometimes the easiest way to move data from another program into Access is to "print to file," that is, to save report output from the other program in a text file. If you print a columnar report to a file, it looks a lot like a fixed-width file.

When you set up the report in the other program, use the following guidelines:

- Don't use page headers and footers, since they will appear in the text file mixed in with lines of data.
- Use the program's "unformatted" printing mode, if available. This approach may suppress margins and page breaks in the file.
- Don't use commas when formatting numbers.

- Choose a format for dates that Access can understand. The easiest is *MM/DD/YY*, the default date format when importing into Access.
- Set the left margin to zero so there are no extra spaces at the beginning of each line.
- Don't apply any character or paragraph styles (bold, italics, under-lined, or other formatting), which place codes in the text file.

Now, you can print the report to the file. (From a Windows application, use the Generic/Text Only printer driver to create an ASCII file.) Before you import the file into Access, edit the file, looking for the following:

- If you couldn't suppress printing headers and footers, delete them from every page of the report.
- Delete the page breaks and the blank lines that make up the top and bottom margins.
- Delete any remaining formatting codes.
- Make sure that the records appear in fixed-width format, that is, that each field appears in the same position on each line of the file.

Now you are ready to import the fixed-width file as described above.

Handling Importing Errors

If your first attempt at importing results in an error table, fix the errors in the text file and import again, making sure not to import any records twice.

If Access has trouble importing records, it creates a table called "Import Errors - *User Name*," where *User Name* is your name. It contains one record for each record that Access couldn't import. The table contains the following three fields:

- Error: A description of the error, such as "Type Conversion Failure" (the data is of the wrong type for the field).
- Field: The field that Access couldn't import.
- Row: The row (record) number in the file in which Access found the error.

If you run into errors when importing, you have two options:

- If you imported into an empty table, delete all the records in the table. Using the Windows Notepad or another text editor, fix the problems in the text file. The row numbers help you find the errors. Then import the file again.

- Make a copy of the text file you imported. Then using the Windows Notepad or another text editor, delete all the records that imported correctly, that is, leave only the records that have errors. Fix the errors, then import this small file. (You may want to import the corrected records into a new empty table first to make sure that the errors were corrected.)

In general, it is a good idea to import into an empty table—which allows you to look at the imported records and make corrections as necessary—before mixing the records with your existing data.

Importing Dates That Access Can't Read

Import the dates into Text or Number fields, create a query that calculates date values from the imported values, and make an update query to correct the table.

There are date formats that Access cannot read. For example, version 1.0 can't read dates in *YYMMDD* or *YYYYMMDD* format. If the parts of the date are not contiguous, that is, if there are several spaces between the day, month, and year, Access can't import the information as dates. If one part of the date is missing—for example, if the dates are in the format *MM/YY* with no day—Access can't convert them to dates. Or if the file uses non-standard or foreign names or abbreviations for the names of months, Access can't understand them. In this situation, you can still import the dates into Access, but you must perform a few extra steps.

For example, the fixed-width text file shown in Figure 2.6, contains dates in *MM/YY* format. Since Access cannot read this format, what can you do if you need to import them as standard format dates, using the first day of the month?

To import the file and convert the partial dates to a Date field, do the following:

1. Import the file. Import the parts of the date as separate Text or Number fields named Month, Day, and Year. To import the dates in Figure 2.6, omit the Day field since there is no day position in the dates. If the dates contain text, for example French dates like *14 juillet 1789*, use a Text field for the text part of the date.

2. Modify the design of the table, adding a Date field to contain the dates.

3. Make a new query to calculate the date based on the fields you imported. Base the query on the table you just imported. In the Field

```
Bodeau   12/90
Brink    01/57
Muder    08/54
Young    05/54
```

Figure 2.6   Fixed-width text file with non-standard dates.

row of the query grid, enter an expression that calculates the date based on the Month, Day, and Year fields. To interpret the dates in our example, use 1 in place of the Day field, since the dates contain no day numbers.

If Year, Month, and Day are Number fields, use the DateSerial() function, like this:

```
DateSerial(Year, Month, Day)
```

To change the dates in Figure 2.6, use this expression:

```
DateSerial(Year, Month, 1)
```

If Year, Month, and Day are Text fields, join the fields into a format that Access can understand, and use the DateValue() function, like this:

```
DateValue(string expression)
```

For example, if Year, Month, and Day are Text fields containing "1994," "12," and "25" respectively, use this expression:

```
DateValue(Month &"/"& Day +"/"& Year)
```

View the results of the query to make sure that the expression calculates the date correctly.

4. When you have figured out the right expression to calculate the dates, change the query into an update query. Copy the expression from the Field row of the query grid to the Update To row, omitting the "Expr1:" that Access adds to the beginning of the expression. Change the entry in the Field row to the name of the Date field you added in step 2. For example, the update query might look like Figure 2.7 (this query updates a field called Date joined with a calculation using fields Year and Month).

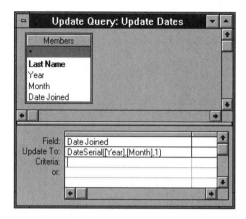

Figure 2.7   Use an update query to calculate dates from Month and Year fields.

5.   Update the table by clicking on the ! button from the toolbar.

6.   Look at the table to make sure that the new Date field is right. When it is, delete the Month, Day, and Year fields.

Interpret Non-Standard Month Names

If the months are abbreviated in a non-standard way, make a new table that contains two fields:

- The non-standard abbreviations (e.g., juillet for July)
- Either the standard month abbreviations or month numbers

In the query, relate the Month field to the field in the new table that contains the matching month abbreviations. This allows you to convert the non-standard abbreviations into either standard abbreviations or month numbers, for use in constructing valid dates.

Importing Data into an Existing Table

Import into an empty table, clean up the data, and append it to the table.

If you want to import information into an existing Access table, create a new, blank table in the database to import it into; don't import directly into the table that will eventually contain the information. Using a temporary table protects the information in your existing table from damage while you are importing. Also, while the imported records are in a separate table, you can clean the data up, if necessary.

Changing Field Names and Types

Once you have imported data into Access, you usually need to modify the design of the resulting tables. You may need to change field names and types, or delete fields you won't need. It is much easier to rename fields immediately, before you create forms, reports, queries, and macros that refer to them by their old names. Here are tips for making these changes easily.

Changing a Text Field to a Yes/No Field

Use update queries to change all the values to Yes or No, then change the field type.

If you have Yes/No information stored in a Text field, it is easy to change the field into a Yes/No field type without losing the existing data. Access recognizes the words *Yes, No, True, False, On,* and *Off* and can convert them into Yes/No data automatically when you change the field type.

However, Access doesn't recognize *Y, N, T, F,* or any other letters as Yes/No data. If you use these in your Text field, you can use an update query to change them into *Yes* and *No* before changing the field type.

1. Make sure that the Text field is at least three characters in size, so that *Yes* and *No* will fit in it.
2. Make a query based on the table, and enter in the query grid the name of the field you want to change into a Yes/No field. (You can enter other field names, as well.)
3. For the criteria, enter one value the field contains, for example, *Y.*
4. Switch to Datasheet view to check the results of the query.
5. Switch to Design view, then choose Query Update from the menu to change the select query into an update query.
6. In the Update To line of the query grid, enter either *Yes* or *No.* For example, if you have selected all the records with values of *Y,* enter *Yes.*
7. Click on the ! button from the toolbar to run the query. Access tells you how many records will be changed.
8. Click on OK if the number of records looks right. Access updates all the records you selected.
9. Repeat steps 6 through 8 for each value in the field. For example, if you just updated all the records containing *Y* to contain *Yes,* do the same thing to change records with *N* to contain *No.*

To change the field type:

1. Choose the table and switch to Design view.
2. Select the Text field.
3. Change the Data Type from Text to Yes/No.
4. Save the change by choosing File Save from the menu or by closing the Table window and clicking on Yes in the dialog box that appears.

As Access converts the Text field to a Yes/No field, if it encounters values that it doesn't recognize, it displays a warning. If this happens, cancel the conversion, fix the values in the Text field, and change the field type again.

After you change the field type, you can change the way the field is displayed in forms or reports, using check boxes, option buttons, or toggle buttons. You can also use a custom format to display other text values, like *Member* and *Non-member* (see Chapter 5).

Changing a Number Field to a Counter

Make a new table in which the Number field is changed to a Counter, then import the records.

If you import a table that contains a Number field containing sequential numbers, you would probably find it helpful if Access could continue numbering records as you enter them. However, to do this you must change the Number field into a Counter. Changing the field type directly wipes out the existing values of the Number field. Instead, follow these steps to retain the existing numbers:

1. Make sure that the primary key field of the table is the Number field that you want to change into a Counter.
2. Create a table with the same structure as the table whose Number field you want to change, except include a Counter field in place of the Number field. Make sure that all the field names are unchanged, including the name of the Number field. (See the next Hot Tip for an easy way to make this new table.)
3. Create an append query to append the records from the original table to the new table. To do this, make a query based on the original table, and drag the * (signifying all fields in the table) from the fields onto the query grid. Choose Query Append from the menu to change the query from a select to an append query. In the Query Properties dialog box, set the table to which you want to append to be the new table. Click on OK.

Now, the append query is ready to run.

4. Click on the ! button from the toolbar (or choose Query Run from the menu). Access tells you the number of rows that will be appended. Click on OK, then close the query—there is no need to save it.

5. Look at the new table. It should contain all the records from the original table. The values in the Number field are now in the corresponding Counter field. If you enter new records, the Counter field automatically fills in a number one greater than the last entry in the field.

6. Delete the original table. Rename the new table with the name of the original table.

Make an Empty Copy of a Table

The easiest way to make an empty table with the same structure is to display the list of tables in the database window, highlight the existing table, press **Ctrl+C** to copy the table, then press **Ctrl+V** to paste a copy of the table. Access displays the Paste Table As dialog box, shown in Figure 2.8. Enter the new name for the table, and choose the Structure Only Paste Option.

Setting the Size of Number Fields

Set the size of each Number field to save storage space.

When Access stores numbers, it needs one, two, four, or eight bytes to store each number. The default size of Number fields is Double, which takes the most storage space. If you know that a Number field will contain only whole numbers, choose Long Integer as the field size if the number may be larger than 32,000, Integer if they may go up to 32,000, or Byte if the whole numbers will be between 0 and 255.

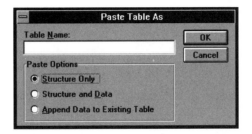

Figure 2.8 Use the Paste Table As dialog box to copy a table.

Use Currency Fields

If the numbers are dollar amounts (or another currency), make the field a Currency rather than Number field. This ensures that Access won't round cents off incorrectly when performing calculations.

Changing Field Names

Change the names in all queries, forms, and reports on which the field appears.

If you change the names of fields in your tables, Access does not automatically change them in the queries, forms, reports, macros, and modules in which the field names appear. If you are going to rename fields, it is easier to do it before you create these other Access objects.

If you have already created queries, forms, reports, and other objects based on your tables, you can use the Database Analyzer that comes with Access to find all the references to the fields you want to rename (see *Renaming Objects in Your Database* in Chapter 3).

Validating Existing Data

Make an update query to apply a new validation rule to the existing records in the table.

When you import a table, it is a good idea to create validation rules for the fields. But what about the records that are already in the table? Validation rules apply only to new records.

After you create the validation rule, create a query that selects records that don't match it. That is, create a query based on the table and include the field you are validating. You may want to include other fields so you can identify the records as you look at the results of the query. For the field you are validating, enter a criteria that is the *opposite* of the validation rule—a criteria that is false when the validation rule is true, and true when the validation rule is false. For example, if you are validating a field called Phone Number, the validation rule might be:

```
Like  "###-###-####*"
```

For the query, enter this criteria:

```
Not Like "###-###-####*"
```

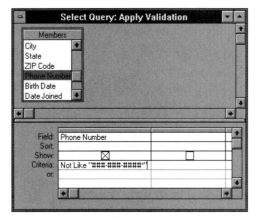

Figure 2.9 Query to select records that don't match the validation rule for a field.

Take a look at Figure 2.9 to see how the Select Query dialog box appears.

Look at the query results, which contain all the records that would fail the validation rule. Correct the entries. Press **Shift+F9** to requery the table. All the records should disappear—if they don't, they still don't pass the validation rule.

Finding Duplicate Key Values

Use a query to identify the duplicate keys.

After you import a table into Access, you should decide which field or fields to use as the primary key. If there are duplicate values of the primary key field, Access displays the message, "Can't have duplicate key; index changes were unsuccessful." You get the same message if you create a No Duplicates index for a field that contains duplicate values.

If the field should be able to contain duplicate values, you must choose another field or combination of fields for your primary key. But what if the field shouldn't contain duplicates? Here is an easy way to find them:

1. Make a new query based on the table. Click on the Totals button on the toolbar to add a total row to the query grid.

2. Drag the name of the desired key field (the field that you want to index or want to make into a primary key) into the query grid.

3. For the Total row of the query grid, choose Group By. This tells Access to include only one row for each value in the desired key field.

4. Drag the same field name into another column in the query grid.

5.   For the Total row, choose Count, which in the Field row of the next column in the query grid, type

```
count: count(*)
```

to tell Access to display the number of records that have the value of the desired key field. Each value of the field should appear in only record— it is the values that appear in more than one record that are causing the problem.

6.   For the Criteria row of this column, enter this:

```
>1
```

This selects only the values of the desired key field that appear in more than one record. The finished query looks like Figure 2.10.

7.   View the results of the query to see the values that are causing the trouble. You can fix them in the original table.

Fixing Referential Integrity Problems

Make an outer join query to find the records that violate the referential integrity rule.

When you create relationships between tables in the Relationships dialog box, and you select the Enforce Referential Integrity box, Access doesn't create the relationship unless all the existing records in the tables satisfy referential integrity. That is, all records in the related table must contain values of the related field that appear in the primary table. If there are any records in the related table that contain values of the related field that

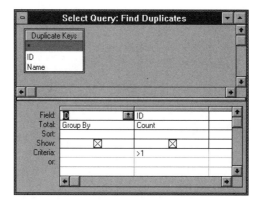

Figure 2.10   Query to identify multiple values of a key field.

don't match the primary table, Access displays the error message, "Existing data in table *table name* violates specified relationship."

For example, in the membership database we designed in Chapter 1, the Members and Donations tables are related by Membership Number. The Payee field in the Donations table is the foreign key field. What if we import donations with invalid membership numbers? How do you find the offending records? Here is an easy way:

1. Create a new query based on the two tables you want to relate. Join them by dragging the primary key field from one table to the matching foreign key field in the other table. For example, drag the Membership Number field from the Members table to the Payee field in the Donations table. This relates the two tables using these fields.

2. Double-click on the line that relates the tables. This selects the relationship and displays the Join Properties dialog box, shown in Figure 2.11.

3. Choose option 3, "Include All records from 'Donations' and only those records from 'Members' where the joined fields are equal." This is called an *outer join* because it includes records that don't exist in both tables. (See *Including Results with Missing Data* in Chapter 9 for more information on outer joins.)

4. Click on OK.

5. Drag the primary key from the primary table (Membership Number from the Members table) and the foreign key from the related table (Payee from the Donations table) to the query grid. View the result of the query.

Any record for which the field from the primary table (Membership Number) is blank is a record that violates referential integrity. There is no record in the primary table for the value in the related table.

When you fix the erroneous records, try creating the relationship again.

Figure 2.11 Finding invalid foreign key values using an outer join.

Fixing the Structure of Your Database

When you set up an Access database, the data you import may not be divided into the tables the way you want. In some cases, you may want to split tables into several related tables. Here are ways to split up or combine related tables.

Combining One-to-One Tables

Use a make-table query to combine two tables with a one-to-one relationship.

If you have two tables with a one-to-one relationship, you may decide later on to maintain them as a single table. For example, if you store personnel information in two tables, with general information about each employee in the Employees table and financial information about each employee in the Salaries table, you may decide to combine them later.

In each table, there is one record for each employee. The two tables are related by Employee Number, which is the primary key in both tables. To combine the tables:

1. Create a query that contains all the fields from one table, and all the fields from the other table except the key field. (If you include the primary key fields from both tables, the field will appear twice in the resulting table.)

2. Choose Query Make Table from the menu. Enter a name for the new, combined table.

3. Click on the ! button on the toolbar to run the query. This creates the new, combined table.

4. In the new table, enter formats, defaults, validation rules, and validation text, because they are not copied from the original tables. Also, define a primary key field.

5. If you plan to delete the two original tables, use the Relationships dialog box to create relationships between the new, combined table and other tables in the database.

6. When you are sure the new table contains the data from both original tables, you can delete the two original tables.

Splitting One Table into Two Related Tables

Use two make-table queries to split one table into two tables with a one-to-one relationship.

To split a table, follow these steps:

1. Make a query based on the table you want to split. Include the primary key field and all the fields you want to include in one of the split tables. Both of the tables must contain the primary key field; this is the field that will relate the two tables. No other fields should be duplicated between the two tables.

2. Choose Query Make Table from the menu, and enter the name for the new, split table.

3. Click on the ! button from the toolbar to run the query.

4. Open the resulting table and make sure that it contains the fields you want.

5. In Design view, enter formats, defaults, validation rules, and validation text for the new table, because they are not copied from the original table. Also, define a primary key field.

6. Repeat steps 1 through 5 for the other table—you'll have created two tables to replace the original table.

7. Create the one-to-one relationship between the two new tables in the Relationships dialog box. Also, create relationships with any other tables in the database.

8. When you have checked the two new tables, you can delete the original table.

Splitting One-to-Many Tables into Separate Tables

Use queries to split a table into two tables with a one-to-many relationship.

In some cases, you may have imported a single table that tries to simulate the effect of two related tables by using duplicate fields. For example, if you are setting up a membership database for a non-profit organization, you might want to track donations by members. The Members table you import might contain these fields:

```
Membership Number
Name
Address
City
State
ZIP
Donation1
Date1
Donation2
Date2
Donation3
Date3
```

This table allows you to store information about the last three donations each member made. But what happens when someone makes a fourth donation? And how could you create a report listing all donations by date, or all donations above a certain amount? It would be hard, because the donation information may be stored in any of three fields.

It would be better to store donations in a separate table, related to the Members table. The new Donations table would contain the Membership Number field, with a one-to-many relationship with the Members table (one member can donate many times). It would also contain Date and Amount fields. The process of changing the tables in a database to a better relational structure is called *normalization*.

You can split the existing table into separate Members and Donations tables by using queries.

1. Make a query based on the original table. Drag the primary key field (Membership Number) to the query grid. For each field about the first donation (Donation1, and Date1), enter an expression in the Field row of the query grid like this:

    ```
    Amount:  [Donation1]
    ```

In this example, Amount is the name that the field will have in the Donations table. Donation1 is the current name of the field. This expression includes Donation1 in the dynaset, while changing its name to Amount. The finished query for the first donation looks like Figure 2.12.

2. Choose Query Make Table from the menu. For the table name, enter the name of the new table (Donations). Click on the ! button from the toolbar to create the table. Now, the Donations table exists, has the fields you want, but only contains data for the first donation for each member.

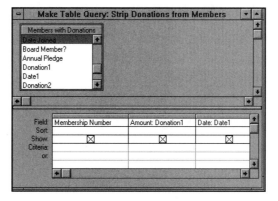

Figure 2.12 Query to select fields about the first donation.

3. Repeat steps 1 and 2 for the fields about the second donation, except name the new table Temp2. (You can't append the records directly to the Donations table, because null values would be appended for the Amount and Date fields.)

4. Repeat steps 1 and 2 for the fields about the third donation, creating a table called Temp3. Now, you can append the Temp2 and Temp3 tables to the Donations table.

5. Make a query based on Temp2 and drag the * (indicating all the fields in the table) from the field list to the query grid.

6. Choose Query Append from the menu, and enter the table name that contains the data about the first donations (Donations). Click on the ! button to run the query.

7. Repeat steps 5 and 6 to append the Temp3 table to the Donations table. Now the Donations table contains all the information about donations that the Members table contains.

8. Enter formats, defaults, validation rules, and validation text for the new Donations table. Choose a combination of fields to use as a primary key. The combination should include the primary key field from the original table (Membership Number) plus another field. For the Donations table, a combination of Membership Number and Date uniquely identifies each donation.

9. Modify the structure of the original table, deleting the columns that contain the information you have moved to the new table. For the Members table, delete the Donation1, Date1, Donation2, Date2, Donation3, and Date3 fields.

10. Create a one-to-many relationship between the original table (the "one" side) and the new table (the "many" side).

CHAPTER

3

Maintaining Access Databases

O nce you have created a database in Access—whether you import data or attach Access to existing databases, or whether you start from scratch—you want to keep it running smoothly. It would be terrible to lose so much careful work, to data loss when a hard disk breaks, to power glitches that cause the computer to reboot, or to well-intentioned but destructive tinkering by a co-worker. This chapter contains tips for documenting, backing up, and maintaining your database.

Documenting Your Database

An Access database contains a number of components that work together. For example, reports are based on queries that pull information from tables, and forms have macros attached to fields that validate data in tables. For a complex application, this can get confusing. To avoid mishaps on your part and on the part of others using the database, you will find it immensely helpful to document the inner workings of the application.

Deciding How Much to Write

Documentation includes comments in the database as well as printed material.

It is a good idea to write some documentation about your Access database, especially if other people will use it or if anyone else might have to maintain it, make changes to it, or add forms or reports. This documentation can come in three forms:

- **Comments and Descriptions:** When you create or modify a table, add comments in the Description column (visible in Design view) for each field. When you create macros, add comments in the Comment column about what each action does.

- **User Instructions:** Include instructions on forms you create. Write procedures for how to enter data and how to print reports. However, if the database has menus and lots of instructions on each form, you may not need detailed additional written instructions.

- **Database Structure:** You can use the Database Analyzer that comes with Access to print out the structure of each table, query, form, report, macro, and module. In the next few pages, you'll find instructions for installing and running the Analyzer.

You can store the documentation for your database in a word-processing document and print it out for your own and others' use.

Use Help Text in Written Instructions

Some of the information you'd like to include in your written instructions may already exist in Access Help. Press **F1** any time you are in Access and browse through the Access Help topics to see if there is material you can use.

If so, follow these steps to copy the text from Access Help to your Windows word-processing program:

1. Press **F1** to display the Access Help window.
2. Select the text you want to use.
3. In the Help window menu bar, choose Edit Copy to store the text in the Windows Clipboard.
4. In your word processor, use the command (usually Edit Paste, or **Ctrl+V**) to paste the text into your documentation.

The Help text has hard carriage returns at the end of each line. To allow the text to wrap properly from line to line in your word-processing document, delete the unneeded carriage returns.

What Is the Database Analyzer?

Use the Database Analyzer to create tables containing information about the tables, queries, forms, reports, macros, and modules in your database.

The Database Analyzer is an Access library database written by Microsoft. You can use it to produce documentation about your databases. It is stored in a file named ANALYZER.MDA, which is installed with Access if you choose to install the sample databases.

To use the Database Analyzer, you create a macro called Analyzer in the database that you want to analyze. (See *Installing the Database Analyzer* in the next section to learn how to create the macro.) When you run the Analyzer macro, it creates tables that contain information about your database. You can analyze the entire database, or you can choose the tables, queries, forms, reports, macros, and modules to analyze. The results of the analysis are written to one or more tables. Each output table and its function is indicated in Table 3.1.

Table 3.1   Database Analyzer Output Tables

Table Name	Objects Analyzed	Fields	Description
@TableDetails	Tables	TableName, Name Type, Length, IndexName	Lists all fields in each table, including their names, types, lengths, and whether they are indexed.
@QueryDetails	Queries	QueryName, Name, Type, Length, SourceTable	Lists all fields (columns) in each query's dynaset, including their names, types, lengths, and what table (or other query) each comes from.
@QuerySQL	Queries	QueryName, SQLStatement	Lists queries with their SQL equivalents.
@FormProperties	Forms	FormName, Caption, LinkChildFields, LinkMasterFields, Modal, OnOpen, OnClose, OnMenu, OnPrint, PopUp, RecordSelectors, RecordSource, ScrollBars	Lists forms including the property settings for each form. (These are settings that apply to the whole form, not individual controls on the form.)
@FormControls	Forms	FormName, AfterUpdate, AllowEditing, BeforeUpdate, Caption, ControlName, OnPush, Visible (see note that follows this table)	Lists all controls on each form, with the property settings for each control.

Table 3.1   Database Analyzer Output Tables (continued)

Table Name	Objects Analyzed	Fields	Description
@Report Properties	Reports	FormName, Caption, LinkChildFields, LinkMasterFields, Modal, OnOpen, OnClose, OnMenu, OnPrint, PopUp, RecordSelectors, RecordSource, ScrollBars	Lists reports including the property settings for each report. (These are settings that apply to the whole report, not individual controls on the report.) The FormName field actually contains the report name.
@Report Controls	Reports	FormName, AfterUpdate, AllowEditing, BeforeUpdate, Caption, ControlName, OnPush, Visible (see note)	Lists all controls on each report, including the property settings for each control.
@MacroDetails	Macros	MacroName, MacroGroup, Action, Condition, Argument1, Argument2, Argument3, Argument4, Argument5, Argument6, Argument7, Argument8, Argument9, Argument10	Lists macros, including the actions, conditions, and arguments contained in each macro.
@Module Procedures	Modules	ModuleName, ProcedureName, Params	Lists the procedures contained in each module, including their parameters.
@Module Variables	Modules	ProcedureType, VariableName, Type	Lists the variables in each procedure, including their names and types.

Note: When you analyze forms and reports, you can choose which control properties to include in the @FormControls and @ReportControls output tables. The default properties to include are shown in the Fields column of Table 3.1, but you can add any other properties of form and report controls to this list. (See *Analyzing Forms and Reports* later in this chapter for information on adding properties to a database analysis.)

You can store the analysis output tables in the database you are analyzing, or in another database. If you want to put the output tables in another database, you will have to create the database before you run the Database Analyzer—the Analyzer can't create a new database to contain the tables.

Installing the Database Analyzer

Edit MSACCESS.INI in the WINDOWS directory, adding a line to include the Analyzer as a library.

The Database Analyzer library database (ANALYZER.MDA) is packaged with Access and is installed when you install Access's sample applications. (If you are not sure if the file was installed, use the Windows File Manager to look for it in your Access program directory.)

For each database you plan to analyze, you must create a macro that calls the analyzer. Here are the steps for preparing to analyze a database:

First you must edit your MSACCESS.INI file to include information about the Analyzer.

1. Using a text editor like the Windows Notepad, open the MSACCESS.INI file in your Windows program directory (usually C:\WINDOWS). If you can't find MSACCESS.INI, use the File Manager to search for it.

2. In MSACCESS.INI, find the line that says:

   ```
   [Libraries]
   ```

There is probably a line beneath it that refers to WIZARD.MDA, the library database that contains FormWizards and ReportWizards.

3. Just below the [Libraries] line, on a line by itself, type **analyzer.mda=**.

4. Save the MSACCESS.INI file.

5. If Access is running, exit, then restart the program. (Access reads the MSACCESS.INI file when it loads.) If Access can't find the Analyzer database, it will display a message saying "Can't find analyzer.mda." If this happens, exit from Access, find ANALYZER.MDA, and move it to the Access program directory. Or check again that the new line in MSACCESS.INI is right. Then restart Access.

Now you're ready to create the macro that runs the Analyzer.

6. Open the database you want to analyze.

7. View the list of macros in the Database window. Click on the New button to make a new macro.

8. When Access displays the Macro window, enter the following in the Action column of the first row (you can either type the action, or choose it from the pull-down list):

   RunCode

9. Notice the Function Name argument, which displays in the lower half of the Macro window. For the function name, enter

   StartAnalyzer()

   StartAnalyzer() is the name of an Access Basic function in ANALYZER.MDA. Your macro should look like Figure 3.1.

10. Close the Macro window, saving the macro. Name it Analyzer.

Now the Database Analyzer is ready to analyze this database.

Copy the Analyzer Macro to Your Other Databases

You have to install the Database Analyzer only once in your MSACCESS.INI file, but each database you want to analyze must contain the Analyzer macro. Once you have created the macro, you can copy it to another database. Follow these steps to copy the Analyzer macro:

1. Open the database containing the Analyzer macro.
2. In the Database window, highlight the Analyzer macro in the list of macros and choose Edit Copy from the menu (or press **Ctrl+C**).
3. Open another database and paste the macro into it by choosing Edit Paste from the menu (or pressing **Ctrl+V**).
4. When Access prompts you to name the macro, type **Analyzer**. (You don't have to call the macro Analyzer, but it will be less confusing if you use the same name in all your databases.)

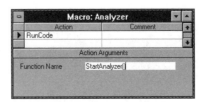

Figure 3.1   You need to create a macro to run the Database Analyzer.

Running the Database Analyzer

Run the Analyzer macro, choose the items to analyze, and specify the output database.

To use the Database Analyzer:

1. If you want to store the analysis tables in a new database, you must create it first. Choose File New Database from the menu and name the database something like ANALYSIS.

2. Open the database you want to analyze.

3. To run the Analyzer macro, select the Analyzer macro from the list of macro names in the Database window and click on Run. Access displays the Database Analyzer dialog box, shown in Figure 3.2.

4. Click one of the six buttons—Table, Query, Form, Report, Macro, or Module—in the left-hand part of the Database Analyzer dialog box to choose which type of database object to analyze. The Items Available box fills with a list of the items of that type in the database. You can choose one or more of these items to analyze from the Items Available list.

5. To select an item, highlight it and click on the right-pointing arrow button in the middle of the Database Analyzer window. The item name moves from the Items Available list to the Items Selected list. To choose all the items on the Items Available list, click on the double right-pointing arrow button. To deselect an item, highlight it in the Items Selected list and click on the left-pointing arrow button.

You can select one or more of each of the six types of database objects to analyze. Depending on what types of objects you include, the Database Analyzer creates one or more output tables (see Table 3.1).

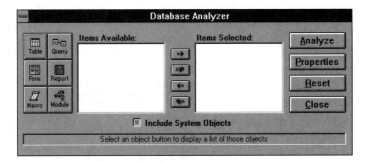

Figure 3.2 The Database Analyzer window.

6. When you have selected all the objects you want to analyze, click on the Analyze button to display the Select an Output Database dialog box, shown in Figure 3.3.

It is a good idea to put the output of the Database Analyzer in one of two places:

- The database you are analyzing
- A separate existing database that contains the output of this and other analyses (you might name this database ANALYZE)

7. Choose an output database and click on OK.

A series of messages appears at the bottom of the Database Analyzer window. When the Analyzer is done, it displays a dialog box saying, "Process Completed."

8. Click on OK.
9. Click on the Close button to close the Database Analyzer window.

Now you can look at the tables the Database Analyzer created.

Analyze System Objects

You may want to choose the Include System Objects check box in the Database Analyzer window. If you do, additional objects appear for some database object types.

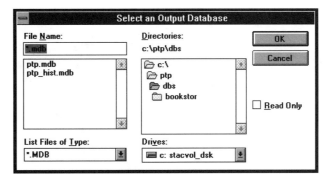

Figure 3.3 Selecting an output database for the Database Analyzer.

Analyzing Forms and Reports

Click the Properties button in the Database Analyzer window to select which properties to list in the output tables.

Controls in forms and reports have a tremendous number of properties, 38 in all. To limit the size of the @FormControls and @ReportControls output tables, you can choose which properties you are interested in. The Database Analyzer selects the following properties by default: AfterUpdate, AllowEditing, BeforeUpdate, Caption, ControlName, OnPush, and Visible.

To change this list, delete any existing @ReportControls and @FormControls tables in the database in which you store the output tables, if necessary. (Access won't let you change the properties if these tables exist.) Then run the Analyzer macro. Click on either the Forms or Reports button. Then, click on the Properties button to display the Form Properties dialog box, shown in Figure 3.4—the dialog box is called Form Properties even if you are viewing reports; the properties you choose apply to both forms and reports.

Use the right-pointing arrow in the center of the Form Properties window to move properties from the Available Properties list to the Selected Properties list. If properties are selected that you are not interested in, use the left-pointing arrow to deselect them, moving them back to the Available Properties list.

Click on Close when you have selected the properties you would like to include in the @FormControls and @ReportControls output tables. The Database Analyzer stores your property choices in the ANALYZER.MDA database, so the new properties remain selected the next time you run the Analyzer.

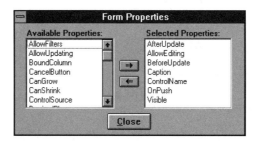

Figure 3.4   Choosing the properties to include in Database Analyzer output tables.

Using the Database Analyzer Output Tables

Create reports and queries using the output tables.

Once you have run the Database Analyzer, you can use its output tables just like regular Access tables. To produce technical documentation for your database, you can create reports that list information from the tables.

You can also use queries to search the output tables. For example, if you want to know which forms contain a particular field, create a query on the @FormControls table using the ControlSource field as the criteria.

Once you have finished using the output tables and have printed any reports based on them, you can delete them. The Database Analyzer will re-create the tables the next time you run it. Or, if you want to leave the tables in the database, the Database Analyzer will update them the next time you run it.

Keeping the Database Analyzer Small

Compact ANALYZER.MDA after you use it.

The Database Analyzer is stored in the Access database ANALYZER.MDA. When you run the Database Analyzer, it creates temporary tables that increase its size on the disk. To make it smaller, compact it just as you would any other Access database. (See the Hot Tip *Compact the Database Analyzer* later in this chapter for information.)

Making a Diagram of Your Database

Use the Query window to draw a picture of the relationships in the database.

Access can draw a diagram of your database, showing the relationships between the tables. If you create a query that includes all the tables in the database, the top part of the Query window shows field lists for the tables, with join lines indicating the relationships. To make a diagram in a Query window:

1. Create a new query.
2. Add all the tables in the database to the query. Don't add any queries.
3. Maximize the Query window so you have lots of room to work. You can also move the split bar (which divides the two parts of the Query window) down as far as possible, since you won't use the query grid.

4. There won't be join lines to attached tables. To create missing join lines, drag the primary key from the field list of one table over to the related field on the field list of the related table.

5. You may need to widen the field lists for tables with long names, so that the whole table name appears at the top of each field list.

6. Move the tables so that the join lines cross as few times as possible, to make a clear diagram. Figure 3.5 shows the top part of the Query window containing a diagram of the MEMBERS database.

7. Save the query, using a name like Database Diagram.

To print the diagram, copy the screen to a drawing program like Microsoft Paintbrush, which comes with Windows. If you have a screen capture program like HotShot or Halo Desktop Imager, use it to capture the top part of the Query window, save the image, and print it. If you don't have a screen capture program, you can use the Windows print-screen facility and Microsoft Paintbrush by following these steps:

1. Move the Query window to the left side of the screen. (Move the Database window out of the way.) This ensures that the Query window will fit on the Paintbrush drawing.

2. Press the Print Screen key on your keyboard to copy the current contents of the screen to the Clipboard.

3. Run Microsoft Paintbrush. In the Windows Program Manager, double-click the Paintbrush icon in the Accessories program group.

4. Make the Paintbrush drawing area as large as possible. To remove the Toolbox and Linesize box from the Paintbrush window, choose View Tools and Linesize. To remove the Palette, choose View Palette.

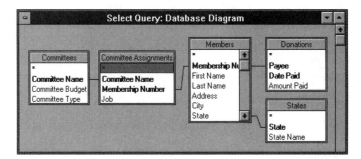

Figure 3.5   Query window showing a diagram of the tables in the MEMBERS database.

5. In Paintbrush, choose Edit Paste from the menu, or press **Ctrl+V**, to copy the screen image from the Clipboard into the Paintbrush drawing. The Paintbrush drawing now contains your diagram, along with the rest of the Access window and whatever else was on screen when you captured the screen image. Now you can isolate just the diagram.

6. Choose View Toolbox and Linesize to display the toolbox again.

7. From the toolbox, choose the Pick tool (the right-hand scissors icon).

8. Select a rectangle that includes the diagram.

9. Press **Ctrl+X**, or choose Edit Cut from the menu, to move the diagram to the Clipboard.

10. Start a new drawing by choosing File New from the menu. When Paintbrush asks if you want to save the current drawing, click on No.

11. Choose Edit Paste, or press **Ctrl+V**, to copy the diagram from the Clipboard to the new drawing.

12. You can edit the drawing, adding titles or other explanations. You may want to type *1* and *M* at the ends of the join lines to show which tables are the master ("one") and detail ("many") tables in one-to-many relationships.

13. To save the drawing, choose File Save from the menu and enter a filename.

14. To print the drawing, choose File Print.

15. To exit Microsoft Paintbrush, choose File Exit.

If the database contains more than about ten tables, you may not be able to fit the whole diagram on the screen. Create two or more diagrams, each showing some of the tables.

Making and Using Backups

Of all the files you store on your computer, the information in database files is the most vital to back up. Up-to-date backups are important in case entire database files are deleted or damaged, individual database objects are deleted or modified incorrectly, or individual records in tables are deleted or badly modified. So many things can go wrong—protect yourself and your data!

An Access database consists of two files: one with the extension .MDB and one with the extension .LDB. The .MDB file contains the actual Access database, while the .LDB file contains the locking information that allows the database to be shared with other users. Access creates the .LDB file automatically—if it is accidentally deleted, Access just re-creates it. Therefore, you only need to back up the .MDB file.

Backing Up the Whole Database

Because Access stores all database objects together in one database file, even if only one object has changed, it is easiest to back up the whole database file.

There are three common ways to make backup copies of database files:

- You can use the Windows File Manager or the DOS XCOPY command to copy your Access database files to diskette. If the files are large (and Access database files always are!), use a compression program like PKZIP (from PKWare, Inc.) to shrink the files before copying. When using File Manager or XCOPY, the file (or its compressed equivalent) must fit on a single diskette. Newer versions of PKZIP can create zip files that span several diskettes.

- A backup program like DOS BACKUP, FastBack, or Central Point Backup allows you to make backup copies of files that are too large to fit on a single diskette by dividing the files up into pieces and copying them to a series of diskettes. Some compress the database as they copy it, reducing the number of diskettes you need. You must use the matching restore program to use files backed up by a backup program. *You can't use DOS COPY or XCOPY or the Windows File Manager to copy files back to your hard disk if they were backed up using a backup program.*

- A tape backup allows you to copy many files, including database files, to tape quickly. Commercial backup programs work with tapes as well as diskettes.

When making backups, be sure to include all the files used by the application. This certainly includes your Access database(s), and might also include external data files or programs. Remember, you need to back up the .MDB file for each database, but you don't need to include the .LDB (locks) file. Be sure to include documentation files and other related files.

Back Up SYSTEM.MDA

The SYSTEM.MDA database in your Access program directory contains passwords and security information for multi-user systems. If you have implemented Access security, be sure to include SYSTEM.MDA in your backups. Without the SYSTEM.MDA file, Access won't run, and without an up-to-date version, you may not have the correct information about users and permissions.

Making a Backup Schedule

Make backups regularly, using rotating tapes or sets of diskettes.

Once you determine how to make backup copies of the database files, decide how often to do so. It is a bad idea to keep just one backup copy of your application—tapes and diskettes can be ruined or misplaced easily. Also, errors in your database may not be discovered immediately. Keep backups for several days or weeks, so that you can return to an older backup to fix the problem.

For applications that are updated every day, you might want to use a backup scheme like this:

- Make five tapes, or five sets of backup diskettes, and label them **Monday**, **Tuesday**, **Wednesday**, **Thursday**, and **Friday**.

- Every day, back up the database using the tape or diskette(s) for that day.

- Every Friday, make an extra backup and keep it for a month.

- Occasionally, take one of the extra Friday backups to another location.

This backup scheme provides daily backups that you keep for a week, weekly backups that you keep for a month, and occasional off-site backups. This may seem like an unnecessary bother, but think of the effort involved in recovering from the loss of all or part of your database!

Put the Backup Command in Your AUTOEXEC.BAT File

To make sure that you do backups, you can put the backup command in your AUTOEXEC.BAT file. For example, if you use PKZIP and DOS BACKUP to compress the database files and related files in C:\ACCESSDB and copy them to diskette(s) in A:, add these lines to your AUTOEXEC.BAT:

```
echo Put backup diskette #1 in drive A:.
pause
pkzip -a c:\db.zip c:\accessdb\*.MDB
backup c:\db.zip a:
echo Backup done! Put away the backup diskette.
pause
```

If your AUTOEXEC.BAT runs Windows (with the command WIN), be sure to put the commands to make the backup before the WIN command. If you use a commercial backup program with diskettes or tapes, refer to the manual for information on entering the necessary command(s) to perform the backup.

Importing Objects for Backup

If the database is large and the objects that change are small, import them into an empty database for backup.

If you have a large database, but make relatively minor modifications to it, you might find a full, daily backup to be a waste of time and diskettes. If the only objects that you change are small, you can import them into a new, empty database and back that up.

First back up the entire database. Then, every time you want to make an additional backup, create a new database and import the objects that have changed. Make backup copies of this database on diskette or tape.

When you use this backup method, you runs the risk of forgetting to import and back up new data. It is a good idea to make a backup of the entire database from time to time.

Restoring Databases

Use the same backup program, or XCOPY (or File Manager) and PKUNZIP, to restore the database file.

Sooner or later, a database file will disappear or get damaged, or an object in the database will get deleted accidentally. When it happens, you can fall back on your backup diskettes or tapes. There are two steps: First, restore the backup copy of the database file. Then, use the restored version to replace the damaged or missing file, or objects in the file.

If the database has been damaged, see *Repairing Damaged Databases* later in the chapter, before giving up and restoring the database from backups.

If the entire database has been deleted, restore the most recent backup of the database. If you used PKZIP and XCOPY or the Windows File Manager to make the backup, use XCOPY or File Manager and PKUNZIP to copy it back to its original location. If you used DOS BACKUP or another backup program, use the corresponding restore program. When you have restored the database file, it may be out of date—it does not contain any updates made since you made the backup. Try to reconstruct the changes you have made since the backup was made, and make them again. Now you know why I encourage you to make backups often!

If one or more objects in the database have been deleted or damaged, but the rest of the database is usable, you may be able to keep the existing database and import the missing objects. This partial restoration approach is better than replacing the whole database with the backup copy, because you won't lose all the edits you made since you backed up the database. Follow these steps to import only the damaged or missing database information:

1. Restore the database, but copy it into a temporary directory or give it a different name.

2. Run Access and open the database with the deleted or damaged objects.

3. Delete any damaged objects.

4. Import the missing objects from the backup database. Choose File Import from the menu, choose Microsoft Access as the Data Source, choose the database file you just restored as the File to import from, and select the objects to import.

5. Repair the database, just in case there is other damage. (See *Repairing Damaged Databases* later in this chapter for details.)

Making Global Changes to Tables

Maintaining a database includes making occasional changes to most or all of the records in a table. For example, you may decide to change the codes you use in a field, and you want to change all occurrences of those codes in a table. Or you may want to raise all of the prices of your products by 5 percent, or all the prices of products from one distributor. Here are techniques for using action queries; to make these kinds of global changes to tables.

Before you begin making global changes, be sure to make a backup of your database. If an update or delete query works incorrectly, it can destroy a lot of information in a hurry.

Updating All Values of a Field

Use an update query to change the values.

You can change the value of a field in every record in a table. For large tables, it would be tedious and error-prone to do this by hand. Instead, use an update query.

For example, for the membership database, you might want to add a field called Target Pledge that is 10 percent above each member's existing annual pledge. You want to store the field in the table, rather than using a calculated field in a query, so that you can edit the amount for certain active members. Follow these steps to add the new field and fill it in automatically:

1. Open the table in Design view and add the new field. Enter a format, default value, and validation rule as needed.

2. Save the change to the table.

3. Create a new query based on the table.

4. Create a calculated field in the query by entering an expression in the Field row of the query grid. For example, enter this expression to calculate the Target Pledge:

   ```
   [Annual Pledge] * 1.1
   ```

   (See Chapter 9 for more information on creating calculated fields in queries.)

5. Drag one or more additional fields to the query grid, so you can check that the calculation is working correctly. For example, drag the Annual Pledge and Last Name fields to the grid. Figure 3.6 shows the finished query.

6. Switch to Datasheet view to check that the calculation works. (The calculated values may not be formatted correctly; this will be fixed when they are stored in the new field.)

7. Switch back to the Query window. Change the query from a select query into an update query by choosing Query Update from the menu. Access adds the Update To row to the query grid.

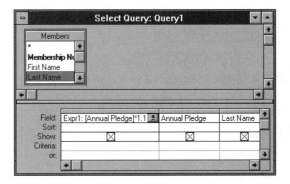

Figure 3.6 Query to calculate target pledges for each member.

8. In the column for the calculated field, move the expression to the Update To row. Select the expression and press **Ctrl+X** to store it in the Clipboard. Delete the temporary name Access gave to the calculation (Expr1) from the Field row. Move to the Update To row and press **Ctrl+V** to copy the expression from the Clipboard to the query grid.

9. Enter the name of the field to be updated in the Field row of the same column (or choose it from the drop-down list). For this example, enter Target Pledge.

10. Delete the other columns from the query grid, since you don't want to update any other fields. Figure 3.7 shows the finished update query.

11. Click on the ! button on the toolbar to run the update query. Access notifies you how many rows (records) of the table will be updated. Click on OK to proceed.

Figure 3.7 Update query to calculate target pledges.

12. View the table to make sure that the new field contains the proper values.

13. Close the query—you don't need to save it.

You can use this method to make many types of corrections to all the records in a table. For example, if some state codes have been entered in lowercase letters, you can use the following expression to capitalize them:

```
UCase([State])
```

Updating Selected Values of a Field

Use an update query with criteria to fix selected records in a table.

You can also select the records to update. For example, if you mistakenly entered many addresses in Quebec using the wrong province code (*QU* instead of *PQ*), you can correct them as a group. Follow these steps to use an update query to make the corrections:

1. Create a new query based on the table.

2. To make a column in the query grid that selects the records that need to be changed, drag the name of the field to be updated from the field list to the query grid. Enter a criterion that selects records with the values to be changed. For example, drag the State field to the query grid and enter **QU** in the Criteria row.

3. You may want to switch to Datasheet view to check that the selection is right, then switch back to continue designing the query.

4. Change the query from a select query into an update query by choosing Query Update from the menu. Access adds the Update To row to the query grid.

5. In the Update To row, enter the correct value. For example, enter **PQ**. Figure 3.8 shows the finished update query.

6. Click on the ! button on the toolbar to run the update query. Access notifies you how many rows (records) of the table will be updated. Click on OK to proceed.

7. View the table to make sure that the updated field contains the proper values.

8. Close the query—you don't need to save it.

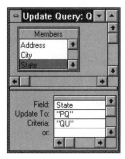

Figure 3.8 Update query to correct a province code.

Replacing Values in One or All Fields of a Table

You can use the Edit Replace command to replace text throughout a table, with Access asking whether to change each occurence.

You can use an update query to replace values in a field. For example, if a town gets a new ZIP code, you can make an update query to change all the values in the ZIP code field for that town. But what if you want to confirm each replacement, because some addresses remain in the old ZIP code and others are in the new ZIP code? You can use the Edit Replace command.

The Edit Replace command is especially convenient if you want to replace information in all the fields of a table or look at and confirm each replacement. However, the Edit Replace command can't calculate the replacement values using expressions, as update queries can.

To replace text in one or all the fields in a table, open the table in Datasheet view or in a form. Then choose Edit Replace from the menu to display the Replace dialog box, shown in Figure 3.9.

You can replace the text in the current field (the field your cursor was in when you chose the command) or all the fields in the table. You can also specify whether the text can be part of a longer entry or must be the entire entry, using the Match Whole Field option. Use the Match Case

Figure 3.9 Replacing text in one or all the fields in a table.

option if you want the capitalization of the entry to match what you typed. When you have entered the text to search for and the text to replace it with, click on the Find Next button to find the next occurrence of the text (starting at the current record). Then, click on Replace if you want the replacement to occur. If not, just click on Find Next again to skip the replacement. To replace all occurrences without confirming them, click on Replace All.

Other Database Maintenance Tasks

Here are few more tips on moving database files to a different directory or disk, hiding database files, renaming database objects, compacting databases to avoid wasting disk space, and repairing damaged databases.

Moving and Renaming Database Files

Close the database and move or rename the .MDB file that contains it.

To rename a database, just close the database and rename the .MDB file that contains it. For example, if your database is named BILLING, Access stores it in a file named BILLING.MDB. You can use the DOS REN (rename) command to change the name, or you can use the File Rename command in the Windows File Manager. Change the filename, but leave the extension as .MDB. If the database has multiple users, make sure everyone has closed the database before you rename it.

Access stores the locking information that allows you to share the database in the .LDB file of the same name. You can either rename or delete this file. If you delete it, Access automatically re-creates it the next time you open the database.

Note: You can't rename a database while it is open: Windows says, "Access denied," and DOS says, "Sharing violation."

To move a database to another directory or disk, close the database and move the .MDB file using the Windows File Manager. You can either move the corresponding .LDB file or delete it.

Hide Database Files

If you don't want others to open a database, you can arrange for a database not to appear on the list of available databases when users choose File Open Database from the menu. For example, if you create a database to contain output tables from the Database Analyzer, you may not want others to open it. To hide the database, just rename it, replacing the .MDB extension with .MDA. Microsoft uses this trick to hide several databases that are usually stored in the Access program directory.

To open a database that has been renamed with the .MDA extension, choose File Open Database from the menu. In the Open Database dialog box, the File Name box contains:

```
*.MDB
```

Edit this entry to read

```
*.MDA
```

and then press **Enter**. The list of files now shows the .MDA files in the directory. Choose one and then click on OK.

The following .MDA files will appear in the File Name list box for the Access program directory:

- SYSTEM.MDA, which contains multi-user database security accounts and passwords, and is encrypted.
- UTILITY.MDA, which contains system objects used by Access itself.
- WIZARDS.MDA, which contains FormWizards and ReportWizards— Access Basic programs that help you create forms and reports.
- ANALYZER.MDA, which contains the Database Analyzer, described earlier in this chapter.

Renaming Objects in Your Database

Highlight the object name in the Database window, choose File Rename from the menu, and use the Database Analyzer to find all references to the renamed object.

In the Database window, you can change the name of any object in the database by choosing File Rename from the menu. But, when you change the name of the object, references to the object aren't automatically changed. For example, you might create a table named MAIL, then create forms, queries, reports, and macros based on the MAIL table. If you rename MAIL as Mailing List, everything that refers to MAIL stops working. You must change the name of the table in all the forms, queries, reports, macros, and modules that refer to it.

You can use the Database Analyzer to find all the references to the object you want to rename. But, you must run the Analyzer *before* you rename the table, because the Analyzer can get confused if it can't find a table that is referred to in queries. For databases with multiple users, make sure no one else is using the database when you rename objects.

The easiest way to rename an object there are a lot of references to is to copy the object, change the references, and delete the original object. Be sure to back up the database first.

To rename a table:

1. Install the Database Analyzer as described earlier in this chapter, creating the Analyzer macro in the database.

2. In the Database window, view the list of macros, highlight the Analyzer macro, and click on Run.

3. Click on the Query button, and then click on the double-right-arrow button to select all the queries.

4. Repeat step 3 for forms, reports, macros, and modules. Now all the objects in your database, except the tables, are selected for analysis. You don't need to analyze the tables, because tables don't contain references to other objects, so no table will contain a reference to the table you want to rename.

5. Click on the Properties button, make sure the Control Source property is selected, then click on OK.

6. Click on the Analyze button.

7. Select the database in which the Database Analyzer output tables should be created, then click on OK.

The Database Analyzer runs and creates the tables described earlier in this chapter. Now you can look in each of the output tables to find the references to the table you want to rename. However, don't make changes to the data in the output tables—make the corrections to the actual objects in the database.

8. Make a copy of the table to be renamed by opening the table in Design view and choosing File Save As. Use the name to which you want to rename the table.

9. To correct any queries that refer to the old table name:

    9a.   Open the @QueryDetails table and search the SourceTable field for the old name of the table.

    9b.   Wherever you find it, look in the QueryName field to find the name of the query that contains the reference.

    9c.   Open that query in design mode.

9d. To fix the query, drag the new table to the top part of the table. Edit the Field entries in the columns of the query grid—correct the table name for those that referred to fields in the original table. If the query contained a column with an asterisk (*) to include all the fields from the renamed table, you may have to drag the asterisk to the grid again.

9e. Delete the field list for the old table from the top part of the query window.

9f. Save the query.

10. To correct any forms that refer to the renamed table:

   10a. Open the @FormProperties table and search the RecordSource field for the old name of the table.

   10b. Wherever you find it, look in the FormName field to find the name of the form that contains the reference to the renamed table.

   10c. Open the form in design mode. Make sure the Property Sheet is visible, and fix the table name in the Record Source property.

   10d. Also open the @FormControls table and search the ControlSource field for the old name of the table. It may appear within Access expressions in the Control Source property of a bound text box that looks up data from other tables. If you find the table name, change it in the expression and save the form.

   10e. Save the forms you change.

11. To correct any reports that refer to the renamed table:

   11a. Open the @ReportProperties table and search the RecordSource field for the old name of the table.

   11b. Wherever you find it, look in the (misnamed) FormName field to find the name of the report that contains the reference to the renamed table.

   11c. Open the report in design mode. Make sure the Property Sheet is visible, and fix the table name in the Record Source property.

   11d. Also open the @ReportControls table and search the ControlSource field for the old name of the table you renamed. It may appear within Access expressions in the Control Source property of a bound text box that looks up data from other tables. If you find the table name, change it in the expression and save the report.

11e. Save the reports you change.

12. To correct any macros that refer to the renamed table:

12a. Open the @MacroDetails table and search the Condition fields and the fields named Argument1 through Argument10 for the name of the table. The old table name may appear by itself or within an expression.

12b. Wherever you find it, look in the MacroName field to find the name of the macro that contains the reference to the renamed table. The MacroGroup field contains the name of the macro within that macro group, if any.

12c. Change the table name in the macro arguments and conditions, and save the macro.

13. To change the name in modules, open each module and choose Edit Find from the menu to search for the old name of the renamed table. Save each module you change.

14. If another Access database is attached to the renamed table, you must also change the name there. Unfortunately, you can't just rename the table; while this changes the name that appears in the attached database, it does not change the name Access looks for in the original database. Instead, follow these steps:

14a. Open the other database.

14b. Delete the renamed table (this doesn't delete the table in the database in which it is stored, it just deletes the attachment).

14c. Attach to the table again, using the new name.

14d. If you don't want to have to update all the queries, forms, reports, macros, and modules in this database that refer to the attached table, you can choose the File Rename command from the menu to rename the database from the new name to the old name. Renaming the table in the attached database doesn't affect the table in the database in which it is stored, it just controls the name used for the table in this database.

15. If you defined relationships to the table you want to rename, you must delete the relationships and re-create them using the new table name. Choose Edit Relationships from the menu to display the Relationships dialog box. For each relationship to the table, delete the relationship and re-create it using the new table name.

16. Now all references to the table have been changed from the old name to the new name. Delete the old table.

Use the same procedure after renaming a query, form, report, macro, or module. As you can see, renaming an object can be a huge job once there are references to it! Ideally, you should rename an object as soon as possible, before creating objects that refer to it. It is a good idea to back up the database before making many changes, such as these involved in renaming a table, and compact it afterwards.

Compacting Databases

Use the File Compact Database command to shrink database files on disk.

As you work with an Access database, creating objects, modifying them, and deleting unwanted objects, the amount of wasted space in your database file increases. To get rid of the wasted space, compact your database by following these steps:

1. Close the database. If the database is shared, make sure all users close the database.

2. Choose File Compact Database from the menu (this command only appears when no database is open). Access displays the Database to Compact From dialog box, shown in Figure 3.10.

3. Choose the database to compact and click on OK. Access then displays the Database to Compact Into dialog box.

You can use the same name for the database to compact into. (Access assigns the database a temporary name while compacting. If the compacting completes successfully, it deletes the original database and substitutes the new one for it.)

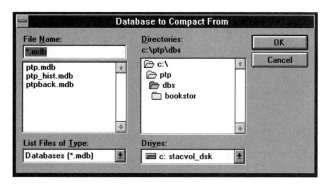

Figure 3.10 Choosing the database to compact.

4. Choose or enter a name, then click on OK. If you chose the name of an existing file, Access asks you to confirm that you want to replace the existing file. (Be sure you didn't enter the name of a *different* existing file!)

5. While compacting, Access displays a measure indicating how much of the process it has completed. Unless the process fails, Access will not notify you when it is done

Note: Compacting your database will not interfere with the Counter fields in your database. After you compact, Counters resume numbering after the highest existing record value.

Compact the Database Analyzer

Remember, Access "hides" files with the extension .MDA; when you want to compact the Database Analyzer (ANALYZER.MDA), the filename won't appear on the list of databases. Change the File Name entry from ***.mdb** to ***.mda** and press **Enter**. Then choose the file ANALYZER.MDA.

Since the ANALYZER.MDA is open as a library whenever you run Access, Access can't replace the existing ANALYZER.MDA with the new, compacted version. Instead, save it as a new database called TEMP.MDB. Exit from Access, then use the Windows File Manager to delete ANALYZER.MDA and rename TEMP.MDB as ANALYZER.MDA.

Repairing Damaged Databases

Use the File Repair Database command. If this doesn't work, import objects into a new database.

A database can become corrupted:

- If the computer or Windows is restarted when Access is running and the database is open, or

- If there is a hard disk error that prevents database information from being saved and read correctly

When you try to open a damaged database, Access may notice the damage and suggest that it try to repair the damage. If you think a database may be damaged even though Access opened it, you can close the database and choose File Repair Database from the menu. Anytime a database acts strangely, it is a good idea to repair it, just in case it was damaged. Repairing an undamaged database will do no harm.

If the database was seriously damaged, Access may not be able to repair it, and you won't be able to open the database. However, you may be able to import objects from it, if Access can read parts of the database file. Create a new database and begin importing database objects from the damaged database.

If you have made regular backups, you should be able to use a recent backup of the database. You may be able to use a combination of objects from the backup copy of the database and from the damaged database to create a new, up-to-date database.

Once you think you have repaired or re-created a damaged database, it is a good idea to use the Database Analyzer to look at all the objects in it. Running the Database Analyzer is described earlier in this chapter.

To use the File Repair Database command:

1. Close the database. For databases with multiple users, make sure everyone closes the database.

2. Choose File Repair Database from the menu.

3. Choose the database to repair.

4. Access begins repairing the database, and displays an indicator showing what percentage has been completed. When it is done, it displays the message "Repair of database "*name*" completed successfully." If the database couldn't be repaired, Access will notify you as well.

5. Click on OK.

Part Overview

PART 2

Forms and Datasheet Shortcuts

When your database is up and running, you will spend most of your time using forms, both for entering data and for selecting information to view. This part of the book describes how to make well-designed, easy to use interactive forms that speed up your work with Access. By using Access' advanced validation and formatting features, you can ensure that information entered in your tables is correct and properly formatted.

Chapter 4 describes keyboard and mouse techniques that will save you time when performing routine edits using both datasheets and forms, including how to get the most out of Access' online Help. Chapter 5 helps you create custom formats for use in fields or in form or report controls. In Chapters 6 and 7, you learn shortcuts for creating and editing forms, including how to create and customize subforms and how to design forms for ease-of-use. Chapter 8 reveals how to make "smart forms"—forms that dynamically display lists of options, trigger macros to format and validate information, and display command buttons to perform a wide variety of tasks.

Data Entry Shortcuts

O nce you create a database, the bulk of your time will be spent entering or viewing data. Whether you work with datasheets or forms, this chapter provides tips for streamlining data entry. Of course, the best way to speed up data entry and editing is to create well-designed forms, with macros that validate and format the information. Chapter 5 discusses formatting, form design is described in Chapters 6 and 7, and tips for using macros with forms are in Chapter 8.

General Shortcuts

These shortcuts can save you time whenever you use Access.

One-Click Functions

Use the toolbar to switch in and out of Design view, to create new queries and forms, to find records, and more.

The toolbar displays buttons (tools) that correspond to the current window. For example, in a Form window, there are buttons for switching to Design view, creating and using filters, finding a record, changing to print preview, and getting help. You can perform the same functions by choosing commands from the menu, but it's much easier to click one button on the toolbar.

The back of the Microsoft Access *User's Guide* shows a list of all the toolbar buttons and their names.

Press Shift+F1 to Get Help

If you aren't sure what a button on the toolbar does, press **Shift+F1** to display the question mark pointer (a question mark is joined to the regular arrow pointer). Then click on the button. Access displays Help about the button.

Getting Back to the Database Window

Press F11 or Alt+F1 to make the Database window active.

Unless you have created your own main menu form, the Database window probably serves as "mission control" in your database. You can switch back to it at any time by pressing **F11**. If your keyboard doesn't have the **F11** key, you can press **Alt+F1**.

In the Database window, you can use menu accelerator keys to view tables, queries, forms, reports, macros, or modules. Press **Alt+V** to display the View menu, and then choose the type of objects to view.

Open Objects in Design View

If you want to use an object while you're in the Database window, simply highlight the object and then press **Enter**. Tables will appear in Datasheet view, Forms will appear in Form view, and so on.

If you want to open any object in Design view, just press **Ctrl+Enter**.

Using your mouse, you can use an object by double-clicking on it in the Database window. To open the object in Design view, double-click using the right mouse button.

Closing the Current Window

Use Ctrl+F4 to close the current window.

When you are done using a window, you can press **Ctrl+F4**, instead of choosing File Close from the menu, to close the window. If you have made changes that have not yet been saved, Access asks if it should save them now.

Switching Windows

Use Ctrl+F6 to move to the next open window in Access.

If you have several windows open in Access, you can cycle through them by pressing **Ctrl+F6**. Each time you press **Ctrl+F6** Access displays the next window until you get back where you started.

Alternatively, you can use the Window menu. At the bottom of the Window menu, Access displays a list of the open windows. Choose one.

Move Dialog Boxes Out of the Way

If the dialog box you are using covers up information you need to see, move the dialog box out of your way. Click on and hold the title bar of the dialog box and drag it out of your way.

If you don't want to use the mouse, you can use the keyboard to do the same thing. Press **Alt+Spacebar** to display the control menu for the dialog box window, then press **M** to choose Move. Use the arrow keys to move the dialog box to its new location. Then press **Enter** to complete the command.

Quick Saving

To quickly save the object you are working with, use Shift+F12 or Alt+Shift+F2.

When using any database program, it's a good idea to save early and often. You never know when the power will go out or when you'll kick the computer's plug with your toes. To save the record you are editing, form or report you are designing, or macro or module you are creating, you can choose File Save from the menu. However, if you are keying in text, you might find accessing the menu somewhat cumbersome. Instead, you can quickly save your object by pressing **Shift+F12** or **Alt+Shift+F2.**

Copying Access Objects

Access provides several ways for copying all types of Access objects.

After you create something once in Access, you never have to create it again. Instead, you can use cut and paste commands, or—even faster—cut and paste shortcut keys. (If you use Windows 3.0, the **Ctrl+X**, **Ctrl+V**, and **Ctrl+C** shortcut keys don't work. You must use **Shift+Del** to cut, **Shift+Ins** to insert, and **Ctrl+Ins** to copy.)

The Edit Cut command (or its shortcut key, **Ctrl+X** or **Shift+Del**) deletes a highlighted object and places it in the *Clipboard*, a temporary storage space maintained by Windows. Once information is in the Clipboard, you can use the Edit Paste command (or **Ctrl+V** or **Shift+Ins**) to copy it back to your database. If you don't want to delete the object from its current location, use the Edit Copy command (or **Ctrl+C** or **Ctrl+Ins**) to copy it to the Clipboard without deleting it.

To copy an Access object—a table, query, form, report, macro, or module, or a control on a form or report:

1. In the Database window, highlight the object.
2. Choose Edit Copy from the menu, or press **Ctrl+C** (or **Ctrl+Ins**).
3. Choose Edit Paste from the menu, or press **Ctrl+V** (or **Shift+Ins**).
4. For most types of objects, Access prompts you to name the copy. Enter the name and click on OK.

The original object is unaffected, and there is a new object, copied from the original object, with the new name. You can modify the new copy as needed—it won't affect the original. You can repeat steps 3 and 4 as many times as you want, creating additional copies of the object.

Once you have cut or copied an object to the Clipboard, you can insert it in a different database. Open the database into which you want to insert the copy, then use the Edit Paste command. Access prompts you for the name (except when pasting a control).

Access also provides another way to copy a table, query, form, report, macro, or module. Follow these steps to save a copy of an object as a separate Access object:

1. Open the object you want to copy.

2. Choose the File Save As command from the menu, or press **F12** or **Alt+F2**.

3. Access asks for the name to give to the new copy. Enter the name and click on OK.

The new copy of the object remains open for editing.

HOT
TIP

Cut and Paste in the Zoom Box

In the Zoom box, you can't choose the Edit Cut, Edit Copy, and Edit Paste commands from the menu. Instead, you must use their keyboard equivalents: **Ctrl+X** (or **Shift+Del**) to cut the marked text to the Clipboard, **Ctrl+C** (or **Ctrl+Ins**) to copy it to the Clipboard, and **Ctrl+V** (or **Shift+Ins**) to paste the contents of the Clipboard at the cursor location.

Moving an Access Object

To move an object, cut and paste it.

You can use Access's cut-and-paste commands to move an object from one place to another. For example, you can move an action from one macro to another by cutting it from one macro and pasting it in the other.

To move a control from one place to another on a form or report, or to a different form or report:

1. Highlight the control you want to move.

2. Choose Edit Cut from the menu, or press **Ctrl+X** (or **Shift+Del**). Access deletes the control and places it in the Clipboard.

3. Highlight the section of the form or report where you want to move the control. You can also move the control to a different form or report.

4. Choose Edit Paste from the menu, or press **Ctrl+V** (or **Shift+Ins**). Access inserts the control, usually near the top-left corner of the section.

5. Move the control to where you want it.

Navigation Techniques

In a datasheet or form, you constantly move from field to field and from record to record. Here are fast ways to get where you want to go, using either the keyboard or the mouse.

Moving with the Mouse

Use the scroll bars to move with the mouse.

When you view a datasheet or form, there can be three scroll bars that let you move around the form, as shown in Figure 4.1. (When you design the form, you can control which of these scroll bars appear.)

The fastest way to move from record to record is by clicking the Next Record and Previous Record buttons on the record scroll bar. If you know the number of the record you want, you can type it into the record number box on the record scroll bar. To get to the first or last record in the table or dynaset, press the First Record and Last Record buttons on the record scroll bar.

Navigating Quickly through Forms

Use the Ctrl key with cursor keys to move quickly from one record to another.

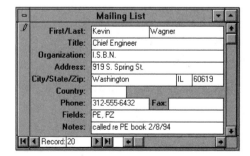

Figure 4.1   A form window with scroll bars.

To move from record to record in forms, you must use the Ctrl key: press **Ctrl+PgDn** to move to the same field of the next record; press **Ctrl+PgUp** to move to the same field in the previous record. This technique is great when you need to change information in the same field in many records. If you want to move to the first field of the next record, press **Ctrl+PgDn** and tap **Home**.

To move quickly to the first or last record in the table or dynaset, you can again use the Ctrl key. To move to the current field in the last record, press **Ctrl+Down Arrow**, and to move to the current field in the first record, press **Ctrl+Up Arrow**.

Appendix A contains a list of keyboard shortcuts you can use when moving around in fields and records, when editing records, when using forms, and when editing modules.

Move from Subforms to Master Forms

Access even provides keyboard shortcuts to move from a subform to fields in the master form. If the cursor is in a subform, press **Ctrl+Tab** to move the cursor to the next field in the master form, just after the subform.

Editing Tips

Once you have moved to the record and field you want to edit, here are quick ways to enter or change data.

Copying Text in Fields or Controls

You know how to cut, copy, and paste objects, but what about the text in a field?

Follow these steps to use Access' copy and paste commands to copy text contained in a field or control:

1. Press **F2** to edit the field or control that contains the text you want to copy.
2. Use the mouse or the selection shortcut keys (listed in Appendix A) to highlight the text you want to copy.
3. Choose Edit Copy from the menu, or press **Ctrl+C** (or **Ctrl+Ins**).

4. Move the cursor to the field or control into which you want to insert a copy of the text.

5. Press **F2** to edit.

6. Move the cursor to the location where you want to insert a copy of the text.

7. Choose Edit Paste from the menu, or press **Ctrl+V** (or **Shift+Ins**).

Moving Text in Fields, Controls, and Properties

Use the Ctrl+X shortcut key to move text.

You can also use the cut and paste commands and shortcut keys to move the text in fields or controls. If you type text in the wrong control, or in the wrong property for a control, or in the wrong field in a form or datasheet, select the text, press **Ctrl+X** or **Shift+Del** to delete it from its current position and place it on the Clipboard. Then, move the cursor to the correct location and press **Ctrl+V** or **Shift+Ins** to paste the text in the new location.

Entering Information Automatically

Use Ctrl shortcut keys to duplicate the same field from the previous record, enter the current date and time, or enter the default value for the field.

If you are entering a number of records, the information in some fields may be the same for all the records. Using Access' shortcut keys, you only have to enter the information once. In the rest of the records, you can press **Ctrl+'** (apostrophe) to duplicate the information from the same field in the previous record.

If you have specified a default value for the field, it will appear in the field when you add a new record. If you have entered a different value in a field with a default value and want to change it back, you can press **Ctrl+Alt+Spacebar**.

If you want to enter the current date and time in a field, you can use your computer's clock. Simply press **Ctrl+;** (semicolon) to enter today's date, or **Ctrl+:** (colon) to enter the current time.

HOT TIP

Delete the Current Record

To delete the current record quickly, just press **Ctrl+-** (minus). This action selects and deletes the current record. If the Confirm Record Changes option is Yes for the database (this is the default setting), Access asks if you really want to delete the record. (To change the Confirm Record Changes option, choose View Options from the menu, choose General for the Category, change the Confirm Record Changes option to No, and click on OK.) Confirmation, especially for a novice user, is better left on. Although confirmation dialog boxes can be a pain when deleting many records, they can be a real gem when your hands are working faster than your brain!

Undoing Mistakes

Access knows that sometimes your fingers fly too fast. If you make a mistake, Access allows you to undo the last change you made by providing several methods for undoing errors: Ctrl+Z, Alt+Backspace, or Edit Undo.

If you make a mistake and notice it right away, you can ask Access to "undo" the last thing you did. Access can only undo your *last* action, so don't do anything before undoing your mistake! Choose Edit Undo from the menu, or press **Ctrl+Z** or **Alt+Backspace**. Depending on what you last did, the Undo command on the Edit menu may appear as Undo Typing, Undo Delete, or other undo actions. If the last thing you did can't be undone, the command may not be available; that is, it will appear in gray.

Using Combo and List Boxes

Use the F4 or Alt+Down Arrow shortcut key to open a combo or list box.

When you are typing in a form, it is usually more efficient to keep using the keyboard than to move your hand to and from the mouse. But what happens when you need to choose a value from a combo or list box?

Access has shortcut keys for using combo and list boxes from the keyboard. To use shortcut keys, move the cursor to highlight the combo or list box. Then press **F4** or **Alt+Down Arrow** to open the combo box (list boxes are already open). Use the **Down** and **Up Arrow** keys and the

PgDn and **PgUp** keys to highlight your choice. Then press **Tab** to select that value and move to the next field.

Entering Special Characters

To enhance the appearance of your forms and reports, you may want to enter special characters into fields or into controls in your forms or reports.

Special characters include letters from foreign alphabets, long hyphens, copyright symbols, and foreign currency symbols. Access can handle these characters in Text or Memo fields. There are two ways for you to enter these special characters into your applications: You can type ANSI character numbers directly into the field, or you can copy the characters from the Windows Character Map accessory.

To type a special character into a Text or Memo field directly, you must know its three-digit number *ANSI* character number. (ANSI is the American National Standards Institute, which establishes standards.) There is a table of special characters in the Microsoft Windows *User's Guide* or you can use the Search button in Access Help to search for "ANSI." Once you know the character number, make sure your numeric keypad is set to type numbers (Num Lock is on), hold down the **Alt** key, type **0** followed by the character number on the numeric keypad, and release the **Alt** key. For example, the ANSI character number for the copyright symbol (©) is 169. To enter this character into an Access Text field, hold down **Alt**, type **0169** on the numeric keypad, and release **Alt**.

The other way to enter a special character is to copy it from the Windows Character Map (CharMap) accessory. CharMap displays a table of special characters available for the current font. Unless you specify otherwise, Access usually uses the MS San Serif font for text. Figure 4.2 shows the CharMap for this font.

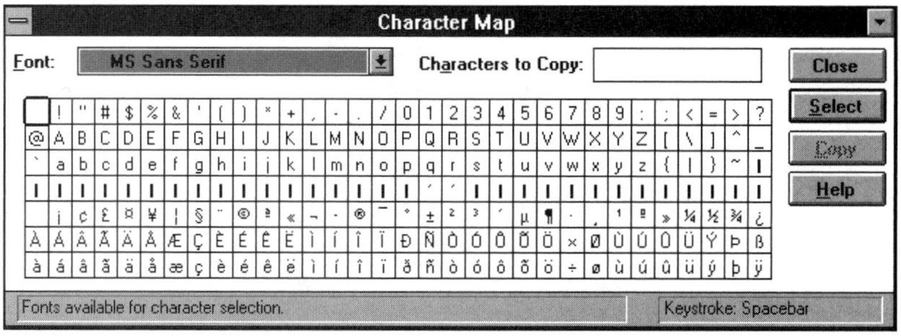

Figure 4.2 These MS San Serif characters can be copied into Access.

To copy one or more characters from CharMap into your Access field:

1. Run the Windows Character Map program, which appears in the Accessories program group.
2. Choose the font you are using (usually MS San Serif) from the Font combo box.
3. Click on the character you want to copy. A dark box appears around the character.
4. Click on Select. The character appears in the Characters to Copy text box.
5. Repeat steps 3 and 4 if you want to copy a series of characters.
6. Click on Copy to copy these characters to the Clipboard.
7. Click on Close to exit CharMap or if you plan to copy other characters, minimize CharMap so that you can return to it quickly by double-clicking the icon.
8. Return to Access.
9. Locate the field in which you want to paste the character, press **F2** to edit the field, position the cursor where you want the character(s) to go, and then press **Ctrl+V** or **Shift+Ins** (or choose Edit Paste from the menu).

Adding New Records

Adding new records is a snap when you use the Ctrl++ shortcut key.

To add new records to a table, you add them in a new, blank row in the datasheet or a new, blank form in the Form window. To position the cursor in a new row or blank form, press **Ctrl++** (Ctrl and the Plus key).

You can also use the Records Data Entry command from the menu. This command "hides" the existing records in the table and positions you in a new, blank record for data entry. To see the existing records again, choose Records Show All Records from the menu.

HOT TIP

Requery after Adding Records

When you add records while using a query, the new records appear at the end of the datasheet. If the query sorts the records, and you want the new records to move to their proper positions in sort order, requery by pressing **Shift+F9** or by choosing Records Show All Records from the menu. Access requeries the original tables, resorts the results, and the records move to their proper places.

Saving the Current Record

Use the Shift+Enter shortcut key to save your changes.

If you plan to make extensive changes to a single record, it is a good idea to save your changes from time to time. For example if you are editing a lengthy Memo field, you may spend half an hour editing a record. To save your changes while continuing to work on a record, choose File Save Record. A quicker way to do the same thing is to press **Shift+Enter** to save the changes.

Customizing Datasheets

If you use datasheets to enter or view data, you can probably improve on the sizes and order of the columns that Access gives you.

Switching the Order of Columns

Select the column and drag it to its new position.

You can change the order in which columns appear in a datasheet. This doesn't affect the way the data is stored in the table, and you can change it any time. For example, if you plan to look at or make changes to two fields in a table, it would be easier if the two columns were side by side in the datasheet.

Select a column in the datasheet by clicking on the top border of the column. You can select several adjacent columns to move by clicking the top border of one column, then holding down **Shift** as you click on the top borders of other adjacent columns. Then drag the column(s) to the new position.

You can also move columns by using the keyboard. First, select the column you want to move by positioning the cursor on any value in the column and then pressing **Ctrl+Spacebar**. You can select several adjacent columns by selecting the first column, then pressing **Shift+Left Arrow** or **Shift+Right Arrow** to extend the selection. Then, press **Ctrl+F8** to begin Move mode. The MOV indicator appears in the status bar at the bottom of the Access window. Use the Right and Left Arrow keys to move the column(s) to a new position. Then, press **Esc** to end Move mode.

When you close the datasheet window, Access asks if you want to save changes to the table or form. This actually refers to changes to the datasheet layout. If you want to make the new column order permanent, click on Yes.

Setting Column Widths

To make columns wide enough to display long entries, move the column dividers.

The first time you use a datasheet, you should adjust the column widths so that entries aren't cut off on screen. Using the mouse, drag the column dividers to the widths you want.

When you close the datasheet window, Access asks if you want to save changes to the table. If you want to make the new column widths permanent, click on Yes.

To set the default column width for new datasheets, choose the View Options Datasheet command and change the value of the Default Column Width setting.

Freezing Columns in View

You usually want to see the primary key field(s) all the time. Access allows you to freeze columns so that they are always visible.

If a table has too many fields to fit on the screen, fields will scroll off the screen. You can "freeze" columns so that they never scroll off the screen and always appear on the left side of the datasheet.

To freeze a column in view, select the column or columns, and choose Layout Freeze Columns from the menu. A dark vertical line separates the frozen column(s) from the rest of the columns. To unfreeze all the columns for a datasheet, choose Layout Unfreeze All Columns.

When you close the datasheet window, Access asks if you want to save changes to the table or form. If you want to make the new column freezes permanent, click on Yes.

Hiding Columns from View

Hide columns you seldom look at, or those you don't want others to see.

To "hide" a field from view, select the column or columns and choose Layout Hide Columns from the menu. The column disappears, but it is still stored in the table. Or you can use the mouse to drag the right edge of the column to the left until the column disappears.

To reveal a hidden column, choose Layout Show Columns from the menu. Access displays the Show Columns dialog box, shown in Figure 4.3.

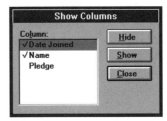

Figure 4.3 Revealing hidden columns in a datasheet.

Columns that are visible have checks by their field names; those that are hidden do not. You can hide or show columns by selecting the field name and clicking on Hide or Show. When you are done, click on Close.

When you close the datasheet window, Access asks if you want to save changes to the table or form. If you want the column display to be permanent, click on Yes.

Choose whether to See Gridlines

You can also control whether Access draws lines between the rows and columns of the datasheet—the *gridlines*. Usually it is a good idea to use gridlines, since they make it easy to tell which row and column a value is in. However, for printing a datasheet, you may want to turn them off. Choose Layout Gridlines from the menu to suppress the display of gridlines. This command is a toggle—the same command is used to turn the feature on and off. Access indicates that gridlines are deselected by clearing the check mark from in front of the command. To turn gridlines back on, choose the same command again.

Formatting Data with Custom Formats

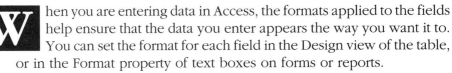

When you are entering data in Access, the formats applied to the fields help ensure that the data you enter appears the way you want it to. You can set the format for each field in the Design view of the table, or in the Format property of text boxes on forms or reports.

In most cases, you can choose a standard format from the list Access offers. However, there may be instances when you'll want to create your own *custom formats* (also called *user-defined formats*). For example, if you work with foreign currencies, you might want some fields formatted to display British pound signs (£). Or, you might want to format Social Security numbers or credit card numbers in a standard way.

You can use custom formats in tables to format fields, or in text boxes on forms or reports to format controls that display either fields or calculated values. This chapter provides tips for creating custom formats for each type of field (except OLE fields, which cannot be formatted).

Formatting Individual Field Types

Access has different rules for formatting text values, numeric values, dates, and Yes/No fields. There are special formatting codes for each type of field to give you complete control over how the information appears.

Formatting Text and Memo Fields

Use custom formats to add fixed punctuation to codes, or to control capitalization.

A custom format for a Text (or Memo) field can contain two parts, which are separated by a semicolon:

- The format to use if the value contains text
- The format to use if the value is blank

If you omit the second format, Access uses the first one for all values. Table 5.1 shows the characters you can use to customize the format for Text fields.

If there are more characters in the field than there are @ (at symbols) or & (ampersands) in the custom format, Access displays the characters anyway. You can't use custom formats to control the number of characters in the field—use validation rules instead. If you want to display only part of a field, make a calculated field that uses the Left(), Right(), or Mid() functions to select the part you want (see Chapter 9).

To include text in the format, such as "SSN " before a Social Security number, enclose the text in quotation marks. Alternatively, precede each

Table 5.1 Custom Format Characters for Text Fields

Character	Description
@	Placeholder for one character. If there is no character in this position, a space is displayed.
&	Placeholder for one character. If there is no character in this position, nothing is displayed.
<	Placeholder for all characters in the field, with capital letters converted to lowercase.
>	Placeholder for all characters in the value, with lowercase letters converted to uppercase.

character with a backslash (\). You can include commonly used punctuation, line dashes, and parentheses, without enclosing them in quotes.

Table 5.2 shows some examples of custom formats for Text fields.

Unfortunately, there is no standard initial capital formatting character—one that would capitalize the first letter of each word and display other letters in lowercase. However, you can create an Access module to do this for you. See Chapter 17 for information on creating Access modules.

Don't Enter Punctuation in Codes

If you use custom formats to insert hyphens and other characters in values for phone numbers, Social Security numbers, and similar fields, don't enter the hyphens into the fields themselves—your custom format adds them when the value appears in a datasheet, form, or report.

This is a more efficient way to store the information, since the hyphens and other fixed characters aren't stored over and over in every field.

Although it can be confusing to enter values without standard punctuation, you will become accustomed to the difference soon.

Table 5.2 Sample Custom Formats for Text Fields

Purpose	Format	This Value...	Appears As...
Social Security numbers	"SSN "@@@-@@-@@@@	123456789	SSN 123-45-6789
Telephone numbers	"("@@@")"@@@-@@@@	1234567890	(123)456-7890
Credit card numbers	@@@@-@@@@-@@@@	123456789012	1234-5678-9012
Nine-digit ZIP codes	@@@@@-@@@@;"Missing"	123456789 (Null)	12345-6789 Missing
Capitalized names	>	Megan	MEGAN

Formatting Number, Currency, and Counter Fields

Use custom formats to display special text for negative, zero, or missing values.

A custom format for a numeric value can contain four parts, which must be separated by a semicolon:

- The format to use if the number is positive
- The format to use if the number is negative
- The format to use if the number is zero
- The format to use if the value is null (blank)

If you omit the second or third formats, Access uses the first one (for positive numbers) for all values. If you skip the fourth format, Access displays nothing for null values.

Table 5.3 shows the special characters you can use in custom formats for numbers.

Table 5.3   Custom Format Characters for Numeric Values

Character	Description
. (period)	Decimal separator, indicating where the decimal point should appear. (The decimal point may appear as a comma if your Windows International setting is for a country that formats numbers this way.)
, (comma)	Thousands separator, indicating that thousands, millions, billions, and so on. should be separated by a comma. (The thousands separator may appear as a period or a space if your Windows International setting is for a country that formats numbers this way.)
0	Digit placeholder, indicating where a numeric digit appears. If there is no digit in this position in the number being formatted, it displays a zero anyway. This is useful for the first digit before a decimal point—a zero appears like "0.25" rather than ".25". It is also used for digits after the decimal point if you always want the same number of decimal places to appear.
#	Same as 0, but if there is no digit in this position in the number being formatted, nothing is displayed.
$	Displays "$".
%	Displays "%" and tells Access to multiply the number by 100.
E-, e-, E+, and e+	Displays the number in scientific notation.

To include text in the format, such as "lbs." after a number, enclose the text in quotation marks. Alternatively, precede each character with a backslash (\). You can include commonly used punctuation, like dashes and parentheses, without enclosing them in quotes.

Table 5.4 shows examples of custom formats for numbers.

When you enter a custom format into an Access property, you don't have to anticipate the maximum number of digits that the number might have. If you enter a zero or pound sign to indicate how you want numbers in the ones place to appear, Access assumes that you want digits for larger numbers to appear the same way. If you enter a comma between the thousands and hundreds places to indicate that you want a thousands separator to appear, Access not only displays the thousands separator before thousands, but also before millions (and billions, if your numbers get that large).

HOT TIP

Scale Numbers by Thousands

For large numbers, you may want to scale the numbers by thousands or millions. If you scale a number by thousands, the value 2,000 appears as 2. The value 2,345 appears as 2.345.

To do this with a custom format, enter one comma (to scale by thousands) or two commas (to scale by millions) just to the left of the decimal separator. If there is no decimal separator in the format, enter the comma(s) just to the right of the last 0 or #. Access then scales the number by thousands or millions. For example, this format scales numbers by one thousand:

```
0,
```

You can still use a comma to indicate that you want thousands separators to appear. For example, the format

```
#,##0,
```

tells Access to scale by thousands and to display commas between the resulting thousands.

You can also control how many decimal places to show in the resulting number. For example, 1,234,567 scaled by millions appears in Access as 1 if you specify zero decimal places. Use the Decimal Places property in the table, form, or report to control the number of decimal places that are displayed.

Table 5.4   Sample Custom Formats for Numeric Values

Purpose	Format	This Value...	Appears As...
Account number	"Acct. No. "00-00-000000	0141123456	Acct. No. 01-41-123456
Balance due on bill	$#,##0.00 "Due";	1.23	$1.23 Due
	$#,##0.00 "Credit";	-4.56	$4.56 Credit
	"Zero balance"	0	Zero balance

Formatting Date/Time Fields

Use custom formats to control how each part of the date and time are displayed.

A custom format for a Date/Time field contains the same four parts as custom formats for numbers, which must be separated by a semicolon:

- The format to use if the date is positive
- The format to use if the date is negative
- The format to use if the date is zero
- The format to use if the date is null (blank)

Access stores dates internally as numbers, where December 30, 1899 is date number zero. The time is stored as the fractional part of the number, where midnight is 0 and noon is 0.5.

Since most dates you are concerned with are positive (that is, since 1899), you can omit the second and third formats—formats for negative and zero values. And unless you want to display something special for missing (null) values, you can omit the fourth format, too. Table 5.5 shows the special characters you can use in custom formats for dates.

Table 5.5   Custom Format Characters for Date/Time Fields

Character	Description
: (colon)	A Time separator, separating hours, minutes, and seconds. (The time separator may appear as a different character if your Windows International setting is for a country that doesn't use colons between hours and minutes.)
/	Date separator, separating days, months, and years
c	General date format
d	Day of the month in one or two digits (1-31)
dd	Day of the month in two digits (01-31)

Table 5.5   Custom Format Characters for Date/Time Fields (Continued)

Character	Description
ddd	First three letters of the weekday (Sun-Sat)
dddd	Full name of the weekday (Sunday-Saturday)
ddddd	Standard Short Date format, e.g., 12/4/90. (This format is set in the International utility of the Windows Control Panel.)
dddddd	Standard Long Date format, e.g., Tuesday, December 4, 1990. (This format is set in the International utility of the Windows Control Panel.)
w	Day of the week (1-7)
ww	Week of the year (1-54)
m	Month of the year in one or two digits, (1-12)
mm	Month of the year in two digits (01-12)
mmm	First three letters of the month (Jan-Dec)
mmmm	Full name of the month (January-December)
q	Quarter of the year (1-4)
y	Number of the day of the year (1-366)
yy	Last two digits of the year (01-99)
yyyy	Full year (0100-9999)
h	Hour in one or two digits (0-23)
hh	Hour in two digits (00-23)
n	Minute in one or two digits (0-59)
nn	Minute in two digits (00-59)
s	Second in one or two digits (0-59)
ss	Second in two digits (00-59)
ttttt	Standard Long Time format, e.g., 9:39:00 PM. (This format is set in the International utility of the Windows Control Panel.)
AM/PM	Display any hours in the time using a twelve-hour clock. Display the uppercase letters "AM" or "PM" here.
am/pm	Display any hours in the time using a twelve-hour clock. Display the lowercase letters "am" or "pm" here.
A/P	Display any hours in the time using a twelve-hour clock. Display the uppercase letter "A" or "P" here.
a/p	Display any hours in the time using a twelve-hour clock. Display the lowercase letter "a" or "p" here.
AMPM	Display any hours in the time using a twelve-hour clock. Display the forenoon/afternoon designators from the Time Format section of the International utility of the Windows Control Panel.

Table 5.6 Sample Custom Formats for Date/Time Fields

Purpose	Format	This Value...	Appears As...
Week number	"Week No." ww	6/28/93	Week No. 26
Day name	dddd"'s Schedule"	4/5/93	Monday's Schedule
Full date	mmmm d", "yyyy	12/25/94	December 25, 1994
Full date and time	mmmm d", "yyyy" at "ttttt	12/4/90 9:39 PM	December 4, 1990 at 9:39 PM

To include text in the format, such as "hrs." after a time, enclose the text in quotation marks. Alternatively, precede each character with a backslash (\).

Table 5.6 shows examples of custom formats for dates.

It can be rather confusing to edit fields that have been formatted with custom date formats. You'll probably find it easier to use these formats only in reports.

Formatting Yes/No Fields

Use custom formats to display descriptive text for True and False values.

A custom format for a Yes/No field contains the same four parts as a custom format for numbers, which must be separated by a semicolon:

- The format to use if the value is positive
- The format to use if the value is negative
- The format to use if the value is zero
- The format to use if the value is null (blank)

However, since Yes/No fields can only be -1 (for Yes, True, or On) and 0 (for No, False, or Off), the first and fourth formats are ignored. You do, however, have to put in a semicolon to "hold the place" for the first, unused, format. You can omit the semicolon after the third format.

The formats can only include text, which must be enclosed in quotation marks.

Table 5.7 shows examples of custom formats for Yes/No fields.

Formatting Tips

In addition to the types of formatting just described, you may have special formatting needs. Printing checks, for example, requires a unique format

Table 5.7 Sample Custom Formats for Yes/No Fields

Purpose	Format	This Value...	Appears As...
Members vs. non-members	;"Member";"Non-member"	-1	Member
Exempt from sales tax?	;"Tax-exempt";"Taxable"	0	Taxable

for numbers. Access lets you specify how to handle Text fields that contain values of different lengths, whether to fill any blank space, and what colors to use.

Handling Text Values of Different Lengths

You can control how Access fills the placeholders in your format if the text value is too short.

When you use a custom format to format a text or memo value, you can use the @ and & formatting characters as placeholders for the characters of the value. For example, in a phone number, you might have ten placeholders for the ten digits of a long-distance phone number. But what if you enter a phone number with only seven digits?

By default, values are *right-aligned*, that is, Access starts filling the data into the format from the left until it runs out of characters in the value. To *left-align* a value, enter the left-alignment character, ! (exclamation point), as the first character in your format. When a format is left-aligned, Access starts filling the data into the format from the right.

For example, here is a custom format for left-aligned phone numbers:

```
!"("@@@")"@@@-@@@@
```

If the phone number has only seven digits (no area code), the digits appear where the last seven @ symbols are in the format. The first three @ symbol placeholders are filled with spaces.

Printing Check Amounts

Use an asterisk in custom formats to fill blank space.

You can fill up the blank space in a report control, to prevent someone from writing in additional information. For example, when printing amounts on checks it is prudent to fill up the space to the left of the number with asterisks.

To fill up blank space in a custom-formatted value, use an asterisk (*) followed by the characters you want to fill the space with. For example, this format fills the space with asterisks to the left of the dollar amount:

`**$#,##0.00`

You can actually use this method to fill blank space in any numeric, text, or date value, and you can enter the asterisk and fill character at the beginning or end of the custom format to fill in the space before or after the values.

Formatting in Color

Add color names to formats in square brackets.

At the end of each of the formats in your custom format, you can indicate what color the information should be. Enclose the color name in square brackets, like this:

`[Red]`

The available colors are Black, Blue, Green, Cyan, Red, Magenta, Yellow, and White.

For example, this numeric custom format displays negative numbers in red:

`$#,##0.00;($#,##0.00)[Red]`

Warning: When formatting controls for reports, use only the colors you can print—stick with black if you don't have a color printer.

6

Making Better-Looking Forms

Once you set up your database, you will probably spend most of your time using forms. Forms are indispensable for data entry, on-screen reports, and easy-to-create menus. If you use command buttons on your forms, you can easily move from form to form, entering information into different tables and printing reports.

This chapter contains tips for creating forms, including how to make changes to forms you create with FormWizards, how to improve the appearance of forms, and how to design forms to be printed as well as viewed on-screen. The next two chapters tell you how to use subforms and multi-page forms and how to make dynamic, interactive forms using macros and command buttons.

What are the determining factors in choosing to create a form or use a datasheet? The following list points out the advantages of using forms in your applications.

- If some entries are long, the columns in the datasheet must be wide, making it impossible to see the whole record at once.

- If there are many fields, you can't see the whole record at once.

- If some fields contain codes, you might like to be able to choose the codes from lists.

- If some fields are Yes/No, you might like to use check boxes, option boxes, or toggle buttons to make selections.

- If some fields contain pictures or other objects that won't show up in the Datasheet view, you must use a form to see them.

- If some fields should be validated based on values entered in other fields (for example, the format of a postal code depends on which country the address is in), then use a form.

- If some fields contain values that can be looked up from other tables (for example, you enter a product code and you'd like Access to fill in the price for you), then a form should be your choice.

- If you want to be able to see one master record and a list of corresponding detail records (for example, one order and a list of the items that make up the order), then a form should be your choice.

Now that you can decide when to create a form, this chapter will provide you with tips for making your forms clearer and easier to use.

The examples in this chapter use a client billing database, which stores information on clients, billable hours for each client, and invoices for hours. The database is named BILLING on the optional Access Insider Companion Diskette.

Creating and Editing Forms

Nine times out of ten, a FormWizard can make a form similar to the one you want. You'll probably find it is usually easier to make a form with a FormWizard and then modify it, rather than making the form from scratch.

Modifying Forms Created with FormWizards

After the FormWizard creates a form, use Design view to move fields and make other changes.

FormWizards are "code generators"—that is, they create a form, then they disappear. You can modify the resulting form just as if you had created it yourself from scratch. Simply open the form in Design view to make your changes (you can click on the Design view button on the last screen of the FormWizard to switch to Design view).

The default grid for a form created by a FormWizard is set to 64 units per inch. When a grid is this fine it's invisible, making it more difficult to align controls to it. To make the grid visible and easier for aligning controls, set the Grid X and Grid Y properties of the form to 12 and 12 (or your favorite grid spacing). If you still can't see the grid, choose View Grid from the menu.

To align all the controls to this new grid, choose Edit Select All from the menu, then choose Layout Size to Grid.

FormWizards leave a lot of space between the controls on forms. You may want to move the controls closer together so you can see more of your information on the screen.

Click into Design View

In the Database, you can open a form in Design view by double-clicking on the form name with the *right* mouse button.

Delete Duplicate Titles

If you create a form using a FormWizard, and you enter a title for the form you end up with the same or similar form title in the title bar of the window (the name of the form) and in the Form Header section of the form. There's no point displaying this title twice—delete it from the Form Header.

If you would rather change the text in the title bar of the Form window, change the Caption property of the form.

Changing the Properties of Forms, Sections, and Controls

The property sheet provides a convenient way to view and modify the properties of your form.

While you are designing a form, you will probably want to change properties of the whole form, sections of the form, and controls on the form. It's convenient to keep the property sheet displayed while you're editing. The property sheet lists the current settings for all of the properties of one object. Choose View Properties from the menu, or click on the Properties button on the toolbar, which is shown in Figure 6.1.

Once the property sheet is displayed, you can choose the item whose properties you want to see. To display the properties of the whole form, select the form by choosing Edit Select Form from the menu. If the horizontal and vertical rulers are displayed, a faster way to select the form is to click on the little white box in the upper-left corner of the form (at the intersection of the rulers).

To display the properties of a section of the form, click on the section header. To see the properties of a control, click on the control.

Display Property Sheets Fast

If the property sheet isn't already displayed, double-click on a section header or control and the property sheet appears showing the properties of the object.

Edit Long Properties

To edit a long entry in a property sheet, press **Shift+F2** to use the Zoom box.

Basing a Form on an Existing Form

If you need to create a new form that is similar to one you already have, you can save the old form with a new name instead of re-creating a new form altogether.

Figure 6.1   Use the Properties, Field List, and Palette buttons when designing forms.

Access sure can make things easy! To create a new form, simply open an existing form in Design view, then choose File Save As from the menu and enter a new name. Saving the form with a new name doesn't change the existing form—it just makes a new form that is a copy of the existing form. You can modify the new form without changing the original.

Copy a Form to Another Database

You can also base a form on a form from another database. To create the form:

1. Open the other database.
2. In the Database window, highlight the form you want to copy.
3. Press **Ctrl+C** to copy the form to the Clipboard.
4. Open the database in which you want to make the new form and press **Ctrl+V** to paste a copy of the form.
5. Name the copy.

You can use the new form as it is or you can make changes to it. Unless the two databases have tables and fields with identical names, you will have to make some adjustments to the Record Source and Control Source properties of the form and its controls.

Sorting and Selecting the Records in the Form

Use queries or filters to sort and select the records.

The *record source* is the table or query that contains the records shown in the form. You enter the table or query name in the Record Source property of the form. The order of records displayed in a form is determined by the record source property of the form:

- If the record source is a table, the records appear in primary key order (or in order of entry, if there is no primary key).
- If the record source is a query, the records appear in the sort order defined by the query.

The record source also controls which records are displayed:

- If the record source is a table, all the records appear.
- If the record source is a query, the records selected by the query appear.

If the record source of your form is a table and you don't want to see the records in primary-key order, or if you want to see a subset of the records, create a query based on the table. Include all the fields in the table that you want to show on the form. Sort the records into the order you want. Use the Criteria row of the query grid to specify which records you want to include. For example, Figure 6.2 shows a query that sorts a table of Clients into order by organization name. Use this query as the record source for the form instead of the original table.

If you want to see the records in different orders at different times, or if you want to see different selections, use a *filter*. A filter is an on-the-fly query that can sort and select the records you see in a form. To create a filter, open the form in Form or Datasheet view. Choose Records Edit Filter/Sort from the menu, or click on the Edit Filter/Sort button on the toolbar (Figure 6.3) to display the Filter window (Figure 6.4). Notice that this window looks very much like the window you use for designing queries.

You create a filter just as you would create the sorting and selection part of a query. There is no Show row in the grid, because all fields are shown when you use filters. Use the Sort row to indicate how you'd like the records sorted. Enter criteria into the Criteria row.

When you are done, close the Filter window by double-clicking on the control-menu box or by choosing File Close from the menu. Access

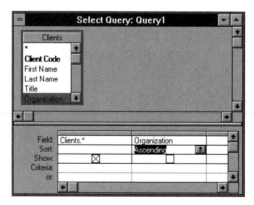

Figure 6.2 Query to sort Clients records alphabetically by organization name.

Figure 6.3 Use the Edit Filter/Sort, Apply Filter/Sort, and Show All Records buttons to create, enable, and disable filters.

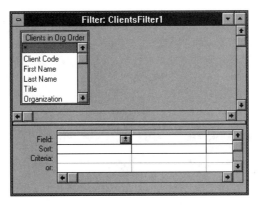

Figure 6.4 Sorting and selecting the records in a form with a filter.

doesn't ask you for a name, because filters don't have names. There can only be one filter at a time for each form. If you want to save the filter for future use, save it as a query (see the next Hot Tip).

To use the filter, choose Records Apply Filter/Sort from the menu, or click on the Apply Filter/Sort button on the toolbar (Figure 6.3). To turn the filter off, choose Records Show All Records from the menu, or click on the Show All Records button. The filter is still available—you can turn it back on by clicking on the Apply Filter/Sort button again.

Save Frequently Used Filters as Queries

Filters are discarded when you close the form, unless you save the filter as a query. In the Filter window, choose File Save As Query and enter a name for the query. (See the next Hot Tip for how to use a query as a filter.)

If you want to switch between two or more filters, you can create buttons on the form that run macros that set the filter (see Chapter 8).

Use a Query as a Filter

You can use a query as a filter if it meets these requirements:

- The query is based on the same table or query as the form.
- The query is a select query.
- The query does not include fields from other tables or queries.
- The query does not include totals.

To load a query as a filter, click on the Edit Filter/Sort button on the toolbar (Figure 6.3) to display the Filters window. Then, choose File Load From Query from the menu. Access displays only the queries it thinks meet the requirements listed above. Choose one and click on OK. The query grid in the Filters window shows the query.

Showing One, Several, or Many Records

Use the Default View property to control how many records you see at a time.

You can display a form in one of three views:

- **Single Form:** Displays one record at a time
- **Continuous Forms:** Displays multiple records, each in a copy of the Detail section of the form
- **Datasheet:** Displays the form fields arranged in rows and columns

To control which view the form is in when you open it, you can set the Default View property to one of the three views. Once you open a form in the default view, you can use the Datasheet View button and the Form View button on the toolbar to toggle between views. For example, if you open the form in Single Form view and click on the Datasheet View button, the form is displayed in Datasheet view. Then, if you click on the Form View button, the form is redisplayed in Single Form view. This same technique is used to toggle between Continuous Forms view (when that view is the default view) and Datasheet view. If, however, your default view is Datasheet view, clicking on the Form View button displays the form in Single Form view.

Making a Form That Looks Like a Datasheet

Using continuous forms, you can make a datasheet with special features that only forms can have.

To make a form that looks almost like a datasheet, but with lots of features that datasheets don't have:

1. Place all the fields in one row in the Detail section of the form.
2. Move the label for each field into the Form Header section, above the text box it describes (see the next Hot Tip). You may also want to delete any colons at the end of the labels.

3. Set the Default View property to Continuous Forms.

Now, you can customize this "datasheet" using all the properties of controls, including formatting, defaults, validation, and alignment. You can include read-only fields by setting the Locked property of the control to Yes. You can use check boxes or option buttons for Yes/No fields, and combo boxes or list boxes to choose values for codes from a list. You can also use macros and command buttons—these items are all explained in Chapter 8.

Figure 6.5 shows a form that looks like a datasheet, but with a check box for a logical field.

If Controls Are in the Wrong Section

If you create controls in the wrong section of the form, you can use Access' cut and paste feature to move them. Simply select the control you want to move and cut (Edit Cut or **Ctrl+X**) the control, placing it in the Clipboard. Then, click on the top border of the section where you want the control to be in and paste (Edit Paste or **Ctrl+V**). The controls you paste are selected when they appear, ready for you to move them to the right location within the section.

Making Read-Only Forms

You can make a form for reference purposes only, not for editing.

If a form is intended for use as a reference, and you don't want to change the information by mistake, make the form *read-only*. This means that when you open the form, editing will not be allowed. You will be able to see all the records but you (and other users) won't be able to change them. To make a form read-only, set the Default Editing property of the form to Read Only and set the Allow Editing property to Unavailable.

Code	First Name	Last Name	Organization	Hourly Rate	Timesheet?
BARAN	Ben	Pieter	Email Ping Software	$35.00	☐
IECC	John	Levine	I.E.C.C./J.C.L.T.	$30.00	☐
SEEK	Doug	Robar	Seek Software	$42.00	☒

Record: 3

Figure 6.5 Simulated datasheet with check boxes.

If, however, some of the information contained in the form needs to be updated occasionally, you will want to be able to switch into editing mode. In this situation, set the Allow Editing property to Available. You will now be able to switch between read-only and editing modes by choosing Edit Editing Allowed from the menu.

You can also make individual controls in the form read-only, by setting their Locked properties to Yes.

Making a Form for Entering New Records

Use Data Entry mode to hide existing records.

If you want to make a special form for entering new records only, set the Default Editing property of the form to Data Entry and the Allow Editing property to Available. When you open the form, you won't be able see or edit the existing records, but you will be able to add new ones. For this type of form, you may find it helpful to include lots of on-screen instructions about what to enter in each field.

In any form, you can use Data Entry mode to conceal existing records. Simply choose Records Data Entry from the menu to conceal their display. To see all the records again, choose Records Show All Records, or click on the Show All Records button on the toolbar (Figure 6.3).

Setting the Width and Length of a Form

Let Access set the size of the window to match the form.

To make the window the right size for the form, display the form in Form view (not Design view) and choose Windows Size to Fit Form from the menu. Issuing this command tells Access to change the size of the window to match the size of the window as closely as it can. If you are viewing a continuous form, it sizes the window to show a whole number of records, eliminating partial records. That is, if the window shows two full records and part of a third, Access resizes the window to show exactly two records.

If you want the window size to match the form size every time you open the form, set the AutoResize property of the form to Yes.

Setting the Style for Your Forms

You can make your own form template to set the defaults for new forms you create.

Whenever you make a new form—by choosing Blank Form, not using FormWizards—Access uses a *form template* to determine the default settings for the new form. Usually, Access uses its own template, which it calls Normal. You can set your own template, however, so that whenever you make new forms, the default sections, section sizes, and properties are the way you want them.

To create your own form template:

1. Choose an existing form with the specifications you want or make a new form. It doesn't matter what controls are on the form—Access just uses the default sections, section sizes, form properties, section properties, and default control properties. If you are using a new form for your template, be sure to set all the properties the way you will want them in new forms, including setting the grid (the Grid X and Grid Y properties of the form).

2. Choose View Options, then choose Form & Report Design.

3. For the Form Template option, enter the name of the form.

4. Click on OK.

Now whenever you create a new form from scratch, Access will use the properties from the template as the defaults for the new form. If you change the form that you designated as the form template, new forms will have the defaults of the current version of the form. Existing forms will remain unchanged—Access uses the template only when it creates the new form.

Note: Changing the form template doesn't affect forms created by FormWizards, which use their own templates.

Create Form Templates in Each Database

Access stores only one form template name, which it uses for all databases. You can't enter different template names in different databases.

When you create a custom template, it is available only in the current database. That is, whenever you make a new form in any database, Access will look in that database for the form with the name you specified. If the form isn't there, Access uses the Normal template instead. If you want Access to use your form template in other databases, copy the form to the other databases. If you want to use different form templates in different databases, create the templates in each database. Make sure the form template in each database has the same name in all the databases, and use that form name for the Form Template item in the View Options Form & Report Design command.

Changing How Text Is Selected in Controls

You can control how the cursor acts as you move from field to field in forms.

Normally, when moving the cursor into a field, the entire field is selected. If you would rather have the insertion point move to the first character of the field without selecting the whole field, choose View Options Keyboard. For the Arrow Key Behavior option, choose Next Character.

This changes the cursor behavior in all datasheets and forms in all databases. If you want to change the behavior for only selected controls on selected forms, you can use a macro instead. To change the cursor behavior for a specific control, attach a macro to the On Entry property so that the macro automatically presses the **F2** and **Home** keys when you enter the control (see Chapter 8).

Saving Forms

Be sure to save your changes to the form design—don't take a chance on losing your work!

If you spend a long time working on a form, you might want to save it from time to time, just in case you delete something accidentally or a power glitch makes your PC reboot. Simply choose File Save Form, or press **Shift+F12** or **Alt+Shift+F2**—a five second task that can save you from raiding the Tylenol and/or Tums bottles.

If you want to save a form with a different name, choose File Save Form As in Design View, or press **F12** or **Alt+F2**.

If you decide to experiment with the design of the form, save it first. Make the changes and switch to Form view to try them out. If you don't like the result, close the form without saving your changes.

Creating and Editing Controls

As you modify a form, you create, move, and modify its controls. Here are tips for working with controls.

Setting Defaults for New Controls

Set the default properties for the types of controls you use, so you don't have to set the properties for each control you create.

Figure 6.6 Create a new control using the toolbox.

To create a control, you choose a control type from the *toolbox*, a window containing a button for each control type. Figure 6.6 shows the toolbox.

When you create a control by clicking on a tool in the toolbox, the control has the default properties for that type of control. Before you create controls for your form, modify the default properties for the types of controls you plan to use. Once you've set the control defaults, you won't have to set the same properties over and over for each control you create in the form. To change control defaults:

1. Click on a tool on the toolbox. The property sheet shows the default properties for new controls you create using the tool.

2. Set the defaults for this type of control. Be sure to set the Auto Label property to determine whether Access should automatically create a label for the control.

If you have already created a control that typifies the way you want controls of that type to work, you can set the defaults to match those of your "perfect" control. Select the control and choose Layout Change Default from the menu. Access copies the properties from the control to the defaults for that type of control.

Note: Changes to the defaults apply to the current form only. Access stores default properties for new controls for each form you create.

Set Properties to the Default

What if you made a control *before* you set the default properties for that type of control? You can set the properties of a control to the current defaults for that type of control by choosing Layout Apply Default from the menu.

Creating Controls for Fields

The most important controls on most forms are those that display field values. It's easy to create these controls.

The quickest way to create new controls is to drag field names from the field list. To use the field list:

1. Choose the type of control(s) to create by clicking on the tool you want on the toolbox. Choose the Text box tool for Text, Number, Currency, Date, or Memo fields. Choose the Check box, Option button, or Toggle button tool for a Yes/No field.

2. Select the field(s) from the field list. To select several contiguous fields from the list, click on the first one, then hold down **Shift** and click on the last one. To select several fields that are not listed contiguously, click on the first one, then hold down **Ctrl** and click the other fields. To select all the fields, double-click on the title bar of the field list.

3. Drag the field(s) to the form, moving the cursor to the upper-left corner of the area where you want the control(s) to go. If you selected more than one field, Access places the controls in a column with space between one control and the next.

View the Field List to Create Controls Quickly

To display the field list, choose View Field List from the menu, or just click on the Field List button on the toolbar (Figure 6.1).

Create Several Controls of the Same Type

If you plan to create several of the same kind of control using the toolbox, you can "lock" the toolbox onto one tool. Simply choose the tool from the toolbox, then click on the Lock button at the bottom of the toolbox. While the Lock button is pressed, the tool remains selected. When the cursor is in the Design window, Access displays the pointer shape appropriate for creating the type of control you chose.

When you are done creating controls of that type, click on the Pointer button at the top of the toolbox to "unlock" the tool.

Also, if you choose a tool from the toolbox then change your mind, you can click on the Pointer button to deselect the tool.

Copying Controls

Forms are easier to use if controls have a consistent look. To make a group of controls with the same sizes and properties, duplicate one control.

If you want several similar controls on a form, it is more efficient to create one, then duplicate it. Once you have made the first in the series of controls, select it and choose Edit Duplicate from the menu. A copy of the control (and its associated label, if any) appears below and to the right of the original. You can then move the copy where you want it. If you duplicate the same control again, Access positions the new control automatically in the same relative position, so the controls are aligned and evenly spaced.

Another way to copy controls is to select the control and then press **Ctrl+C** to copy the control and **Ctrl+V** to paste the copies. This technique is useful for copying controls into other sections of the form, or onto other forms.

Making Changes to Several Controls at Once

Select a group of controls, then move them, copy them, format them, or align them.

You can select a group of controls in one of three ways:

- Click on the first control, then hold down **Shift** and click on each additional control.

- Start at a point outside any control and drag the pointer through or around all the controls you want to select. Access draws a dotted line around the selected area. If any part of a control is within the dotted line, the control is selected.

- Choose Edit Select All from the menu to select all controls on the form.

There are some settings you change for the whole group of controls, but there are others that you cannot. For example, if you select the Font, Size, Bold, Italic, Underline, Align-Left, Center, Align-Right, or General Alignment buttons from the toolbar when a group of controls is selected, the change affects all the selected controls. But, you can't set properties on the property sheet for a group of controls at once. When more than one control is selected, the property sheet is blank.

Lining Up Controls

Controls are easier to use if they look neatly organized.

It is easier to use a form if the controls are organized. One important aspect of control layout is alignment—making the left, right, top, or bottom edges of a group of controls line up straight.

If you set the Grid X and Grid Y properties of the form to 16 units per inch or less, the grid appears on the screen and you can see if controls are aligned to it.

To tell Access to automatically align the upper-left corner of controls to the grid whenever you move or create them, choose Layout Snap to Grid. A check mark appears next to the command when Snap to Grid is on. When you drag the edges of controls to resize them, Access only lets you drag them to line up with the grid; that is, Access "snaps" the border you are resizing to the nearest gridline.

If you have already created one or more controls and you want to move them so that their upper-left corners align with the grid, select the control(s) and choose Layout Align To Grid from the menu. You can also resize the controls so that all four sides of each control are aligned with the grid. Select the control(s) and choose Layout Size to Grid. The edges of each control you selected snap to the nearest gridline.

You may also want to line up a group of controls with each other; for example, moving a group of controls so that their left edges are aligned. Once you have selected a group of controls, you can choose Layout Align from the menu. Then choose one of the follow four options:

- Left: Move the controls so that their left edges are aligned with the left edge of the leftmost control.

- Right: Move the controls so that their right edges are aligned with the right edge of the rightmost control.

- Top: Move the controls so that their top edges are aligned with the top edge of the top control.

- Bottom: Move the controls so that their bottom edges are aligned with the bottom edge of the bottom control.

If you don't like the positions Access moves the controls to, you can choose Edit Undo Align from the menu to restore them to their former positions.

Suspend Snap to Grid Temporarily

If you use Snap to Grid, Access won't let you move or resize controls except in alignment with the grid. If you want to move or resize one particular control so that it doesn't match the grid, hold down the **Ctrl** key while you place, move, or resize the control. This suspends Snap to Grid while you work with the control. When you release the **Ctrl** key, Snap to Grid resumes, but the control stays where you put it.

Use the Grid in New Forms

To control whether the grid appears in new forms you create, and whether Snap to Grid is selected, choose View Options Form and Report Design from the menu. Set the Show Grid and Objects Snap to Grid options.

Displaying Long Text

Use scroll bars to display long Text or Memo fields in a text box.

To display a Text or Memo field that may be very long, use a text box. You can make the text box taller than one line of text, and Access will wrap the text onto additional lines.

If the text still can't fit in the text box, you can scroll down through the text by pressing **F2** to edit the field and then use the arrow keys to move the cursor through the text. Access does, however, provide an easier method for viewing and editing long text—you can display a vertical scroll bar along the right side of the text box. Simply set the Scroll Bars property for the text box to Vertical. Now, when you press **F2** to edit a value that is too long to fit in the text box, Access displays a vertical scroll bar for the field, shown in Figure 6.7.

Sizing Controls

Look at the form in both Form view and Design view to check that controls are large enough for their contents.

When you create controls in Design view, especially text boxes and labels, you can guess how large they must be to fit their contents. But you can't be sure your guess was correct until you see the form in Form view. After creating or resizing controls on a form, be sure to switch to Form view to look them over—text that fits into a label in Design view may not fit in Form view.

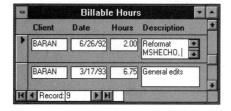

Figure 6.7 A vertical scroll bar for editing long values in a text box.

If the text in a label control is short, and you want to make the control smaller, you can select the control and choose Layout Size to Fit. Access shrinks the control until it is just big enough to show the text.

Controlling the Appearance of a Form

Access lets you dress up your forms with colors, lines, boxes, pictures, and 3-D effects. Some of these techniques are also useful when you're designing reports. By using lines and boxes, you can divide the form up into areas, and make the form look more like paper forms. Here are tips for using these special effects.

Changing the Text in the Title Bar of the Form

Set the Caption property of the form to the text you want to appear in the title bar.

If you don't set the Caption property of a form, the title bar displays "Form: *FormName*." When you use FormWizards to create a form, you are prompted for a form title when you create the form; Access uses this name as the caption.

HOT TIP

Center Labels

To make a good-looking form, you may want to center labels in the window. It is easy to center text within a label box—just set the Text Align property to Center, or click on the Center button on the toolbar. To center a label in the window, make the label box span the full width of the form.

Making Color Controls

You can set the background, text, and border colors of text boxes, labels, and other controls.

You can set the colors for the components of controls:

- **Text:** The text that appears in the control
- **Fill:** The background of the control
- **Border:** The line around the control, if any

Depending on the type of control, some of these options may be unavailable (appear in gray). If you have a monochrome monitor, you can choose among shades of gray.

To display the palette of available colors shown in Figure 6.8, choose View Palette from the menu, or just click on the Palette button on the toolbar (Figure 6.1). Select the control you'd like to add color to, and use the palette to specify the colors. As you click on the color choices on the palette, Access fills in the corresponding color numbers on the property sheet for the control. (Access stores the colors of objects as color members rather than as words. For example, the color number for white is 16777215. By using the palette, you don't have to remember or type these color numbers!)

If you plan to print the form, be sure to pick color combinations that are supported by your printer. Unless you have a color printer, Access translates the colors you choose into shades of gray. For example, dark red on light teal is readable on the screen, but appears as black-on-black when printed on a non-color printer.

Drawing Lines

Use lines for dividing the form into areas, highlighting controls, and dividing a column of values from its total.

To draw a line on a form (or on a report), click on the Line tool on the toolbox, then position the control on the form. If you want a line that is horizontal or vertical, rather than angled, press **Shift** after you click on the Line tool, and hold it down while you draw the line. Once you have drawn the line, you can drag its ends to change its length or position. To change the width of the line, change its Border Width property.

You can also set the width color of a line by using the palette. For line controls, only the Border and Width sections of the palette are active. If you choose Clear for the Border, the line is transparent (invisible) on the form.

If you draw a line at a slant, and you want a matching line at the exact opposite slant, copy the line and change the Line Slant property of the copy to the opposite slant (the settings are / or \).

Figure 6.8 Using the palette to set the color of a control.

Drawing Boxes

Using rectangles, you can divide the form into areas, create shadows behind controls, and create grids.

To draw a rectangular box on a form (or on a report), click on the Rectangle tool on the toolbox. At this point, you can draw a rectangle in one of two ways:

- Click on the form to have Access draw its default rectangle with its upper-left corner at the position you clicked. (You can change the default Width and Height properties of the Rectangle tool by clicking on the tool and changing the values in the property sheet.)
- Create a rectangle of any size by dragging the mouse on the form. Position the mouse where you want the upper-left corner of the rectangle, drag down and to the right, and release the mouse button when the size is correct.

Once you have created a rectangle, you can choose colors for the background and border of the rectangle using the palette, as well as adjusting the width of the border.

Rectangles usually surround one or more objects. If you create a rectangle to enclose existing objects, the rectangle appears *in front* when you first create it, covering the other objects. To tell Access to display the rectangle *behind* the other objects, select it and choose Layout Send to Back from the menu.

Draw a Border around a Label or Text Box

If you want a border to display immediately around the value in a label or text box, you don't have to create a separate rectangle control. Instead, set the Border Style property of the label or text box to Normal instead of Clear, and adjust the Border Color and Border Width properties accordingly. The result is a border for the control. Borders appear on both forms and reports.

Creating Shadows Using Overlapping Controls

Use rectangles or lines to create shadows behind text boxes or labels.

If you put two controls in the same position on the form, one control is *in front*, and is entirely visible, and the other control is *in back*, and is partly covered up. You can use the Layout Bring to Front and Layout Send to Back commands to specify which control is in front.

Using overlapping controls, you can create shadows behind controls to give them depth. This technique works on both forms and reports. To give a text box (or other box) a shadow:

1. Create a rectangle that is the same size as the text box. To make the rectangle the same size, copy the Width and Height properties from the text box to the new rectangle.

2. Using the palette, fill the rectangle with the color you want for the shadow. Choose the same color for the border, or make the border clear. (Shadows don't look right with visible borders.)

3. Position the rectangle slightly below and to one side of the text box.

4. With the rectangle selected, choose Layout Send to Back to display the rectangle behind the text box.

If you make several shadowed controls in this way, the illusion of shadows will be heightened if all the shadows are the same color and in the same position relative to their controls (bottom right, bottom left, top right, or top left).

Another way to create a shadowed effect is to draw lines along the bottom and one side of the control. Make the two lines the same width and color. Figure 6.9 shows one control with a rectangular shadow and another control with a line shadow.

Move the Shadow with the Control

You can attach a label to a text box, but you can't attach a rectangle. Once you have created a rectangular shadow behind a control, if you decide to move the control, remember to move its shadow, too! The easiest way is to select both the control and the shadow and move them together, so that the shadow stays in the same relative position to the control.

Figure 6.9   Controls with shadows.

Make Small Shadows Using Special Effects

You can also use the Special Effects property of a control to give it small shadows. The Raised and Sunken special effects give controls highlighting along two sides and shadows along the other two sides, resulting in a 3-D effect, shown in Figure 6.10.

The Appearance section of the palette displays three special-effect options, which provide an easy way to apply special effects to a control. When you select a control, you can click on the Raised or Sunken buttons on the palette to get the special effects.

For the Raised and Sunken effects to look their best, use the same background (Fill) color for the section of the form and for the control. This way the highlighting looks like shadows on an otherwise "flat" surface. However, if you make a raised label or text box with a gray background, it looks a lot like a command button, which may be confusing.

Placing Labels in Boxes with Values

Put a text box inside a large label to give the illusion that they are one object.

Another effect you may want for your form is for the label for a text box to appear "inside the box," as in Figure 6.11. Rather than putting a label inside a text box, follow these steps to make a large label with a text box inside it:

1. Make a text box and associated label.
2. Select the label and make it big enough to contain the text box, too.

Figure 6.10   Raised and sunken text boxes.

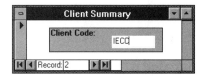

Figure 6.11   Label appears to be inside the text box.

3. Using the palette, choose colors for the background and borders of the label.

4. Drag the text box into the label. Make sure it's on top, by choosing Layout Bring to Front. (If the label is attached to the control, it's always behind the control.) Make sure that the text box is entirely inside the label so the label's box isn't obscured. (Switch to Form view to check this.)

5. Using the palette, set the borders of the text box to Clear. You can use the same color for the background of the text box that you used for the label, or you can choose a different one—see which effect you like. Using a different background color makes it more obvious where to type the value when using the form.

Using a Scanned Form as the Background

You can make your Access look like an existing paper form by displaying an image of the paper form.

If your Access form is based on an actual paper form, you can scan the paper form and use the resulting image as the background of your Access form. For example, if customers fill in printed forms asking to be placed on your mailing list, you can use a scanned image of a blank form as the background of the Access form for adding records to a mailing list table—this makes the Access form look more familiar to data entry staff who have used the printed form. To create a form or report with a scanned background:

1. Make the form look as much as possible like the printed form. Don't worry about lines, boxes, colors, or the exact text of labels, since these will be provided by the scanned form. Concentrate on putting the bound controls in more or less the right places, and make sure that there are fields in your tables that correspond with all the blanks on the printed form.

2. Scan a blank form and store it in a format that Access can read, like a Paintbrush picture in .BMP or .PCX format.

3. Place the image on your form. Click on the Unbound object frame tool on the toolbox, and then click on the upper-left corner of the detail section of the form. When you see the Insert Object dialog box, choose Paintbrush Picture, then click on the File button to load an existing file. Choose the directory and filename of the file containing the scanned image and click on OK. Access creates an unbound object frame control containing the image.

4. Size the unbound object frame control. Choose Layout Size to Fit to make the control big enough to show the whole image. You can change the size of the control by dragging its edges or by entering values for the Width and Height properties. You can also determine how the scanned image fits into the control by setting the Scaling property.

5. With the object control selected, choose Layout Send to Back. The controls that were originally on the form now appear on top of the scanned image.

6. Move the controls to the positions on the scanned form, deleting unnecessary label controls. To size the text boxes, you may need to change the grid for the form (enter different values for Grid X and Grid Y). To temporarily disable Snap to Grid while you position a control, hold down the **Ctrl** key while you drag it into position or while you size the control precisely.

Figure 6.12 shows a subscription form for a journal, based on a printed subscription form.

Printing Forms

Although Access provides reports as the best way to produce printed output from your database, you can also print forms. To keep paper records of the records you enter, you can use a form for entering

Figure 6.12 Subscription form with scanned image as the background.

information and then print the form. If you intend to print a form, keep the following tips in mind.

Choosing Which Records to Print

Use filters to select the records to print.

When you print a form, Access prints all the records in the record source, that is, in the table or query on which the form is based. If a filter is active, Access limits the printing to the records selected by the filter. (See *Sorting and Selecting the Records in the Form* earlier in the chapter for information on using filters.)

To print one or a few contiguous records, select the record or range of records by clicking on the record selectors on the form. Then choose File Print from the menu.

Modifying the Page Setup for a Form

The way a form appears on the page can add to or detract from its readability. Set the width of the form to fit on the paper, and specify when Access should start a new page.

Choose File Print Setup to see the Print Setup dialog box which shows page size, margins, orientation, and other settings. These settings are saved with the form, so you can have different settings for different forms (and reports). See *Choosing the Printer and Page Format* in Chapter 12 for information on these settings.

Set the size of your form to fit the page. (To display the ruler if it is not already visible, choose View Ruler from the menu.) If the form is wider than your paper, Access will try to print the form in two or more vertical strips, and you may end up with extra blank sheets of paper after each printed form. To make your form the right width, either enter a measurement in the Width property for the form, or drag the right edge of the form leftward. Subtract the left and right margins on the Print Setup dialog box from your paper width to find the maximum width of the form.

If you want each record to print on a separate page, create a page break. Otherwise, Access prints one record after another down the page. To add a page break after each record (at the end of each Detail section), select the Detail section of the form and set the Force Page Break property to After.

You can also control where Access inserts page breaks if the length of the Detail section varies. The section size may vary if there are fields that may get larger because their Can Grow property is set to Yes. (The Can

Grow property is discussed in Chapter 11.) If a form or section of a form is too long to fit at the bottom of the current page, you can instruct Access to print the rest of the record on a new page. Set the Keep Together property of the form or section to Yes.

You can also insert page breaks within the Detail section of the form. If you plan to print several pages of information for each record, insert a page break control at the position in the Detail section where you want a new page to start. To insert a page break control, choose the Page break tool from the toolbox, then click at the location in the Detail section. Access inserts the page break control at the left edge of the form.

Note: If you print a form while it is displayed in Datasheet view, Access prints the datasheet, not the form. Make sure you switch to Form view before printing a form.

Choosing Fonts for Printed Forms

Choose the printer before you design the form, and use Layout For Print to see your printer font options.

Choose File Print Setup and select the printer you plan to use for printing the form. When you select the printer first, you can tell Access to use the fonts that are available for the specified printer. For the form, set the Layout for Print property to Yes to display printer fonts rather than screen fonts on the toolbar, and to control which font sizes and other typographical options are available.

TrueType fonts look approximately the same on the screen and on paper and can be used whether Layout for Print is Yes or No.

Note: If you decide to print on another printer later, and choose another printer on the Print Setup dialog box, your font options may change depending on the type of printer you use.

Choosing Colors to Print

Make the background white and choose colors that print clearly.

If you plan to print your form, you will probably want to make the background of all sections of the form white. Unless you have a color printer, Access translates all the colors on your form into shades of gray and you will use up lots of ink or toner printing forms. Choose colors for the controls that print clearly on your printer, and that contrast appropriately. You'll have to print the form a few times until you like the colors on the screen and the way the form looks when printed.

Printing Headers and Footers

You can create two sets of headers and footers: one for on the screen and one for printing.

For an on-screen form, the header may contain command buttons or instructions for using the form. When you print the form, you probably want a very different header, one that displays the title of the form, perhaps the name of the organization, today's date, and other information. Similarly, the on-screen footer may contain command buttons for saving the form or printing it. The printed footer should contain the page number or other information.

Luckily, Access provides two sets of headers and footers for forms:

- **Form Header and Footer:** They appear at the top and bottom of the Form window. Unless their Display When properties are set to Screen Only, the Form Header prints once at the beginning of the form printout and the Form Footer prints once at the end of the printout.

- **Page Header and Footer:** They appear at the top and bottom of every printed page. They never appear on the screen in Form view.

To add a Form Header and Footer as a pair, or Page Header and Footer as a pair, choose Layout from the menu. Choose Form Hdr/Ftr or Page Hdr/Ftr to turn these sections on or off (they are on if a check mark appears before the menu item).

To specify when the Form Header and Footer appear, set the Display When property of the Form Header and Footer sections. The possible settings are Always (appears in Form view and when printed), Print Only (appears only when printed), or Screen Only (appears only in Form view).

If you want one set of headers and footers to appear on-screen and another to be printed, turn on both sets of headers and footers by using the Layout Page Hdr/Ftr and Layout Form Hdr/Ftr commands. Then set the Display When properties of the Form Header and Footer sections to Screen Only.

Print the Date, Time, and Page Number

In the Page Header or Footer section of the form you may want to include the current date or time and the page number. To do this, create an unbound text box in the Page Header or Footer, then enter an expression for the Control Source of the text box. For the current date or time, enter:

```
=Now()
```

Then choose a date or time format for the Format property of the control. For the page number, enter:

```
=Page
```

or

```
="Page " & Page
```

Specifying Non-Printing Controls

If there are command buttons or screen-oriented instructions that you don't want to print, you can tell Access not to print them.

To make a control appear on the screen but not when the form is printed, set its Display When property to Screen Only. You can set this property for form sections, too.

Command buttons on forms should usually be non-printing controls.

Printing a Blank Form

You can print a blank form to use for writing down information on paper in preparation for data entry.

To print a blank form, you need to tell Access not to print any records. Make a filter that eliminates all the records, that is, a filter with criteria that no records match.

In the grid for the filter, choose a field and enter a criterion that is impossible—for example, specify that a price is negative, or that a code matches a non-existent code like "XXX." When you apply the filter, no records match, and Access displays a form with no data in it. When you print the form, it will be blank.

Preview a Form before Printing

To see how the form will look when it is printed, display the form in Form view, then choose File Print Preview from the menu or click on the Print Preview button on the toolbar. See *Previewing Reports and Forms* in Chapter 12 for additional information on using Print Preview.

Filling in a Printed Blank Form

Choose the Data Only option in the Print Setup dialog box to fill in pre-printed forms.

You can tell Access to print only the values of the bound controls, with none of the unbound controls on the form. This is useful if you want to print information onto a pre-printed form. If the pre-printed form already has labels, boxes, lines, and other items, you just need to print the actual values from the table or query on which the form is based.

To suppress the printing of unbound controls, choose File Print Setup to display the Print Setup dialog box. Then choose Data Only and click on OK.

When you print the form, the labels, lines, rectangles, and unbound controls do not print. Only the bound controls print—controls that contain data. If you want to create a label that does print in Data Only mode, create a text box instead of a label. For the Control Source property, enter an expression like

```
="labeltext"
```

but, of course, using the text you want to appear.

Changing a Form into a Report

Save the form as a report, then remove screen-specific controls and add page headers and footers.

It is easy to convert a form into a report. In Design view, choose File Save As Report from the menu. Access asks for the name to give the new report. Remember, saving a form as a new report will not affect the original form.

The resulting report has the same structure as the form, with the same controls. The Form Header and Footer sections become the Report Header and Footer section, and the page header and footer and detail section are retained.

Before you can use the report, you must:

- Size the report for your printer and paper, using the File Print Setup command. (You may already have done this if you designed the original form to be printed.)

- Remove or edit macros in the On Open or On Close properties of the report, which may no longer work, since they may refer to menu items available in a Form window. The macros that you entered as properties for controls are not retained when Access converts the form to a report, since report controls don't have the same properties.

To make the new report look better, you may also want to:

- Remove command buttons, which are meaningless on a printed report.
- Add Page Header and Footer sections, if the form didn't already have them.
- Change background colors to white and text colors to black, unless you have a color printer. Use white text against gray or black backgrounds for small areas that you want to emphasize.
- Change fonts and font sizes to make the form more readable on paper, if needed.

Streamlining Data Entry with Forms

Y ou can do more with forms that just looking at the fields from one record on the screen. Using subforms, you can display a record from a master table and all the related records from a detail table at the same time. Using multi-page forms, you can organize the information stored in large records. This chapter contains tips for using subforms and multi-page forms, as well as techniques for making forms easier to use for data entry.

The examples in this chapter are based on the client billing database (BILLING) on the Companion Diskette.

Using Subforms

In a database with related tables, it is extremely useful to be able to see one record from a master table (the "one" table in a one-to-many relationship) and all related records from a detail table (the "many" table) on a form at the same time. Using subforms, it is easy to do this in Access. Usually, you use the Main/Subform FormWizard to create a form with a subform, and then make modifications to the form. This section provides tips for creating subforms without a FormWizard, which is necessary if you want two subforms on the same form. You will also find information on formatting and using subforms.

Linking a Subform Manually

Drag the subform onto the form in Design view, then check the linkage between the forms.

To create a subform manually—without using a FormWizard—there must be a field in the record source of the subform that links it to a field in the record source of the main form. And there must be a one-to-many or one-to-one relationship between the main form's record source and the subform record source. For example, in a client billing database, you would have a table of clients and a table of hours that can be billed to the clients. If the main form contains information about a client, the subform can contain the records of hours billable to that client, as shown in Figure 7.1.

The subform and main form are *linked* by two properties of the subform control:

- Link Child Fields, which is the field name(s) in the record source of the subform.

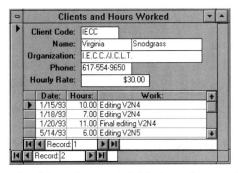

Figure 7.1 Form with subform showing billable hours for one client.

- Link Master Fields, which is the field name(s) in the record source of the main form.

The linkage between the main form and the subform usually consists of one field, which must have the same data type in both record sources, but not the same field name. (For example, the field can be called Code in the Clients table and Client Code in the Work Hours table.) When you are looking at a record in the main form, the linkage tells Access which records to display in the subform—those with the same value of the linked field.

To create a subform, and its linkage:

1. Create a form to use as the subform, including the fields in the order in which you want them to appear. Create it like any other form. If it will always appear in Datasheet New as a subform, the layout of controls on the form doesn't matter, only their order.

2. Save the subform.

3. Open the main form in Design view.

4. Make space on the main form for the subform control.

5. Select the subform in the Database window and drag it to the Design New of the main form. Access creates a subform control on the main form, containing the subform you selected (the Source Object property for the new subform control contains the name of the form you dragged).

6. Move and size the subform control.

7. Display the property sheet for the subform control to check the Link Master Fields and Link Child Fields properties. The Link Master Fields property should contain the name of the link field in the record source of the main form. The Link Child Fields property should contain the name of the link field in the record source of the subform.

Display the Subform in Design View

If you are designing the main form and want to see the subform in Design view, too, double-click on the subform control in the main form. Access opens another Design view window, to display the subform. Now, you can make changes to both forms.

Using a Different Subform

Change the Source Object property of the subform control.

You can use any form as a subform. If you want to use a different subform, you must first create and save the new subform. Then, display the main form in Design view and display the property sheet for the subform control. In the Source Object property for the subform control, enter the name of the new subform.

Formatting Columns in Subforms

To set the subform column widths, change them while viewing the subform by itself in Datasheet view.

To adjust the width and order of the columns of a subform that appear as a datasheet, you must modify the subform in Datasheet view. Once you move the columns and change the column widths, save the subform. You may have to adjust the column widths a few times until the subform just fits into the subform control on the main form.

   To change the column headings in the subform, switch to Design view and change the labels that are attached to the text boxes on the form.

Update the Subform

If you are designing the main form and the subform at the same time, and you have saved your changes to the subform, you can tell Access to load the newly changed subform into the main form. In Design view of the main form, select the subform control, then press **Enter**. This (usually) loads the latest version of the subform.

   If this doesn't work reliably (and it doesn't for me!), display the property sheet for the subform control, click on the Source Object property, and choose the updated subform from the list.

Viewing a Subform in Form View

Access allows you to display subforms in Form view, not only as datasheets.

You will usually want a subform to appear as a datasheet. However, you can also view the subform in Form view if you want to see just one record in the subform at a time. That is, a single subform form appears in the subform control instead of a datasheet. For example, Figure 7.2 shows the same client billing form as Figure 7.1, but with the subform in Form view.

You can toggle the subform between Form view and Datasheet. Simply select the subform and choose View Subform Datasheet from the menu. A check mark appears in front of the command name to indicate that the subform is currently displayed in Datasheet view. To switch back to Datasheet view, choose the command again.

If the Views Allowed property of the subform is set to Datasheet, Access won't let you switch into Form view. Change the Views Allowed property of the subform to Both.

To make Form view the default view for the subform, set the subform's Default View property to Single Form or Continuous Forms instead of Datasheet. You may also want to move the controls on the subform into an arrangement that matches that of the main form. The subform can have Form Header and Footer sections, if you want.

Making the Subform Read-Only

You can make the subform or the whole form read-only to prevent unauthorized modifications.

If you don't want to allow edits to a main form and a subform, you can change the Default Editing property of the main form to Read Only. If you

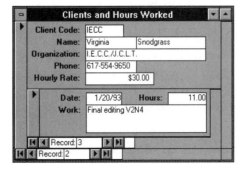

Figure 7.2   Form with subform in Form view.

only want the subform to be read-only, open the subform in Design view and change the Default Editing property to Read Only. With this approach, the main form is editable but the records in the subform are not.

One added advantage of a read-only subform is that Access won't display the extra blank row at the bottom of the subform.

Totaling Records from Subforms

To display a total of values in the subform, you must create controls on both the subform and the main form.

If the information shown in the subform includes quantities, you may want to display a total on the main form. For example, in the client billing example (Figure 7.1), each client is billed for a number of hours worked. The main form shows one client and the subform shows the days on which billable work was done. It would be nice to see total hours worked for each client.

Unfortunately, you cannot make a control on the main form that calculates a total for records on the subform. You can, however, make a control in the form footer of the subform that calculates the total, and then make a control on the main form to display the value of this calculated control.

Here are the steps to follow to calculate a total of values of a control on the subform and to display it on the main form. You create two controls: one in the form footer of the subform and one in the Detail section of the main form. It is important when you enter the expressions for calculating and displaying the total that you follow the instructions carefully—in some cases, you must use the name of the *field* in the record source in the expression, and in other cases, you must use the name of the *control.* It can get confusing!

1. Open the subform in Design view and display its property sheet.
2. Make sure that the subform has a Form Footer section in which to put the total control. Choose Layout Form Hdr/Ftr if the form doesn't have a Form Footer.
3. Note the name of the field (not the control) that contains the values you want to total (in the Detail section of the form). For example, in Figure 7.3, the control named Work contains a field named Hours, which is the value to be totaled.
4. In the form footer of the subform, make a text box. For the Control Source property of the control, enter the expression that will total the

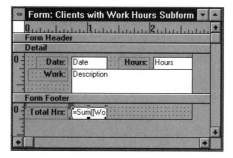

Figure 7.3 Subform with subtotal control.

field. For example, the Hours Subtotal control in Figure 7.3 contains the expression:

```
=Sum([Hours])
```

5. Enter a descriptive Control Name and set the Format for the total as Fixed, as shown in Figure 7.4.

6. Switch to Form view so you can see if the subtotal control works. Since you are now viewing the subform as an independent form, the subtotal control totals all the records in the record source—right now it acts like a total, not a subtotal. When this form is used as a subform, the linkage between the main form and the subform restricts the records in the subform to one client at a time, and the control will act like a subtotal.

7. If you plan to display the subform in Form view, not just Datasheet view, hide the form footer section by setting its Visible property to No. Otherwise, you'll display the subtotal once on the subform and once on the main form.

8. Note the name of the subtotal control (Hours Subtotal in this example), and save the subform.

9. Open the main form in Design view and display the property sheet.

10. Create a text box to contain the subtotal, as shown in Figure 7.5. For the Control Source of the control, enter an expression that refers to

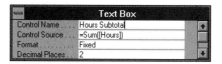

Figure 7.4 Properties of subtotal control.

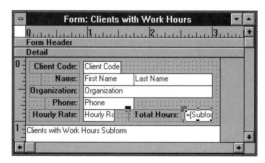

Figure 7.5　Control on main form to display the subtotal.

the subtotal control in the subform. This expression uses a special syntax for referring to controls on subforms:

```
=[subform control name].Form![subtotal control name]
```

The *subform control name* is the name of the subform control on the main form; that is, the Control Name of the control on the main form that contains the subform. The control name is usually the same as the name of the subform. In this example, the name of the subform control is Subform.

The *subtotal control name* is the name of the control on the subform that calculates the total—the control we made above in steps 4 and 5. In this example, the control is named Hours Subtotal.

Therefore, the expression needed to display the subtotal on the main form is:

```
=[Subform].Form![Hours  Subtotal]
```

11. Set the Format for this new control to Fixed, then set the Decimal Places property to 2, as shown in Figure 7.6.

12. Switch to Form view so you can see if the subtotal control works. If you see *#Name* or *#Error* instead of the subtotal, check the expression for the control carefully, and make sure that you entered the name of the control on the subform correctly.

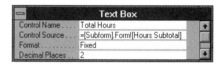

Figure 7.6　The properties of the control to display the subtotal.

Counting Records in a Subform

The form can display a count of subform records—for example, the days worked per client.

You might also want a control on the main form to show the number of records on the subform. For example, on the client billing form, you might want to show the number of days in which billable work was done for each client—a count of the records in the subform.

You can use the same method we used for totaling records to create controls that count the number of records in the subform. For example, in the client billing form, you could create a control named Record Count in the form footer of the subform with this expression as the Control Source:

```
=Count([Hours])
```

Be sure to count a field that doesn't contain null values for any records.

In the main form, you can create a control using this expression as the Control Source:

```
=[Subform].Form![Record Count]
```

Printing Subforms

Make sure that the subform control can grow to fit all the records when you print it.

If you want to see a subform when you use the main form, but you don't want to include it when you print the form, set the Display When property for the subform control to Screen Only.

If you do want to include the subform when you print the form, it is a good idea to make sure that all of the records in the subform are printed, regardless of whether they fit on the screen. Set the Can Grow property of both the subform control and the detail section of the form to Yes. To omit the subform altogether when it contains no records, set the Can Shrink property of the subform to Yes.

Using Multiple Subforms

You can include more than one subform on a form.

To place two subforms on a form, create and link each subform as described in *Linking a Subform Manually* earlier in this chapter. Figure 7.7 shows a form for the client billing database—for each client, the form shows a list of hours worked and invoices issued.

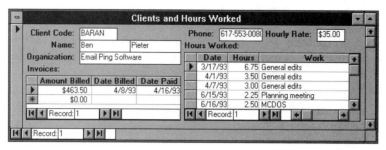

Figure 7.7   A form with two subforms.

Making Multi-Page Forms

If you include a lot of information on a form, it might be too large to fit on the screen. In order to view all the data, you can add page breaks to create a *multi-page form.*

Dividing Forms into Pages

Add page break controls in the Detail section to divide the form into pages.

To divide a form into pages, both on the screen and when the form is printed, add page break controls. Click on the Page break tool on the toolbox and click on the form where you want the break to appear. A dotted line appears at the left margin of the form to indicate where the page breaks. To avoid splitting the information in controls, make sure that all other controls are either entirely above or entirely below the page break, as shown in Figure 7.8. You usually use page break controls in the Detail section of the form, since this section can contain many controls from records in the form's record source.

Note: Page breaks only work on the screen if the Default View of the form is Single Form.

Using Headers and Footers in Multi-Page Forms

Put identifying information about the record in the form header.

If the form has form Header and Footer sections, they appear all the time, regardless of which page of the form you see. When you are looking at a multi-page form in Form view, it may not be obvious which record you are looking at. If the general information about the record is in the first

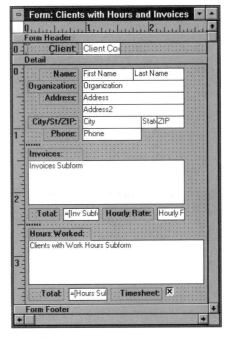

Figure 7.8 A multi-page form in Design view.

page of the form and you are looking at the second page, you may not know what record the information pertains to.

You might find it helpful to put one or more controls containing identifying information about the record in the Form Header. For instance, the client billing example in Figure 7.8 shows a multi-page form with a Form Header that shows the client code.

Designing Each Page of a Multi-Page Form

Make all pages the same size.

Because the size of the Form window doesn't change as you move from page to page of the form (by using the **PgDn** and **PgUp** keys), it is a good idea if all the pages of the form are the same size. Use the vertical ruler along the side of the form to position the page breaks evenly. You can also look at the Top property of the page break control, which tells you the distance from the top of the section. Divide the total size of the Detail section evenly into pages.

For example, for a three-page form, you might want to put page breaks at the 2-inch mark and the 4-inch mark, with the bottom edge of the Detail section at the 6-inch mark. This way, each page of the Detail section is 2 inches high.

After you divide the form into pages, switch to Form view and choose Window Size to Fit Form from the menu. This sizes the Form window to display one page of the form.

You might also find it convenient to have command buttons that allow you to move from page to page of a multi-page form—see Chapter 8 for information on creating command buttons.

Printing Multi-Page Forms

Create a page header and footer to print on each page, and use the Force New Page property to make additional page breaks when printing.

The same page break controls that divide a form into multiple pages on the screen also tell Access to skip to the top of the next page when printing. If you have inserted two page break controls to split a form into three pages on-screen, Access will skip to the top of a page after the first page and after the second page when printing the form.

However, it won't skip to the top of the page after the last page of the form unless you tell it to (you end up with the last page of one form and the first page of the next printed on the same piece of paper). You can set the Force New Page property of any section (except the Page Header and Footer sections) to No, Before Section, After Section, or Before & After. To skip a page at the end of each form, set the Force New Page property of the Detail section to After Section.

You will probably want to create page headers and footers to print on each page of the form. Page Header and Footer appear only when printed, not on the screen. You can use page headers to print your company name and the form name as well as the date, the time, and page numbers (see the Hot Tip, *Print the Date, Time, and Page Number*, in Chapter 6). You can also decide whether to print the form header and footer by setting the Display When property of the Form Header or Footer sections to Always (to print) or Screen Only (to suppress printing).

Entering Data Using Forms

Forms are more than passive arrangements of data on the screen—you use forms for entering and editing data. Using good form design as well as learning Access' shortcut keys can speed up data entry considerably. This section presents tips for efficient data entry using forms.

Controlling Tab Key Order

After you move controls around on a form, make sure you correct the tab order.

When you've moved a control on a form, you must verify that the *tab order*—the order in which the cursor moves from control to control when you press the Tab key—is still correct. Choose Edit Tab Order from the menu to display the Tab Order dialog box, shown in Figure 7.9. Then choose the section of the form you have changed. Click on Auto Order to set the tab order to left-to-right, top-to-bottom. Make further corrections by dragging the rows in the list of controls into the right order.

It is usually confusing if the tab order doesn't follow the left-to-right pattern. However, if you have controls in columns, you may want the cursor to move down each column, then up to the top of the next one.

Skip a Control in Tab Order

If you do not want to include a control in the tab order (that is, you don't want the user of the form to be able to select the control), set the Enabled property of the control to No and the Locked property to Yes. The control can't be selected using the mouse, and pressing **Tab** skips over the control, even though it appears in the list of controls in the Tab Order dialog box.

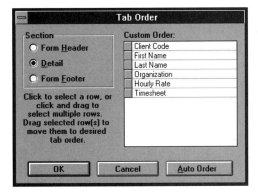

Figure 7.9 Setting the tab order of a form.

Navigating through Forms and Subforms

When you are entering data, you will probably find it convenient to use the keyboard rather than the mouse to move through your forms.

Table 7.1 shows shortcut keys for moving among your records in Form view. To move among the fields of one record, use the keys shown in Table 7.2. In Datasheet view, you can use the keys shown in Table 7.3.

When you use a form that contains a subform, you can use the keys shown in Table 7.4.

Moving Directly to Controls

You can assign an access key to a control so you can move the cursor there quickly.

You can assign an Alt+key combination to a control so that you can move the cursor directly to the control. To assign this *access key* to a control, must include an ampersand (&) immediately preceding the character key in the Caption property of the label control attached to the editable control. For example, if you enter

`&Total`

the label displays

`Total`

To move the cursor directly to the editable control to which the label control is attached, you press the **Alt** key and the character key, in this case **Alt+T**.

Table 7.1   Shortcut Keys for Moving Among Records

Action	Shortcut
First record	Ctrl+Home or Ctrl+Up Arrow
Last record	Ctrl+End or Ctrl+Down Arrow
Next record	Ctrl+PgDn
Previous record	Ctrl+PgUp
New record	Ctrl++
Search (Find dialog box)	F7
Repeat previous search	Shift+F4

Table 7.2 Shortcut Keys for Moving Among Controls

Action	Shortcut
Last field	End
First field	Home
Next field	Enter
Next page	PgDn
Previous page	PgUp
Previous field	Shift+Tab

Table 7.3 Shortcut Keys in Datasheet View

Action	Shortcut
First record	Ctrl+Home
Last record	Ctrl+End
Next record	Down Arrow
Previous record	Up Arrow
New record	Ctrl++

Table 7.4 Shortcut Keys for Subforms

Action	Shortcut
Requery records for subform	Shift+F9
Move from subform to next field in main form	Ctrt+Tab
Move from subform to previous field in main form	Ctrl+Shift+Tab
Move to first field in main form	Ctrl+Shift+HomeTable

You will find it is particularly convenient to assign access keys to controls in multi-page forms, so you can move quickly from one page to the next.

Undoing Changes in Forms

Use these shortcut keys to undo changes to the field or record.

As always in Access, you can use the undo feature when you make a mistake. Use the Undo feature right away, without making any other change first, since Access can undo only the last change you made. When you use a form, Access provides three types of undo:

- To undo changes to the current field, press **Esc**
- To undo changes to the current record (all fields), press **Esc** twice
- To undo your last change, press **Ctrl+Z** or **Alt+Backspace**

Providing Instructions on the Status Bar

Use the Status Bar Text property to provide instructions on the status bar.

The *status bar*, the left side of the bottom line in the Access window, can be used to display helpful information to someone filling out a form. The Status Bar Text property of each editable control on the form contains the text that appears in the status bar when the cursor is in that control.

It is a good idea to include instructions about the format of phone numbers and other codes, when information should be capitalized, where the information comes from, and other information about the field displayed in the control.

Seeing Others' Changes in a Multi-User System

If several people are editing records at the same time, you can refresh your data to see the changes.

In a multi-user system, several people can be editing records at the same time. You can choose the Records Refresh command to see any changes that have been made to the data by other people.

8

Making Dynamic Forms

Access provides several ways to make "smart" forms—forms that provide you with lists of choices, that respond to your entries, and that contain buttons you can click to do other tasks. This chapter describes how to use these features, with tips for making your forms work for you.

The first section describes ways to use combo boxes, list boxes, and option groups for choosing values. Then, there are tips for creating macros that you can attach to forms for validating entries, calculating codes, and avoiding accidental deletions. Finally, this chapter includes ways to use command buttons to execute macros from your form.

The examples in this chapter refer to the BILLING database (a client billing system), the MAILLIST database, and BOOKORD, the booksellers order entry database.

Offering Choices

As you know, when you are entering records into a detail table, you must use values from matching master records. For example, in a client billing system, when you enter the billable hours you have worked, you must use the client code from an existing record in a table of clients.

In a large database, you might have difficulty remembering the matching values in the master table. Access solves this dilemma. Instead of making you guess codes, Access can display a list you can pick from. The following topics provide tips for using combo boxes, list boxes, and option groups on your forms.

Creating Combo and List Boxes

It's not much harder to make a combo or list box that to create a simple text box.

Here is the easiest way to make a combo or list box that is bound to a field:

1. Select the Combo or List box tool from the toolbox.
2. Drag the field that you want bound to the control from the field list. Access creates the specified control and enters the field name for the Control Name and Control Source properties.
3. Set the Row Source Type and Row Source properties to tell Access where to get the list of values to display.

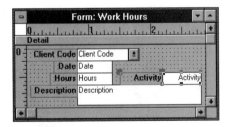

Figure 8.1 Design view of a form with a combo box.

To display a list that is stored in a table or query, choose Table/Query for the Row Source Type and enter the name of the table or query as the Row Source. The first field in the table is the one that appears in the combo or list box. (For information on creating multiple-column combo and list boxes, see *Making Multiple-Column Combo and List Boxes* later in this chapter.)

Figure 8.1 shows a form in a client billing database. When entering billable hours, the user of the form can choose the client code from a combo box. The properties of the combo box are shown in Figure 8.2.

Entering a List to Display

If the matching values are not stored in a table, you can enter the list right in the Row Source property of the control.

If the matching values are not stored in a table, simply type the values you want into the Row Source property, separated by semicolons. Set the Row Source Type property to Value List.

For example, the Activity code in the client billing system indicates the type of work that was done during each group of billable hours. If the values are the codes E (editing), I (indexing), and W (writing), you can enter these directly into the Row Source property of a combo or list box. Figure 8.3 shows a combo box for the Activity code with the three codes entered in the Row Source, separated by semicolons.

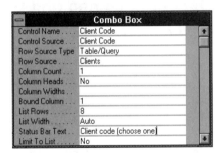

Figure 8.2 Properties of a combo box.

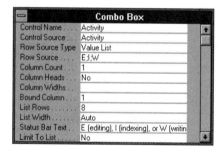

Figure 8.3   Entering a list of values for the Row Source property.

Sounds foolproof, right? Well, most of the time it's not. If the codes change, or if you add or delete the codes, you must change the properties of the control. If the same codes appear on several forms, you must make the changes in each form. And there is no explanation of what the codes mean—you can, and should, include explanations in the Status Bar Text property, but this space is limited.

A better approach is to create a new table to contain the codes that should appear in a combo or list box. The table can contain not only the codes but their meanings too, as shown in Figure 8.4. Now, because the codes are stored in a table, if the codes change, you change them in only one place.

The only circumstances in which it is a good idea to enter a list of values into the Row Source property are when:

- The values have no meaning elsewhere in the database
- The values will rarely or never change
- There is no need to explain the meanings of the choices

For example, in a mailing list, you might want to store the salutation for each person. The choices might be Mr., Ms., Dr., and Prof., and you never expect to use any others. These codes would probably not be used anywhere else in the database, and no explanation would be necessary.

Sorting Options in Combo and List Boxes

Use a query as the Row Source for the list.

Figure 8.4   Table containing activity codes and their meanings.

You can decide what order you want the drop-down list of choices to be in. For example, you can display clients alphabetically by code or by full name.

When you use a table as the Row Source of a combo or list box, the records appear in the primary key order of the table (if there is no primary key, they appear in the order they were entered). If you want them to appear in another order, use a query instead of the table as the Row Source.

Create the query to include the field(s) that you want in the drop-down list. If you want to display more than one field in the combo or list box, include the fields in the query in the same order in which you want them to appear in the drop-down list (see *Making Multiple-Column Combo and List Boxes* later in this chapter).

Sort the query so that the records appear in the order you want and save the query. Figure 8.5 shows a query that sorts the client code and organization name from the Clients table into alphabetical order by organization name. It doesn't include the fields containing address information, because we don't want them in the drop-down list.

In Design view of the form, set the Row Source Type property of the combo or list box to Table/Query, and set the Row Source property to the query you just made. To avoid creating unnecessary queries, see *Avoiding Extra Queries for Filling Combo or List Boxes* later in this chapter.

Entering Other Values in a Combo Box

Use the Limit To List property of combo boxes to control whether you can type in new values.

Using a combo box (but not a list box), you can enter values that are not on the drop-down list by typing them in. If you enter new values, they are stored in the Record Source of the form. However, they are not stored in the Row Source of the combo box. If you don't want to allow this, set the Limit To List property of the combo box to Yes.

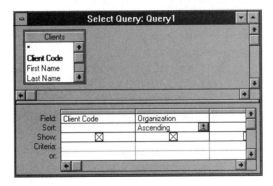

Figure 8.5 Sorting clients by organization name to appear in a combo box.

For example, Figure 8.1 shows a form in the client billing database for entering billable hours worked into the Work Hours table. It uses a combo box to choose the client code, displaying a list from the Clients table. If you type a new value into the combo box, the new client code is stored in the Work Hours table, but it isn't stored in the Clients table. In this case, a relationship with referential integrity has been defined between the Clients and Work Hours tables, and Access won't let you enter a record in the Work Hours table if there is no record for the client in the Clients table. It would be better not to let the user of the form enter client codes that aren't on the drop-down list. To make sure that no new values are entered, either use a list box or set the Limit To List property of the combo box to Yes.

If you do want to allow values that aren't on the list, set the Limit To List property to No (the default setting).

Making Multiple-Column Combo and List Boxes

Tell Access how many columns to display, set the column widths, and choose one column to be bound.

You can display more than one column of information in a combo or list box. Although only one field is stored for each record, you can display several fields in the list. For example, a list box might let the user of the form choose a client by displaying both the client code and organization name. However, the list box actually stores only the client code. The column that provides the value to be stored in the record is called the *bound column*. You use the Column Count property of the combo or list box to tell Access how many columns to display.

You will find it helpful to store the codes and their descriptions in a separate table, because you may want these descriptions to appear on other forms or on reports. In our example, the codes and descriptions are stored in the Clients table. A query called Clients for Combo Box sorts the clients by organization name, and includes only the fields that will appear in the combo or list box. Note that the fields to appear in the combo or list box must be the first ones in the table or query.

To make a multiple-column combo or list box:

1. Make a query that includes the fields, in the cor`rect order, that you want to display in the combo or list box. In our example, the Clients table doesn't store the Client Code and Organization as the first two fields in the table. So instead, we can use the Clients for Combo Box query (Figure 8.5) as the Row Source. The query can also sort the records to appear in the order you want. If the table containing the

codes stores the fields in the same order in which you want the columns to appear in the combo or list box, you can use the table as the Row Source. (To avoid creating unnecessary queries, see *Avoiding Extra Queries for Filling Combo or List Boxes* later in this chapter.)

2. In Design view of the form, display both the field list and the toolbox.

3. Click on the Combo box or List box tool.

4. Drag the field name to which the control will be bound from the field list to the form. For example, if the combo or list box will be used to pick the client code, drag the Client Code field to the form. Position the field where you want the combo or list box to appear.

5. Access automatically fills in the Control Name and Control Source properties with the name of the field you dragged. The Row Source Type defaults to Table/Query. For the Row Source, choose the name of the table or query that contains the codes and descriptions (in this example, the query named Clients for Combo Box).

6. Switch to Form view to make sure that the combo or list box works. At this point, only one column displays.

7. Switch back to Design view. Set the Column Count property to the number of columns you want. In this example, we want two columns (client code and organization name).

8. Set the Column Widths property to the width of each column in inches (or centimeters), separated by semicolons for example, 0.5in; 1.5in. To hide a column, set its width to 0. To let Access choose a default width for the column, omit the width (but do include the semicolon after it).

9. For combo boxes only, set the List Width property to the total of the column widths, plus about 1/4 inch for the scroll bar. If you use the default List Width setting (Auto), the drop-down list will be the same width as the combo box control, which is frequently too narrow to display multiple columns.

10. Enter the number of the column (1 for first, 2 for second, and so on) that contains the value to store in the Bound Column property.

Figure 8.6 shows the settings for the combo box for selecting a client code—the drop-down list contains two columns (Client Code and Organization), which are .5 and 1.5 inches wide. The total width of the list is 2.25 inches. The bound column is the first column.

11. Switch to Form view to try out the control. Figure 8.7 shows the two-column combo box for choosing client codes.

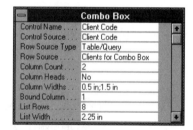

Figure 8.6   Properties for a multiple-column combo box.

Displaying Descriptions while Storing Codes

If you want the user to see a description of a code instead of the code itself, you can make a multiple-column combo or list box that contains both the code and the description, and hide the code column.

Sometimes codes can be so cryptic to the user that displaying them is not useful. Access solves this problem by allowing you to display a different value in the combo or list box than the value stored in the control.

You can create a multiple-column control and then designate the code as the value to store, but hide the code column.

As I mentioned in the previous topic, you can hide a column by setting its column width to zero. For example, for the two-column combo box we made for choosing the client code, the list could display only the full name of the client's organization, hiding the code column. In other words, you would hide the first column by using this entry in the Column Widths property:

```
0 in;1.5 in
```

Figure 8.8 shows the combo box with the first column hidden. Using this method, the user never sees the underlying cryptic codes.

Dressing Up List Boxes and Combo Boxes

Choose colors and special effects for combo and list boxes.

Figure 8.7   Two-column combo box.

Figure 8.8 Multiple-column combo box with one column hidden.

You can set the color for the background, text, and border of combo boxes and list boxes, and you can adjust the width of the border and select a 3-D appearance by using the palette. Combo and list boxes usually look best if they match the general appearance of the text boxes on the form.

Control the Size of a Combo Box

Set the List Rows property to the maximum number of rows the drop-down list should display when the combo box is opened.

Avoiding Extra Queries for Filling Combo or List Boxes

Use an SQL statement as the Row Source instead of a query.

To specify which fields appear as columns in a combo or list box, and what order the records are listed, you usually create a query to use as the Row Source of the combo or list box. You may end up with many queries that are used only for this purpose. To avoid filling your database with these queries, you can enter an *SQL statement* as the Row Source. SQL provides an on-the-fly query for use in the combo or list box.

Every time you create a query, Access translates your entries in the query grid into an SQL (Structured Query Language) statement. You don't have to be familiar with SQL to use an SQL statement as the Row Source — let Access create the SQL statement for you.

For example, in the client billing database, there is a Billable Hours form with a multiple-column combo box for selecting the client code for billing purposes. Rather than using a query to present the Client Code and Organization fields, sorted by Organization, you can use a more efficient SQL statement as the Row Source.

To use an SQL statement as the Row Source of a combo or list box:

1. Create a new query that provides the fields and records you want, in the order they should appear in the combo or list box.

2. While viewing the query in Design view, choose View SQL from the menu. Access displays the SQL dialog box, shown in Figure 8.9.

3. In the SQL dialog box, select the entire SQL statement, then press **Ctrl+C** to copy it to the Clipboard.

4. Switch to the Design view of the form containing the list box or combo box control. View the property sheet for the control.

5. Set the Row Source Type property to Table/Query.

6. Click in the Row Source property box in the property sheet.

7. Press **Ctrl+V** to paste the SQL statement into the property box. You can then press **Shift+F2** to view the entire SQL statement in the Zoom box.

8. Set the other properties of the control.

9. Unless you need the query for other purposes, close the query without saving it.

Displaying Possible Duplicates

Use an unbound combo or list box to display possible duplicate records.

You can use a combo or list box to show possible duplicates when you enter records. For example, in a mailing list database, it is important not to enter the same person more than once. When you enter a new address, you might find it useful for Access to display other records that might be duplicates.

You can use an *unbound* combo or list box for this purpose. Because the control is unbound, it doesn't store information in the record you are editing. Instead, it just displays information that helps you to discover duplicate records. To make a control unbound, leave its Control Source property blank.

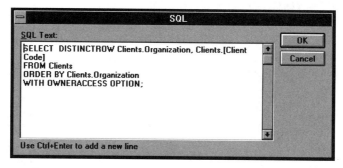

Figure 8.9 The SQL statement constructed by Access.

For example, a mailing list database has a form for entering new addresses. When the user enters a last name, an unbound combo or list box could display a list of existing addresses with the same last name. Figure 8.10 shows the form in Design view, and Figure 8.11 shows the properties of the list box.

The list box is unbound, that is, the Control Source property is blank. For the Row Source enter this SQL:

```
SELECT [First Name],[Last Name] from [Mailing List]
WHERE [Last Name] = [LName];
```

This statement selects records from the Mailing List table, the same table to which the form adds records. Only the First Name and Last Name fields display in the list box, and all of the records that have the same last name as the one in the LName control on the form are included—the last name of the address that the user is adding.

Notice that the Column Count property is set to 2 to show two columns, First Name and Last Name.

To use the list box in Form view, move to a new record and enter a name in the first three fields of the record. Because the values in a list or combo box are based on values in the new record, you must requery to

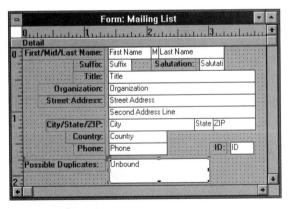

Figure 8.10 Mailing list form with list box to show possible duplicates.

Figure 8.11 Properties for unbound list box to show duplicates.

update the list. Access doesn't update the list box automatically when you enter a last name in the LName control. Press **F9** to update the list box so it selects records based on the new value of LName. Figure 8.12 shows how the form looks in use.

To tell Access to press **F9** automatically when you enter a new last name, you can use a macro (see *Attaching Macros to Forms* in this chapter for more information on using macros).

Choosing Yes/No Values

Use check boxes, option buttons, or toggle buttons to choose values for Yes/No fields.

Check boxes, option buttons, and toggle buttons may look different but they do the same thing—they let you enter a value of Yes or No. Which type of control you choose depends on the look you want. Generally, it is better not to use a toggle button by itself for a Yes/No field, because it looks like a command button.

The easiest way to make one of these controls is to select the Check box, Option button, or Toggle button tool from the toolbox. Then drag a Yes/No field from the field list to the form. Access makes a control of that type, and enters the field name for the Control Name and Control Source of the new control. If you entered a description of the field when you designed the table, it copies the text to the Status Bar Text property. Access also sets the Default Value property if the field has a default.

Using Groups of Buttons to Choose among Values

Create an option group for the field, and create a toggle button for each value of the field.

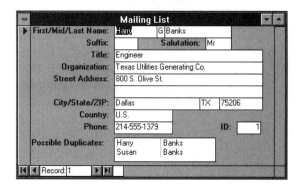

Figure 8.12   Mailing list form showing possible duplicates.

For numeric codes, you can use an *option group* to let the user of the form choose a value. An option group includes one check box, option button, or toggle button for each numeric value the user can pick. Usually, toggle buttons are the most effective control to use in an option group—the user "presses" the button for the desired option. Option groups are great if there are only a few values the field might have. If you need more than five buttons, however, a list box will probably be more effective.

For example, in the client billing database there might be a table of activities that can be done, so that clients can be billed at different rates for different types of work. If the activity codes are numeric, you can use an option group to allow users to make selections. (You can't use option groups with fields that are not numeric.) Figure 8.13 shows a table with numeric activity codes. Figure 8.14 shows an option group with a button for each activity code.

To create an option group with toggle buttons (or check boxes or option buttons), you must first create an option group control, which is usually bound to a field. Then, you create one toggle button for each value of the field. For the activities values, the options group is bound to an Activity field in the table that the form is editing. There are three activities codes, so the option group contains three toggle buttons.

When toggle buttons (or check boxes or option buttons) are part of an option group, Access allows only one button in the group to be selected at a time. The button that is selected provides the value for the field to which the option group is bound. For example, the client billing form can include an Edit button (activity code 1), an Index button (activity code 2), and a Write button (activity code 3). If the Edit button is selected, the

Table: Activities	
ActivityCode	**ActivityDescription**
1	Editing
2	Indexing
3	Writing
0	

Record: 1

Figure 8.13 Numeric codes to be selected using an option group.

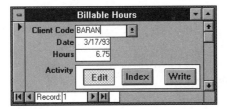

Figure 8.14 Option group with a toggle button for each activity code.

Activity field has the value 1. If the Index button is selected, the field has the value 2. And if the Write button is selected, the field has the value 3.

To create an option group to select values for a numeric field:

1. Click on the Option group tool from the toolbox.
2. From the field list, select the field to which the option group will be bound, and drag it onto the form where you want the option group to appear. For example, drag the Activity field onto the form. Access creates a frame for the option group into which you will place toggle buttons.
3. You can use the palette to set the background color for the option group frame (the area in which the toggle buttons will go), the color of the border around the frame, and the border width. Don't worry about selecting the exact size for the option group frame—once you have placed the buttons, you can choose the final size.
4. Set the Default Value for the option group to the most commonly selected value for the field.

For each value of the numeric field that the option group is bound to, do the following:

- Click on the Toggle button tool on the toolbox.
- Click inside the option group frame where you want the upper-left corner of the button to appear. Notice that when you move the cursor into the option group frame, Access highlights the frame. This tells you that the toggle button will be part of the option group. When you click inside the option group, Access creates a toggle button.
- Enter the caption to appear on the button in the Caption property.
- Enter the numeric value for this button in the Option Value property. This is the value to which the bound field will be set when this button is chosen. For example, if the activity code for editing the client billing form is 1, the button with the "Edit" caption has an Option Value of 1.

You can use the Edit Duplicate command to copy a toggle button once you have made the first one. You can also use the Layout Align command to align the buttons horizontally or vertically.

Figure 8.15 shows a form in Design view with an option group that contains three buttons. Figure 8.16 shows the properties for the third button.

Warning: The only connection between the descriptions of the numeric codes and the codes themselves is the caption on each button. If this information isn't stored elsewhere, make a note of what each value means. You might want to place the information in the Design view of the table, in the description for the field that contains the numeric codes.

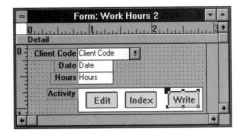

Figure 8.15 Option group for selecting a numeric activity code.

Figure 8.16 Properties of a toggle button in an option group.

Creating a Toggle Button with a Picture

You can display a bitmap picture on a toggle button.

To display a bitmap picture on a toggle button, enter the path and filename of the file containing the picture in the Picture property for the toggle button control. After Access finds the bitmap picture, "(bitmap)" is displayed for the Picture property in the property sheet.

You can use any paint or draw program to create bitmap (.BMP) files. Because there are no commands in Access for scaling or trimming the picture that is displayed on the button, the picture must already be the right size. To create a picture that is the right size using Microsoft Paintbrush (which comes with Windows), draw the picture the same size that it will appear on the button, that is, quite small. You can use Paintbrush's Pick Shrink + Grow command to scale your picture until it fits on your button. Then, select the part of the picture that you want on the button using the Pick tool from the toolbox. In Paintbrush, choose Edit Copy To and enter the filename (and path) for the selected part of the picture.

Enter the Picture Path Name as the Caption

Once you enter the path and filename of the bitmap file into the Picture property, Access displays "(bitmap)" in the property. There is no way to see the path name again. You might find it helpful to enter the path and filename in the Caption property of the control—when there are entries for both Picture and Caption, Access ignores the caption and displays the picture. You will now be able to see the filename of the picture you are using. If you want to use the same picture on a button on another form, you can copy the path and filename from the Caption.

Attaching Macros to Forms

Because Access is an object-oriented database system, the objects in the database can have their own intelligence. You can make a form intelligent by attaching macros to the controls on the form. When you use the form, moving from control to control can trigger macros that check your entries, change the controls that are displayed, or format your entries.

To attach a macro to a form, you enter the name of the macro in a property of the form or of a control on the form. You can attach macros to the following form properties:

- **On Open**: Runs the macro before opening a form
- **On Close**: Runs the macro before closing a form
- **Before Update**: Runs the macro before saving a record
- **After Update**: Runs the macro after saving a record
- **On Current**: Runs the macro when you open the form and Access loads the first record, and also before moving to a different record
- **On Insert**: Runs the macro before inserting a new record
- **On Delete**: Runs the macro before deleting a record

You can also attach a macro to these control properties:

- **Before Update**: Runs the macro before saving data in the control
- **After Update**: Runs the macro after saving data in the control
- **On Enter**: Runs the macro before the cursor enters the control
- **On Exit**: Runs the macro before the cursor leaves the control
- **On DblClick**: Runs the macro when you double-click on the control
- **On Push**: Runs the macro when you click on a command button

This section provides tips for creating macros that make your forms smarter. For more ideas about creating macros, see Chapter 16.

Creating Macros for Forms

Store all the macros for a form in one macro group.

As you create macros to attach to forms, you may end up with many small macros. Rather than saving each macro separately, make one macro group that contains all the macros for one form. For example, if you plan to create a number of macros for a form called Work Hours, make one macro group called Work Hours Form.

To make a macro group:

1. Choose Macro from the Database window and click on New to display the Macro window.

2. If the Macro Name column is not displayed, choose View Macro Names from the menu to display the column.

    Now, you can store a number of macros in this macro group by entering a macro name in the Macro Name column, then adding the actions and arguments for the macro. (See Chapter 16 for information about entering actions and arguments.)

    Use a macro name that indicates which control, or which form property, the macro is attached to. For example, for a macro that is run by a button whose caption is "Add," name the macro AddButton.

3. Save the macro group. If you plan to use this group to contain all the macros for one form, name it after the form—for example, Work Hours Form.

    To attach a macro in a macro group to a property of a form, use the name of the macro group followed by a period (.) followed by the macro name. For example, if the Work Hours Form macro group contains a macro named AddRecord, you can enter this macro name in a form or control property:

    ```
    Work Hours Form.AddRecord
    ```

Display Macro Names Automatically

If you create macro groups rather than individual macros, you'll usually want to see the Macro Name column in the Macro window. To tell Access to display this column whenever you open the Macro window, choose View Options Macro Design from the menu, and set Show Macro Names Column to Yes.

If you frequently use conditions in your macros, you can also set Show Conditions Column to Yes.

Pressing F2 Automatically

Use a macro to switch into edit mode when the cursor enters a control.

When you need to make changes to a record, you'll probably find it more efficient to edit the values rather than simply overwriting the current contents. You can create a macro that switches to edit mode so that you don't have to press F2. You could avoid writing a macro by setting all controls to remain in edit mode. Simply choose View Options Keyboard from the menu and set the Arrow Key Behavior to Next Character.

But, what if you want to change this behavior for only specific controls? You can make a macro that presses **F2** and **Home**. If you run this macro when you enter the control, it prevents accidental erasure.

To create this macro:

1. Create a new macro group, or open the existing macro group for this form.

2. Enter a name in the Macro Name column—for example, "PressF2."

3. For the Action, choose SendKeys.

4. The SendKeys action has two arguments, shown in the lower part of the Macro window. For the Keystrokes argument, type:

   {F2}{HOME}

   For the Wait argument, choose No. The macro now looks like Figure 8.17.

5. Save the macro.

To attach the macro you just created to a control:

1. Open the form in Design view.

2. Display the property sheet for the control.

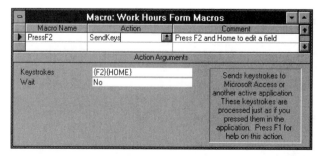

Figure 8.17   Macro to switch to edit mode when you enter a control.

3. For the On Enter property, choose the name of the macro group you just saved. Then, edit the property, adding a period (.) followed by the macro name. For example, if the macro group is named Work Hours Form and the macro is named PressF2, the On Enter property should contain:

```
Work Hours Form.PressF2
```

Now when the cursor enters the control, Access automatically presses **F2** to enter edit mode, and **Home** to move the cursor to the beginning of the field.

You can use the same macro for many controls. For example, on a form used for data entry, you might want to attach the PressF2 macro to all the text box controls.

Requiring an Entry

Attach a macro to the form to require entries in controls.

Validation rules can't prevent a field from being left blank. Instead, you can create and attach a macro to the Before Update property of the form that requires the user to make an entry. Table 8.1 shows a macro that requires that the Hourly Rate field contain a value.

Warning: You must make sure to attach this macro to the *form's* Before Update property; if you attach it to the Before Update property of the control that displays Hourly Rate, the macro is never run if the user doesn't move the cursor to that control.

The macro checks whether Hourly Rate is null (blank) using a condition. If so, it displays a message box, cancels the update, and returns the cursor to the Hourly Rate control so the user can enter a rate. The ellipsis (...) in the Condition column indicates that this action should be taken only if the preceding condition was true, so if Hourly Rate is not null, the macro does nothing.

Table 8.1   Single-Field Required Entry Macro

Macro Name	Condition	Action	Arguments
RequireRate	[Hourly Rate] Is Null	MsgBox	Message: Enter an hourly rate. Beep: Yes Type: Information Title: Hourly Rate Required
	...	CancelEvent	
	...	GoToControl	Control Name: Hourly Rate

To require entries in several controls in a form, the macro can check several conditions. For each condition that is met, it can display an appropriate message and move the cursor to the control with the offending value. Once it finds one missing value, the macro stops to allow the user to fix the problem. Table 8.2 shows a macro that checks three fields for null values.

Moving the Cursor with Macros

A macro can move the cursor to different controls depending on what value you enter.

Based on what you enter in one control, you can create a macro that moves the cursor to the next appropriate control. You can even move to

Table 8.2   Multiple-Field Required Entry Macro

Macro Name	Condition	Action	Arguments
RequireEntries	[Hourly Rate] Is Null	MsgBox	Message: Enter an hourly rate. Beep: Yes Type: Information Title: Hourly Rate Required
	...	CancelEvent	
	...	GoToControl	Control Name: Hourly Rate
	...	StopMacro	
	[Client Code] Is Null	MsgBox	Message: Choose a client code from the list. Beep: Yes Type: Information Title: Client Code Required
	...	CancelEvent	
	...	GoToControl	Control Name: Client Code
	...	StopMacro	
	[Organization] Is Null	MsgBox	Message: Enter the name of the client's organization. Beep: Yes Type: Information Title: Client Organization Required
	...	CancelEvent	
	...	GoToControl	Control Name: Organization

another page of the form. Use the After Update property of the control, then use the GoToControl or GoToPage action.

For example, in an order entry database (see the BACKORD database on the companion diskette), the order entry form might have a Payment Method control that is set to 1 (check), 2 (charge), or 3 (purchase order). If the value is 1, the cursor can move to the Cust Check Number control. If it is 2, it can move to the Card Number control. And if it is 3, it can move to the Cust PO control. Table 8.3 shows a macro that makes entries and moves the cursor depending on the value of Payment Method.

Hiding Unnecessary Controls

A macro can make unneeded controls invisible.

You can even hide controls depending on their values. For example, if the Payment Method for an order is 1 (check) or 3 (purchase order), you don't need to use the Card Number control. The macro can hide the control by setting its Visible property to No. Table 8.4 shows part of a macro that hides the Card Number field if the Payment Method is 1 (check).

The second SetValue action sets the Visible property of the Card Number control to No, hiding the control.

Setting the Default to the Last Value Entered

Attach a macro to the form's On Insert property to set up new records.

In some data entry situations, each record differs from the preceding one by only a few fields. You can use a macro to set the defaults for some fields

Table 8.3   Conditional Cursor Movement Macro

Macro Name	Condition	Action	Arguments
Payment	[Payment Method] = 1	SetValue	Item: [Cust PO] Expression: "check"
	...	GoToControl	Control Name: Cust Check Number
	[Payment Method] = 2	SetValue	Item: [Cust PO] Expression: "VISA/MC"
	...	GoToControl	Control Name: Card Number
	[Payment Method] = 3	GoToControl	Control Name: Cust PO

Table 8.4 Conditional Cursor Movement Macro

Macro Name	Condition	Action	Arguments
Payment	[Payment Method] = 1	SetValue	Item: [Cust PO] Expression: "check"
	...	SetValue	Item: [Card Number]. Visible Expression: No
	...	GoToControl	Control Name: Cust Check Number

in each new record to the values from the preceding record. Then you can enter information for only the fields that are different. This is similar to pressing **Ctrl+"** for each field of the record, except that it happens automatically when you start a new record. You can also decide which fields should be duplicated and which should be left blank.

Table 8.5 shows a macro that can be attached to the On Insert property of the Work Hours form of the client billing database. It duplicates four fields (Client Code, Date, Hours, and Description), then returns the cursor to the first field for editing. To duplicate the fields, it sends the keystrokes

^"

(that is, Ctrl+") and

~

(that is, Enter) for the first three fields, to copy the value from the previous record and move to the next field. For the last field, it again sends

Table 8.5 The SetUp Duplication Macro

Macro Name	Action	Arguments
SetUp	SendKeys	Keystrokes: ^"~ Wait: No
	SendKeys	Keystrokes: ^"~ Wait: No
	SendKeys	Keystrokes: ^"~ Wait: No
	SendKeys	Keystrokes: ^"+{TAB}+{TAB}+{TAB} Wait: No

```
^"
```

and then three

```
+{TAB}
```

(Shift+Tab) to move back to the starting field. (You can also combine the Keysrokes into one long string and use one SendKeys action to type them.)

Avoiding Accidental Deletions

Use a macro to check that a record can be deleted.

If you have defined a one-to-many relationship between two tables with referential integrity, Access won't let you delete a record from the master table (the "one" side of the relationship) if there are related records in the detail table (the "many" side). However, if you haven't defined (or can't define) a relationship with referential integrity, you can use a macro to do this checking.

For example, if the master table is an attached table, Access won't let you define a relationship. Instead, you can use the On Delete property of the form for the master table to run a macro. The macro can do a lookup in a related table, checking that there are no related records. If there are, the macro can cancel the deletion.

The macro that you run from the On Delete property might look like Table 8.6. The Deletion macro uses the DCount() function to count the records in the detail table. DCount() uses three arguments:

```
DCount("*", "table", "criterion")
```

The first argument tells Access what field to count, and entering "*" tells it to count any record that matches the criterion. The *table* is the table, query, or SQL statement containing the records to count. The *criterion* is the true-or-false expression that describes the records to be counted.

Table 8.6 Macro to Check for Related Records in an Attached Table

Macro Name	Condition	Action	Arguments
Deletion	DCount("*", "Order Details","[Product Code] = Forms![Products]! [Product Code]") > 0	MsgBox	Message: There are orders for this product,so you shouldn't delete it. Beep: Yes Type: Warning! Title: Do Not Delete
	...	CancelEvent	

The macro uses this condition to determine if there are records in the detail table:

```
DCount("*", "Order Details", "[Product Code] =
  Forms![Products]![Product Code]") > 0
```

This counts the records in the Order Details table that have the same Product Code as the one the user is trying to delete. If there are any records in Order Details, the count is greater than zero and the macro cancels the deletion.

Maximizing the Form

When you open a form, you can maximize it automatically.

If a form is large, you may want to use it maximized, that is, expanded to take up the entire Access window. You can maximize the form automatically when it is opened, using a macro attached to the On Open property of the form.

The macro contains just one action: Maximize, which maximizes the current window.

Displaying List or Combo Boxes Based on Previous Choices

Use a macro to display only the controls that are appropriate, based on what the user has entered.

What if you want to choose something from a list or combo box (or other control), and have an appropriate second list or combo box (or other control) appear based on the choice? For example, if you choose Check for the payment method, you want to choose between Check, Money Order, and Travelers Cheques. If you choose Charge for the payment method, you want to choose between VISA, Mastercard, and Discover. And if you choose Purchase Order for the payment method, you don't want make any additional choice.

Follow these steps to attach a macro to the On Exit property of the first combo or list box, which displays another combo or list box visible based on the user's choice.

1. Create the first-level combo or list box. For example, make a combo box called Payment Method.

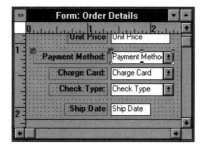

Figure 8.18 Three combo boxes.

2. Create each second-level combo or list box. For example, make two combo boxes called Check Type and Charge Card. Figure 8.18 shows a form with the three combo boxes.

3. Make sure each combo or list box works in Form view.

4. Set the Visible properties of all the second-level combo or list boxes to No, to suppress their display when the form first opens.

5. Create a macro to run after the user chooses a value from the first-level combo or list box. Table 8.7 shows a sample macro.

Access interprets the macro like this: If the Payment Method is "C" (check), display the Check Type combo box and move the cursor there.

Table 8.7 Macro to Display Second-Level Combo or List Box

Macro Name	Condition	Action	Arguments
DisplayBoxes	[Payment Method]="C"	SetValue	Item: [Charge Card].Visible Expression: "No"
	...	SetValue	Item: [Check Type].Visible Expression: "Yes"
	...	GoToControl	Control Name:[Check Type]
	[Payment Method]="R"	SetValue	Item: [Charge Card].Visible Expression: "Yes"
	...	SetValue	Item: [Check Type].Visible Expression: "No"
	...	GoToControl	Control Name:[Charge Card]
	[Payment Method]="P"	SetValue	Item: [Charge Card].Visible Expression: "No"
	...	SetValue	Item:[Check Type].Visible Expression: "No"
	...	GoToControl	Control Name: [Ship Date]

If the Payment Method is "R" (charge), display the Charge Card combo box and move the cursor there. And if the Payment Method is "P" (purchase order), don't display either combo box and move the cursor to the next control on the form.

6.   Attach this macro to the On Exit property of the first-level combo or list box, in this case the Payment Method control.

7.   Test out the macro by trying each value of the first-level combo or list box.

8.   When the macro works, move the second-level combo or list boxes on top of each other. Only one is visible at a time, so they can both occupy the same space on the form.

Using this method, you can make any type of controls appear as needed.

Setting Two Fields from One Combo Box

Use a macro to copy the value of unbound columns of a combo box to text box controls.

Although you can bind just one of the columns in a multiple-column list box or combo box to a field in the underlying table or query, you can fill in data from the other columns as well. You create a macro that copies the value(s) from the other column(s).

For example, in the booksellers order entry database, when you enter the orders you can make a combo box from which the user chooses the product code that has been ordered. The combo box can display both the product code and the unit price of the product. Although the combo box is bound to a Product Code field on the form, you also want to store the price in a Unit Price text box on the form. (You should store the price for each order, because when prices change, it is important to know what price was current when the order was placed.) To create a combo box:

1.   On the form, create the combo box shown in Figure 8.19. Set the Column Count property to 2 (or more, if you want to display other columns), then set the Bound Column property of the combo box. In Figure 8.19, the bound column is 1, the Product Code column.

2.   Create the text box that you want to fill with the other column of the combo box. In Figure 8.19 it is the Unit Price text box.

3.   Create a macro that copies the value of the column from the combo box to the text box. For the SetValue action which copies the value,

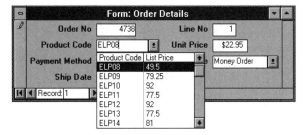

Figure 8.19 Setting two controls from a combo box with two columns.

use the following expression to refer to the value of the column of the combo box:

```
[comboboxname].Column(n)
```

In this expression, *comboboxname* is the name of the combo box control. *N* is the column number in the control. The first column is column 0, the second column is column 1, and so on. Table 8.8 shows a macro that copies the value of the second column of the Product Code combo box to the Unit Price text box.

4. Enter this macro name in the After Update property of the combo box, so that after the user chooses a product, the macro copies the price.

If you prefer, you can hide the column from which you copy the value. For example, you can hide the price column in the Product Code combo box, so the user doesn't see the list of prices. To hide the column, enter zero for its width in the Column Widths property.

Calling an Access Basic Function

You can call an Access Basic function defined in a module.

If you have written an Access Basic function in your database, you can call the function from a form. In a property into which you would usually enter a macro name, type the function name instead, using this format:

```
=functionname()
```

Table 8.8 Macro to Fill Text Box from Combo Box

Macro Name	Action	Arguments
CopyPrice	SetValue	Item: [Unit Price] Expression: [Product Code].Column(1)

The equal sign and parentheses are required, so Access knows this is a function and not a macro name. If the function returns a value, Access discards it.

To run an Access Basic function from within a macro, use the RunCode action. See Chapter 17 for information on Access Basic functions.

Choosing How to Attach Macros to Forms

Attach your macro to the right property so it runs at the right time.

It is important to attach your macro to the right property, either of the form or of a control on the form. Otherwise, the macro may not run at the right time. Here is the order in which events happen as you use forms.

When you open a form, macros attached to the following properties are run in this order:

- **On Open**: Before the form is displayed
- **On Current**: Before the first record is displayed
- **On Enter**: For the first control in the form

When you close a form, macros attached to the following properties are run in this order:

- **Before Update**: For the control the cursor is in, if its value was changed
- **After Update**: For the control the cursor is in, if its value was changed
- **Before Update**: For the form, if the value of the current record was changed
- **After Update**: For the form, if the value of the current record was changed
- **On Exit**: For the control that the cursor is in
- **On Close**: Before the form disappears

When you move the focus to a new record, macros attached to the following properties are run in this order:

- **On Exit**: For the control the cursor is in
- **On Current**: Before the new record is displayed
- **On Enter**: For the first control in the new record, before the cursor enters it

- **On Insert**: When you create the new record by typing the first character in the record

If you have added or changed a record, macros attached to the following properties are run in this order:

- **Before Update**: For the control the cursor is in, if the value has changed
- **After Update**: For the control the cursor is in, if the value has changed
- **Before Update**: For the form, before the record is updated
- **After Update**: For the form, after the record is updated
- **On Exit**: For the control the cursor is in
- **On Current**: For the form, before the new record is displayed
- **On Enter**: For the control the cursor is in

(To run the Before Update and After Update macros without running the On Exit macro, save the record using the File Save Record command.)

When you leave a control after changing its value, macros attached to the following properties are run in this order:

- **Before Update**: Before the value is updated
- **After Update**: After the value is updated
- **On Exit**: As you leave the control

When you delete a record, macros attached to the following properties are run in this order:

- **Before Update**: For the form, when you select the record to delete (only runs if you have changed the data in the current record)
- **After Update**: For the form, when you select the record to delete (only runs if you have changed the data in the current record)
- **On Exit**: For the control the cursor is in, when you select the record to delete
- **On Delete**: When you delete an existing record, but before it is actually deleted
- **On Current**: For the record the cursor moves to after the record is deleted
- **On Enter**: For the first control in that record

Using Macros for Calculations and Lookups

Some of the most powerful macros you can attach to forms fill in data automatically, or format existing data. Here are some useful macros to speed up data entry.

Capitalizing Text

You can create a macro to convert text entries to uppercase letters.

You can use a macro to capitalize the entry in a text box, or to do other data cleanup. (You might think that you could use the ">" custom format to capitalize text, but this only *displays* text in capital letters. It doesn't save the capitalized text in a field.)

For example, state codes should be capitalized. The macro in Table 8.9 converts the value of the State field to uppercase letters using the UCase( ) function.

To run this macro, attach it to the After Update property of the State control.

Looking Up a Value

Use a macro to look up a value in a related table.

A macro can automatically look up a value in a related table. For example, in an order entry system, when you enter the product code, it is useful for a macro to look up the unit price in the table of products. If you choose the product code from a combo box, you can use the method described in *Setting Two Fields from One Combo Box* earlier in this chapter.

If you don't use a combo box, on the After Update property of the field use the SetValue action to perform a DLookUp( ) on the related table. DLookUp( ) uses these three arguments:

```
DLookUp("fieldname", "table", "criterion")
```

Table 8.9 Capitalization Macro

Macro Name	Action	Arguments
StateCaps	SetValue	Item: [State]
		Expression: UCase([State])

The *fieldname* is the name of the field in *table*—the table, query, or SQL statement specified for the lookup procedure—that contains the information you want to store. The *criterion* tells Access which record(s) in *table* to look in.

For example, in an order entry form, when you enter a value into the Product Code field, you might want to look up the price in the Products table and enter it into a Unit Price field on the form. The lookup expression is:

```
= DLookUp("[List Price]","Products","[Product Code] =
Form.[Product Code]")
```

This expression tells Access to look in the Products table and search for a record for which the Product Code is the same as the Product Code control on the form. When it finds the record, it returns the value of the field named List Price. Table 8.10 shows a macro to do this.

The macro stores this price in the Unit Price control of the form.

HOT TIP

Refer to Fields on Forms

In macro arguments, you frequently need to refer to fields on the current form. To refer to a field on the form from which the macro was called, use this format:

```
Form.[fieldname]
```

To refer to a control on another open form, use this format:

```
Forms![formname]![fieldname]
```

To refer to a control on a subform, use this format:

```
Forms![mainform]![subform].Form![fieldname]
```

Checking for Duplicates

Attach a macro to a control to look for existing duplicate values.

Table 8.10 The ProductPrice Lookup Macro

Macro Name	Condition	Action	Arguments
ProductPrice		SetValue	Item: [Unit Price] Expression: = DLookUp("[List Price]","Products","[Product Code]= Form.[Product Code]")

You can prevent duplicate values in a field by making a no-duplicates index on the field. In Design view of the table, set the Index property of the field to Yes (No Duplicates). Creating a no-duplicate index sure sounds like a winner; however, each index slows down data entry and editing. Also, a no-duplicate index is completely inflexible—what if you want to be able to enter companies with the same name as long as they are in different cities? Use a macro instead. (Alternately, you can use a list box for this job—see *Displaying Possible Duplicates* earlier in this chapter.)

Table 8.11 shows a macro that checks for a duplicate organization (company) name. The DCount( ) function in the condition scans the Clients database, counting all records for which the Organization field has the same value as the current value in the form. It will always find one occurrence—the one the user is entering. If it finds two or more occurrences, there is a duplicate, and the macro displays a warning.

Attach the DuplicateOrg macro to the Before Update property of the Organization control so that the macro runs after the user has entered the organization name, but before the new value is saved.

To allow two companies with the same name to be entered if they are in different towns or states, the condition could be expanded to this:

```
DCount("*", "Clients", "[Organization] = Forms!Clients!Organization
  And [ZIP] = Forms!Clients!ZIP") > 1
```

This checks for records with the same organization name and ZIP code.

Recording Add and Edit Dates

Use macros that set controls to DATE( ).

Table 8.11   The DuplicateOrg Checking Macro

Macro Name	Condition	Action	Arguments
DuplicateOrg	DCount("*", "Clients", "[Organization] = Forms!Clients! Organization") > 1	MsgBox	Message: There is already a client with this organization name. Don't add this one. Beep: Yes Type: Warning! Title: Duplicate Client
		CancelEvent	

It can be very useful to see the date on which a record was originally added, or when it was last changed. These dates allow you to tell if the information is up to date. You can create macros to do this automatically.

To add entry and modification dates to a table and to a form that updates the table:

1. Add Date fields named Date Entered and Date Modified to the table. For the Format property of each field, choose a date format.
2. Add text boxes for the two fields to the form.
3. Create macros to update the text boxes in the form. Table 8.12 shows the two macros, which use the Date() function to enter today's date.
4. Enter the AddDate macro name in the On Insert property of the form.
5. Enter the ModDate macro name in the Before Update property of the form.

Calculating Codes

Use a macro to create codes automatically based on fields in the record.

You can use a macro to create codes from information entered in the record. For example, you could make an ID code that consists of the first three letters of the last name plus the first five characters of the ZIP code. The expression to calculate the code might be:

```
UCase(Left([Last Name], 3) & Left([ZIP], 5))
```

This expression also capitalizes any letters in the code.

In the Before Update property of the form (or alternatively in the After Update event of the last field on which the code is based), run a macro like the one in Table 8.13.

The macro first checks that there are entries for the Last Name and ZIP code fields, because without them, the ID code would be incomplete.

Table 8.12 Date-Stamping Macros

Macro Name	Condition	Action	Arguments
AddDate		SetValue	Item: [Date Entered] Expression: Date()
ModDate		SetValue	Item: [Date Modified] Expression: Date()

Table 8.13   Code Creation Macro

Macro Name	Condition	Action	Arguments
MakeCode	[Last Name] Is Null	MsgBox	Message: Enter a last name. Beep: Yes Type: Information Title: Last Name Required
	...	CancelEvent	
	...	GoToControl	Control Name: Last Name
	...	StopMacro	
	[ZIP] Is Null	MsgBox	Message: Enter a ZIP code. Beep: Yes Type: Information Title: ZIP Code Required
	...	CancelEvent	
	...	GoToControl	Control Name: ZIP
	...	StopMacro	
	[ID Code] Is Null	SetValue	Item: [ID Code] Expression: UCase(Left([Last Name], 3) & Left([ZIP], 5))

Then it uses a SetValue action to calculate the code and store it in a field called ID Code. It sets the value only if the ID Code field is blank. This allows the user to enter an ID code or to modify the one that the macro creates, in case of duplicates.

Automatically Numbering Records

You can number records automatically without using Counter fields.

To number records automatically, you can use a Counter field in the table. But what if you want more control over the numbers, such as the ability to edit them so you can fill in missing numbers when records are deleted? Or you might want to number groups of records separately (numbering products from each manufacturer using separate sequence numbers). Using a macro on a form, you can number records without a Counter field.

    The macro can find the highest existing value of the Counter field and add one to it, creating the next number. To find the highest existing value in a table, use the DMax( ) function.

For example, in the client billing database, it would be useful for each record in the Work Hours table to be uniquely identifiable. Rather than using a Counter field to number all the records using one sequence of numbers, you can have a separate sequence for each client. The Work Hours records for client A are numbered 1, 2, 3, and so on, and the records for client B are also numbered 1, 2, 3, and so on. The client code plus the sequence number uniquely identifies each record. The number might be stored in a field called Work Number.

To automatically assign a work number to a record when you enter it, create a macro that calculates the next work number for that client. This expression finds the highest existing Work Number value for the client entered on the form:

```
DMax("[Work Number]","Work Hours","[Client Code] = Form![Client Code]")
```

If you add one to the highest existing number, the result is the next work number for the client.

To make a macro that assigns values to the Work Number field automatically:

1. Create a form for entering work hours. Make the first control contain the client code, as shown in Figure 8.20. The user must enter the client code before Access can calculate the new work number.

2. Create a macro that calculates the new number and assigns it to the Work Number control. The macro does the calculation only if the Work Number control is null, so that it doesn't change existing numbers. Table 8.14 shows a macro that does this.

The macro runs only if the Client Code has been entered and the Work Number field is blank. It calculates the new work number using the expression explained above. If this is the very first record for this client, the DMax() function in the first action of the macro returns null, the result

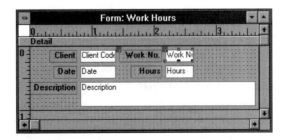

Figure 8.20 Form for assigning work numbers automatically.

Table 8.14 Macro to Assign New Numeric Code

Macro Name	Condition	Action	Arguments
NewCode	([Client Code] Is Not Null) And ([Work Number] Is Null)	SetValue	Item: [Work Number] Expression: DMax("[Work Number]","Work Hours", "[Client Code] = Form![Client Code]")+1
	([Client Code] Is Not Null) And ([Work Number] Is Null)	SetValue	Item: [Work Number] Expression: 1

of the expression is null, and Work Number is set to null. If the Work Number is still null after the first action is complete, this must be the first record for this client. Therefore the second action of the macro assigns a value of 1 to the Work Number field in this case.

3. Set the Default View property of the form to Single Form. The expression in the macro always works when the form is in Single Form view, but it doesn't always work in Continuous Forms view. (In Continuous Forms view, the last record you entered may not have been stored in the table before the DMax() function in the formula is calculated for the next record.)

If you are working in a multi-user environment, it is possible that more than one user will receive the same calculated work number. Although a user can change the work number by hand, you may want to track the highest number portion in a separate table and use either a macro or Access Basic code to maintain it. (See *Creating a Multi-user Custom Counter* in Chapter 17 for more info on multi-user counters.)

Automatically Assigning Codes That Mix Letters and Numbers

Use a macro that isolates the numeric part of the code, adds one, and reassembles the code.

You can also automatically number records with codes that contain letters. The macro can remove the letter portion before adding one to the number portion.

For example, an order entry system for a mail order bookseller assigns book (product) codes to each book, consisting of a two-letter publisher code followed by a three-digit number. For each publisher, the numbers are assigned in order. You can create a macro that can calculate the book's product code when the user enters the publisher code in a new record. The first two letters are the value of the Publisher control. To calculate the numeric part of the code (the last three numbers), use the following expression to find the last code used for the particular publisher:

```
DMax("[Book Code]", "Books", "Left([Book Code], 2) = Form![Publisher]")
```

For example, if the user entered the publisher code CB, the last book code for this publisher might be CB005. To find the next code, the last three characters of the book code (the number) must be isolated, then one is added, and the number is converted back to a three-character string, and concatenated after the publisher code. This long expression does the trick:

```
[Publisher] & Format(Mid(DMax("[Book Code]", "Books", "Left([Book
  Code], 2) = Form![Publisher]"),3,3)+1, "000")
```

The Mid() function isolates characters from the book code starting at character 3 and continuing for 3 characters (the third through fifth characters of the code, which are the numeric portion). To this is added a value of 1. The Format() function converts this to a three-character string using the format "000." (See Chapter 5 for information on creating custom formats.) This number is concatenated after the publisher code.

To make a macro that assigns book codes to new books as they are entered:

1. Create a form for entering books. Make the first control contain the publisher code and the second the book code, as shown in Figure 8.21. The user must enter the publisher code before Access can calculate the new book code.

2. Create a macro that calculates the new book code and assigns it to the Book Code control. The macro does the calculation only if the Book Code control is null, so that it doesn't change existing book codes. Table 8.15 shows a macro that calculates book codes that contain both letters and numbers.

The macro runs only if the publisher code has been entered and the book code is blank. It calculates the new book code using the expression explained above. If this is the first record for this publisher, the DMax() function in the first action of the macro returns null, the result of the expression is null, and Book Code is set to just the publisher code with

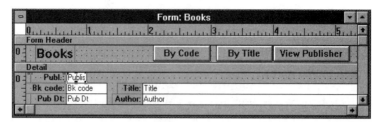

Figure 8.21 Form for assigning book codes automatically.

Table 8.15 Macro to Assign New Codes with Mixed Letters and Numbers

Macro Name	Condition	Action	Arguments
NewCode	([Publisher] Is Not Null) And ([Book Code] Is Null)	SetValue	Item: [Book Code] Expression: [Publisher] & Format(Mid(DMax ("[Book Code]", "Books", "Left([Book Code], 2) = Form![Publisher]"),3,3) +1, "000")
	Len([Book Code]) = 2	SetValue	Item: [Book Code] Expression: [Publisher] & "001"

no number. If the Book Code is only two characters long after the first action is complete, this must be the first record for this publisher. Therefore the second action of the macro adds a sequence number of 001 in this case.

3. Set the Default View property of the form to Single Form.

Creating Command Buttons on Forms

In addition to attaching macros to form and control properties, you can create command buttons that run macros when you click on them. Here are tips for creating command buttons that change the records displayed on a form, print records, find records, and close the form.

Creating a Command Button

For users, command buttons are the best way to issue a series of commands to Access. And they aren't hard to make.

The easiest way to create a command button on a form is to drag the name of a macro from the Database window onto the form. To add your own command buttons to a form:

1. Create a macro group for the form to contain all the macros associated with the form. (See *Creating Macros for Forms* earlier in the chapter for information on creating macro groups.) Display the Macro Name column in the Macro window (choose View Macro Names if this column doesn't appear).

2. Create the macro that you want the command button to run. Enter a name for the macro in the Macro Name column.

3. Save the macro group. (Don't close the Macro window, since you will probably want to make changes or additions to the macro.)

4. Open the form in Design view.

5. From the Database window, drag the macro group name to the form and drop it where you want the command button to appear. Access creates a new command button at that location. It enters the macro group name in the On Push and Caption properties of the button.

6. Change the Caption for the button to the word(s) you want on the button. (If you want the button to display a picture instead of text, see the next topic, *The Appearance of a Command Button.*)

7. Size the button.

Notice that the On Push property of the button contains the name of the macro group, but not the name of the individual macro in the group. (If you don't use macro groups to store groups of macros, skip the next step.)

8. Edit the On Push property of the command button, adding a period (.) and the macro name after the macro group name. For example, if you drag a macro group called Clients Form to the form, the On Push property of the new button is set to Clients Form. To run a macro in this macro group named AddNew, you would need to edit the On Push property to display

```
Clients Form.AddNew
```

9. Switch to Form view and test the macro.

10. If you plan to print the form and don't want the button to appear when printed, remember to set its Display When property to Screen Only.

Command buttons are usually placed in the form header or footer, so that they are always visible. This is important on multi-page forms. You can also place command buttons in the Detail section of the form near a control they relate to. For example, you might place a button for searching by client code near the Client Code control.

Changing the Appearance of a Command Button

A button can display text, a picture, or be invisible.

When you create a command button, Access adds default text to its Caption property. To change the text on a command button, edit the text in the Caption property of the button control. You can use the palette to set the color of the text on the button, but you can't change the background or border color.

To display a picture, enter the name of a bitmap file containing the picture you want in the Picture property of the control (see *Creating a Toggle Button with a Picture* earlier in this chapter for more details on displaying pictures on buttons).

You can also make a button transparent by setting its Transparent property to Yes. (Don't set its Visible property to No, because this also disables the button.) By placing the transparent button on top of another control, you can make the other control appear to respond to a click. For example, on the Clients form of a client billing database, you can make a transparent button that allows the user to search for a client. By placing this transparent button on top of the Client Code text box, when the user clicks in the text box, the button is pushed and the macro runs. Because this technique prevents editing, use it with read-only (locked) controls.

Give the Button an Access Key

If a command button has a caption, you can give the button an *access key*, that is, an Alt+key combination that moves the cursor directly to the button. Include an ampersand (&) immediately preceding a character in the button caption. For example, for a button with the caption "Print," change the caption to "&Print." The character following the ampersand is the access key, so pressing **Alt+P** would move the cursor to the Print button. The ampersand does not appear on the button; instead, the character following the ampersand appears underlined (For instance, Print).

Adding a New Record

Create a macro that displays a new, blank record.

If you use a form for data entry, you might find it convenient to have a button for adding records. To make an Add or New button, create a command button that runs a macro like the one in Table 8.16.

The macro can also perform other actions to set up the new record, like entering defaults.

Deleting a Record

Use a macro to delete the current record, after checking for related records, if necessary.

Normally, you delete a record from a form by first selecting it, pressing **Del**, and then responding to the warning dialog box. Instead, you can create a Delete command button that will run a macro and skirt these tasks altogether. You can also program the macro to check that there isn't a reason not to delete the record (see *Avoiding Accidental Deletions* earlier in this chapter).

Table 8.17 shows a macro to be run from a command button named Delete. The macro selects the current record, turns off warnings, and

Table 8.16   The AddRecord Macro

Macro Name	Condition	Action	Arguments
AddRecord		DoMenuItem	Menu Bar: Form Menu Name: Records Command: Go To Subcommand: New

Table 8.17   The Deletion Macro

Macro Name	Condition	Action	Arguments
DelRecord		DoMenuItem	Menu Bar: Form Menu Name: Edit Command: Select Record Subcommand:
		SetWarnings	Warnings On: No
		DoMenuItem	Menu Bar: Form Menu Name: Edit Command: Delete Subcommand:

deletes the record. It turns off warnings so that Access doesn't display a dialog box to confirm the deletion. Because warnings are turned off, it is important for the macro to check for conditions under which the record shouldn't be deleted.

If deleting the record would violate the referential integrity of a relationship with another table, this macro won't delete the record. Instead, it will display the usual dialog box regarding enforcing referential integrity and the macro will halt. But what if the relationship isn't defined to enforce referential integrity? For example, if the related table is an attached table, Access can't enforce the relationship. If you are deleting records in a master table (a table on the "one" side of a one-to-many relationship), the macro should check for related records in detail tables. The macro in Table 8.18 will not delete a record in the Clients table if there are related records in the Work Hours table.

Table 8.18   Deletion Macro That Checks for Related Records

Macro Name	Condition	Action	Arguments
DelRecord	DCount("*", "Work Hours", "[Client Code] = Form![Client Code]") > 0	MsgBox	Message: There are related records for this client, so don't delete it.
			Beep: Yes
			Type: Warning!
			Title: Do Not Delete
	...	CancelEvent	
	...	StopMacro	
		DoMenuItem	Menu Bar: Form
			Menu Name: Edit
			Command: Select Record
			Subcommand:
		SetWarnings	Warnings On: No
		DoMenuItem	Menu Bar: Form
			Menu Name: Edit
			Command: Delete
			Subcommand:

Sorting and Selecting the Records

Use command buttons to apply filters to change the order or selection of records.

Using filters, you can control whether all or selected records are displayed in the form and in what order they appear. Since creating and applying a filter takes several commands, it is much more efficient to make a command button for each filter you commonly apply. To create a command button for your filters:

1. Create a filter that selects and sorts the records as you want them to appear. (See *Changing the Order of Records in the Form* and *Selecting which Records Display* in Chapter 6.)

2. Save the filter as a query. (See the *Save Frequently Used Filters as Queries* Hot Tip in Chapter 6.)

3. Create a macro that applies the filter.

   The macro in Table 8.19 applies a filter called Work Hours by Date. Another button might sort the Work Hours by client.

4. Create a command button that runs the macro. The button might have the caption "By Date."

   You can create several command buttons that apply filters, one for each selection of records you usually use. You can also create a button that returns the form back to the original selection and sort order—use the DoMenuItem action to choose the Records Show All Records command from the menu.

HOT TIP

Avoid Making Unnecessary Queries as Filters

If you create a command button to apply a filter that selects records, you don't have to create a query to use as the filter. Instead, you can enter an *SQL WHERE clause* in the macro.

Table 8.19 Macro That Applies a Filter

Macro Name	Condition	Action	Arguments
ByDate		ApplyFilter	Filter Name: Work Hours by Date Where Condition:

The SQL WHERE clause is the part of the SQL statement in a query that selects the records to be included. It can only select records; it can't sort them.

To create an SQL WHERE clause to use for filtering records with a command button, create the query that selects the records you want. Choose View SQL from the menu to view the SQL equivalent of the query. Highlight the line that begins with WHERE (the WHERE clause may take several lines, if the criterion is complex) and copy it to the Clipboard by pressing **Ctrl+C**.

Next, enter an SQL WHERE clause in the macro that applies the filter. In the line of the macro that contains the ApplyFilter action, paste the SQL WHERE clause in the Where Condition argument by pressing **Ctrl+V**. Leave the Filter Name blank.

Finding a Record

Create a command button that finds a record that contains the value you enter in an unbound text box.

When using forms, you frequently need to find a particular record. Normally, you do this by moving the cursor to the field that contains the value you are looking for, clicking on the Find button on the toolbar, entering the value, and then clicking on Find Next. Such tedium! Of course, you can follow these steps to create a command button that makes this process much simpler:

1. In the form header, make an unbound text box named Client ToFind to contain the value for which you want to search. Figure 8.22 shows the unbound text box next to the command button we will create later.

2. Create a macro that searches for the record based on the value in the text box you just created. Table 8.20 shows a macro that searches the

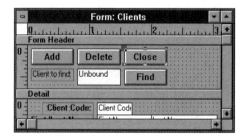

Figure 8.22 Text box to contain the value to search for.

Table 8.20 Search Macro

Macro Name	Condition	Action	Arguments
FindClient		GoToControl	Control Name: [Client Code]
		FindRecord	Find What: =Form ![ClientToFind] Where: Match Whole Field Match Case: No Direction: Down Search As Formatted: No Search In: Current Field Find First: Yes

Client Code field for the record that contains the value in the ClientToFind unbound text box on the form.

3. Create a button on the form that runs this macro. Place the button just to the right of the unbound text box that contains the value to search for. You can also create a label on the form that tells the user to fill in the value and then click on the button.

Note: Instead of creating an unbound text box in step 1, you can make an unbound combo box from which the user can select the value to search for. Leave the Control Source property blank so the combo box is unbound. For the Row Source property, choose a table or query that lists the values of the control you search. For example, when searching for clients by Client Code, use the Clients table as the Row Source, since it contains a list of Client Codes.

You can also write a macro that displays a pop-up box prompting for the value to search for.

Another alternative is to omit creating the command button in step 3. Instead, attach your search macro to the On Exit property of the text box you made in step 1. When you enter the value to search for and press **Tab** or **Enter**, the macro runs.

Closing the Form

You can easily make a command button that closes the form.

Although this is the same as double-clicking on the window's Control-menu box, or choosing Close from the Control menu, or pressing **Ctrl+F4**, if you have other buttons for frequently used form tasks, you will probably find it convenient to make a Close command button too.

Table 8.21 shows a macro that closes a form named Clients.

If you have several forms open at once, you can make a command button on one form that closes another form. In the macro run by the button, use a Close action and enter the name of the other form as the Object Name argument.

Displaying Records as Read-Only

Use command buttons to switch between read-only and edit mode to avoid accidentally modifying or deleting data.

To avoid making accidental changes to the data in a form, you can display the form as read-only by setting the form's Default Editing property to Read Only. When the user wants to make changes, you can provide an Edit button that switches from read-only to edit mode. The macro issues the Records Editing Allowed command, which switches between these two modes.

Unfortunately, there is no direct way that this macro can tell whether the form is currently in read-only or edit mode. And there is no obvious signal to the user of the form that editing is not allowed. Instead, the macro must store the editing mode itself—but how? One way for the macro to keep track of the editing mode is to make one control visible when the form is in read-only mode and another control visible when the form is editable. A macro condition can tell if a control is visible, and the macro can run accordingly. Also, the user can tell which mode the form is in. In effect, the Visible property of a control stores the edit mode.

For example, you can make two command buttons, with captions *Edit* and *Done*. When the form is in read-only mode, the Edit button is visible and the Done button is hidden. When you press the Edit button to switch to edit mode, the macro also hides the Edit button and makes the Done button visible. When you press the Done button to indicate that you are done making changes, a macro switches the form back to read-only mode, hides the Done button, and displays the Edit button.

This is confusing, but it works! See for yourself:

1. Make the form open in read-only mode by setting the Default Editing property to Read Only.

Table 8.21 Macro to Close a Form

Macro Name	Condition	Action	Arguments
CloseForm		Close	Object Type: Form
			Object Name: Clients

2. Create a macro named EditRec to be run by the Edit command button. This macro, laid out in the upper half of Table 8.22, issues the Records Editing Allowed command, hides the Edit command button, and displays the Done command button. The macro must also move the cursor away from the Edit button before it hides the button. (Access doesn't allow you to hide the control the cursor is on.)

3. Create a macro named DoneEditing to be run by the Done command button. This macro, laid out in the lower half of Table 8.22, issues the Records Editing Allowed command again, displays the Edit command button, and hides the Done command button.

4. Create a command button named EditButton with the caption Edit that runs the EditRec macro.

5. Create a command button named DoneButton with the caption Done that runs the DoneEditing macro. (The easiest way is to copy the Edit command button control, then change the Control Name, Caption, and On Push properties.) Hide the control by setting its Visible property to No since the form opens in read-only mode.

6. Switch to Form view to test the Edit and Done buttons.

Table 8.22 Macro to Switch between Read Only and Editing Modes

Macro Name	Condition	Action	Arguments
EditRec		DoMenuItem	Menu Bar: Form Menu Name: Records Command: Editing Allowed
		GoToControl	Control Name: [Client Code]
		SetValue	Item: [EditButton].Visible Expression: "No"
		SetValue	Item: [DoneButton].Visible Expression: "Yes"
DoneEditing		DoMenuItem	Menu Bar: Form Menu Name: Records Command: Editing Allowed Subcommand
		GoToControl	Control Name: [Client Code]
		SetValue	Item: [EditButton].Visible Expression: "Yes"
		SetValue	Item: [DoneButton].Visible Expression: "No"

7.   In Design view, move the Done button on top of the Edit button. Since only one is visible at a time, they can occupy the same space.

In addition, you can make the form switch to read-only mode whenever you move to another record. The On Current property of the form can run a macro that checks which button is visible (Edit or Done). If the Done button is visible, the form is currently editable, and the macro can switch to read-only mode.

Later in this chapter, in the topic *Hiding or Displaying a Subform,* I will discuss another method for switching between two modes. This technique uses a toggle button instead of a command button to control the switching.

Appear to Change the Caption on a Button

A macro can't use the SetValue action to change the caption on a button because SetValue can't change the Caption property of a control. Instead, you can make separate buttons for each caption, make all but one button hidden, and place the buttons on top of each other on the form. The macros run by the buttons can change which button is visible, because the SetValue can change the Visible property of a control. Make sure that only one button is visible at a time!

While creating and testing the buttons, don't stack them up, so you can see what caption(s) appear. When the buttons work, move them on top of each other, and make sure that all the buttons are the same size.

Copying All Fields from a Previous Form

A macro can enter values in controls for a new record.

Earlier in this chapter, you saw how to make a macro that repeated the values from the previous record in a new record. The macro ran automatically whenever a new record was inserted. Instead of making this automatic for every new record, you can make a command button that repeats the values at your request.

Create a command button. For the macro used in the On Push property of the button, use the same macro shown in Table 8.5, but as the first action in the macro, add a GoToControl action to move to the first editable control in the detail section of the form. You can add conditions to prevent the macro from overwriting existing entries in controls, so that it repeats the value only when the control is blank (null).

Printing the Form

Use a macro to print the current record.

It is easy to make a command button that prints the current record. Table 8.23 shows the macro to do it.

The macro saves the current record in case it has been changed. Then it selects the current record and prints the selection.

Hiding or Displaying a Subform

Use a toggle button to control whether a subform, or other detail information, is displayed.

You can use a button to display more information on a form. For example, you can add a button to hide or display a subform that contains details about the record.

Instead of using a command button, you can use a toggle button. This has the visual advantage of appearing "pressed" when the subform is visible, and "popped out" when the subform is hidden. This gives the user of the form a visual cue regarding the status of the button. Command buttons never appear pressed.

Table 8.23 Print Macro

Macro Name	Condition	Action	Arguments
PrintRec		DoMenuItem	Menu Bar: Form Menu Name: File Command: Save Record Subcommand:
		DoMenuItem	Menu Bar: Form Menu Name: Edit Command: Select Record Subcommand:
		Print	Print Range: Selection Page From: Page To: Print Quality: High Copies: 1 Collate Copies: Yes

To make a toggle button that hides or displays a subform:

1. Create an unbound toggle button control on the form by clicking on the Toggle button tool on the toolbox and then clicking on the form where you want the button to appear.

2. For the Control Name property, enter ShowToggle.

3. For the Caption, enter Show Subform or the caption you want on the button.

4. Create a macro that makes the subform visible or hidden depending on whether the toggle is pressed (True, or -1) or not (False, or 0). (A sample macro is provided in Table 8.24.)

5. In the After Update property of the toggle button, enter the name of the macro you just created. This runs the macro whenever the toggle button is pushed, because pushing the toggle button changes its value.

6. For the subform control, set the Visible property to No, so it starts out hidden.

7. Switch to Form view to test the toggle button.

Hot Tip

Use Toggle Buttons to Run Macros

You can use a toggle button instead of a command button to run any macro. It makes sense to use a toggle button for macros that switch between two modes or activities, so that the value of the toggle button controls what the macro does.

The macro should have two parts: what to do if the toggle button control is true (that is, not equal to zero), and what to do if it is false (that is, equal to zero).

Table 8.24 Macro to Toggle between Visible and Hidden

Macro Name	Condition	Action	Arguments
ShowHours	[ShowToggle]=0	SetValue	Item: [Subform].Visible Expression: "Yes"
	[ShowToggle]<>0	SetValue	Item: [Subform].Visible Expression: "No"

Opening a Related Form

You can use the On Dbl Click property or a transparent command button to open a form with more information about a value on the form.

When you are looking at information on a form, you may want to open another form to see related data. For example, when looking at billable hours in the client billing database, you may want to see details about the client the hours are billed to.

You can create a command button to run a macro that opens a form showing the related record. Or you can use the On Dbl Click property of a control to run the macro. For example, you can make a command button with the caption "View Client" to open the Clients form and see information about the client. Or you can double-click on the Client Code control to do the same thing.

To make double-clicking on a control display more information:

1. Create a macro that opens another form. For example, in the client billing database, create a macro that opens the Clients form. Table 8.25 shows a macro to do this.

If the Client Code control is empty, the macro does nothing. If there is a Client Code, the macro opens the Clients form and displays the record with the same Client Code as the one currently on the form.

2. Enter the macro name in the On Dbl Click property of the control. In this case, use the Client Code control.

3. Switch to Form view to test the macro.

Table 8.25 Macro to Open Another Form

Macro Name	Condition	Action	Arguments
ViewClient	[Client Code] Is Not Null	OpenForm	Form Name: Clients View: Form Filter Name: Where Condition: [Client Code]=Forms![Work Hours]![Client Code] Data Mode: Edit Window Mode: Normal

4. Move the two forms to different screen locations, so the second form doesn't obscure the first one. Close and save the forms so that these locations are saved.

Double-Click to Run a Macro Related to a Control

Instead of creating a command button, use the On Dbl Click property of a control to run a macro if the macro relates directly to the control. Because it is not obvious which controls run macros this way, be sure to include instructions on the form, perhaps in the Status Bar Text property of the control.

However, if a control is disabled (that is, the Enabled property is No), the control cannot "get the focus"—the cursor can't move there and the mouse can't click there.

If you want to run a macro when you double-click a disabled control (perhaps a non-editable primary key field), create a transparent command button, put it right on top of the disabled control, and enter the macro name in its On DblClick property.

Double-Clicking on Command Buttons

You can run different macros from the same command button by setting the properties accordingly.

You can make a command button run one macro when you move the cursor to the button (by entering a macro name for the On Enter property of the button), run another macro when you click on the button (using its On Push property), and run a third macro when you double-click on the button (using its On Dbl Click property). It's hard to imagine a situation in which this wouldn't be very confusing for the user of the form!

To confuse matters even more, if you double-click a command button, Access runs the macros attached to the following properties in this order:

- On Push
- On Dbl Click
- On Push

To prevent the second On Push macro from running, put a CancelEvent action in the On DblClick macro.

Using the On Enter property of a command button is usually not a good idea. If the command button does not already have the focus when you click on it, Access runs the macros attached to the following properties in this order:

- On Enter
- On Push

Generally it is best to use only the On Push property of command buttons.

Making Forms Easy to Use

Careful form design can make a huge difference in the usability of your database. Be consistent in your form design, so that similar controls appear in similar formats and locations on all the forms in the database. Here are other thoughts on good form design.

Organizing Controls

Put controls, especially command buttons, in the right positions on the form.

Use the form header and footer for titles, command buttons, instructions, and other general information about the form. This is especially important in multi-page forms, so that the controls are available on all pages of the form.

Choose a sensible tab order for the controls and buttons on the form. To skip locked controls, set the Locked property to Yes and the Enabled property to No.

Set Defaults and Validation

Use the Default Value and Validation properties, or attach macros to the On Enter and Before Update properties of controls.

If you have not set defaults and validations in your tables, set them in form controls. To provide a default value, attach a macro to the On Enter property of the control, or the On Insert property of the form. The macro should use a condition to make sure that the control is blank (null) before filling in a value, so that defaults only appear when the control is blank.

To validate a control, attach a macro to its Before Update property. The macro can compare the entry to other entries on the form or look values up in other tables. See *Requiring an Entry* earlier in this chapter for information on preventing blank controls.

Including Buttons for Common Actions

Create buttons with the captions Done (or Close), Find, Add (or New), and Print for all forms.

If you plan to put any command buttons on a form, it is a good idea to include buttons for these standard tasks. If you plan to print the form, make the command buttons non-printing by setting their Display When property to Screen Only.

Making Your Own Toolbar

Create a row of small buttons with icons on them in the form header.

If you are worried about the buttons taking up too much space on the form, make your own toolbar. Draw or copy tiny pictures to display on the buttons. Use a screen capture program to capture icons from other programs you use. For example, you can capture a printer icon to use on a button that prints a form or report.

When you capture the icon, store it as a Windows Bitmap (.BMP) file. Do not include the box or button edges when you capture the icon. Icons on gray backgrounds will look the best, since Access uses gray for button backgrounds.

If you draw your own icons, use a gray background, make the picture small, and save it as a .BMP file.

To display the icon on a command button, enter the path name of the file that contains the icon in the Picture property of the control. Make the button small and square. Figure 8.23 shows a form with a toolbar, including buttons to add, delete, print, close, and find. Figure 8.24 shows the properties of the first command button on the toolbar.

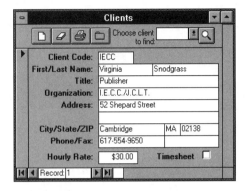

Figure 8.23   Form with a toolbar.

Figure 8.24   Properties of a command button on the toolbar.

Part Overview

Learn to create queries that contain just the information you need for forms and reports— as well as how to avoid making unnecessary queries.

Enhance your Access skills by using total and crosstab queries to create meaningful summaries of large tables. You will also find out how to solve the pernicious problem of duplicate records.

PART 3

Powerful Query Techniques

Behind most forms and reports are queries that sort, select, combine, and summarize the information from tables. This part of the book explains how to use select, crosstab, and total queries to provide information for your forms and reports.

Chapter 9 describes shortcuts for creating and modifying queries, as well as for creating calculated fields, sorting, and selecting records. The section on multi-table queries explains the mysteries of equi-joins and outer joins. Chapter 10 shows you how to summarize the data from one or more tables using totals, counts, averages, crosstabs, and other summarization methods.

CHAPTER

9

Selecting and Relating Records with Queries

Databases usually contain too many records to use all at once. Queries allow you to select the records you want to see, sort them, and total them. A select query produces a *dynaset*, that is, a set of records containing the fields and records selected or summarized by the query. Dynasets are frequently used as the source of data for forms and reports. Here are techniques for creating and modifying queries that select and sort records from one or more tables. Chapter 10 contains tips for summarizing data—calculating totals, subtotals, and crosstabs.

The examples in this chapter are based on the order entry database for a mail-order book distributor. The database contains tables for the books offered for sale, orders received, publishers, and mailings to promote the books. It is named BOOKORD on the optional companion disk.

Tips for Creating and Modifying Queries

It can take several tries before a query works the way you want it to. This section provides tips for creating new queries and modifying existing ones.

Selecting Multiple Fields from the Field List

You can select ranges of fields by Shift-clicking for contiguous fields or by Ctrl-clicking for non-contiguous fields.

If you want to drag several fields from the field list to the query grid, you can select many fields at once. To select several fields that are listed together, click the first field you want, then hold down **Shift** and click the last field. Access selects all the fields between the first and last fields you selected.

To select several fields that do not appear together on the list, click the first field you want, then hold down **Ctrl** and click each additional field. Access selects *only* the fields you click.

Switch between Parts of the Query Window

To move quickly between the field lists in the top part of the Query window and the query grid in the bottom part, press **F6**.

Including All the Fields in a Table

To include all the fields in the dynaset, drag the asterisk from the field list to the query grid.

If you want the dynaset to contain all the fields from the original table, include all the fields in the query grid. There are two ways to do this: Drag all the field names from the field list to the grid or use the asterisk in the field list.

To drag all the field names to the query grid, double-click on the title bar of the field list to select all the fields, then drag them to the grid. Access enters each field name in a separate column of the grid. You can then delete any fields you don't want. If you add a field to the table later, Access does not automatically add it to the query—you must add it manually.

If you drag the asterisk from the field list to the query grid, Access enters this in the Field row:

```
tablename.*
```

If you add fields to the table later, Access will include them in the query automatically. However, you can't use the asterisk in queries that calculate totals.

Sort or Select Records Using the Asterisk

You can't enter criteria or sort information in the column that contains the asterisk as the field name. To select or sort by a field, you must drag the desired field to the grid. Now it is in the query twice: once as part of the asterisk, which includes all fields, and once in the column you just created. To prevent the field from appearing in the dynaset twice, clear the Show box in the new column. That is, click on the Show box so that the X disappears. Finally, enter sorting information or selection criteria for the field.

Include All Fields from All Tables

To include all the fields from all the tables in the top part of the query grid, choose View Query Properties to display the Query Properties dialog box. Clear the checkbox for the Restrict Available Fields option and choose OK.

Naming Fields in the Dynaset

To rename a field, enter the new name and a colon in the Field row.

In the dynaset, fields can have different names from those in the underlying tables. To rename a field in a query, edit the entry in the Field row, adding the new field name and a colon (:) at the beginning, as shown here:

```
newname: oldname
```

For example, a field might be called Book Code in the Books table. To rename it Code in the query, enter the following in the Field row:

```
Code:  [Book Code]
```

Naming Queries

You can't use the same name for a table and a query.

When you save a query, don't use the same name as an existing table. Because tables and queries can be entered interchangeably as the record source for forms and reports, a database cannot contain a table and a query with the same name. If you do try to save a query with the name of an existing table, Access asks, "Replace existing table?" If you choose Yes, Access deletes the table with that name and saves the query. *Watch out!*

Open a Query for Design

To open a query quickly for modification, highlight the query name in the Database window and double-click with the *right* mouse button.

Viewing the Source of Each Field

Display the Table row in queries that contain multiple tables, so you can see which table each field comes from.

For queries that include fields from more than one table, it is useful to see which table each field comes from. Choose View Table Names from the menu to display a Table row that shows the table name below each field name.

Show Table Names for All New Queries

If you want all new queries to contain the Table row, choose View Options Query Design and set Show Table Names to Yes.

Omitting Selection Fields

Clear the Show box if you don't need the field in the query dynaset.

You may need to include a field in a query because you use it to select records, but you don't need the values of the field in the resulting dynaset. For example, in a mail-order bookseller database, you might make a query that selects all orders on a given date. You don't need to store the order date over and over in each record of the dynaset.

To omit a field from the dynaset, click on the Show box in the query grid to remove the X in it. You can still use the field for sorting and selecting in the query, but you can't use it in forms or reports based on the query.

Copying a Query

Many of your queries may be similar, perhaps including most of the same fields but using different selection criteria. To make a new query if you already have a similar one, save yourself some time by copying the existing query.

If you want to create a new query that is similar to an existing query, it is usually more efficient to modify a copy of the existing query rather than starting from scratch. There are two ways to copy a query:

- Open the query and choose File Save As from the menu to save it with a different name.

- In the Database window, highlight the query. Copy it to the Clipboard by pressing **Ctrl+C**. Then paste a copy of it back into the database by pressing **Ctrl+V**. Access asks you for the name to give to the new copy.

The second method is useful when you need to copy a query from one database into another.

Save a Query Fast

To save a query after making changes, simply press **Shift+F12** or **Alt+Shift+F2**. To save it using a different name, press **F12** or **Alt+F2**.

Copying and Moving Information in a Query

Use the Clipboard for moving and copying expressions, field names, criteria, and other text in the query grid.

If you type information into the wrong cell of the query grid, you don't have to retype it; simply move the information to the right cell. Highlight the text and press **Ctrl+X** to cut the text to the Clipboard. Move the cursor to the cell that should contain the text and press **Ctrl+V** to paste the text from the Clipboard into the cell.

If you need the same criteria or expression in several cells, you can copy it. Highlight the text and press **Ctrl+C** to copy the text to the Clipboard. Move to another cell that should contain the same or similar text and press **Ctrl+V** to paste it into the cell. You can paste the text as many times as you want, and you can edit it after you paste it. Text remains on the Clipboard until you replace it by cutting or copying something else.

Canceling a Query

Use Ctrl+Break to cancel a query

If you begin running a query that takes a long time, and you decide you don't want to run it, stop the query by pressing **Ctrl+Break**. Access cancels the query and discards the unfinished result.

Avoiding Unnecessary Queries

Use SQL statements in forms and reports instead of queries.

Queries can be used as sources of data for several Access objects, including forms, records, combo boxes, and list boxes. Instead of creating a query to be used in these instances, you can use an SQL statement in place of a query name and avoid creating an extra query. It takes less space to store an SQL statement than an entire query.

Access translates all queries into SQL statements, which you can copy and paste into your form or report. Use the View SQL command to display the SQL equivalent of your query. You can then copy the statement to the Clipboard and paste the statement in place of the query name.

SQL statements can be used in the following places:

- In the Record Source property of forms and reports
- In the Row Source property of combo and list boxes on forms. (See *Avoiding Extra Queries for Filling Combo or List Boxes* in Chapter 8.)

For example, in the mail-order bookseller database, a form shows all the books that are listed on a particular brochure or catalog. You can use an SQL statement to avoid making a single-purpose query. To use an SQL statement in place of a query:

1. Create a query that selects and sorts the records. Figure 9.1 shows part of the query grid, including the columns that sort records by title and select records based on the brochure code.

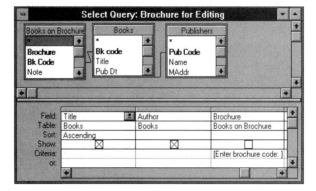

Figure 9.1 Query to select and sort records for a form.

2. Choose the View SQL command from the menu. Figure 9.2 shows the SQL dialog box containing the SQL statement that Access constructed from the query.

3. Select the entire SQL statement (make sure that you highlight to the end, scrolling the box downward as needed).

4. Press **Ctrl+C** to copy the SQL statement to the Clipboard.

5. Click on Cancel to close the SQL dialog box without saving changes (just in case you changed something accidentally). Leave the query open.

6. Open the form or report that uses the records from the query.

7. In Design view, display the property sheet (click on the Properties button on the toolbar if the property sheet isn't displayed).

8. Click in the Record Source property of the form or report and press **Ctrl+V** to paste the SQL statement. Because the SQL statement is likely to be quite long, you may want to press **Shift+F2** to see it in the Zoom box.

Figure 9.2 SQL equivalent of the query.

9.   Switch to Form view to test the change to the form. If you are using the SQL statement as the record source of a report, switch to Print Preview.

10.   Close the Query window without saving the query.

If the SQL statement is too long (longer than 255 characters), Access can't fit it in the Record Source property, and you'll have to use the query. In this case, return to the Query window, save the query, and enter the name of the query in the Record Source property of the form or report.

Calculating Additional Information

In addition to including fields from tables, a query can create calculated fields using Access' operators and built-in functions. To create a calculated field, enter an expression in the Field row of the query grid. The expression can contain the names of fields, enclosed in square brackets, in any table in the query. The fields don't have to be in the query grid.

Once you have added calculated fields to a query, you can use the fields for sorting, selecting, or subtotaling, or you can display them in forms and reports based on the query.

Combining Values

Use concatenation to combine two or more values.

To combine two values, use the concatenation operator: the ampersand (&). For example, to combine the First Name and Last Name fields for an order, you might try this expression:

```
[First Name] & [Last Name]
```

Access concatenates the two text values, placing one after the other with no space in between. To leave a space between the first and last name, enclose a space in quotation marks and concatenate it between the two fields:

```
[First Name] & " " & [Last Name]
```

Access converts all values to text automatically when concatenating. For example, you can use the ampersand to combine a date value with some text:

```
"The order date is " & [Order Date] & "."
```

Access automatically converts the date into text, and concatenates it with the other text value. This also works for concatenating numeric values:

```
"Please pay this amount: " & [Total Order]
```

HOT TIP

Edit Long Expressions in the Zoom Box

When entering or editing a long expression, you can see only part of the expression in the query grid. To see the whole expression, press **Shift+F2** to use the Zoom box for editing.

Using Parts of Text Fields

Use Access' built-in string functions to select parts of text values.

To use parts of a text value in an expression, use Access' built-in *string functions* (text fields are called *strings* in Access Basic). These functions extract part of a text value:

- Left(*textvalue, n*): Select the leftmost *n* characters of the text value
- Right(*textvalue, n*): Select the rightmost *n* characters of the text value
- Mid(*textvalue, start, length*): Select characters from the text value starting at character *start* and continuing for the next *length* characters. If you omit the *length*, Access uses all the rest of the characters in the text value.

For example, in the mail-order bookseller database, each book has a unique code, the first two characters of which indicate the publisher of the book. You can create a calculated field that shows just the publisher code. This expression calculates the publisher code from the book code:

```
Left([Book Code], 2)
```

Naming Calculated Fields

Enter the name and a colon before the expression in the Field row.

You can name calculated fields so that the column headings in the dynaset are descriptive. When you enter an expression in the Field row of the query grid, Access adds the temporary name "Expr*n*:" in front of the expression, where *n* is 1 for the first expression in the query, 2 for the second, and so on. You can edit this, replacing the temporary field name with a more useful one.

You can also enter a field name when you type in the expression. For example, to create a calculated field named Publisher, you can enter this in the Field row of a new column:

```
Publisher: Left([Book Code], 2)
```

Access won't assign this calculated field a temporary name — it uses the name you provided.

Changing the Case of Text

Use UCase( ) and LCase( ) to change case.

You can convert text into all capital or small letters, using these functions:

- UCase(*textvalue*): Convert to capital letters
- LCase(*textvalue*): Convert to small letters

For example, this expression capitalizes the customer's last name:

```
UCase([Last Name])
```

See *Capitalizing the First Letters of Words* in Chapter 17 for how to write ProperCase( ) functions.

Making Calculations Based on Number and Currency Fields

Use arithmetic operators for numeric calculations.

You may want a query to sort or select records based on the result of a calculation. For example, in the Orders table in the mail-order bookseller database, you might want to see the orders in which the gross profit is above a certain amount. The gross profit might be calculated like this:

```
[Total Order]-[Amt Refund]-[Sales Tax]
```

You can use the arithmetic operators in Table 9.1 to create numeric calculations.

To calculate a percentage, divide two numbers and multiply by 100. For example, here is the percentage of the total sale represented by shipping and handing charges:

```
[S & H]/[Total Order]*100
```

Table 9.1 Access' Arithmetic Operators

+	Addition
-	Subtraction
*	Multiplication
/	Division
\	Division, rounding off the answer to an integer
^	Exponentiation
Mod	Division, keeping only the remainder (modulo)

HOT TIP

Calculate Currency Values

If you divide a Currency value by a Number, the result is a Number size of Double. If you want the result to be Currency, use the CCur() function:

```
CCur(expression)
```

The CCur() function converts the results of the expression to a value of type Currency.

For example, if you calculate a half-price sale price based on the current list price, you may want to change the resulting price to be a Currency value. Use this expression:

```
CCur([Cur List$]/2)
```

If you plan to do further calculations with the currency amounts, you should usually round them off to the nearest cent so that your totals will be correct. Use the CInt() function to round off the amount to two places, then convert to Currency:

```
CCur(CInt([List Price]/2*100)/100)
```

Formatting Calculated Numbers

Use the Format() function to set the format of calculated numeric fields.

Once you have created a calculated numeric field, you may want to control its format. For example, if you calculate a ratio or percentage,

Access displays as many decimal places as it has calculated, usually far more than you want to see!

You can use the Format() function to tell Access how to display the number:

```
Format(expression, "formatstring")
```

The *expression* is the numeric calculation you want to format. The *formatstring* is a custom format (see Chapter 5 for information on custom formats). For example, to format a ratio as a percentage, the format string is:

```
"0%"
```

This format tells Access to multiply the ratio by 100 and follow the value with a percent sign. To show the percentage of each order represented by shipping and handling charges, use this expression in the Field row of the query:

```
Format([S & H]/[Total Order],"0%")
```

Finding the Difference between Two Dates

Use the DateDiff() function to find the number of periods between two dates.

To calculate the number of days, weeks, months, or other periods between two dates, use the DateDiff() function:

```
DateDiff(timeperiod, firstdate, seconddate)
```

The *timeperiod* indicates the periods you want to count. Table 9.2 defines the time periods and their usage.

Firstdate and *seconddate* are the two dates. If *firstdate* is before *seconddate*, the result is a positive number representing the number of periods from one to the other. If *firstdate* comes after *seconddate*, the number is negative.

For example, this expression calculates the number of days from when books are ordered to when they ship:

```
DateDiff("d", [Order Date], [Ship Date])
```

You can also find the lapse between a Date field and a fixed date. To enter a fixed date in an expression, enclose it in pound signs (#). For example, to find the number of weeks until the end of 1994, you could use this expression:

```
DateDiff("w", [Order Date], #12/31/94#)
```

Table 9.2   TimePeriod Indicators

TimePeriod Indicators	Function
"d"	Days
"w"	Weeks
"ww"	Calendar weeks (number of Sundays)
"m"	Months
"q"	Quarters
"yyyy"	Years
"h"	Hours
"m"	Minutes
"s"	Seconds

This works fine for orders placed through 1994, but when you begin to receive orders in 1995, the value will become negative because the order date is later than 12/31/94. What if you want to know the number of weeks until the end of whatever year the order is placed in?

Access provides a special time period code to do this. Use the time period "y," enclose the fixed date in quotation marks instead of pound signs, and omit the year. For example, this expression calculates the number of weeks until the end of the year in which the order is placed:

```
DateDiff("y", [Order Date], "12/31")
```

Calculating a New Date

Use addition to add days to a date; use the DateAdd() function to add time periods other than days.

You can add and subtract days from a date to produce a new date. For example, to calculate the date on which payment is due from the order date, you can use this expression:

```
[Order Date] + 30
```

If you want to add weeks, months, quarters, or years to a date, you can use the DateAdd() function:

```
DateAdd(timeperiod, number, date)
```

The *timeperiod* is the same code described for the DateDiff() function, and is used to tell Access what periods you want to add to the date. The *number* is the number of these periods to add. The *date* is the date to add the periods to.

For example, this expression finds a due date that is three weeks after the order date:

```
DateAdd("w", 3, [Order Date])
```

Using Today's Date and the Current Time in an Expression

When you use the Date( ) and Time( ) functions, Access supplies the current date and time.

The Access Date() function provides the current date, based on your computer's internal clock. You can use the Date() function in expressions, for example, to find the number of days since orders were placed:

```
DateDiff("d", [Order Date], Date())
```

If you want the current time, use the Time() function. The Now() function supplies both the current date and time.

Be sure to include the parentheses after the function names for Date(), Time(), and Now(), so that Access knows you want to use a function, not a field named Date, Time, or Now.

Using Part of a Date

Access has functions to use part of a date in an expression.

You can use just the day, month, or year of a date in an expression, or you can find the day of the week or the week number. Use the functions shown in Table 9.3.

For example, to select all orders for the fourth quarter, create this calculated field:

```
DatePart("q", [Order Date])
```

and enter this criterion:

4

Creating Conditional Calculations

Use the IIf( ) function to make if-then calculations.

Table 9.3 Functions to Include a Portion of a Date in an Expression

Function	Usage
Day(*date*)	Day number of the month (for instance, for 12/25/94, this is 25)
DatePart("w", *date*)	Week number in the year (1 to 52 or 53)
Weekday(*date*)	Number indicating the day of the week, where 1 is Sunday and 7 is Saturday
Month(*date*)	Month number (1 to 12)
DatePart("q", *date*)	Quarter number (1 to 4)
Year(*date*)	Year number

Sometimes you want to do a calculation one way for some records and another way for other records. For example, if your business is located in Massachusetts, which has a 5-percent sales tax, you calculate sales tax one way for Massachusetts residents and another way for everyone else. Access has a useful function for this purpose:

```
IIf(condition, iftrue, iffalse)
```

This function (which is called "immediate if"), calculates the *condition*. If it is true (non-zero), it calculates the *iftrue* expression; otherwise it calculates the *iffalse* expression. *Iftrue* and *iffalse* can be values, field names, or expressions.

For example, to calculate Massachusetts' sales tax, use this expression:

```
IIf([State] = "MA", [Total Order] * 0.05, 0)
```

Converting Data Types

Access includes functions to convert fields or expressions to specific data types.

If you need to convert a field or expression into a specific data type, you can use the functions shown in Table 9.4.

Using Calculated Fields

Calculated fields don't always work the same as other fields.

There are some limitations to how you can use calculated fields. For one thing, you can't use the name of a calculated field in the expression for

Table 9.4 Conversion Functions

Function	Usage
Str(*expression*)	Convert to Text (string), or use the Format() function described earlier in this chapter
DateValue(*expression*)	Convert to Date
CCur(*expression*)	Convert to Currency
CInt(*expression*)	Convert to Number of size Integer
CSng(*expression*)	Convert to Number of size Single
Val(*expression*)	Convert to Number of size Double
CLng(*expression*)	Convert to Number of size Long

another calculated field. Instead, include the expression for one calculated field within the expression for the other.

When you view the query dynaset, you can't edit the values of calculated fields. Access updates the calculations automatically when the information on which they are based changes.

Calculations Based on Controls in a Form

You can refer to form controls in an expression.

If you know that a form will be open when the query is run, you can refer to controls on the form in an expression for a calculated field. Use this format to refer to a control:

```
Forms![formname]![controlname]
```

See *Using Forms to Prompt for Parameters* in Chapter 16 for examples of how to use forms to provide information for running queries.

Selecting and Sorting Records

One of the main purposes of queries is to select records from tables and then sort them. (The other main purpose is to combine information from related tables.) This section provides tips for selecting and sorting with queries.

Selecting Records Based on Parts of Values

You can search for text values by specifying only part of the value, using either wild card characters or Access string functions.

The easiest way to select records based on parts of values is to use *wild card characters*. The wild card characters are the asterisk (*), which matches any sequence of characters, and the question mark (?), which matches any single character. For example, to specify the first letter of the value, enter a criterion like this:

```
Like "A*"
```

Access interprets this expression as "any string that begins with the letter A."

Note: When you use Access wild card characters, be sure to use the Like operator, not an equal sign. For example, to search for entries that start with "Chemical," type

```
Chemical*
```

or

```
Like "Chemical*"
```

but not

```
= "Chemical*"
```

If you enclose a wild card character in quotation marks and use an equal sign, Access looks for an actual asterisk or question mark, instead of interpreting them as wild card characters. (This can be useful if your data contains asterisks and question marks!)

You can use square brackets to include a range of values. For example, to specify that the first letter be in the range of letters from A to L, enter this:

```
Like "[A-L]*"
```

To find values that include the same sequence of letters at the beginning of the value, regardless of the letters at the end of the value, put the asterisk at the end, like this:

```
Like "Unitarian*"
```

To find values that include the same sequence of letters at the end of the value, regardless of the letters at the beginning of the value, use the asterisk at the beginning, like this:

```
Like "*Corp."
```

To find values that contain the same sequence of letters anywhere in the value, you can use more than one asterisk, like this:

```
Like "*Canadian*"
```

Asterisks match any number of characters, including none. The previous example would match the value "Canadian," with nothing before or after it. To match a specific number of characters, you can use the question mark wild card character. For example, if the brochure codes used by the mail-order bookseller contain the year as the fourth and fifth characters, this criterion would select all the records for 1994:

```
Like "???94"
```

But wild card characters work only to describe records you want to include. What if you want to *omit* those values; that is, what if you want all the records *except* those for 1994?

Instead of using a wild card to refer to part of a value, make a calculated field. For example, to create a calculated field that contains just the year portion of the order date, you can use this expression:

```
Year([Order Date])
```

Then, you can specify all orders except those in 1994 by entering this criterion:

```
<> 1994
```

You can also enter the calculation as part of the criterion. For example, to select all books except those with "CB" as the first two characters of the book code, you could use the Left() function in the Criteria row:

```
Left([Book Code], 2) <> "CB"
```

When you use this as a criterion in the Book Code column of the query grid, save the query, and then close and reopen it. Access creates a new column in the query grid for this calculated field:

```
Left([Book Code], 2)
```

It enters this as the criterion:

```
<> "CB"
```

The Show box for this field is empty, so that the expression doesn't appear as a field in the query's dynaset. Access uses it only for selecting records.

To select books for which the third character of the Book Code is not "a zero," you can use the Mid() function, like this.

```
Mid([Book Code], 3, 1) <> "0"
```

Sorting Records Based on Parts of Values

Use string functions to sort records based on parts of values.

You can also sort the records in a query based on parts of values. Using the Left(), Right(), and Mid() functions described earlier in this chapter, you can create calculated fields in the query. Then, tell Access how to sort based on those field.

For example, to sort a list of brochures by year, where the year is in the fourth and fifth characters of the brochure code:

1. Enter an expression in the Field row of the query grid. For example, this expression creates a text value containing just the fourth and fifth characters from the brochure code:

    ```
    Brochure Year: Mid([Brochure],4,2)
    ```

2. In the Sort row of the query grid, choose how you want Access to sort by this value.

3. If you don't want the value to appear in the dynaset, click on the Show box to clear it.

Selecting Records by Date

You can select records that contain a specific date, or those that fall within a specified month, quarter, year, or other range.

When selecting by date, enclose dates in pound signs (#) so that Access can tell they are dates. If you omit the pound signs, Access usually puts them in for you. If there are no pound signs enclosing a date, Access has interpreted it as a text or numeric value rather than as a date.

To select records that contain a particular date, use this expression in the Criteria row for the date field:

```
= #12/25/94#
```

To select records within a range of dates (including the beginning and ending dates), enter this criterion:

```
Between #1/1/94# And #6/30/94#
```

To select dates in a given a year, enter this expression in the Criteria row:

```
Year([fieldname]) = 1994
```

Use the name of the Date field in the expression. When you save, close, and reopen the query, Access will re–interpret this expression and create a new column in the query grid for the expression you entered, with the year you entered as the criterion, as shown in Figure 9.3. The Show box is empty, so that the expression doesn't appear as a field in the dynaset.

To select dates in a given quarter, enter this expression in the Criteria row for the date field:

```
DatePart("q", [fieldname]) = 1 And Year([fieldname]) = 1994
```

When you save, close, and reopen the query, Access creates new columns for the DatePart() function and the Year() function.

To select dates in a given month or year, you can use a wild card character as part of the date. When you use a wild card, remember to use the Like operator, and don't use pound signs to enclose the date. For example, enter this expression in the Criteria row to select dates in December, 1994:

```
Like "12/*/94"
```

Or you can use the Month() function (this is useful if you plan to use parameters to prompt for the month and year):

```
Month([fieldname]) = 12 And Year([fieldname]) = 1994
```

To select all dates in 1994, you can also use this expression:

```
Like "*/*/94"
```

To select dates that are older than a certain age, you can use the Date() function to provide today's date. Enter this expression to select records that are more than 30 days old:

```
< (Date() - 30)
```

Searching for Missing Values

To find records with blank values, search for Null.

Figure 9.3 New column created by Access for Year.

You can easily find all the records in which there is no entry in a particular field. For the criterion for the field, enter this:

```
Is Null
```

If you want all the records that *do* contain a value, enter this:

```
Is Not Null
```

Avoiding Errors When Values Are Null

Use the IIf() function to handle the possibility that values are blank.

Access cannot evaluate some functions if a value is null, and you may get unexpected errors from a criterion like this:

```
[Book Code] Is Not Null And Left([Book Code], 2) = "CB"
```

If the Book Code is blank (null), then the Left() function won't work and will cause an error. You can avoid errors by using the IIf() function, which looks like this:

```
IIf(condition, iftrue, iffalse)
```

As I mentioned earlier, if the condition is true, Access uses the *iftrue* expression; otherwise it uses the *iffalse* expression. For example, here is an expression that does not cause an error if Book Code is blank:

```
[Book Code] Is Not Null And IIf([Book Code] Is Null, Null, Left([Book
  Code], 2) = "CB")
```

Selecting Values in a List

Use the In operator to provide a list of values to match or exclude.

If you want to select records based on a list of values, you can use the In and Not In operators to list the values that you want to either match or exclude. For example, if you want all orders for books with certain codes, you can use the In operator like this:

```
In ("BW010", "BW014", "BW017")
```

Be sure to enclose the list of values in parentheses and separate the values with commas. Enclose text values in quotation marks.

If you want all records *except* those on the list, you can use the Not In operator:

```
Not In ("BW010", "BW014", "BW017")
```

The records in the dynaset are sorted by the field in which you used the In operator, in the order in which the values are listed in the In list.

Multi-Table Queries

To include information from more than one table in a form or report, create a query that includes fields from multiple tables. You can also include records from one query's dynaset in another query. This section provides techniques for making and using multi-table queries.

Adding Tables to a Query

You can add tables to the top part of a query.

To add a table to a query so that you can include fields from the table in the query, highlight the table name in the Database window and drag it to the top part of the query window. Or, choose Query Add Table from the menu and click on the table name(s).

You can also add existing queries as tables. Highlight the name of an existing query in the Database window and drag it to the top part of the Query window. You can use fields from the existing query in the new query.

Joining Tables in a Query

Drag a field from the field list to its related field.

To use multiple tables in a query, you usually want to relate them. If you have defined relationships between the tables using the Edit Relationships command, related tables will automatically be joined when you create queries. Otherwise, when you create a query you can tell Access how tables are related.

Drag the related field from the field list for one table to the related field in the second table. Access draws a line, called a *join line*, to show that the fields are now joined. The relationship is saved as part of this query, but doesn't extend to other queries in the database.

When you create a join in a query, or when Access creates one automatically because of an existing relationship between tables, it is called an *equi-join*. With an equi-join, the query dynaset will include records that have related records in all the tables in the query. If there are

Table: Books	
Book Co	**Title**
BW004	J & P Transformer Book, 11th Ed., Completely Revised
BW021	Loss Prevention in the Process Industries
BW023	Power Transformer Handbook
BW039	Circulating Fluidized Bed Boilers: Design and Applicatio
BW040	Fluidization Engineering, 2nd Ed.
BW041	Mixing in the Process Industries, 2nd Ed.
BW042	Principles and Practices of Slurry Flow

Record: 1

Figure 9.4   Books table in the mail-order bookseller database.

no related records in any table in the query, the dynaset doesn't contain the records from the other tables.

For example, Figure 9.4 shows records in the Books table of the mail-order bookseller database, including book codes and titles. Figure 9.5 shows orders for books in the Order Details table. There are many orders for some books, but no orders for others.

The dynaset of a query with an equi-join between these two tables will include one record for each record in Order Details, because there is a corresponding record in the Books table for each one. However, it won't contain a record for each record in the Books table, because for many books there are no orders. Figure 9.6 shows a query with the two tables, and Figure 9.7 shows the resulting dynaset.

Table: Order Details					
Order No	**Line**	**Book Code**	**Qty**	**Price**	**Ship Date**
4760	1	CB002	1	$22.95	
4761	1	CB005	1	$26.95	2/23/93
4762	1	CB002	1	$22.95	2/25/93
4763	1	CB005	1	$26.95	2/25/93
4764	1	CB003	1	$26.95	2/25/93
4765	1	CB005	1	$26.95	2/25/93

Record: 1

Figure 9.5   Order Details table in the mail-order bookseller database.

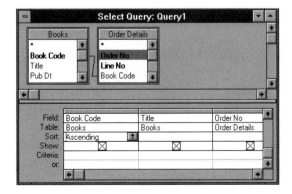

Figure 9.6   Query with an equi-join between Books and Order Details.

Book Code	Title	Order No
BW004	J & P Transformer Book, 11th Ed., Completely Revis	4770
BW023	Power Transformer Handbook	4770
CB002	Complete Guide to PC-File, 5.0/0.1	4774
CB002	Complete Guide to PC-File, 5.0/0.1	4762
CB002	Complete Guide to PC-File, 5.0/0.1	4766
CB002	Complete Guide to PC-File, 5.0/0.1	4768

Figure 9.7 Dynaset with records for all orders, but not for all books.

Join Tables from Different Databases

You can even join tables from different databases in a query. From the Database window, use the File Attach Table command to attach to the table in the other database. Make a new query including the attached table and any other tables in the database. Join the tables by dragging fields from one field list to another.

You can't use the Edit Relationships command to join an attached table to other tables, but you can re-create the join in each query.

Including Records with Missing Data (Outer Joins)

Use an outer join to include all the records from both joined tables.

An equi-join is supposed to include records for which there is a related record in both tables as explained in the previous topic. For most queries, an equi-join produces the result you want. However, you may sometimes want to include all the records from both joined tables in the query's dynaset.

For example, what if you want a report showing all the books the mail-order business carries, with the number sold for each one? Because this should include records in Books for which there are no records in Order Details, an equi-join won't work. Instead, you can use an *outer join.* An outer join retrieves all the records in one table whether or not they have related records in the other tables in the query. When you create an outer join between two tables, you select one of the tables to be the one for which all the records are included.

To make an outer join between two tables:

1. In the top part of the Query window, display two joined tables. Remember, the tables can be joined automatically by Access because there is a relationship defined between them, or you can join the two tables by dragging one or more fields from one field list to the other.

2. In the top part of the Query window, double-click on the join line between the two tables. Access displays the Join Properties dialog box, shown in Figure 9.8.

Option 1 on the dialog box produces an equi-join. Options 2 and 3 define outer joins, choosing one table or the other as the table from which to include all records.

3. Choose Option 2 or 3 and click on OK. For example, to produce the listing of all books, choose Option 2.

In the Query window, the join line now has an arrowhead on one end that points away from the table for which all records are included.

4. View the dynaset. Now the dynaset contains at least one record for each record in the Books table, as shown in Figure 9.9. For books with no orders, fields from the Order Details table are blank. For books with multiple orders, there are many records, one for each order. You can use totals to create a count of orders for each book — Chapter 10 describes how to add a total row to the query grid.

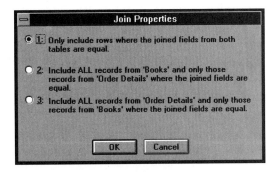

Figure 9.8 Defining an outer join between two tables.

Book Co	Title	Order No
BW004	J & P Transformer Book, 11th Ed., Completely Revised	4770
BW021	Loss Prevention in the Process Industries	
BW023	Power Transformer Handbook	4770
BW039	Circulating Fluidized Bed Boilers: Design and Applicatio	
BW040	Fluidization Engineering, 2nd Ed.	
BW041	Mixing in the Process Industries, 2nd Ed.	
BW042	Principles and Practices of Slurry Flow	
CB002	Complete Guide to PC-File, 5.0/0.1	4778
CB002	Complete Guide to PC-File, 5.0/0.1	4783

Figure 9.9 Result of an outer join that includes records for all books.

Avoiding Ambiguous Outer Joins

If Access can't process a query with several joins, break it into several queries.

Access can get confused if you join several tables in a query and define one of them as an outer join. For example, if you want to join tables A and B with an outer join, and tables B and C with an equi-join, Access can't process the query, and you get this message: "Query contains ambiguous (outer) joins."

If you have trouble getting the results you want, break the query up into several queries. For example, make one query that joins tables A and B with an outer join. Save the query and call it AB. Make another query based on query AB and table C, and join them by dragging fields from the field lists in the top part of the Query window. Now Access can tell exactly how you want to join the tables.

For example, the mail-order bookseller might want a list of all the books, with the order number and order date for each book that has been ordered. The book codes and titles come from the Books table, the order numbers come from the Order Details table, and the order dates come from the Orders table. You might try the query in Figure 9.10, in which there is an outer join between Books and Order Details and an equi-join between Order Details and Orders.

To permit Access to process this query, you must break the query into two queries one combining Order Details and Order, and one combining that query with the Books table.

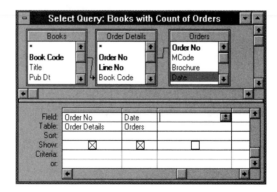

Figure 9.10   This is an example of an ambiguous outer join—Access can't process this query.

When Are Dynaset Fields Editable?

In a multi-table query, you can usually edit only the fields from the detail table.

When you create a multi-table query that contains tables with a one-to-many relationship, you cannot edit all the fields in the resulting dynaset. The fields that come from the detail table (the "many" side of the relationship) can be edited, but those from the master table (the "one" side) are read-only. This is because many records in the dynaset may contain data from one record in the master table, and Access cannot update all the matching records.

If the dynaset includes fields that occur in both the master and detail table, be sure to use the fields from the detail table, not the master table, so that they will be editable. For example, if you create a query based on the Orders and Order Detail tables, the Orders table is the master table and the Order Details is the detail table. The tables are linked by the Order No field. If you want to include the Order No field in the query, drag it from the Order Details field list, not the Order field list.

There is one situation in which you can update fields from the master table: If the query doesn't contain any fields from the detail table, there is at most only one record for each record of the master table, and the fields are editable. But why include the detail table in the query if you don't include any of its fields in the query's dynaset? Here's why: You can include a field from the detail table on the query grid for sorting or selecting, as long as you clear the Show box so that it isn't included in the dynaset.

Here are other types of queries in which some or all of the fields may not be editable:

- Queries with totals
- Crosstab queries
- Queries in which Unique Values Only is selected on the Query Properties dialog box
- Calculated fields in queries (Access updates them automatically when you change the values of the fields on which the calculations are based).

Prompting for Query Criteria

Once you have designed a query, you may want to use it with a variety of values. For example, having made a query that selects books from one publisher, you may want to search for books from another publisher. You can do this without creating another query—simply use query parameters.

Creating Parameter Queries

Replace fixed information in the Criteria row with parameter prompts in square brackets.

A query that uses parameters is called a *parameter query*. To make a parameter query, first create a select query. Then, in the Criterion row of the query grid, replace any fixed values with

```
[parametername]
```

The *parametername* is the text that you would like to appear in a pop-up box that asks for the value.

For example, if the query contained this criterion:

```
= "CB"
```

you could change the criterion to this:

```
= [Enter publisher code:]
```

When you run the query, you see a pop-up dialog box like the one in Figure 9.11.

Make sure that the parameter name is not the same as a field name in the query, because this could confuse Access. If the parameter name is the same as a field name, Access thinks you want to use the field value.

Use different parameter names if you use more than one parameter. If two parameters use the same prompt, Access only asks for a value once, and uses the same value for both parameters.

Once you have created parameters in the query grid, you can tell Access what data type to accept for each parameter. Use the Query Parameters dialog box to tell Access the data type of each parameter, so that values of the wrong data type will be rejected. Because you must also include the parameter name in the dialog box, it is a good idea to copy the prompts

Figure 9.11   Access prompting for a query parameter.

from the query grid to the dialog box (without the brackets) since the text must match. Follow these steps for each parameter in the query:

1. Highlight the parameter name in the query grid, not including the square brackets.
2. Press **Ctrl+C** to copy the parameter name to the Clipboard.
3. Choose Query Parameters from the menu. Access displays the Query Parameters dialog box.
4. Press **Ctrl+V** to paste the parameter name in the next blank row of the Parameter column.
5. Choose the data type for the parameter.
6. Click on OK to close the Query Parameters dialog box.

If, when you run the query, Access prompts you for the same parameter twice, the parameter is spelled differently in the query grid and in the Query Parameters dialog box. Check the spelling, spaces, and punctuation, or recopy the text from one place to the other.

Controlling the Order of Prompts

You can control the order in which Access prompts for parameters. In the Query Parameters dialog box, list the parameters in the order you want the prompts to appear. You can't drag rows to change the order, but you can cut and paste the field names to move them to different rows.

Prompting for a Range

Use two parameters to select a range of values.

If your criterion is a range of values, you can prompt for two parameters, like this:

```
Between [Enter starting date:] And [Enter ending date:]
```

Make sure to use different names (prompts) for the two parameters, so that Access will prompt for them individually.

Prompting for the First Letter of Values You Want

What if you want all the book titles that start with "S"? Use a parameter and an asterisk to select values that start with a particular letter.

If you want to select text values that start with a particular letter, you can prompt for that letter. Enter a criterion like this:

```
Like [Enter the first letter of the title: ] & *
```

This prompt for a letter, then uses that letter followed by an asterisk as the selection criterion.

Using Parameter Values in Forms and Reports

When a report is based on a parameter query, you usually want the parameter value to appear as part of the title of the report. For example, for a listing of titles for one publisher, the publisher code or name should appear in the title.

If you create a form or report that uses a parameter query as its Record Source, the values of parameters can appear on the form or report. For example, the mail-order bookseller database might contain a report of all the books from one publisher, to be mailed to the publisher for confirmation of titles and prices. The Record Source for the report could be a query with a parameter in the selection criterion for the publisher.

To display the publisher code in the title, make a text box and enter the parameter name as the Control Source. Enclose the parameter name in square brackets if it contains a space at the end, or punctuation that might confuse Access.

Using Parameters and Wild Cards with the SQL Server

Use the SQL Server wild card characters, not Access wild card characters, when entering parameters.

If you use Access to connect to an SQL Server database, you should be aware that wild cards in parameters will not work normally. Access' wild card characters (the asterisk and question mark) are not valid wild card characters in parameter SQL Server queries, and the SQL Server interprets them as text. For queries that do not include parameters, Access translates asterisks and question marks in the query into their SQL Server counterparts, but this translation doesn't apply to parameters.

When entering parameters for parameter queries, use the SQL Server wild card characters instead: Replace the asterisk with a percent sign (%) and replace the question mark with an underscore (_).

Summarizing Data with Total and Crosstab Queries

O nce you have selected the records and fields you are interested in, you may want to summarize the information by totaling numeric fields or counting records. This chapter presents useful techniques for summarizing, totaling, and cross-tabulating information in queries.

The examples in this chapter are based on the mail order booksellers database which is called BOOKORD on the optional companion diskette.

Calculating Totals and Subtotals

By adding a Total row to the query grid, you can tell Access how to total or subtotal the records in the dynaset. Rather than including individual records copied from the input tables, the dynaset includes records that contain consolidated information—totals, averages, minimum values, or maximum values.

Calculating Totals and Averages

You may want to calculate the total of one or more numeric fields for all or selected records in a table. For example, you might want to total all the sales for one month. Or instead of calculating totals, you may want to summarize the records by counting or averaging them.

To calculate any type of summarized values:

1. Create a new query based on the table that contains the information you want to summarize. In the mail-order bookseller database, the Order Detail table contains the prices of the books that were sold and their ship dates.
2. Click on the Totals button from the toolbar to add the Total row to the query grid.
3. Drag each field by which you want to select the records to total to the query grid. For example, if you want to select records for a particular month, drag the Ship Date field to the grid. If you want to include all records when totaling, don't drag any fields, and skip to step 7.
4. Set the Total row to Where for each of the fields to indicate that you want to use these fields for selecting values.
5. For each of the fields, enter a value or expression in the Criteria row. Figure 10.1 shows a query that selects orders with a ship date in January 1993.

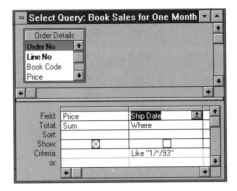

Figure 10.1 Totaling book sales for January 1993.

6. For each of these fields, make sure that the Show box is cleared. Since these are not fields you are totaling, you don't want Access to show them in the dynaset.

7. Now drag the field(s) you want to summarize to the query grid. For example, drag the Price field to the grid (the sale price of the book).

8. For each field you want to summarize, choose the type of calculation for the Total row. You can choose any of the following summarization methods:

- **Sum:** Totals a numeric field
- **Avg:** Calculates the average of a numeric or date field
- **Min:** Calculates the smallest value in a numeric field, the earliest date in a date field, or the first value in alphabetical order in a text field
- **Max:** Calculates the largest value in a numeric field, the latest date in a date field, or the last value in alphabetical order in a text field
- **Count:** Counts the number of entries in any field (not including blank entries)
- **StDev:** Calculates the standard deviation of the values in a numeric field (this is a statistical calculation)
- **Var:** Calculates the statistical variance of the values in a numeric field
- **First:** Shows the value of a field from the first record
- **Last:** Shows the value of a field from the last record

For example, to total the Price field, choose Sum for the Total row.

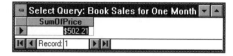

Figure 10.2   Result of totaling book sales for January 1993.

9.   Now that all the entries in the Total row have either Where (for fields you are selecting by) or one of the summarization calculations listed above, click on the Datasheet View button from the toolbar to see the dynaset shown in Figure 10.2.

Rename Total Fields

Access creates a name for each total field, combining the summarization method (like Sum) with the field name. For example, the field in Figure 10.2 is named SumOfPrice.

You can rename summarized fields by entering a name on the query grid. Edit the Field row, adding the name you want to use for the total, followed by a colon (:), then followed by the field name to total. For example, if you want the total book sales to be named Total Sales, the Field row of the query grid would look like this:

```
Total Sales: Price
```

Calculating More than One Total

You can mix sums, averages, counts, and other types of totals in the same query.

When calculating totals, you can include more than one field to total. For each field, you can use any type of summarization method. You can even do two different calculations for the same field. For example, Figure 10.3 shows a query that both sums and averages book sales, and counts the number of books sold.

Subtotaling by Field

Group by the field or fields for which you want subtotals.

Queries can also calculate subtotals for one or more fields. To calculate subtotals, you specify one or more fields to group by. Access will calculate subtotals for each value of this field. For example, if you want to see the

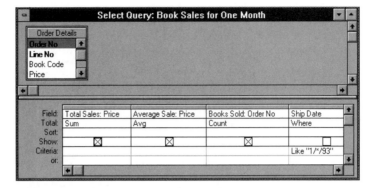

Figure 10.3 Calculating sums and averages for the same field.

total book sales for each title you sell, the field to group by would be Book Code, which uniquely identifies each book. Subtotals can use any of the summarization methods listed earlier.

To make a query with subtotals:

1. Create a new query based on the table that contains the information you want to total.

2. Click on the Totals button from the toolbar to add the Total row to the query grid.

3. Drag the subtotal grouping field to the query grid. For example, drag the Book Code field to the grid to calculate a subtotal for each book. Access automatically enters Group By in the Total row of the field. Leave this entry unchanged.

4. Drag each field you want to summarize to the query grid. For example, drag the Price and Order No fields to the grid, so you can total the prices and count the orders.

5. For each field to summarize, change the Total row from Group By to the type of summarization calculation. For example, choose Sum for the Price column and Count for the Order No column. Figure 10.4 shows the query.

6. Switch to Datasheet view to see the dynaset, shown in Figure 10.5.

If you don't want to include all the records in the table when calculating subtotals, you can add fields to select by. For each of these fields, choose Where for the Total row and enter criteria in the Criteria row. Clear the Show box so the field doesn't appear in the resulting dynaset.

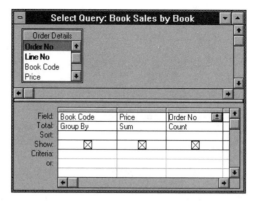

Figure 10.4 Query to subtotal book sales by book.

Book Code	SumOfPrice	CountOfOrder No
BWP04	$130.00	1
BWP23	$95.00	1
CBP01	$79.95	1
CBP02	$536.75	25
CBP02-3	$318.51	12
CBP02-5	$323.40	12
ELP20	$239.50	1
MDP17	$99.75	1
PTP01-3	$14.00	3
PTP01-5	$15.00	3

Figure 10.5 Subtotaling book sales by book.

Subtotaling by Parts of Fields

You can use expressions to subtotal parts of fields or the result of any calculation.

You can use a calculated field to create subtotal groups. For example, if the first two characters of the Book Code indicate the publisher of the book, you might want to subtotal book sales by publisher.

To do this, enter this in the Field row of the query grid:

```
Publisher: Left([Book Code],2)
```

When you enter a calculation in the Field row, Access automatically enters Expression in the Total row. Change this to Group By. Figure 10.6 shows a query that totals by an expression, and Figure 10.7 shows the result.

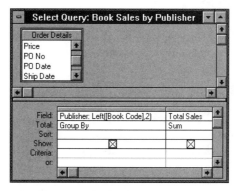

Figure 10.6   Subtotaling by part of a field.

Figure 10.7   Result of subtotaling by part of a field.

Group by Memo Fields

Access doesn't let you group by a Memo field when doing subtotals. However, you can group by part of a Memo field by using the Left() function.

For example, if the Comments field in the Books table is a Memo field that contains "OP" as the first two characters for books that are out of print and "IP" for those that are in print, enter this in the Field row of the query:

```
OP/IP: Left([Comments], 2
```

Access enters Expression in the Total row. Change this to Group By.

Counting Records

Use Count(*) to count all records, including blank entries.

When counting records, decide whether you want all the records or only those that contain an entry for a particular field. If you want to count all records, count a field that doesn't have any blank entries. Use the primary key for the table to be safe.

Alternatively, enter this expression in the Field row of the query grid:

```
Count(*)
```

Access changes this to

```
Expr1: Count(*)
```

and enters Expression in the Total row. This entry indicates that you have entered a total expression in the Field row instead of a field name. You can change Expr1 to a more descriptive name for the count:

```
Number of Orders: Count(*)
```

This expression counts all the records in the query, regardless of blank values in any field. You can use Count(*) when calculating totals and subtotals.

Calculating Ratios for Subtotal Groups

Enter your own expression to calculate ratios, using the Sum() function.

Although Access provides a complete set of standard types of calculations for summarizing records, you may also want to create your own. The most common type of custom total is the ratio—one total divided by another. For example, you may want to know the amount paid for shipping and handling as a percentage of the total amount paid. You can also use calculations for making adjustments. For example, you might want to know the total amount paid less the amount refunded.

To calculate a ratio, use the Sum() function to do the summing, and then divide. For example, the expression to calculate shipping as a percentage of total paid is:

```
Shipping Percent: Sum([S & H])/Sum([Total Order])
```

In other types of calculations, you can also use the Sum() function. For example, here is the expression to adjust the total amount paid by the amount refunded:

```
Total Net of Refunds: Sum([Total Order])-Sum([Amt Refund])
```

In addition to the Sum() function, here are other functions (called *aggregate functions*) you might want to use when calculating your own totals:

- **Avg():** Calculates the average
- **Count():** Counts the non-blank entries in the field
- **Min():** Calculates the smallest value (for numeric fields), the earliest date (for date fields), or the first value in alphabetical order (for text fields)
- **Max():** Calculates the largest value (for numeric fields), the latest date (for date fields), or the last value in alphabetical order (for text fields)
- **First():** Uses the value from the first record
- **Last():** Uses the value from the last record

You can also use the Format() function to format the result, especially for ratios that you want to show as percentages. The Format() function works like this:

```
Format(expression, formatstring)
```

The *expression* is the calculation you want to format. The *formatstring* tells Access how you want to format the value of the expression. You can use any of the custom formats that are described in Chapter 5, enclosed in quotation marks. For example, to format a ratio as a percentage, use this expression:

```
Shipping Percent: Format(Sum([S & H])/Sum([Total Order]), "0%")
```

Figure 10.8 shows the results of calculating Shipping Percent and Total Net of Refunds.

Handling Duplicate Records

The bane of every database user's existence is duplicate records. One way to find them is by making a query that smokes them out. You may consider two records to be identical if every field contains the same value, or if only certain key fields do. For example, in a table of book orders, two records with the same date, phone number, and total amount are probably duplicates, even if the addresses are spelled differently.

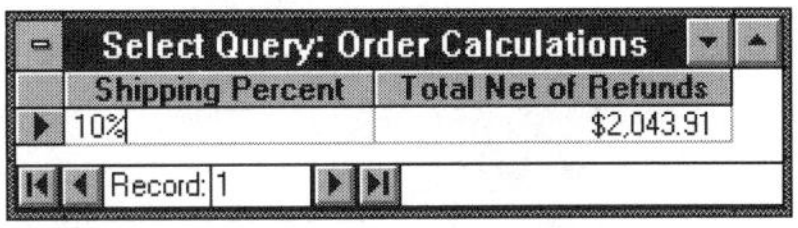

Figure 10.8 Calculating ratios and totals with adjustments.

Finding Duplicate Records

Group fields that identify duplicate records, and use a second query to see the details.

You can find duplicate records by making a query with a Total row, and counting the number of records with the same values. Group the fields that would be the same in duplicate records.

To make a query that finds duplicate records:

1. Create a new query based on the table. In the mail-order bookseller database, the query would be based on the Orders table to find duplicate orders.

2. Click on the Totals button from the toolbar to add a Total row to the query grid.

3. Choose one or more fields that identify duplicate orders. For example, to see if there are multiple orders from the same person, choose the Last Name and First Name fields. Drag these fields to the query grid and set the Total row for each of these fields to Group By.

4. Make a column to count the number of records for each value (for example, for each name). In the Field row of the new column, enter:

```
Count: Count(*)
```

Access enters Expression for the Total row of this column.

5. In the Criteria row for the Count field, enter:

```
>1
```

This tells Access to include rows only if there appears to be duplicate records. Figure 10.9 shows a query for finding duplicate orders in the Orders table of the mail-order database.

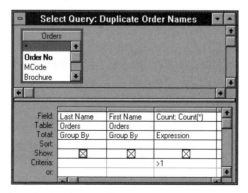

Figure 10.9 Finding duplicate records.

Figure 10.10   Possible duplicate orders.

6.   View the datasheet for the query. You will see the identifying fields, with the number of records for each value, as shown in Figure 10.10.

Now you can look in the original table for the records with those values, and determine if they are duplicates. Or, you can continue with the steps that follow to create another query that shows the records that may be duplicates.

7.   Save the query as Duplicate Order Names.

8.   Create a new query based on the query you just made. The easiest way to do this is to highlight the query name in the Database window and click on the New Query button on the toolbar.

9.   Add the original table to the query. For example, if the Duplicate Order Names query was based on the Orders table, add the Orders table to the query.

Now, you must join the fields that match.

10.   For each field in the first query, except for the Count field, drag the field from the field list to the same field in the field list for the table, as shown in Figure 10.11. Link First Name to First Name and Last Name to Last Name.

11.   Drag the asterisk from the field list for the table (not the field list for the original query) to the query grid.

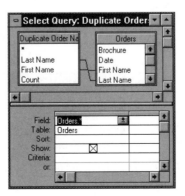

Figure 10.11   Query to display details of possible duplicates.

12.   View the datasheet for the query. It includes all the fields from the original table for only those records that may be duplicates.

Omitting Records in which All Fields Are Duplicates

Use the Unique Values Only property to omit duplicate records.

If you are worried about records that are exact duplicates—that is, in which every field in one record duplicates the field in the other record—you can tell Access to eliminate them from the query dynaset. Choose View Query Properties from the menu (or click on the Properties button on the toolbar) to see the Query Properties dialog box, shown in Figure 10.12. Select Unique Values Only. Any records that would be exactly the same in the dynaset are included only once. This method doesn't help with records in which some fields match but other fields don't.

There is one caveat: If you choose Unique Values Only, you can't edit the values of the dynaset.

If you want to keep the results of the query as a new table without duplicates, change the query from a select query to a make-table query (choose Query Make Table from the menu). Now you can edit the values of the new table, but changes aren't reflected in the original table.

Cross-Tabulating Records

Using a crosstab query, you can create a dynaset that looks like a spreadsheet, with the values of one field labeling the rows and the values of another field labeling the columns. The summarized values of a third field appear in the cells of the "spreadsheet."

For example, you might want to see a cross-tabulation in which the rows represent the months in which orders were placed, the columns represent the brochures mailed to market the books, and the values in the grid are the sales. Figure 10.13 shows such a crosstab query.

Figure 10.12   Omitting exact duplicates from the dynaset.

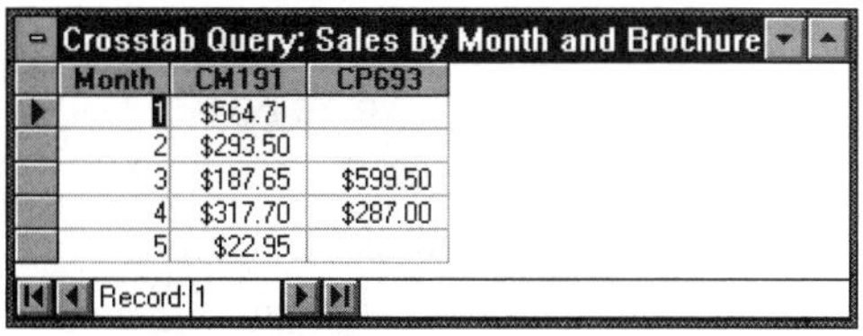

Crosstab Query: Sales by Month and Brochure
Month CM191 CP693
1 $564.71
2 $293.50
3 $187.65 $599.50
4 $317.70 $287.00
5 $22.95
Record: 1

Figure 10.13 Cross-tabulating sales by month and mailing.

Cross-Tabulating Two Fields

Convert a query with totals to a crosstab query by choosing the fields to use for the row and column headings and the values to show in the crosstab cells.

To make a crosstab query that tabulates two fields:

1. Create a query that generates the totals you want to see. For example, Figure 10.14 shows a query that groups orders by month and brochure, summing the total order amount, and Figure 10.15 shows the resulting dynaset. The query should contain two Group By fields and one total (Sum) field.

Select Query: Sales by Month
Orders
*
Order No
MCode
Brochure
Field: Month: Month([Date] Brochure Sales: Total Order
Total: Group By Group By Sum
Sort:
Show:
Criteria:
or:

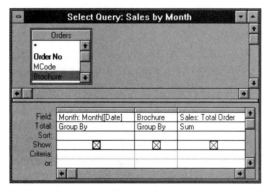

Figure 10.14 Creating a query with totals to convert to a crosstab.

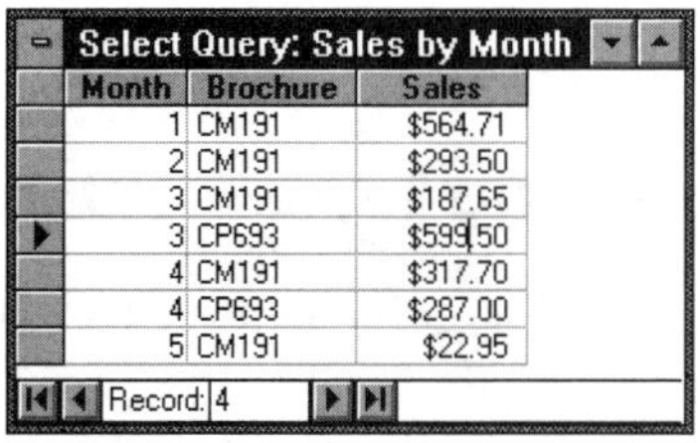

Select Query: Sales by Month
Month Brochure Sales
1 CM191 $564.71
2 CM191 $293.50
3 CM191 $187.65
3 CP693 $599.50
4 CM191 $317.70
4 CP693 $287.00
5 CM191 $22.95
Record: 4

Figure 10.15 A query dynaset with totals to be used in a crosstab.

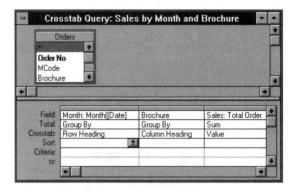

Figure 10.16   This is an example of a crosstab query.

2.   Choose Query Crosstab to add a Crosstab row to the query.

3.   Choose one of the Group By fields as the row heading field, and set the Crosstab row in the query grid to Row Heading. For example, make Month the row heading field.

4.   Set the Crosstab row for the other Group By field to Column Heading. For example, make Brochure the column heading field.

5.   Set the Crosstab row for the total field to Value. For example, make Sales (the sum of the total order field) the value field. Figure 10.16 shows the finished query.

6.   View the dynaset.

Name Crosstab Queries to Explain the Values

When you look at the result of a crosstab query, there is nothing in the dynaset that indicates the meaning of the values in the cells or the values in the column headings. The column heading for the first column indicates what the row headings mean.

When you save a crosstab query, be sure that the query name contains this information. For example, if the row headings are months, the column headings are brochure codes, and the values in the cells are sales, give the query a name like "Sales by Month and Brochure."

Cross-Tabulating Three Fields

Use two row headings and one column heading.

You can use more than one field as the row heading of a crosstab query. For example, in the two-way crosstab explained in the previous topic, the

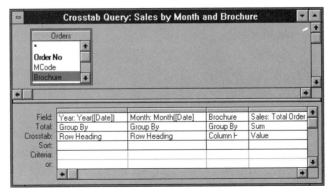

Figure 10.17 Query to create a three-field crosstab.

row heading is the month of the sale. But once the company has been in operation for more than one year, this will mix together orders from the same month in different years (the orders in month 1 will include orders from January 1993 and January 1994). It would be a good idea to add a column for the year, as shown in Figure 10.17.

You can have more than one row heading in the query, but only one column heading. Figure 10.18 shows the result of the three-way crosstab.

Creating a Form or Report to See Crosstabs with Totals

Use a form or report to calculate row and column totals for a crosstab.

A crosstab query looks like a spreadsheet with rows and columns for the fields you are tabulating. But what about totals for the rows and columns? For example, in the crosstab query described in the previous topic, it would be useful to see total sales for each month and for each brochure.

A crosstab query can't display these totals, but if you create a form or report to show the results, the form or report can create the totals.

The dynaset of a crosstab query contains one field for each value of the column heading field. In our example, the column heading field is

Year	Month	CM191	CP693
1993	1	$564.71	
1993	2	$293.50	
1993	3	$187.65	$599.50
1993	4	$317.70	$287.00
1993	5	$22.95	

Figure 10.18 A three-field crosstab query result.

Brochure. The dynaset contains one variable called CM191 for the monthly sales from the CM191 brochure and another variable called CP693 for the monthly sales from the CP693 brochure. You can display these fields on the form or report, and create controls in the footer to sum them. To create a form that displays a crosstab query with row and column totals:

1. Create the crosstab query described in *Cross-Tabulating Two Fields*.

2. Create a new, blank form. Base it on the query you just created. (Make sure to choose Blank Form rather than FormWizards.)

3. Add Form Header and Footer sections by choosing Layout Form Hdr/ Ftr from the menu.

4. Set the Default View property for the form to Continuous Forms.

5. For each field in the field list, drag the field to the form. Move the label for each field from the Detail section to the Form Header section by dragging it. The Form Header and Detail section should look like Figure 10.19 (without the totals in th Form Fotter section, which we'll create next).

6. Create an unbound text box in the Detail section to the right of the other controls. Move its label to the Form Header section. Enter Total for the Caption property of the label and RowTotal for the Control Name of the text box.

7. For the Control Source property of the RowTotal text box, enter an expression that sums the controls that display values (don't include the controls that display row headings). For example, if the controls that display sales in the Detail section are named CM191 and CP693, the Control Source of the RowTotal control would be

```
=[CM191]+[CP693]
```

8. Create one unbound text box in the Form Footer section below each text box in the Detail section, except those that display the row

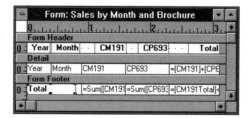

Figure 10.19   Form to display a crosstab query with row and column totals.

heading(s). For example, create unbound text boxes below the CM191 and CP693 controls. Enter descriptive names in the Control Name properties, like CM191Total and CP693Total.

9. For the Control Source property of each text box in the Form Footer, enter an expression that sums the values of the text box above it. For example, the text box below the CM191 control would contain the expression

```
=Sum([CM191])
```

10. For the Control Source property of the text box in the Form Footer below the RowTotal control, enter an expression that sums up the controls in the Form Footer, like this:

```
=[CM191Total]+[CP693Total]
```

11. For all the unbound text boxes on the form, choose values for the Format and Decimal Places properties so that the formats of the totals match those of the rest of the values.

This method of generating row and column totals relies on the values of the column heading field remaining unchanged. What happens if the mail-order bookseller sends out a new brochure, for example, a brochure with code PE993? When orders are generated by the new brochure, the crosstab query creates a new field, named PE993, for orders from the new brochure. But the form or report won't automatically contain controls to display and total the new field. When a new field appears in the crosstab dynaset, you must manually update the form or report, using the following technique:

- Add a new control in the Detail section (as in step 5).

- Add a new control to total the field in the Form Footer section (as in steps 8 and 9).

- Modify the expression in the rightmost control in the Detail section, the text box that totals the row (this is the control you created in step 7). Add the new field name to the expression.

- Modify the expression in the rightmost control in the Form Footer, the text box that totals the column totals (this is the text box you created in step 10). Add the name of the text box you just created to total the field.

Designing Effective Reports

Access can create an amazingly wide array of reports—from columnar reports to mailing labels to form letters to faxes. This part of *Access Insider* contains shortcuts for creating the many controls most reports require, as well as determining what sections you need in each report. This series of chapters also shows you how to print calculations, subtotals, and totals on reports, and includes step-by-step instructions for creating many common report formats.

Chapter 11 helps you speed up report creation and editing with a variety of shortcuts. Chapter 12 discusses printing reports and forms on both conventional printers and using printer drivers or fax boards. If you plan to use a word processor or other program to print output from Access, you will want to read the section on designing reports to be printed to file, either directly from Access or using the OutputAs library. Chapter 13 helps you avoid the pitfalls of calculated controls on reports. Chapter 14 focuses on such common report formats as snaking-column reports, form letters, mailing labels, envelopes, membership rosters, invoices, and transaction registers.

Part Overview

Report Tips

O nce you have created your database and have begun entering information, you can create endless reports—invoices, packing slips, inventory reports, analyses by month or by product, form letters, mailing labels, envelopes, or even faxes. This chapter contains tips on creating and modifying reports and the controls they contain, including how to handle multi-page reports and subreports. Some of the techniques are similar to those presented in Chapter 6 for creating and editing forms, while others are unique to report design.

The reports in this chapter refer to the mail-order bookseller database, BOOKORD, described in Chapters 9 and 10.

Creating and Editing Reports

As with form creation, when you are creating a report, you can use the ReportWizard, a new report, or you can copy an existing report and make modifications. This section contains tips for creating new reports and modifying the properties of existing ones.

Editing Reports Made with ReportWizard

After running ReportWizard, use Design view to move fields, customize labels, and add calculated controls.

A ReportWizard works like an automatic report generator—it asks you questions, then creates a new report based on your answers. You can modify the resulting report just as if you had created it from scratch. To open the new report in Design view, simply click on the Design button on the last screen of the ReportWizard. To make changes to a report later, you can click on the Design button in the Database window.

By default, ReportWizards set the grid to 64 units per inch. Of course, when the grid is this fine, it is invisible; you may want to adjust the settings to make it easier to align controls. Set the Grid X and Grid Y properties of the form to 12 and 12, 16 and 16, or your preferred grid settings. If the grid still isn't visible, use the View Grid command. To align all the edges and the controls to the new grid, choose Edit Select All to select all the controls, then choose Layout Size to Grid.

Editing the Properties of Forms, Sections, and Controls

The property sheet shows all the properties of an object so you can easily modify them.

If you find that you are constantly changing properties for an object, keep the property sheet displayed by choosing View Properties from the menu or by clicking on the Properties button on the toolbar. The Properties, Field List, and Palette buttons on the toolbar are shown in Figure 11.1.

To see the properties of the whole report, choose Edit Select Report from the menu. If the horizontal and vertical rulers are displayed, you can quickly select the whole report by clicking on the little white box at the intersection of the rulers. To see the properties of a section, click on the section header. To display the properties of a control, click on the control.

Display Property Sheets Fast

If the property sheet isn't already displayed, double-click on a section header or control—Access displays the property sheet showing the properties of the object.

Changing the Source of the Records

Modify the Record Source property of the report to change which records are included.

If you have created a report but you now want to include a different set of records, you can change the Record Source property of the report. The *record source* is the table or query that contains the records shown in the report. You can change the Record Source property by editing the property in the property sheet for the report.

Most reports use queries as the record source. The following list points out the advantages of using a query rather than a table:

- You can select which records to include, using the Criteria row in the query grid
- You can create calculated fields to print, by entering expressions in the Field row of the query grid (see Chapter 9)
- You can calculate totals and crosstabs (see Chapter 10)

Figure 11.1 Use the Properties, Field List, and Palette buttons on the toolbar when designing reports.

Basing a New Report on an Existing Report

If you already have a report that is similar to the report you want to create, copy it and make the necessary changes.

Open the existing report in Design view, then choose File Save As from the menu to save the report with a new name. Remember, this technique *doesn't change the existing report* — it makes a new report by copying the existing one. Now you can modify the copy without changing the original.

Open and Save Reports Fast

To open a report in Design view, select the report name in the Database window and double-click with the *right* mouse button. To save a report, you can press **Shift+F12** or **Alt+Shift+F2**. To save a report with a new name, press **F12** or **Alt+F2**.

Copy a Report from Another Database

You can even copy a report from one database to another. Open the other database and highlight the report in the Database window. Press **Ctrl+C** to copy the report to the Clipboard. Open the database in which you want to make the new report and press **Ctrl+V** to paste a copy of the report into the database. Access asks you for a name to give the new report.

If the two databases have tables and fields with identical names and types, you can use the report as it is. Otherwise, you will have to adjust the record source of the report and its sections and controls.

Setting the Sizes of Report Sections

Don't leave extra blank space in the sections of your report.

The size of each section of the report specifies how much space it will take on the page. If there is blank space at the bottom of a section, Access leaves the same amount of blank space on the page when it prints the report. After you have placed the controls in each section of the report, make sure you adjust the bottom margin of the section.

Don't leave space at the top of the Page Header section—Access sets a margin at the top of each page (see Chapter 12 for more information on page setup). However, you do need to leave space below the heading information to separate it from the following text.

As with page headers, page footers don't need blank spaces following the section—Access takes care of the bottom margin.

For group headers, leave blank space at the top of the section if you want a gap between one group and the next. Alternatively, you can leave the space at the bottom of group footers.

In the Detail section, any blank space you include will be printed for each record in the report. If you want one line of information for each record, include one row of controls for each record with no blank space above or below the row.

Make Double-Spaced Reports

To double space a report, include one row of controls in the Detail section for each record. Leave a space, approximately the same height as the controls, below the row of controls. Figure 11.2 shows a double-spaced listing of book titles. Be sure to leave space at the bottom of the Page Header section as well.

Avoiding Blank Pages

Check the width of the report to make sure it fits on the page.

Almost every Access user has wound up with blank pages between each printed page of a report. The blank pages appear in Print Preview, but what causes them?

Access knows the width of your paper and how much space to leave for the left and right margins because these sizes are specified on the Print Setup dialog box. Access adds the width of your report to the left and right margins on the Print Setup dialog box. If the total is wider than your paper, Access splits the report into vertical bands, and prints the left and right halves of your report on separate pieces of paper. If the report is just a little

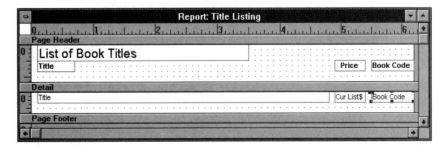

Figure 11.2 A double-spaced report in Design view.

bit too wide to fit, the text of the report is in the left half, leaving the right half blank. It is these "right halves" that are the blank pages Access prints.

If you are getting blank pages between each page of a report:

1. Choose File Print Setup from the menu to display the Print Setup dialog box, shown in Figure 11.3.

2. Subtract the left and right margins from the page width shown in the Paper Size setting. This should be the maximum width of the report. If the left and right margins are too wide, make them smaller by changing the settings. For example, if your paper is 8-1/2 inches wide and you have half-inch left and right margins, don't make your report more than 7-1/2 inches wide.

3. Click on OK to exit from the Print Setup dialog box, saving any changes you made.

4. Check the width of the report. You can look at the right edge of the report in the Design window (if the rulers aren't visible, choose View Rulers from the menu). Alternatively, look at the Width property in the property sheet for the report.

5. If the report is too wide to fit on the page, drag the right edge of the report leftward. If the edge won't move, a control extends to the right of where you want the page to end. Move or shrink any control that extends too far to the right, and move the right edge of the report to the left. Alternatively, modify the Width property of the report.

Another possible reason for blank pages is an incorrect setting for the Force New Page property of one of the sections of the report. If you have used the Before & After setting for the Force Page Break property of any

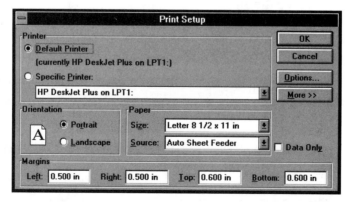

Figure 11.3 Check the left and right margins of the report before printing.

section, try changing it to Before Section. Preview the report to see if this change eliminates the blank pages.

Check the Report Width after Adding or Moving Controls

If you place a new control on a report or move an existing control, and the right edge of the control won't fit in the report, Access automatically makes the report wider. After adding or moving controls, check that the report hasn't become to wide to fit on the page.

Setting the Style for Your Reports

You can set the defaults for new reports you create by making your own report template.

Whenever you make a new report—by choosing Blank Report, not by using a ReportWizard—Access uses a *report template* to determine the default settings. Usually, Access uses its own template, called Normal. You can create your own template, however, so that new reports contain the defaults you want.

The report template controls these parts of each new report you create:

- The properties of the report
- The sections to include in the report (report header or footer, or page header or footer)
- The size of each section
- The properties of each section
- The default properties for each type of control you can create; the template cannot create controls

To create your own report template:

1. Choose an existing report or make a new report to be the template. Remember, the template cannot create controls so it doesn't matter what controls are on the report. Be sure these properties are set the way you want them in future reports.
2. Choose View Options, then choose Form & Report Design.
3. For Report Template, enter the name of the report.
4. Click on OK.

Now, whenever you create a new report from scratch, Access will use the properties from this report for the new report. If you change the report that you designated as the report template, new reports will have the defaults of the current version of the report. Changing the report template doesn't affect reports created by the ReportWizard.

Make Report Templates in Each Database

Access stores just one report template name, which it uses for all databases. Whenever you make a new report in any database, Access will look for a report template with the name you specified. If the report isn't in the database, it doesn't look in any other databases—instead, it uses its Normal template.

If you want Access to use your report template in other databases, copy the report to the other databases. If you want to use different report templates in different databases, create the report templates in each database, making sure to use the same name in all the databases.

Set the Default Report Options

To set the margins for new forms and reports you create, choose View Options Printing from the menu. Access lets you enter default left, right, top, and bottom margins. To control other options, choose View Options Form & Report Design from the menu. You can set the following options:

- **Objects Snap to Grid:** Turns Snap to Grid on or off
- **Show Grid:** Controls whether the grid appears
- **Selection Behavior:** Controls which objects are selected when you select multiple objects in Design view. If you choose Partially Enclosed and any part of any objects is is the area you select, the object is selected. If you choose Fully Enclosed, an object must be entirely within the area you select (see *Modifying Several Controls at the Same Time* later in this chapter).
- **Show Ruler:** Controls whether the ruler appears

Sorting and Selecting Records

Selecting records for a report is similar to selecting records for a form, using a query as the record source. But reports have a special facility for sorting records—the Sorting and Grouping dialog box. In this section, I'll provide tips for sorting and selecting the records that appear in the report. Chapter 13 contains techniques for creating groups with the Sorting and Grouping dialog box.

Selecting Records to Include

Use a query as the record source for the report.

To select records for the report, you must use a query as the record source. Use the Criteria row in the query grid to select the records to include in the report. Be sure that the query includes all the fields you use in the report.

To change the source of the records for the report, display the property sheet for the report and set the Record Source property to the name of the query.

HOT TIP

If You Change the Query

While you have the report open in Design view, you may want to work on the query that provides the records included in the report. If you make changes to the query used as the record source for the report, save the query when you are done. You don't have to close the Query window—until you are sure that you are done changing the query, leave it open. The next time you preview the report, it will run the updated query.

Sorting the Records in the Report

Use the Sorting and Grouping dialog box to sort records by one or more fields.

If you don't use the Sorting and Grouping dialog box, Access prints the records in the order in which they appear in the record source for the report. If the record source is a table, the records are sorted in primary key order. If it is a query, the order of the records is determined by the Sort row of the query.

To change the order in which records appear, use the Sorting and Grouping dialog box, shown in Figure 11.4. The sort order specified on the Sorting and Grouping dialog box overrides the sort order of the table or query used as the record source.

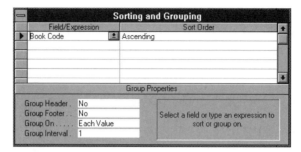

Figure 11.4 Sorting the records in a report.

To sort the records in a report by a field:

1. Click on the Sorting and Grouping button on the toolbar, or choose View Sorting and Grouping to display the Sorting and Grouping dialog box.

2. Enter the field name by which you want to sort in the Field/Expression column. You can also choose the field name from the drop-down list, which contains all the fields in the record source.

3. Choose Ascending or Descending for the Sort Order.

4. Double-click on the Control-menu box (the white box at the left end of the title bar) to close the dialog box. *Don't choose File Close from the menu—that closes the Design window containing the report.*

5. Choose File Print Preview from the menu or click on the Print Preview button on the toolbar to preview the report and confirm the sort order.

Sorting the Records by Two or More Fields

Enter the sort fields in the Sorting and Grouping dialog box in order of precedence.

To sort the records in a report by two fields, decide which field is the *primary sort field* and which is the *secondary sort field.* The secondary sort field is used only when two or more records have the same value of the primary sort field. Access uses the secondary sort field as a tie-breaker. For example, to sort orders by customer name, you would probably sort by last name (the primary sort field), then first name (secondary sort field).

If you have a large number of records, you can designate more than two fields to sort by. For example, a field containing middle initials might be the next field to sort by. You can sort up to ten fields, though it is rarely useful.

To sort on more than one field:

1. Display the Sorting and Grouping dialog box.
2. Enter the name of the primary sort field in the first row of the Field/Expression column (for example, Last Name).
3. Choose Ascending or Descending for the Sort Order.
4. Enter the name of the secondary sort field in the second row of the Field/Expression column (for example, First Name).
5. Choose Ascending or Descending for the Sort Order.
6. Repeat Steps 4 and 5, adding information in the next available row, for each additional field by which you want to sort.
7. Close the dialog box.
8. Preview the report.

Sorting by a Calculation

You can enter an expression in the Field/Expression column of the Sorting and Grouping dialog box.

You can sort by a calculated value that is not one of the fields in the record source of the report. For example, the mail-order bookseller database could contain a listing of books that includes the markup on each book (the difference between the publisher's list price and the price the mail-order bookseller charges). The markup is calculated in a field on the report, using this expression:

```
= [Our Price] - [List Price]
```

To sort the books in descending order of markup (that is, highest markup first), enter the same expression in the Field/Expression column of the Sorting and Grouping dialog box. (You can omit the equal sign at the beginning of the expression.) Choose Ascending or Descending for the Sort Order. For our example, choose Descending.

Sorting by a Field That Is Not on the Report

Base the report on a query, add the field to the query, and use the field in the Sorting and Grouping dialog box.

You may also want to sort by a field that doesn't appear in the record source of the report, but appears in a related table. For example, the mail-order bookseller database includes a report that lists the sales for each book. The record source of the report is the Order Details table.

But what if you want to sort the report on Order Date, a field that doesn't appear in the Order Details table? Order Date is stored in the Orders table.

If the record source of the report is a query rather than a table, add a calculated field to the query. Then, use this field both to display the calculation on the report and to sort the records. If the record source of the report is a table, make a new query and add the calculated field to it.

For example, to sort the book sales listing by order date:

1. If the record source of the report is a table, you must first create a new query. If the record source of the report is already a query, skip to step 4.

2. Create a new query based on the table the report is based on. For example, if the record source of the report is the Order Details table, create a query based on the Order Details table.

3. Drag the asterisk from the field list to the Field row of the query grid, to include all the fields from the table. If the report uses only a few fields from the table, you can drag just the first names that appear on the report instead of using the asterisk. This keeps the query dynaset smaller.

4. The related table that contains the field you want to sort on must appear in the top part of the query. If it doesn't, add the table to the query by dragging the table name from the Database window to the Query window. For example, if you want to sort by Order Date, which is contained in the Orders table, add the Orders table to the query.

5. Make sure that there is a join line between the two tables. If not, create a join by dragging the primary field from one table to the related field in the other table. For example, the Orders and Order Details tables are related by Order No.

6. Drag the field by which you want to sort to the query grid. For this example, drag the Order Date field from the Orders field list to the grid.

7. Save the query.

8. If the report was based on a table, change the Record Source property of the report from the table name to the name of the query you just created.

9. Click on the Sorting and Grouping button on the toolbar or choose View Sorting and Grouping to display the Sorting and Grouping dialog box.

10. Enter the name of the field you just added to the query in the first row of the Field/Expression column. You can also choose the field name from the drop-down list, which contains all the fields in the record source. For our example, sort by the Order Date field.

11. Specify the Sort Order.

12. Double-click on the Control-menu box to close the dialog box.

Controlling Page Breaks

Different reports require different types of page breaks. You may want to print one record per page—for example, a detailed report with information about each employee, to be distributed to each employee's supervisor Or, you may want each page to show a group of related records — for example, records grouped by invoice number (groups on reports are discussed in detail in Chapter 13). You may also want a separate cover page at the beginning of the report, or a summary page at the end of the report. This section describes techniques for inserting page breaks in your reports.

Adding Page Breaks to a Report

Use the Force New Page property of a report section, or add a page break control.

You can add page breaks to a report in several ways:

- To start a new page after each record, set the Force New Page property of the Detail section to either Before Section or After Section. (If you choose the Before & After setting for this property, Access prints a blank page after the page for each record.)

- To start a new page after each group of records (see Chapter 13 for grouping records), set the Force New Page property of the group footer to After Section. This option tells Access to print the Group Header section, the Detail section for each record in the group, the Group Footer section, and then to start a new page.

- To start a new page within a section of your report, use a page break control. For example, if the Detail section of the report is too long to fit on one page, the page break control tells Access to begin a new page.

To create a page break control, click on the Page break tool from the toolbox. Then, click where you want the page break to occur. Access places the page break control at the left margin of the report.

Note: Don't place page break controls in the Page Header or Page Footer sections.

Printing One Record Per Page

When you print invoices, packing slips, or other reports, you may need to distribute the pages of the report separately, with one record per page.

To print one record per page, set the Force New Page property of the Detail section to either Before Section or After Section. You don't need to use Page Header or Page Footer sections in this type of report—you can put the page header information right at the top of the Detail section, since each Detail section starts at the top of a new page. You only need to use Page Header and Page Footer sections if the Detail section for one record might spill onto a second page.

Making a Cover Page

You can print one or more pages at the beginning of the report, including a cover page or a page with introductory text or instructions.

To create a cover page for your report, use a Report Header section in the report:

1. Choose Layout Report Hdr/Ftr from the menu to add both a Report Header and Report Footer section to the report.
2. If you don't want anything to print at the end of the report, close up the Report Footer section by dragging the bottom edge of the section upward to meet the top edge.
3. If the report has a page header and footer, decide whether you want them to print on the cover page. On the property sheet for the report, set the Page Header and Page Footer properties to All Pages or Not with Rpt Ftr if you want the page header and footer to print on the cover page. Otherwise, set the properties to Not with Rpt Hdr or Not with Rpt Hdr/Ftr.

4. Tell Access to print the report header on a separate page by setting the Force New Page property for the Report Header section to After Section.

Now you are ready to create the controls in the Report Header section to display the text or graphics you want to print. If you want more than one cover page, insert page break controls in the Report Header section.

Creating a Report Summary Page

At the end of a report, you can print a page with totals, counts, or other summary information, or a page containing an order form or other text.

To create a summary page for a report, or any other page that prints at the end of the report:

1. Choose Layout Report Hdr/Ftr from the menu to add both a Report Header and Report Footer section to the report.

2. If you don't want a cover page to print at the beginning of the report, close up the Report Header section by dragging the bottom edge of the section upward to meet the top edge.

3. If the report has a page header and footer, decide whether you want them to print on the summary page. On the property sheet for the report, set the Page Header and Page Footer properties to All Pages or Not with Rpt Hdr if you want the page header and footer to print on the summary page. Otherwise, set the properties to Not with Rpt Ftr or Not with Rpt Hdr/Ftr.

4. Tell Access to print the report footer on a separate page by setting the Force New Page property for the Report Footer section to Before Section.

Now you are ready to create the controls in the Report Footer section. The summary page can contain totals, counts, and other summary information (see Chapter 13 for how to include summary calculations in a report). You can also include text and graphics in the report footer. For example, in the mail-order booksellers database, the Brochure report includes a listing of books for sale with an order form in the Report Footer section, shown in Figure 11.5. If you want more than one summary page, insert page break controls in the Report Footer section.

Note: A report footer may not print correctly on multiple-column reports—Access may print it on a separate page even if the Force New Page property is set to None for the Report Footer section.

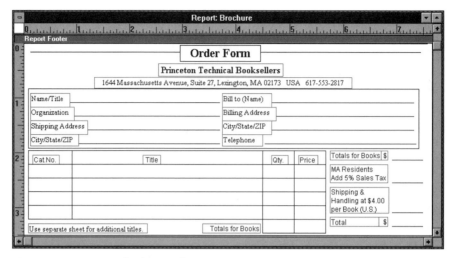

Figure 11.5   An order form in the Report Footer section.

Avoiding Blank Space at the Bottom of the Page

If you want Access to fill up each page, make sure that the Keep Together properties of each section are set to No.

Access may leave blank space at the bottom of a page if it is trying to keep a section together on a page. If you don't mind having a page break in the middle of a section, set the section's Keep Together property to No.

Creating and Modifying Controls

As you create a report, you create new controls and modify existing ones. Here are techniques for working with report controls.

Setting Defaults for New Controls

Set the default properties for the types of controls you use, so you don't have to set them each time you create a new control.

Access stores a set of default properties for each type of control. When you create a new control by clicking on the tool in the toolbox, Access sets the control's properties to the defaults for that type of control. After you create the new control, you can then modify any of its properties.

Before you create controls for your report, modify the default properties for the types of controls you plan to use, so you won't have to set the same properties over and over for each control you create. To set control defaults:

1. Click on a tool on the toolbox. The property sheet shows the default properties for new controls you create using this tool.

2. Set the defaults for this type of control. Be sure to set the Auto Label property to determine whether Access should automatically create a label for the control. Also set the Add Colon property to indicate whether Access should add a colon to the end of the automatic label.

3. If an existing control typifies the way you want controls of this type to work, select the control and choose Layout Change Default from the menu. Access copies the properties from the control to the defaults for that type of control.

Note: The default properties are stored as part of the report—each report has its own set of defaults for each type of control. Changes to the defaults apply only to the current report. To set the default properties of controls for new reports, set them in the report template.

Apply Defaults to Existing Controls

What if you made a control *before* you set the default properties for that type of control? To set the properties of the control to the defaults for that type of control, choose Layout Apply Default from the menu.

Creating Controls for Fields

The most important controls on a report are those that display field values. They are easy to create.

The quickest way to create new controls that display fields from the record source is to drag field names from the field list. To use the field list:

1. Choose the type of control to create by clicking on the appropriate tool on the toolbox. Choose the Text Box tool for Text, Number, Currency, Date, or Memo fields. Choose the Text Box, Check Box, or Option Button tool for a Yes/No field.

2. Select the field(s) from the field list. To select several contiguous fields from the list, click on the first one, then hold down **Shift** and click on the last one. To select several fields that are not listed contiguously, click the first one, then hold down **Ctrl** and click on the other fields. To select all the fields, double-click on the title bar of the field list.

3. Drag the field(s) to the report, moving the cursor to the upper-left corner of the area where you want the control(s) to go. If you selected more than one field, Access places the controls in a column.

When you create a control by dragging a field from the field list to the report, Access copies the Decimal Places and Format properties from the table design. If you change these properties of the table later, make sure you change them for the control too.

View the Field List to Create Controls Quickly

To display the field list, choose View Field List from the menu, or just click on the Field List button on the toolbar (Figure 11.1).

Create Several Controls of the Same Type

If you plan to create several controls of the same type using the toolbox, you can "lock" the toolbox onto one tool. Choose the tool on the toolbox, then click on the Lock button at the bottom of the toolbox. While the Lock button is pressed, the tool remains selected. When you are done creating controls of that type, click on the Pointer button at the top of the toolbox to "unlock" the tool.

Copying Controls

Reports look more professional if controls have a consistent look. To make a group of controls with the same sizes and properties, duplicate a control.

If you want to create several similar controls, it is more efficient to create one and duplicate it. Once you have made one control, select it and choose Edit Duplicate from the menu. A copy of the control (and its associated label, if any) appears below and to the right of the original. You can move the copy where you want it. If you duplicate the same control again, Access positions the new control automatically in the same relative position, so the controls are aligned and evenly spaced.

Another way to copy controls is to select the control and then press **Ctrl+C** to copy the control to the Clipboard press **Ctrl+V** to paste copies. This technique is especially useful for copying controls to other sections of the report, or onto other reports.

Modifying Several Controls at the Same Time

Format a group of controls together so that they match in font and alignment.

You can make some changes to a group of controls at one time by selecting a group of controls in one of two ways:

- Click on the first control, then hold down **Shift** and click on each additional control.
- Start at a point outside any control and drag the pointer through and around all the controls you want to select. Access draws a dotted line around the selected area. If any part of a control is within the dotted line, the control is selected.

Once you have selected a group of controls, you can select the Font, Size, Bold, Italics, Underline, Align-Left, Center, Align-Right, or General Alignment buttons on the toolbar to modify the whole group of controls at once. Unfortunately, you can't simultaneously set properties on the property sheet for a group of controls—when multiple controls are selected, the property sheet is blank.

HOT TIP

Select All the Controls

To select all the controls in the report, choose Edit Select All from the menu.

Aligning Controls

To create neatly organized reports, make sure that controls are lined up straight.

A report looks ragged if the columns and row of information aren't lined up straight. Access can help you line up your controls by using the grid and alignment features of reports.

Use the grid to limit where controls can appear. If you set the Grid X and Grid Y properties of the report to 16 units per inch or less, the grid appears on the screen and you can see if controls are aligned to it.

To tell Access to automatically align the upper-left corner of controls to the grid whenever you move or create them, choose Layout Snap to Grid. A check mark appears next to the command when Snap to Grid is on. When you drag the edges of controls to resize them, Access only lets you drag them to line up with the grid; that is, Access "snaps" the border you are resizing to the nearest gridline.

If you have already created one or more controls and you want to move them so that their upper-left corners align with the grid, select the control(s) and choose Layout Align to Grid from the menu. You can also resize the controls so that all four sides of each control are aligned with the grid. Select the control(s) and choose Layout Size to Grid. The edges of each control you selected snap to the nearest gridline.

You may also want to line up a group of controls with each other, for example, moving a group of controls so that their left edges are aligned. Once you have selected a group of controls, you can choose Layout Align from the menu. Then, choose one of the following four options:

- Left   Aligns the left edge of each selected control with the left edge of the leftmost control in the group
- Right   Aligns the right edge of each selected control with the right edge of the rightmost control in the group
- Top   Aligns the top edge of each selected control with the top edge of the uppermost control in the group
- Bottom   Aligns the bottom edge of each selected control with the bottom edge of the lowest control in the group

If you don't like the positions Access moves the controls to, you can choose Edit Undo Align from the menu to restore them to their former positions.

Suspend Snap to Grid Temporarily

If you use Snap to Grid, Access won't let you move or resize controls except in alignment with the grid. If you want to move or resize a control so that it doesn't match the grid, hold down the **Ctrl** key while you place, move, or resize the control. This suspends Snap to Grid while you work with the control. When you release the **Ctrl** key, Snap to Grid resumes, but the control stays where you put it.

Center Text on the Page

To center text boxes or labels on the page, make the text box or label control the full width of the page. Then click on the Center button on the toolbar to center the text in the control.

Displaying Long Text

Access can expand a text box control to fit the text it contains.

If a field in your report contains more than a few words of text, you may want it to "wrap" onto additional lines. For example, in the mail-order booksellers database, the Books table contains a Memo field that stores a description of the book. The contents of the Description field may be only a few words or it may be several paragraphs. You could display the field in a very large text box control that can fit the largest description in the table, but Access would leave a large empty space in the report after short descriptions. Instead, you can tell Access to expand the text box control to fit the amount of text in the field.

To make a text box that can grow, make it big enough to fit just one line of text. Then set its Can Grow property to Yes. When Access prints each record, it expands the text box control downward until the entire value of the field fits. The controls below it in the section move down the page.

When you set the Can Grow property of a control to Yes, Access automatically sets the Can Grow property to Yes for the section that contains the control. When Access prints the report, it expands the section as well as the control. If you don't want the section to expand, you can change its Can Grow property to No. Information that doesn't fit in the section is omitted. This is useful when printing on forms of a predetermined size, like mailing labels. (See Chapter 14 for details on printing mailing labels.)

Displaying Fields That May Be Empty

Access can also shrink a control when it is empty, to avoid printing blank lines.

To avoid leaving blank lines when a field is blank, set the Can Shrink property of the text box to Yes. For example, in the mail-order bookseller database, the Books table contains a Memo field for the table of contents of each book. For many books, this field is blank. On a report, you may not want to leave a blank space for these books.

To make a text box that can shrink when the value is blank, make it big enough to fit the longest value in the table. Then set its Can Shrink property to Yes. When printing the report, Access omits the control if the field value is blank (null).

When you set the Can Shrink property of a control to Yes, Access does not automatically change the Can Shrink property of the section that contains the control. Leave the Can Shrink (and Can Grow) properties of the Detail section of the report set to No if the Detail section must always be the same size—for example, for mailing labels. Otherwise set these properties to Yes.

Rounding Off Calculations

If you print calculations on your report, be sure to round them off before totaling them!

You can print a calculated field the same way you display one on a form—create a text box and enter an expression in the Control Source property. However, if you create calulations based on Number or Currency values and you don't round them off, your totals may be wrong.

For example, you can discount a price with an expression like this:

```
=[Price] * .9
```

Using the Format property, you can display the value rounded to two decimal places (dollars and cents). But Access remembers any additional decimal places and uses them when totalling the values (described in Chapter 13). Instead, tell Access to round off the value using a expression. Since Access doesn't have a Round() function (a major omission!) you must use the CInt() function to round the value off. For example, this expression rounds a discounted price off to two decimal places:

```
=CInt([Price] * .9 * 100) /100
```

The expression calculates the discounted price, multiplies it by 100, rounds it to the nearest dollar, then divides it by 100, so that it is rounded to the nearest cent.

Prompting for Information to Print

When you print the report, Access can prompt you for the date, title, or other information.

Just as Access can prompt for parameters when running a query, it can prompt for parameters to print in a report. This feature allows you to specify the information—usually in the Report or Page Header or Footer sections—that you want printed. For example, the mail-order booksellers database contains a report called Title Listing, a general-purpose list of books by title. You might want to print it with the heading "Titles for May 1994" or "Alphabetical Listing" or "Call 617-553-2817 to Order" depending on whom the report is for.

To include parameters in a report:

1. Create a text box control (not a label control) to contain the parameter. Place it where you want to the information to print, usually in the Report or Page Header section.

2. For the Control Source property of the text box control, enter the parameter name in square brackets. For example, enter:

```
[Enter title line]
```

Figure 11.6 shows a report with a parameter.

Note: Ampersands (&) have a special meaning in Access prompts (they define access keys). If you want an ampersand to appear in your prompt, enter two ampersands.

3. Set the alignment for the text by clicking on the Left-Align, Center, or Right-Align buttons on the toolbar. If you plan to enter a number for the parameter, you can't use the Format property to format it. Type the number exactly as you want to see it on the report, including currency symbols and commas.

Rather than entering the parameter when prompted by Access, you can enter the report parameters on a form. See Chapter 16 for information on creating forms that contain query and report parameters.

Figure 11.6 Printing a report parameter in a text box.

Print Query Parameters

If the record source for the report is a query with parameters, you can also print the value of the query parameters. For example, the Brochure report in the booksellers database prints a brochure, including information about each book and an order form in the report footer. The record source for the report is the Brochure for Printing query, which contains this parameter:

```
[Enter brochure code]
```

You can print the brochure code on the brochure, using the value the user enters for the query parameter. Create a text box and enter the parameter name, enclosed in square brackets, in the Control Source property. Make sure that you enter the parameter exactly as it appears in the query—you may want to copy it from the query grid via the Clipboard.

When you print the report, Access prompts for the query parameter to run the query. It doesn't ask you again for the parameter when it prints the report—it uses the value you entered for the query.

Controlling the Appearance of a Report

Access lets you dress up your reports with lines, boxes, pictures, and 3-D effects. Here are techniques for using these special effects. Also refer to the section on *Controlling the Appearance of a Form* in Chapter 6 for techniques for drawing boxes, drawing lines, creating shadows, and using scanned images in the background. You use the same methods for reports as for forms.

Choosing Fonts

Choose fonts that make your report readable and effective, and use boldface, italics, and underlining sparingly for emphasis.

When you select the printer to use for the report using the Print Setup dialog box (discussed in Chapter 12), Access knows what fonts will be available when it prints the report. You can select a font to use for a control in one of two ways:

- Set the Font property in the property sheet.
- Select a font from the Font box on the toolbar.

To make a control bold, italicized, or underlined, use one of these two methods:

- Set the Font Weight, Font Italic, and Font Underline properties in the property sheet.
- Click on the Bold, Italic, or Underline buttons on the toolbar.

Note: You can't make part of the text bold, italicized, or underlined—the property applies to the whole control.

Use Printer Fonts When Designing Reports

Make sure that the Layout for Print property of the report is set to Yes, so that Access displays the available printer fonts, not screen fonts, when you design the report.

Choosing Colors

You can set the background, text, and border colors of text boxes, labels, and other controls, but make sure that the result is readable when printed.

Using the palette, you can set the colors for the components of controls:

- **Text:** The text that appears in the control
- **Fill:** The background of the control
- **Border:** The line around the control, if any

Depending on the type of control, some of these options may be unavailable (appear in gray).

To display the palette, which is shown in Figure 11.7, choose View Palette from the menu, or just click the Palette button on the toolbar (Figure 11.1). Select the control you'd like to add color to, and use the palette to specify the colors. As you click on the color choices on the palette, Access fills in the corresponding color numbers on the property

Figure 11.7 Using the palette to set the color of a control.

sheet for the control. (Access stored the colors of objects as color numbers—for example, the color number for white is 16777215. By using the palette, you don't have to remember or type these numbers.)

Be sure to pick color combinations that are readable when printed. Unless you have a color printer, Access translates the colors you choose into shades of gray. For example, dark red on light teal is readable on the screen, but appears as black-on-black when printed on a non-color printer. Stick to black, gray, and white when designing reports—save colors for forms!

Displaying the Values of Yes/No Fields

Use check boxes or option buttons to show Yes/No values graphically.

Check boxes and option buttons display values of Yes/No fields. Which type of control you choose depends on the look you want. The easiest way to make one of these controls is to select the Check Box or Option Button tool from the toolbox, then drag a Yes/No field from the field list to the report. Access makes a control of that type, and enters the field name for the Control Name and Control Source of the new control.

Alternatively, you can display Yes/No fields in text boxes and use a custom format to show the values as *Yes* and *No*, *True* and *False*, *On* and *Off*, *Member* and *Non-Member*, *Shipped* and *Not Shipped*, or any other pair of words or phrases. See Chapter 5 for information on creating a custom format for a Yes/No field.

Displaying Number Fields as Groups of Buttons

You can use an option group to display the value of a Number field that contains only integers.

If you used an option group on a form to enter the values of a Number field, you can also use one to display its values on a report. See *Using Groups of Buttons to Choose among Values* in Chapter 8 for information on creating an option group.

Avoiding Extra Spaces

Concatenate fields to close up the gaps between values.

When you display several fields in a row, you may not want to leave gaps between them. For example, in a mailing label or form letter, you may want to print fields containing first names and last names with only one space between them. To eliminate extra space between fields, regardless of the length of the values in the fields, concatenate them.

To concatenate two or more fields, create a text box control and enter an expression as the Control Source. Use the ampersand (&) operator to do the concatenation. For example, this expression concatenates fields named First Name and Last Name with a space between them:

```
= [First Name] & " " & [Last Name]
```

See *Combining Values* in Chapter 13 for more information on concatenating fields.

Printing a Standard Form as Part of a Report

Use a scanned image of the form as the background of the report, and fill in the blanks using text boxes.

In *Using a Scanned Form as the Background* in Chapter 6, you saw how to display a paper form, such as a subscription form, in the background of an Access form. In the same way, you can place a scanned form in the background of an Access report, so that you print the standard form as well as filling it out.

For example, Figure 11.8 shows a report that prints the standard quarterly Massachusetts sales tax form. The mail-order bookseller data-

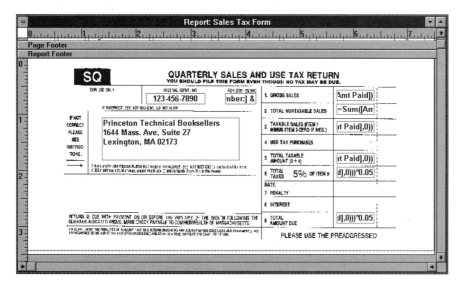

Figure 11.8 Sales tax report including a scanned image of a Massachusetts tax form.

base contains orders for books that are taxable in Massachusetts. Because the standard form is too small to feed into most printers, it would be convenient for Access to print the whole form—text, lines, boxes, and all. In Figure 11.8, the Report Footer section contains an unbound object frame that contains the scanned image of the tax form. On top of the image are labels that display fixed text, like the name of the company and its tax identification number, and text boxes that display calculated totals of sales and tax due for the quarter.

Printing Page Headers and Footers

For reports that are longer than one page, it is important to use page headers and footers to print the report name, date, page number, and other identifying information on each page. To create Page Header and Page Footer sections in a report, choose Layout Page Hdr/Ftr from the menu. This section contains techniques for designing effective page headers and footers.

Numbering Pages

Create a text box in the Page Header or Page Footer section to display page numbers.

To print page numbers, create a text box that contains the following expression:

```
= Page
```

The text box can appear in either the Page Header or the Page Footer section. To display the word *Page* as well as the number, use this expression:

```
= "Page " & Page
```

Printing Today's Date

A text box can display the computer's system date, time, or both.

To print the current date or time (assuming that your computer's system date and time are correct), create a text box containing this expression:

```
= Now()
```

The Now() function returns both the current date and time. If you don't select a format for the text box, you see date and time like this:

```
6/25/94 1:55:48 PM
```

If you want to see only the current date, format the text box as a date. If you want only the current time, format it as a time.

Printing Telephone Book-Style Headers

When printing a long listing, it is easier to find an entry is on if the first entry on each page is highlighted, perhaps displayed in the Page Header.

It is easy to display the first value of a field in the Page Header—just create a text box in the Page Header section that is bound to the field. For example, the booksellers database contains a report called Title Listing that lists all the books the bookseller carries. At the top of each page, the page header includes the title of the first book on the page. Figure 11.9 shows the report in Design view, with a text box in the Page Header displaying the Title field.

You can also print the value of the last record on the page in the Page Footer.

Omitting Headers and Footers on Selected Pages

You can format the cover and summary pages of a report differently from the rest of the report.

You can skip printing the Page Header or Page Footer sections on pages that contain the report header or report footer. You use the Page Header and Page Footer properties of the report to tell Access when to suppress

Figure 11.9 Printing a value from the first record on the page in the Page Header.

printing the Page Header or Page Footer sections. There are four options for the Page Header and Page Footer properties:

- All Pages
- Not with Rpt Hdr
- Not with Rpt Ftr
- Not with Rpt Hdr/Ftr

The most common use of these properties is to stop the page header from printing on the cover page of a report. Set the Page Header property to Not with Rpt Hdr.

Printing Combined Reports

You can combine two or more reports in a number of ways. One way is to print a subreport for every record in the main report—this is analogous to using a subform on a main form. It allows you to print additional information for each record in the report, using data from additional tables and queries.

Another reason to combine reports is to print two unrelated reports together—the reports are not based on related information, but you always want to print them at the same time. In other words, you will be able to print two or more reports with one print command.

This section contains tips for using subreports to print combined reports.

Printing Unrelated Reports Together

If you always print two or more reports at the same time, include them as subreports in a new, unbound report.

You can create an *unbound report* to contain other unrelated reports as subreports. An unbound report is not connected to any table or query— its Record Source property is blank. Its only purpose is to provide an "envelope" to contain two or more subreports. For each report you want to print, create a subreport control on the main, unbound report. When you print the unbound report, all its subreports are printed, too.

For example, the mail-order bookseller always prints the Packing Slips, Invoice to Customers, and Charge Confirmation reports at the same time, when processing a batch of orders. You can make a report called Order

Processing that prints all three reports, one after the other. Figure 11.10 shows the report in Design view, with three subreport controls.

Make sure that all the reports require the same type of paper. For example, don't combine a report that prints on blank paper with one that prints on letterhead, unless your printer has multiple printer bins. Access won't know to pause and let you change paper between reports. For example, the bookseller's combined report doesn't include the Mailing Labels for POs report, since this report prints on sheets of labels.

Note: The page header and footer and report header and footer are determined by the main report, not the subreports. Also, the page numbering will not automatically restart at 1 for each subreport.

Use a Form for Parameters of Subreports

If the record source of one or more subreports is a parameter query, Access asks you for the parameters at least twice. It prompts for each parameter two times when Access formats the report, because Access formats the report in two passes. In Print Preview, as you move from page to page, Access may prompt for the parameters again. This can be very annoying.

To solve this problem, use a form to provide the parameters for the queries (see Chapter 16 for how to create forms that contain parameters for reports).

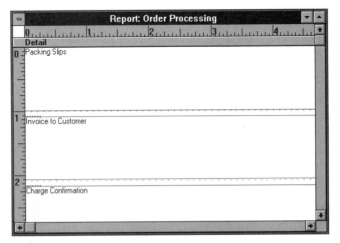

Figure 11.10 Printing three unrelated reports as subreports.

Printing a Subreport for Each Record

Use subreports to provide additional information about each record in a report.

A subreport can provide detail information from other tables. For example, the mail-order bookseller database contains a report that prints one page per book, with general information about the book from the Books table. After the general information is a subreport that lists all the sales for that book. Figure 11.11 shows the report in Design view. The subreport is shown in Figure 11.12.

Unlike the subreports in the previous topic, this subreport is bound to the main report—that is, it is related to the records in the main report. *Bound subreports* work like bound subforms (see Chapter 7 for information on creating subforms). The subreport appears in a subreport control on the main report and is linked to the main report by two properties, Link Child Fields and Link Master Fields. Bound subreports allow you to print information from a one-to-many relationship: The main report displays

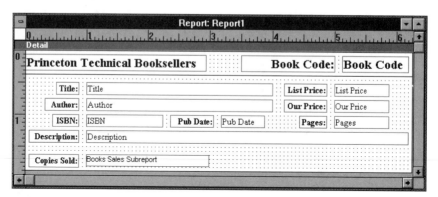

Figure 11.11   Book report with a subform listing sales.

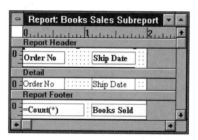

Figure 11.12   Subreport showing order number and ship date for each book sold.

information from the master ("one") table, and the subreport includes data from the detail ("many") table.

To create a subreport like the book sales report:

1. Create the report you plan to use as a subreport. For example, Figure 11.12 shows the subreport that lists the sales for each book. When you preview the subreport by itself, you see sales for all books. When it appears as a bound subreport on the main report, the sales for one book will appear on each page of the main report.

2. Save the subreport.

3. Open the main report in Design view.

4. Make space for the subreport control (also called a Subreport/Subform control) in the Detail section. By including the subreport in the Detail section of the main report, you tell Access to print the subreport once for each record (book) in the main report.

5. In the Database window, select the subreport and drag it to the main report. Access creates a subreport control on the main form, containing the subreport you selected (the Source Object property for the new subreport control contains the name of the report you dragged).

6. Move and size the subreport control.

7. Display the property sheet for the subreport control to check the Link Master Fields and Link Child Fields properties. These properties contain the name of the field that links the main and subreports: The Link Master Fields property should contain the name of the linkage field in the Record Source property of the main report, and the Link Child Fields property should contain the name of the linkage field in the Record Source of the subreport.

Display the Subreport in Design View

If you are designing the main report and want to see the subreport in Design view, too, double-click on the subreport control in the main report. Access opens another Design window in which you see the subreport. Now you can make changes to both reports.

Use a Form as a Subreport

If you have created a form that contains the information you want to include in a subreport, you can insert the form as a subreport. Drag the form from the Database window to the report in Design view.

Using a Different Subreport

Change the Source Object property of the subreport control.

If you want to change the report used as the subreport, make the new subreport first. Then display the main report in Design view and display the property sheet for the subreport control. Change the Source Object property to the name of the new subreport.

Update the Subreport

If you are designing both the main report and the subreport, save the subreport when you have finished making changes. You can now tell Access to load the newly changed subreport into the main report.

In Design view of the main report, select the subreport control, then press **Enter**. This (usually) loads the latest version of the subreport.

If this doesn't work reliably (it doesn't for me), display the property sheet for the subreport control, click on the Source Object property, and reselect the same subreport from the list.

Referring to Controls on a Subreport

You can display totals from a subreport on the main report.

Just as you can display totals from a subform on a main form, you can print totals from a subreport on a main report. (See *Totaling Records from Subforms* in Chapter 7 for information on creating a control on the main report to display a total from a subreport.)

When entering the expression in the control on the main report, use this format:

```
= [subreport control name].Report![report control]
```

For example, if the subreport control on the main report is called Book Sales Subreport and the control on the subreport containing the total is called Total Sales, enter this expression in the text box control on the main report:

```
= [Book Sales Subreport].Report![Total Sales]
```

Printing Reports and Forms

As you design a report you must think about the printer and paper you will use to print it. When you use the Print Setup dialog box, you tell Access the fonts and paper sizes that will be available when you are ready to print a form or report. This chapter contains tips for setting up reports and forms to work with your printer, as well as for "printing" these items to disk or to a fax board for direct faxing.

Choosing the Printer and Page Format

Access stores print setup information with each report, so you can design different reports to be used with different printers, or with different paper sizes on the same printer. Choose File Print Setup to display the Print Setup dialog box, which contains the options for specifying a printer and other print settings.

Setting Margins

Use the Print Setup dialog box to set margins for each report and form.

There are several ways of displaying the Print Setup dialog box for a form or report:

- Highlight the form or report name in the Database window and choose File Print Setup from the menu.
- In Design view, choose File Print Setup from the menu.
- In Print Preview, click on the Setup button.

The Print Setup dialog box, shown in Figure 12.1, contains settings that pertain to the report's size and how it will be printed. You can enter

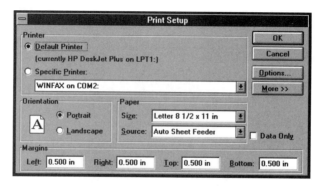

Figure 12.1 Setting the margins in the Print Setup dialog box.

margins in inches by following margin measurements with *in,* or in centimeters by following the measurements with *cm.*

Change the Default Margins

Unlike other print defaults (such as printer, orientation, and paper), you can change the default margins by using the View Options command. Choose Printing for the Category to display the printing options, shown in Figure 12.2.

Changing the margins in the Options dialog box changes the way Access will print datasheets, modules, or new forms and reports. It won't change the margins for existing reports, because the print settings are stored separately for each form and report.

To change other printing defaults, see *Changing the Printing Defaults for Access* later in this chapter.

Solving Blank Page Problems

Blank pages are usually the result of margins that are too wide.

Make sure that the total of the left margin, right margin, and the form or report width does not exceed the width of the paper. If this should happen, Access will print the report in vertical strips. If the report is just a little too wide to fit on the page, the right-hand vertical strip will be blank, and you will get a blank page between each page of your report. You can avoid this situation by adjusting your margins and/or report width, or print on wider paper.

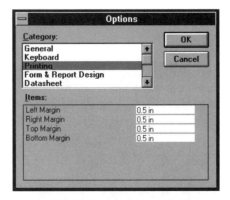

Figure 12.2 Changing the default margins for Access printing.

Choosing Landscape or Portrait Printing

If your printer can print in landscape orientation, Access can print reports and forms using landscape orientation, too.

One of the settings on the Print Setup dialog box is *Orientation*. The orientation of a printed page determines whether the text is printed across the width or the length of a page. Orientation, therefore, has two possible options:

- **Portrait**: Prints text across the width of a page; that is, text runs left to right across the 8-1/2-inch width of the paper
- **Landscape**: Prints text across the length of a page; that is, the text runs along the 11-inch length of the paper

To change page orientation, open the Print Setup dialog box, choose the appropriate Orientation setting, and click on OK. Landscape printing is especially useful for printing columnar reports and documents that will be folded, such as a brochure, so that you can fit more columns across the report.

Printing Drafts Quickly

If your printer has a draft mode setting, you can use it to print reports faster.

Some printers can print in draft mode, which is faster and usually uses less ink or toner, but the quality of the printed page is not professional. Think of draft mode as you would any first draft document—for your previewing eyes only!

You set the print quality for your printouts in the Print dialog box, shown in Figure 12.3.

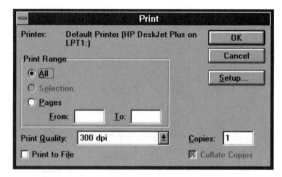

Figure 12.3 Setting the print quality in the Print dialog box.

To specify draft mode for your report or form, highlight the report or form in the Database window and choose File Print from the menu. Access displays the Print dialog box. Depending on your printer, different settings, or modes, are available for the Print Quality setting.

For some Print Quality settings, Access will not be able to print graphics. If your report or form contains any graphic images, Access may omit them from the printout. Experiment with the Print Quality options that your printer offers to find the best combination of appearance and speed.

Changing the Print Defaults for Access

To change the print defaults Access uses, you must change the Windows defaults.

When you print a datasheet or module, or when you create a new form or report, Access uses the print defaults—which printer to use, how it is connected to the computer, and the size and orientation of the paper—specified in the Windows Control Panel's Printers application. (Margins are an exception—you can set the defaults using the View Options command. See *Change the Default Margins* earlier in this chapter.) To change the printer defaults:

1. In the Windows Program Manager, open the Main group window and double-click on the Control Panel icon.

2. In the Control Panel window, double-click on the Printers icon to display the Printers dialog box, shown in Figure 12.4. This dialog box includes a list of the installed printers. (See *Using Multiple Printers,* later in this chapter, if the printer you want to use isn't installed.)

One of the installed printers is designated as the *default printer.* This is the printer that most Windows applications, including Access, will use for printing unless you specify otherwise.

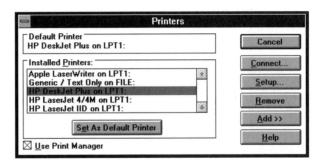

Figure 12.4 Displaying installed printers in the Windows Control Panel.

3. Choose your default printer by highlighting the printer name from the list of installed printers and then clicking on the Set As Default Printer button.

4. To view the options that are selected for a particular printer, highlight the printer name from the list of installed printers and click on Setup to display a dialog box with the current settings for that printer. Figure 12.5 shows a sample printer dialog box. You can set the default page orientation (portrait or landscape) and paper size here. Depending on the printer, there may be other options. Click on OK when you have finished looking at or changing the print setup.

5. After checking that a driver for your printer has been installed in Windows, close the Printers dialog box by clicking on Close (if you have made changes) or Cancel (if you have not). Exit from the Control Panel program by double-clicking on its Control-menu box.

Access uses the default printer and its default setup when you print, unless you specify otherwise. However, Access stores individual print setup information, using the settings specified with the File Print Setup command in Access, for each form and report. That means that you can change the print setup for a specific document without altering the print setup for other forms and reports. For example, if you want to print only one report in landscape orientation, you can set the default page orientation to Portrait in the Printers dialog box, which you can then override from within Access for the one report (see *Choosing Landscape versus Portrait Printing* earlier in this chapter).

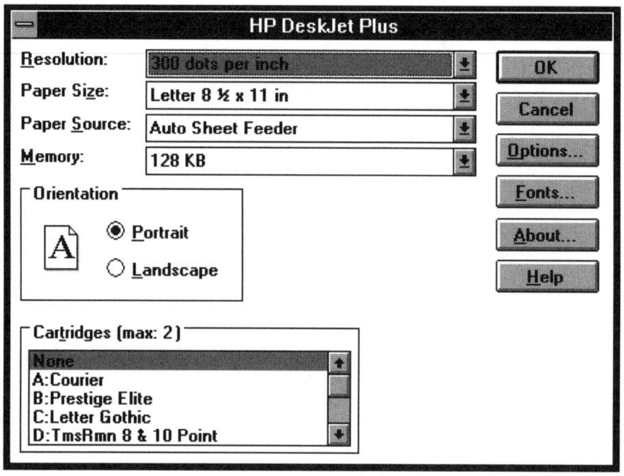

Figure 12.5   Default setup for a printer.

Using Multiple Printers

When you design a report, choose the printer you plan to print it on.

If your computer is connected to several printers, or to a network with several printers, you can install several printer drivers for use with Windows. To see which printer drivers are installed:

1. In the Program Manager, open the Main group window and double-click on the Control Panel icon.
2. In the Control Panel window, double-click on the Printers icon to display the Printers dialog box (Figure 12.4).
3. If the printer you want to use is not on the list of installed printers, refer to your Microsoft Windows *User's Guide* for how to install a new printer driver. (I also recommend Chapter 13: *Using Windows with Your Printer* in *Windows 3.1 Insider.*)
4. After checking that a driver for your printer has been installed in Windows, close the Printers dialog box by clicking on Close (if you have made changes) or Cancel (if you have not). Close the Control Panel window by double-clicking on its Control-menu box.

For each report and form in the database, you can choose the printer on which to print it. Along with the other print settings, Access stores the printer you choose with the form or report. For example, if you have a dot matrix printer for mailing labels and a laser printer for other printing, Access remembers which reports print on which printer.

What if you are designing a database that will be used on other machines with other printers than yours? If you don't know which printers other users might have, always use the default printer. Access will then print to the default printer on each system on which it runs.

Using Printer Fonts

Tell Access to show you the fonts that are available for the printer you have selected for the report.

As you design a report, you choose which fonts to use for each control. When you choose a font, the characters on the screen may not look exactly like those that appear on the printed page because *printer fonts* and *screen fonts* can differ.

Screen fonts are the characters that Windows displays on the screen. Many are installed when you installed Microsoft Windows, including MS

Sans Serif, the screen font Access usually uses. When you install a printer, additional screen fonts may also be installed, so you can see an approximation of the fonts that the printer can print. You can also install screen fonts on your own.

Printer fonts are the characters that are actually printed by your printer; the fonts available depend on your printer.

In Design view, the toolbar displays a Font box and Font size box that list the available fonts and sizes. You can control whether the Font box and Font size box list screen fonts or printer fonts by setting the Layout For Print property of the report. If you choose Yes for Layout For Print, the Font box and Font size box display the fonts and point sizes available for the printer you selected for the report.

Note: If you select a scalable font, such as a TrueType font, the screen and printer characters look the same and the same fonts and font sizes are available for the screen and printer. It doesn't matter if you choose Layout For Print.

Use the HP LaserJet II

If you use an HP LaserJet II, you must select the Print TrueType As Graphics option in the Print Setup dialog box because the LaserJet II driver does not support printing True Type graphics. If you don't select this option, you may see the following problems:

- In Print Preview you see white text on a blank background, but the printer prints a solid black line.
- Reports that contain line controls print the first line of text correctly, but subsequent text appears too far to the right.

Faxing Access Reports

Use a fax board and Windows fax software to send a fax directly from Access.

If your computer contains a fax board, you may be able to send faxes directly from Access. Before you can do this, make sure that:

- The fax board is installed.
- The fax software that runs under Windows is installed.
- You can send faxes using the fax software.

Most Windows fax software installs the fax board as a "printer." The fax board appears as a printer in the Specific Printer list in the Print Setup dialog box. For example, if you install WinFaxPro (a windows fax program), a printer driver appears called WINFAX.

To send a fax directly from Access using a fax printer driver:

1. Highlight the report name in the Database window, or view the report in Print Preview.
2. Choose File Print Setup to display the Print Setup dialog box.
3. Click on Specific Printer and choose your fax printer driver from the list.
4. Click on OK to exit from the Print Setup dialog box.
5. Print the report as usual. Your fax printer driver will prompt you for the phone number of the fax machine you want to send the report to.

If you want to add a cover page or other information to the fax, you may want to make a special report format for faxes. To create the fax cover sheet:

1. Open the Print Setup dialog box, click on Specific Printer and choose the fax driver, then exit the dialog box.
2. In Design view, use the Report Header section to add a cover page, and set the Force New Page to After Section, so that the rest of the report will start on a new page. (See *Making a Cover Page* in Chapter 11 for more information)
3. Create text box controls in the report header with prompts for the information you want to appear on the cover page or with fields from the record source of the report.

Figure 12.6 shows a fax cover page for a report in Design view.

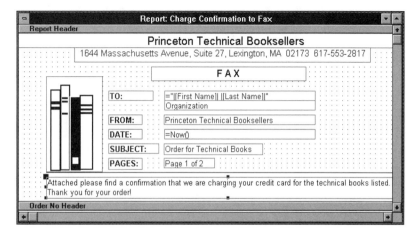

Figure 12.6 Fax cover sheet.

Note: When you select the fax printer driver, Access will change the format of the report accordingly. Use Print Preview to make sure that the report fits in the margins. Also, because fax printers use a lower resolution than laser printers (200 dots per inch rather than 300 or 600), don't use very small or fine characters or lines, because they may not show up clearly. I recommend using at least 11-point type on faxes.

Printing ASCII Text

You can use the Generic/Text Only printer driver to send ASCII text to your printer to speed up printing.

When Access prints a report, it sends the information to the printer in graphics mode. That is, Access does the job of translating the characters to be printed into tiny dots that will appear on the page. This allows Access to control the fonts and sizes that are used for each control on the report, but it also slows down printing. Most printers can print more quickly using the printer's own built-in fonts. By using the Generic/Text Only printer driver instead of your usual printer driver, you can tell Access to send the ASCII text of the report to the printer, so that the printer does the translation into dots:

1. In Design view or Print Preview of the report, display the Print Setup dialog box.

2. Click on Specific Printer and choose the Generic/Text Only printer driver. If the driver is not there you'll need to install it following the steps presented later in this topic.

3. Click on OK to exit from the Print Setup dialog box.

Now Access will print the report by sending ASCII text to the printer rather than graphic information, which should be much faster for most printers. You may need to rearrange the fields on the report, because the font your printer uses to print text is probably different from the font specified for the controls in the report. Most printers use a fixed-space font to print text, and less text will fit in the same space.

In addition, when Access prints using text rather than graphics, it makes some mistakes. See the topic *Creating an ASCII Text File without the OutputAs Library* at the end of this chapter for suggestions on designing reports to be printed as text.

If the Generic/Text Only driver doesn't appear in your Printer Setup dialog box, follow these steps to install it in Windows:

1. In the Program Manager, open the Main group and Control Panel windows.

2. Double-click on the Printers icon to display the Printers dialog box.

3. Look on the list of installed printers for the Generic/Text Only printer driver. If it does not appear, click on the Add button to expand the Printers dialog box to include the list of all the printer drivers available in Windows. Figure 12.7 shows the expanded dialog box.

4. Choose the Generic/Text Only printer driver from the List of Printers list box (it appears near the top of the list).

5. The Printers program may prompt you for Windows program diskettes if it cannot find the printer driver on the hard disk.

6. The printer driver is installed connected to LPT1:. If you always plan to use the Generic/Text Only for printing to file, change this connection from LPT1: to FILE:. If you plan to use it both for printing to file and for printing ASCII text to a printer, change this connection to the printer port to which the printer is attached. To change the printer port, click on the Connect button to display the Connect dialog box (Figure 12.8). Choose the printer port from the Ports list. For printing to file, choose FILE:. Then click on OK to exit from the Connect dialog box.

7. When you are done installing the printer driver, close the Printers dialog box by clicking on Close.

8. Close the Control Panel window by double-clicking on its Control-menu box.

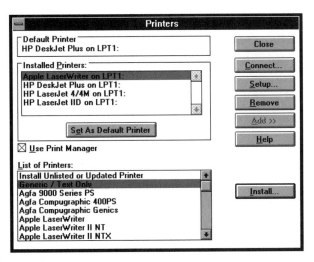

Figure 12.7 Adding a printer driver to Windows.

Now the Generic/Text Only printer driver will appear as an option when you display the Print Setup dialog box

Note: If the Generic/Text Only printer driver appears as "Generic/Text Only on FILE:" in the list of installed printers in the Print Setup dialog box, the driver is configured to print to file rather than to a printer. To change the connection for this printer driver from FILE: to the printer port to which your printer is connected (usually LPT1:, LPT2:, COM1:, or COM2:):

1. In the Program Manager, open the Main group and Control Panel windows.

2. Double-click on the Printers icon to display the Printers dialog box.

You may have noticed that the printer driver name indicates the way it is connected to the computer by using the word *on*. The way the printer is connected to the computer is called the *printer port*. For example, if you use an HP DeskJet, you might see this entry in the list of installed printers:

```
HP DeskJet on LPT1:
```

This entry indicates that the printer is connected to the computer via LPT1: (the computer's parallel printer port #1). The colon (:) is part of the printer port's name.

3. Highlight the Generic/Text Only printer driver in the list of selected printers.

4. Click on the Connect button to display the Connect dialog box, shown in Figure 12.8.

5. For the Port setting, select the appropriate printer port. For example, select LPT1:.

6. Click on OK to exit from the Connect dialog box.

7. Click on Close to exit from the Printers dialog box.

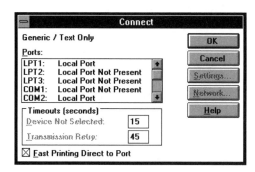

Figure 12.8   Specifying how a printer is connected to the computer.

8. Close the Control Panel window by double-clicking on its Control-menu box.

Speeding Up Slow Reports

Some Access reports can take a long time to print—minutes, or even hours. You can speed up printing many reports.

If your reports take a long time to print, try these approaches:

- If the report is long, split it into several smaller reports and print them separately.
- Remove as many lines, borders around controls, and graphics objects as possible. These print much more slowly than text.
- Turn off the Windows Print Manager. When you use the Print Manager, nothing prints until Access has formatted the entire report and sent it to the Print Manager, which stores it temporarily in a file on disk.

To turn off the Windows Print Manager for a printer:

1. In the Program Manager, open the Main group and Control Panel windows.
2. Double-click on the Printers icon to display the Printers dialog box.
3. Select the printer you are using for the report.
4. Clear the Use Print Manager check box.
5. Close the Printers dialog box by clicking on Close.
6. Close the Control Panel window by double-clicking on its Control-menu box.

Handling Out-of-Memory Errors when Printing

When you print a complex report, especially one with many sections, Access may tell you that it cannot print the report because it has run out of memory!

Access creates temporary hidden queries, one per section, when it prints reports. It uses these queries in the form of SQL statements to compile the information for the report. If your report is complex, with many sections, Access may exceed an internal limit on the total size of the SQL statements required to format the report.

If your table and field names are long, the SQL statements Access creates will be long, too. To solve out-of-memory problems, you may need to shorten your table names or field names. Alternatively, if the report is based on a query that contains many tables and fields, you may want to use a make-table query to create a temporary table. Then use this temporary table as the record source for the report. Using a temporary table as the record source means that when Access prints the report, it only has to process its temporary hidden queries.

This problem was more serious in Access 1.0. If you encounter out-of-memory problems in Access 1.0, upgrade to a more recent version.

Previewing Reports and Forms

Access allows you to see how the report or form will look when printed *before* you spend the time, paper, and toner to print. Using Print Preview, you can see on the screen whether your controls are positioned as you want them, whether the correct information appears in each control, and whether headers and footers appear correctly. There are two ways to preview a report on the screen:

- When looking at the report in Design view, click on the Print Preview button on the toolbar
- From the Database window, highlight the report and click on Preview

This section presents techniques for getting the most out of Print Preview—you can save a lot of paper by getting the report right on the screen first!

Navigating in Print Preview

You can preview all the pages in the report.

When you use Print Preview, Access shows you the top of the first page of the report. To see the rest of the page, use the scroll bar on the right side of the window or press **Down Arrow** and **Up Arrow** or **PgDn** and **PgUp**. To see the full width of the report, press **Left Arrow** and **Right Arrow**. To see other pages of the report, use the navigation buttons in the lower-left corner of the window.

Seeing a Reduced View of the Report

Use the Zoom feature to see the whole page at once, then zoom in on the part you want to see.

Because you can't see a whole page of the report at once (unless you have a large, high-resolution screen), Access lets you "zoom" in and out on the report in Print Preview. In the Print Preview window, the cursor looks likes a magnifying glass. If you click on the report, Access "zooms out" to show the whole page. The type is usually too small to see, but you can get an idea of the overall layout.

Once you have zoomed out, click on the part of the page you want to see. Access "zooms in" on that part of the report. You can also zoom in and out by clicking on the Zoom button on the toolbar.

When the whole page is visible, press the **Down Arrow** and **PgDn** keys to move forward one page, and press the **Up Arrow** and **PgUp** keys to move back one page.

Changing the Printer or Page Format

Use the Setup button to display the Print Setup dialog box.

When you view the report in Print Preview, you may see that you need to make changes to the margins, page orientation, or paper size. You can display the Print Setup dialog box directly from Print Preview—just click on the Setup button on the toolbar.

Previewing Reports with Parameters

You can view the report again with a new set of parameters.

If your report contains parameters, or if it is based on a parameter query, Access prompts you for the parameters before it displays the report in Print Preview. Once you have looked at the report, you may want to try it again with another set of parameters. To force Access to ask you again for the parameters, close and reopen the report, or return to Design view and make a minor change to the report (like selecting the same value for a property).

Previewing Reports Fast

In Design view, choose File Sample Preview to quickly see how your report will look.

Previewing a report can take an annoyingly long time, especially if the record source for the report is a query. Access must run the query, prompting you for any query parameters, before it can show you the report. Waiting for queries can really slow down report design.

Luckily, there is a faster way if the report is open in Design view. When you choose File Sample Preview from the menu, Access displays a few sample records, but it doesn't actually run the query on which the report is based. This allows you to check fonts, type sizes, and control placement. Don't count on the actual data to be correct, since the records don't come from the actual query. (Before saving the report, it is a good idea to do a full preview of the report so that you can see the report with the actual data.) If your report is based on a parameter query, Access prompts you for the parameters but doesn't actually use them, since it doesn't run the query. Just click on OK when Access prompts for parameters.

Printing to File

There are two ways to copy information from an Access database into another type of file: exporting and printing to file. When you use the File Export command, you create a file that contains copies of records in a table in one of the industry-standard formats that Access supports. For example, you can use File Export to create data files for use in mail merge operations with Word for Windows and other word processors. To create any other type of file, design a report that contains the information in the format you want, and print the report to file, that is, save in a file the information that Access usually sends to the printer. When you print a report to file, the file you create is called a *print file*.

This section contains the reasons for creating print files and techniques for creating them. The best way to print most reports to file is by using the OutputAs library described later in this chapter. You can use this technique to create print files in ASCII text format, RTF document format, and XLS Excel spreadsheet format.

Creating a Print File for Later Printing

Make a print file containing the information Access would normally send to the printer, including formatting and graphics codes.

If you want to print a report later, perhaps because the printer you want to use is not available, you can create a print file containing the report. Later, you can send this file to the printer.

To create a print file:

1. With the report selected, choose File Print to display the Print dialog box.
2. Choose the printer you plan to use.
3. Click on the Print to File check box so that it contains an X.
4. Set the Print Range to the pages you want to print.
5. Click on OK. Access displays a message saying that it is printing the report (actually, it is formatting it). Then you see the Print To File dialog box, shown in Figure 12.9.
6. Enter a filename. You might find it helpful to use a file extension like .OUT to remind yourself that this file is Access output waiting to be printed.
7. Click on OK.

Access creates a file that contains the information it would normally send to the printer. It can be printed only on the type of printer you selected for the report (in the Print Setup dialog box), or on compatible printers. To print the file, copy the file to the printer using the Windows File Manager program or DOS.

To copy the file using the File Manager, highlight the filename and choose File Copy from the menu or press **F8**. For the name of the file to copy to, type the printer port to which your printer is connected, for example, **LPT1:**. Click on OK. Access asks if you want to replace the

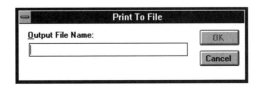

Figure 12.9 Entering the name of the printer port.

existing file named LPT1 (this is clearly a bug in File Manager, since LPT1 isn't a file!). Click on Yes to print the file.

To copy the file using DOS, double-click on the MS-DOS icon in Program Manager, and type this command at the DOS prompt:

```
copy /b filename port
```

For *filename*, enter the path and filename of the file. For *port*, enter the printer port to which the printer is connected. The /B switch tells DOS that your print file contains binary information, not text. For example, to print a print file named REPORT.OUT on a printer connected to COM1:, type this:

```
copy /b report.out com1:
```

To exit from DOS, type **exit**.

Creating a Word for Windows Data File

You can create a file for use in mail merge operations in Word for Windows to print mailing labels, form letters, and envelopes.

You can use a word processor to combine mailing list information with documents to produce mailing labels, form letters, envelopes, and other "personalized" documents. If you want to use name and address information from your Access database and you use Word for Windows (or another word processor that uses the same format for data files), you can export a table in a format that Word for Windows can read. Word for Windows calls the file that contains names and addresses for mail merge operations the *data file*.

You can't print a report to file in this format, but you can create a temporary table that contains the fields you want to print in your Word for Windows document, then export the table.

Choose or create a table to export. If a table in your database contains all the fields you want to use, you can export all the records in the table. If you want to select which fields and records to export, or if the fields you want to use are stored in more than one table, follow these steps to create a temporary table for export:

1.   Create a query that contains the fields and records you want to export. View the query in Datasheet view to make sure the information is complete.

2. Convert the query to a make-table query by choosing Query Make Table. Access displays the Queries Properties dialog box.

3. Enter a name for the new, temporary table. To remind you that this table is only temporary, and should be re-created every time you want to export the data so that it contains up-to-date information, call it something like Temp for Export. Click on the OK button.

4. To run the make-table query and create the temporary table, click on the Run button on the toolbar.

To export the table you have chosen (or created):

1. In the Database Window, choose File Export from the menu. Access displays the Export dialog box.

2. For the Data Destination, choose Word for Windows Merge and click on OK. Access displays the Select Microsoft Access Object dialog box, containing a list of the tables in the database.

3. Choose the table you want to export and click on OK. Access displays the Export to File dialog box.

4. Enter a name for the data file and click on OK. Access displays the Export Word Merge Options dialog box shown in Figure 12.10.

5. The dialog box shows the settings for the format of dates and numbers in the file. Change the settings if you want your dates or numbers formatted differently and click on OK. Access creates the data file in the Word for Windows mail merge format. Now you can use this information in mail merge operations in Word for Windows or other word processors that can read the Word for Windows data file format.

Note: This feature is not available in Access 1.0.

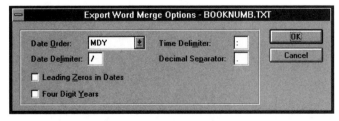

Figure 12.10 Selecting options when creating a Word for Windows data file for mail merge.

Installing the OutputAs Library

Using the OutputAs library, you can print a report to a file as ASCII text or in either RTF or XLS format. These file formats make it easy to import a report into a word processor or spreadsheet program.

If you want to save the output of an Access report so that you can edit it with a word processor, you can use the OutputAs Library to print the report to an *RTF file*. RTF (Rich Text Format) is Microsoft's standard format for documents, and can be read by Microsoft Word, Lotus AmiPro, and WordPerfect for Windows. Using a word processor to edit the output from Access lets you get around certain Access limitations. For example, in Access you can't make just one word within a text box italics or bold—it's all or nothing. And you can't control inter-line spacing in multi-line text boxes in Access. But once the report is in your word processor, you can customize the formatting in ways Access doesn't allow.

Similarly, you can export a report from Access for use in a spreadsheet program by creating a print file in *XLS format*. XLS format is the format in which Microsoft Excel saves its spreadsheets. The OutputAs Library calls this format *BIFF* (binary interchange file format).

You may also want to create an ASCII text file to be imported into another application, printed, or posted on a bulletin board. You can create an ASCII text print file by using the Generic/Text Only printer driver (see *Creating an ASCII Text File without the OutputAs Library* later in this chapter), but the driver has bugs that may garble your reports.

To create an ASCII text, RTF, or XLS file from Access, you can use the OutputAs Library from Microsoft. The library is available on the MSACCESS forum on CompuServe in library 5, in a file named OUTPUT.ZIP. You will also need PKUNZIP or a compatible program to "unzip" the OUTPUT.ZIP file to create the four files it contains. You can download PKUNZIP from section 10 of the PCVENC forum on CompuServe, from most bulletin boards, or you can order it from PKWare, Inc., at 414-354-8699.

The OutputAs library consists of two files:

- OUTPUTAS.DLL: Dynamic link library containing routines used to create the file

- OUTPUTAS.MDA: Access library database containing the Access Basic modules to create the file (see Creating Library Databases in Chapter 17 for an explanation of libraries).

To use the OutputAs library, you must first install it into Access. This adds a new command, Save As Report, to the Help menu. Then you can print a report to a file using this new command.

To install the OutputAs library:

1. The library comes in a .ZIP file named OUTPUT.ZIP. Store OUTPUT.ZIP in your Access program directory. To unzip the OUTPUT.ZIP file, double-click on the MS-DOS icon (located in the Main program group in Program Manager), go to the Access program directory, and type the following command at the DOS prompt:

   ```
   pkunzip output.zip
   ```

2. Use the Windows Notepad program to add OUTPUTAS.MDA to your MSACCESS.INI file. This file contains initialization information for Access (see *Customizing Settings in MSACCESS.INI* in Chapter 15 for more information). To run Notepad, double-click on the Notepad icon (located in the Accessories program group in Program Manager). Choose File Open to load the MSACCESS.INI file in your Windows program directory, usually C:\WINDOWS.

3. Find the [Libraries] section of the file. To install OUTPUTAS.MDA as a library database, add this line below the [Libraries] line and above the [OBDC] line:

   ```
   c:\access\outputas.mda=ro
   ```

If Access isn't stored in C:\ACCESS, make sure to substitute the path name of the Access program directory.

4. To add a new command to Access to allow you to run the OutputAs library, you must create a new section in the MSACCESS.INI file, called [Menu Add-ins]. At the end of the MSACCESS.INI file, add these lines:

   ```
   [Menu Add-ins]
   &Save Report As==SaveReportAs()
   ```

   Don't forget the square brackets in the first line and the two equal signs in the second line. (If your MSACCESS.INI file already has a [Menu Add-ins] section, just enter the second line.)

5. To save the MSACCESS.INI file, choose File Save from the Notepad menu.

6. If Access is running, exit from Access and restart it. Access reads the MSACCESS.INI file only when it loads.

Using the OutputAs Library to Create a Print File

Once you have installed the OutputAs library, you can print any report to a file by using the new Save Report As command.

Using the OutputAs library, you can print any report to an ASCII, an RTF file, or XLS file by using the new Save Report As command on the Help menu. (Unfortunately, menu add-ins appear on the Help menu, even though this isn't a location that you would expect.) Depending on the file format, the report's layout won't match the way it looks in Access. For example, OutputAs can't print information from subreports or subforms in your report. Also, make sure there are no overlapping controls in the report.

To print a report to a file using the OutputAs library:

1. Choose Help Save Report As from the menu. Access (actually, OutputAs) displays the Select Report dialog box, shown in Figure 12.11.

2. Choose a report name from the list, and click on OK.

3. Access displays the Output As dialog box, shown in Figure 12.12. Choose the type of file you want to create from the List Files of Type box. Your choices are:

   - Ascii (*.TXT): ASCII text file

Figure 12.11   Selecting a report to output to a file.

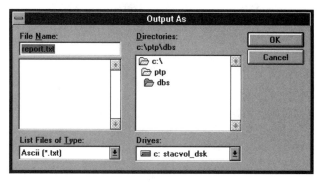

Figure 12.12   Selecting the format and filename for the print file.

- RTF (.RTF): Word-processing file
- BIFF (*.XLS): Excel spreadsheet file

4. Enter a filename in the File Name box, or choose one from the list. OutputAs suggests a filename, but you can replace this with the filename you want.

5. Click on OK.

6. The OutputAs library prints the report to the file. If the report is based on a parameter query, or if the report has parameters, Access prompts for them as usual.

7. Load the file into a text editor (for ASCII text files), a word processor (for RTF files), or a spreadsheet program (for XLS files) to see how the report looks.

The following topics describe how to reformat reports so that the OutputAs library produces better-looking print files.

Create Separate Reports for Printing to File

If you want to print the same report to the printer and to an RTF or ASCII file, make two reports. The report format for creating files is different from normal report formats (see the following topics). When you decide to print an existing report to a text file, make a copy of the report, including "To Text," "ASCII," "To RTF," or "To XLS" in the name. Then make the necessary format changes before printing the report to file.

Creating an Excel Spreadsheet File

You can create an Excel spreadsheet arranged in Excel's own database format.

Excel can store tables in spreadsheet files in a special database format. In Excel, a table of records is called a *database*—the word doesn't refer to a collection of related tables as it does in Access. An Excel database is structured so that each row contains one record, with each field in a separate column. The first row contains the field names for the columns.

To create an Excel spreadsheet file, use the OutputAs library to print a report as a BIFF file. (BIFF is the name that OutputAs uses for XLS files.) This creates a file that is compatible with Microsoft Excel version 3 and later.

When you save a report as an Excel spreadsheet file, OutputAs ignores the layout of controls on the page, and instead creates a spreadsheet formatted as an Excel database with each record on one row. It creates one column for each text box in the report. OutputAs includes only the data in text boxes, omitting all other types of controls. The first row of the spreadsheet contains the Control Names of the text boxes as field names. OutputAs preserves the data format (such as Currency) and the text format (such as font, font size, and color) of the data.

Once the information is in Excel or another spreadsheet program, you can use the spreadsheet's ability to analyze and graph the data.

Because OutputAs ignores the format of your report, just make sure that the text box controls appear in the order in which you want to store them in your Excel Spreadsheet.

Note: Excel limits the number of characters in a cell to 255, so Access truncates text values longer than 255 characters when it creates the file.

Creating an RTF Word-Processing File

Using the OutputAs library RTF file format, you can import an Access report into a word-processing program for further formatting.

If you want to format a report with more precision than Access allows, print it as an RTF file using the OutputAs library and import it into a word processor like WordPerfect for Windows, AmiPro, or Microsoft Word for Windows. Using a word processor, you can control aspects of text formats that Access doesn't support, like the inter-line spacing of multi-line controls, justified text, lines between the columns of multi-column reports, wrapping text around pictures, and desktop-publishing features like tables of contents and indexes.

When you use the OutputAs library to save a report as an RTF file, it preserves the layout of the report as much as possible. However, because the RTF option stores text on a line-by-line basis, some reports may not look exactly like the original Access reports. For example, Access can print a report in which one text box is to the right of and slightly below another text box. When the report is stored as an RTF file, the two text boxes must either be stored on the same line or on successive lines— overlapping lines aren't supported.

The RTF file that OutputAs creates includes the data from both text boxes and label controls. It preserves the data format (such as Currency) and the text format (such as font, font size, boldface, italics, underlining, and color). It doesn't preserve the alignment of values (such as center alignment) within controls. It creates tab stops at the left edge of each text box and uses tabs between values. If a value in a text box is too long to fit in the text box, Access includes only the amount that fits, omitting the rest. For multi-column reports, Access stores the information in the RTF file in a single column. You can use the column features of your word processor to create multiple columns in the word-processing document.

For example, the mail-order bookseller database contains information about each book to be used in marketing brochures. The Brochure report can be printed to create a usable brochure, but you might want to format it further, justifying the text, adding a line between the two columns of the report, and include one or two pictures. Figure 12.13 shows the Brochure report in Design view, and Figure 12.14 shows the report in Print Preview. The two-column report includes the book codes, title, and other information about each book. But what if you want to justify the text and reduce the inter-line spacing? The Description and Contents fields are displayed on the report by using text boxes for which the Can Grow property is set to Yes, but there is no way to set the spacing for the additional lines.

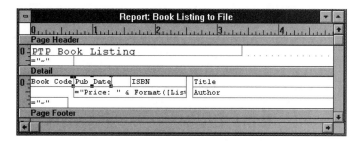

Figure 12.13 Brochure report in the booksellers database.

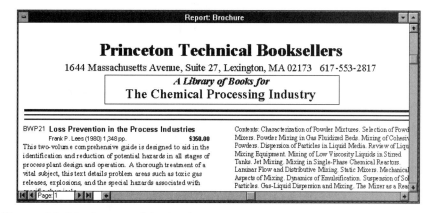

Figure 12.14 Preview of the Brochure report.

If you save the Brochure report shown in Figure 12.14 as an RTF file, it looks like Figure 12.15. Access has added extra blank lines, and the Description and Contents fields have become mixed together.

You can modify the report so that it exports an RTF file suitable for importing into a word processor for formatting. First, make a copy of the report and then modify its contents using the following steps:

1. Eliminate the Page Header and Page Footer sections of the report. Let your word processor handle headers and footers, since the formatting will affect where the pages breaks occur. Use a report header and footer if you want to include information once in the text file, either at the beginning or at the end.

2. Display the property sheet for the report, and set Grid Y to 6. Since the standard line spacing for most printers is six lines per inch, this sets the grid to match. Access creates RTF files with fewer extraneous carriage returns if controls are 1/6 inch high.

   Now, you need to size all the controls to be multiples of 1/6 inch.

3. Select all the controls by choosing Edit Select All from the menu. Then choose Layout Size to Grid. If any control is still too tall, make it smaller, so it is one row tall on the grid. For controls that contain text in a large font size, make the control tall enough so that the text appears completely—otherwise, OutputAs will omit the control during the print to file process.

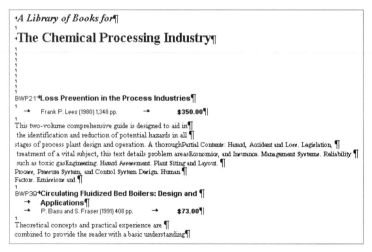

Figure 12.15 Brochure report as an RTF file.

4. Move the bottom edge of each section to line up with the grid, so that it falls on a 1/6 inch boundary.

5. Experiment with using different fonts for the text box and label controls on the report. Setting all font sizes to 10 pitch and sizing controls to be 1/6 inch high eliminates most but not all of the extra carriage returns OutputAs inserts in the RTF file. To change the font for all the controls, select them all by choosing Edit Select All from the menu. Then choose the font from the Font box on the toolbar.

6. For multi-column reports, set the number of columns back to 1. Let your word processor handle creating multiple columns. Choose File Print Setup from the menu and click on More to display the multi-column part of the Print Setup dialog box. For the Items Across setting, enter **1**. For Item Size, select Same as Detail. (Chapter 14 describes these settings in more detail, including how to create multiple-column reports.) Click on OK to exit from the Print Setup dialog box.

7. The Can Grow property of text box controls doesn't always work correctly when exporting to an RTF file. Make text boxes as wide as possible so that text doesn't have to wrap to more lines than necessary. Your word processor can handle the word wrap.

Note: The OutputAs library is limited to outputting 255-character fields. If your Text or Memo fields are longer than this, the OutputAs library only includes the first 255 characters of each value.

If your Text or Memo field contains some values that are longer than 255 characters but not longer than 512 characters, you can add an extra text box that displays the next 255 characters in the field. Enter an expression like this:

```
=IIf(Len(fieldname)>255,Mid(fieldname,256,256),"")
```

This expression checks whether the field is longer than 255 characters—if so, it uses the Mid() function to return characters sharing with the 256th character.

Figure 12.16 shows the Brochure report adapted for export to the RFT file format, and Figure 12.17 shows the resulting RTF file.

You will still need to do some cleaning up to an RTF file created by the OutputAs library, including the following types of changes:

*   You may need to delete extra carriage returns. Use your word processor's global replace command to replace all occurrences of two carriage returns with one carriage return.

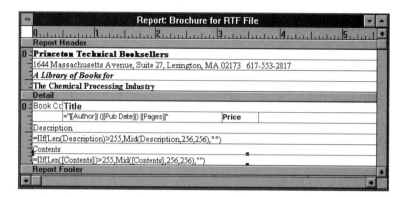

Figure 12.16   Report design modified for output as an RTF file.

- If you use the Can Grow property of a text box control to create multiple-line output, you may need to delete carriage returns that appear at the ends of the lines, so that your word processor can fill the lines.

- If you want text to be centered or right-aligned, you must do this in the word processor, since Access left-aligns all text in the RTF file.

- For a multi-column report, use your word processor's columns feature to format the report with multiple columns.

- Add lines, boxes, and pictures using your word processor's line-drawing and object import features.

When you are done cleaning up the RTF file, save it using your word processor's document format. For example, if you use Word for Windows, save the file as a Word DOC file.

Figure 12.17   Resulting RTF file.

Creating an ASCII Text File

To create a text file with Access data, use the OutputAs library to save a report.

If you want to create an ASCII text file containing data from your Access database, you can create a report with the information in the format you need. Then you can use the OutputAs library to save the output of the report as an ASCII text file. (See the following topic if you don't have the OutputAs library.)

There are several reasons you might need an ASCII text file:

- You may want to create a file that can be read on the screen using Windows Notepad or the DOS TYPE command.

- You might need to export information from Access in a format that isn't supported by the File Export command. For example, when doing a large-scale mailing, a mail-order bookseller might need to provide a mailing list of potential customers in a format specified by a direct-mail service company. If the format isn't one that Access can export to, creating an ASCII file from a report is the best way to make the file.

- Your word processor might not import RTF files, so using an ASCII text file is the only way to transfer data from Access into a word-processing document.

Saving a report as an ASCII text file using the OutputAs library is similar to saving one as an RTF file. OutputAs includes the data in text boxes and label controls, preserving the data format (such as Currency), but not saving text formatting (color, font, and font size). Follow the instructions in the previous topic to customize a report for output to an ASCII text file.

Creating an ASCII Text File without the OutputAs Library

To create an ASCII text file to be read by another application, you can print the report to file using the Generic/Text Only printer driver.

If you don't have the OutputAs library, you can still make a print file containing only ASCII text, not graphical print information, by using the Generic/Text Only printer driver. Using this method to create an ASCII text file, you encounter many more bugs, either in Access or the printer driver itself, but this is the best method to use if you need to print a report that contains subreports, or if you don't have the OutputAs library.

First, choose the correct printer driver, then create a report designed to print the information in the format you want. You must design your report to work with various bugs in Access' print-to-file feature. After printing the report to file, you will probably have to clean up the text file.

The Generic/Text Only printer driver is designed to print text at 10 characters per inch and six lines per inch. Access assumes that all text in the report will be printed at this size. This is very different from a normal Access report, in which you can use text in many sizes and fonts. For this reason, the format of a report to be printed to an ASCII file is very limited. When you design the report, set the grid to six lines per inch and 10 characters per inch (that is, Grid X should be 10 and Grid Y should be 6) to match the positions where Access can print characters.

To create a report to print to a text file, you must first install the Generic/Text Only printer driver in Windows, which is described in *Printing ASCII Text,* earlier in this chapter,.

To design the report to be printed to a text file:

1. Create a new report using a ReportWizard or starting with a blank report, or copy an existing report that is similar to the format you need.

2. Choose File Print Setup from the menu to display the Print Setup dialog box. Click on Specific Printer and then choose the Generic/Text Only printer driver. Set the Left Margin to 0 to avoid blank spaces at the beginning of every line of the text file.

3. Click on Options to display the Generic/Text Only dialog box, shown in Figure 12.18. Choose Continuous for the Paper Feed setting and turn on the No Page Break check box. Click on OK to exit from the Generic/Text Only dialog box.

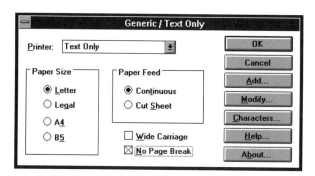

Figure 12.18   Setting options for the Generic/Text Only printer.

4. Click on OK to exit from the Print Setup dialog box.

5. Display the property sheet for the report, and set the Layout For Print property to Yes. Set Grid X to 10 and Grid Y to 6.

6. If the text file is to be imported into another database program, don't use page headers or footers. Headers and footers would interrupt the flow of records in the file. Similarly, if the text file is to be imported into a word-processing program, let the word processor handle the page headers and footers. Omit them from your Access report.

On the other hand, if the text file is to be distributed to others for viewing or printing, you may want to include page headers and footers.

7. Use a report header and footer if you want to include information once in the text file, either at the beginning or at the end.

8. Set the font for all the controls on the report to a fixed-pitch font. To select all the controls, choose Edit Select All from the menu. Then choose a fixed-pitch font like Roman 10cpi from the Font box on the toolbar. It doesn't matter what size you choose for the text—Access ignores font size when it prints the report to a text file.

9. Size all the controls to be 1/6 inch high. Select all the controls by choosing Edit Select All from the menu. Then choose Layout Size to Grid. If any control is still too tall, make it smaller, so it is one row tall on the grid.

10. Access does not print labels correctly when printing to file using the Generic/Text Only driver. For each label control on the report, delete the control and create a text box control in its place. For the Control Source property of the text box, enter an expression containing the label text like this:

```
="labeltext"
```

Replace *labeltext* with the text you want to appear.

11. Delete all the line controls, rectangle controls, and object frame controls, because they cannot be printed as text. To create horizontal lines in the report, create text boxes that contain expressions like this for the Control Source:

```
="———"
```

12. To create blank space in a report, you usually just leave blank space in the Design view of the report. This doesn't always work when printing to file with the Generic/Text Only driver. Access doesn't

always create blank lines in the text file to correspond to the blank space in the report. Instead, you can create "placeholders" by making text box controls that display a unique character not used elsewhere in the report, like a tilde (~) or caret (^). For example, create text controls with this expression as the Control Source:

```
="~"
```

Later, you can replace these characters with carriage returns to create blank lines.

13. Formatting doesn't always work correctly when Access prints a report to a text file. You may need to use the Format() function to format numbers, like this:

```
=Format([List Price],"$0.00")
```

This function formats the List Price field as currency. Refer to Chapter 5 for information on using custom formats with the Format() function.

14. Move the bottom edge of each section to line up with the grid, so that it falls on a 1/6 inch boundary.

15. Don't use boldface for any controls—the Generic/Text Only printer driver tries to simulate boldface by overprinting characters three times, so your text appears in the text file three times!

16. Preview the report to see how it looks. Figure 12.19 shows a report in Design view and Figure 12.20 shows the same report in Print Preview. In Print Preview you can check whether Access is adding blank lines where you want them or if you need to create placeholders. You can also see if Access is formatting numbers correctly.

Now, it's time to print the report.

17. Choose Print from the toolbar to display the Print dialog box and

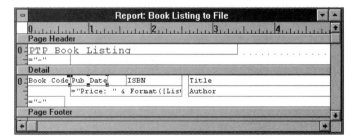

Figure 12.19   Designing a report to print to a text file.

```
┌─────────────────────────────────────────────────────────────────┐
│ ▭              Report: Book Listing to File                 ▼ ▲  │
├─────────────────────────────────────────────────────────────────┤
│ PTP Book Listing                                             ♦   │
│ ~                                                                │
│ BRP01    1985        0-903056     Crystal Structures of Clay Min │
│          Price:  $120.00          G.W. Brindley and G. Brown     │
│ ~                                                                │
│ BRP02    1985        0-904357     Creep of Metals and Alloys     │
│          Price:  $73.50           R.W. Evans and B. Wilshire     │
│ ~                                                                │
│ BRP03    1985        0-904357     Dislocations and Properties of ▼│
├─────────────────────────────────────────────────────────────────┤
│ |◄ ◄ Page:1  ►  ►|  ◄                                          ►  │
└─────────────────────────────────────────────────────────────────┘
```

Figure 12.20   Previewing the text file report.

choose Print to File. (This step isn't necessary if you selected FILE: as the printer port for the Generic/Text Only printer driver, but it doesn't hurt.) Click on OK.

18. Access prompts you for the name of the file to create. Enter a filename. Use the file extension .TXT, or the extension required by the application into which you will import the file. Click on OK.

Access creates the text file. Follow the next set of steps to clean up the file using a text editor or a word-processing program that can save files in ASCII text format. You can use the Windows Write program, which comes with Windows, by double-clicking on the Write icon in the Accessories program group in Program Manager.

1. Open or import the text file into the editor or word processor. In Write, choose File Open from the menu. Choose Text Files (*.TXT) from the List Files of Type box. Choose the filename and click on OK. Write asks if you want to convert the file to Write format. Choose No Conversion.

2. Look at the report. When Access prints a report to a text file, it sometimes switches the order of fields, omits text, and makes other errors. You may need to experiment with the placement of controls on the report to get a format that works.

3. If you used placeholders for blank lines, replace them with carriage returns (also called paragraph marks). In Write, you can use the Find Replace command to replace all tildes with carriage returns: In the Find What box, enter ~ and in the Replace With box enter **^p**. Choose Replace All.

4. Clean up any other mistakes as needed.

5. Save the file as a text file. In Write, choose File Save As from the menu, then choose Text Files (*.TXT) from the Save File as Type box.

As you can see, Access has strange problems making ASCII text files. If you can, use the OutputAs library. I hope a future version of Access will make creating text files easier!

CHAPTER 13

Printing Subtotals, Totals, and Other Calculations

Most reports include calculated values. By including calculations in your reports, you can count, sum, and average the information in the records, and by grouping records, you can calculate subtotals. Access also makes it easy to create running sums, ratios, and other types of calculations. In fact, without leaving Access, you can do most of the calculations you might otherwise do with a spreadsheet.

This chapter contains tips for making reports with calculations and groups. Examples in this chapter refer to the mail-order booksellers database (BOOKORD) described previously.

Printing Calculations for Each Record

First, we need to take a look at how to display the result of a calculated field for each record in a report, including calculated numbers, dates derived from other dates, combinations of Text fields and punctuation, and Yes/No values based on conditions in the record.

There are two ways to print a calculated value for each record:

- You can create a text box in the Detail section of the report and enter the calculation in its Control Source property

- You can create a calculated field in a query, use the query as the record source for the report, and display the field in a text box by entering its name as the control source

Calculated Fields in Queries versus Calculations in Text Boxes

If you want to display a calculation in several places, or use it for the basis of other calculations, you will find it useful to create a calculated field in the record source query.

Here are some situations in which you should create a calculated field in the record source query rather than in a text box in the report itself:

- You want to display the same calculation in several places on the report. Rather than creating several duplicate text boxes, each containing the same calculation, it is more efficient for Access to compute the value once in the record source query and store the result for display.

- You want to sort the records in the report by a calculation that appears on the report. Rather than entering the expression both in a text box and in the Sorting and Grouping dialog box, it is more efficient to compute it once.

- You want to do further calculations based on the calculated field—for example, you want to display counts, averages, or totals. If you use a function like Sum( ) to enter an expression in a text box to create a total, you cannot refer to a text box that contains the calculated field, you can only refer to fields in the record source.

For example, the Sales Ledger report might calculate an estimated profit for each order. If you want to print the orders with the highest profit first, you could enter an expression to calculate the profit in two places: a text box in the Detail section of the report to display the value, and in the Sorting and Grouping dialog box to sort by the value. But why double your effort when it would be more efficient to calculate the value in the record source query?

However, if it makes more sense to calculate the value on the report, follow these steps to create a calculated text box that prints for each record:

1. In the Detail section of the report, create a text box control.

2. Display the property sheet for the control. (If the property sheet is not visible, select the control, then click on the Properties button on the toolbar to display the property sheet.)

3. Enter an expression in the Control Source of the text box control. Begin the expression with an equal sign. For example, this expression calculates the profit for each record in the Orders table in the bookseller database, based on a 33-percent publisher discount:

    ```
    (Int(=[Total Book Amt]*0.33 * 100)/100
    ```

4. Choose a format for the text box (Access does not automatically format calculated values to match other values in the report). For example, format the profit value as Currency with two decimal places.

Note: To calculate numeric, text, date, and other values in text boxes, you can use the same expressions you use to make a calculated field in a query. See *Calculating Additional Information* in Chapter 9 for more information on creating a calculated field in a query, as well as combining text values, using parts of text fields, capitalizing text, performing numeric calculations, performing date arithmetic, and creating conditional (if-then-else) calculations.

Edit Long Expressions

Press **Shift+F2** to edit a property in the Zoom box. The Zoom box allows you to see long expressions in their entirety. You will find this technique especially useful when entering a long expression into the Control Source property.

Combining Values

Combine values and punctuation by using concatenation, or by using vertical bars to enclose field names within text.

The topic *Combining Values* in Chapter 9 described how to concatenate, or combine, two or more values. For example, this expression uses the ampersand (&) concatenation operator to combine three fields and some punctuation into the last line of an address:

```
= [City] & ", " & [State] & "   " & [Zip]
```

You can also use vertical bars around each field name to create an expression that displays the same result:

```
= "|[City]|, |[State]|   |[Zip]|"
```

By enclosing a field name in vertical bars (around the square brackets), you can include field names within quoted text values. The quotes around the whole expression tell Access that the expression is a text value. The vertical bars around the field names tell Access to substitute the value of the field at that location. When Access prints the report it substitutes the value of the City field for the |*[City]*| portion of the text value, substitutes the value of the State field for the |*[State]*| portion, and so forth for each record.

You don't have to convert non-text values to text values before using either of these two techniques—Access converts them automatically before combining the values. To control how Access converts a numeric value to text, you can use the Format( ) function, described in Chapter 5.

Using Conditional Calculations

Create a text box with an IIf( ) expression to display text conditionally.

You can use the IIf( ) function (described in *Creating Conditional Calculations* in Chapter 9) to print different values depending on conditions in the record. For example, the bookseller database contains a PO report, which prints purchase orders sent to publishers. (The PO report is described in more detail in Chapter 14.) Some publishers require prepayment, while others invoice. The PO report contains a text box with this expression as the Control Source:

```
= IIf([Must Prepay?], "Our check is enclosed.", "Please invoice us.")
```

The Must Prepay? field is a Yes/No field. You can enter any type of condition in the IIf( ) function, using comparison operators. For example, to print a message for large orders, you can use the > operator:

```
= IIf([Total Order]>500, "You are eligible for a special discount!", "")
```

Note: When you create a conditional control, be sure to make a text box, not a label control, since label controls cannot contain expressions.

Handle Null Values

If a field mentioned in an expression is blank (null), the result of the expression is often blank as well. Null values can produce blank text boxes when you expect values. To handle this situation, use the IIf( ) function with the *Is Null* condition. For example, on the PO report, there may not be an order contact for each publisher. This expression prints *Order Department* if the Order Contact field is null:

```
=IIf([Order Contact] Is Null, "Order Department", [Order Contact])
```

Naming Controls That Contain Calculations

Don't use a field name as the control name for a text box that contains an expression.

When you create controls, Access names them automatically, although you can change the names later. If you create an unbound text box, Access names it Field$n$, using the next unused number as n, starting with 1. If you drag a field name from the field list to create a control, Access uses the field name as the control name.

However, when you create a control that contains an expression, make sure that the name of the control isn't the same as any field mentioned in the expression. For example, the expression in the previous Hot Tip refers to the Order Contact field. If the text box containing the expression is also named Order Contact, Access gets confused about whether the reference to Order Contact is to the control or the field, and the report displays *#Error*. If this happens, change the name in the Control Name property of the text box.

Printing a Field from Another Table

Access provides four ways to display information from a related table.

You may want to include a field that doesn't appear in the record source of the report. For example, in the PO report, the shipping method indicates how the book should be shipped to the customer. Rather than displaying the Ship Via code from the Orders table (for example, U.S. Book Mail), you may want to show the corresponding description that is stored in the Shipping Methods table.

You can use one of the following four ways to display a related field in a report:

- **Add the field to the record source query:** If the record source of the report is a table, you must create a new query containing all the fields in the report. View the query in the Query window and add the related table that contains the related field you want to display. For example, add the Shipping Methods table to the query, then add the related field to the query grid. When you use this query as the record source of the report, you can create a control that displays the field. This method is usually the simplest way to display a related field on a report.

- **Use a combo box:** Although combo boxes don't work on reports for their primary purpose—selecting values from a list—they are useful for displaying one or more values from a related table or query. To display a related value using a combo box control:

  1. Select the Combo Box tool from the toolbox and drag the field name from the field list.

  2. On the property sheet for the combo box control, select the name of the related table for the Row Source property, for example, the Shipping Methods table.

     The combo box displays fields from the related table starting with the first field.

  3. For the Column Count property, enter the column number of the field you want. For example, if the Shipping Method field, which contains the full description, is the second field in the Shipping Methods table, enter **2** for the Column Count property.

  4. For the Column Widths property, enter widths for the columns, separated by semicolons. For fields you do not want to display,

enter a column width of 0. For example, this entry hides the first column and displays the second with a width of 2 inches:

```
0 in;2 in
```

5. Set the Border Style property to Clear if you do not want a box around the entry.

6. Set the Font Name and Font Size properties to match the other text on the report.

On the report, the combo box looks just like a text box, and this is an easy way to display a related value on a report. By setting the Column Count property to display more columns, you can also display more than one field from the related table.

- **Make a subreport:** If you want to display several records of related values, a subreport is perfect. For example, the booksellers database includes a report called Books with Sales, shown in Figure 13.1. The listing of copies sold is a subreport. See *Printing a Subreport for Each Record* in Chapter 11 for how to create a subreport.

- **Use the DLookUp() function in an expression in a text box control:** This method works if the value you want to look up is also displayed on the report. The DLookUp function looks like this:

```
=DLookUp("[targetfield]", "table", "[lookupfield] =
  Report.[controlname]")
```

The *targetfield* is the field in the related table that you want to display. In our example, it is the Shipping Method field in the Shipping

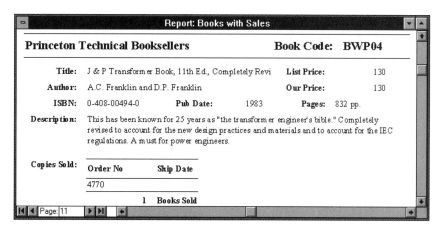

Figure 13.1   Books report with a subreport listing sales.

Methods table, which displays a description like *U.S. Book Mail*. The *table* is the related table (Shipping Methods). The *lookupfield* is the field in the related table that contains the code that relates to the field in the report. For example, the Ship Via field in the Shipping Methods table contains the codes we want to look up. And the *controlname* is the name of the control on the report that displays the code you want to look up, also named Ship Via in this example. For example, the DLOOKUP() function would load like this:

```
=DLookUp("[Shipping Method]", "Shipping Methods", "[Ship Via] =
    Report.[SV]")
```

To use the DLookUp() function, you must make two text box controls, one to display the code you are looking up, and the other to display the result of the lookup. For example, you must make one text box to display the Ship Via field. To use the DLookUp() function:

1. Make a text box to display the code, that is, the field that you want to look up (Ship Via). You can make the text box invisible if you don't want the code to appear on the report (just set the Visible property to No). Don't name this control with the field name; give it another name, like SV.

2. Make a text box with the expression containing DLookUp(). For example, to look up the Shipping Method in the Shipping Methods table, the second text box could use the expression shown above.

This function looks up the value of the SV control (which contains the Ship Via field) in the Shipping Methods table, looking for the record with the same code in the Ship Via field, and returning the corresponding value of the Shipping Method field. Don't forget to enclose each of the three parts of the DLookUp() function in quotes, and to use square brackets around field and control names.

As you can see, this last method is confusing, error-prone, and requires that you make an extra control on the report. I highly recommend using another method to display a related value!

Printing a Running Sum

Access makes printing a running sum easy—use the Running Sum property of a text box control.

In reports with numeric values, you may want to see a running sum—for example, a running sum of sales. To print a running sum for each record:

1. In the Detail section of the report, create a text box control.
2. For the Control Source property of the text box, enter the name of the field you want to sum.
3. For the Running Sum property, select Over All.

You can also print a running sum of a calculated control. For example, in a sales report, you might calculate the profit on each sale in a text box control named Profit. You can make another text box with this expression in the Control Source property:

```
=[Profit]
```

If you set the Running Sum property to Over All, Access displays a running sum of the calculated control.

Use Control Names in Expressions

Access allows you use a control name in an expression in the Detail section of the report, though it is not allowed when calculating totals using Sum() and other functions (see *Summarizing the Records* later in this chapter). Enclose the control name (in the previous topic example, Profit) in square brackets just as if it were a field in the record source of the report.

Number the Records in a Report

Use the Running Sum property to number the records, starting with 1, in a report.

To number the records in a report, create a running sum text box as described in the previous topic. For the Control Source property, enter this expression:

```
= 1
```

This expression tells Access to add one to the displayed value for each record, starting at the first record and continuing for the whole report.

Printing a Control at Fixed Intervals

You can print a line or other text every n records by using a running sum control to count the records.

A report with a long list of items may be easier to read if you include a line every few records. Here's how it works: create one control containing a running sum and another control with a conditional calculation The expression in the second control will use the value of the first control to determine when *n* records have been printed first. To display a line every five records:

1. Create a hidden running sum control. That is, create a text box in the Detail section of the report with these property settings:

    Control Name: Record Count

    Control Source: =1

    Running Sum: Over All

    Visible: No

2. Create another text box in the Detail section that contains an expression like this:

    ```
    =IIf([Record Count] Mod 5=0, "_____", "")
    ```

The Mod (modulo) operator divides Record Count by five and looks at the remainder. If Record Count is a multiple of five, the remainder will be zero and the expression will display a line (a series of underscore characters). Otherwise, it will display nothing. You can use graphics characters instead of underscores to produce other types of lines (see *Entering Special Characters* in Chapter 4), or use asterisks. Figure 13.2 shows a report in Design view containing a list of book titles that the mail-order bookseller carries.

3. To avoid leaving blank space between each record, set the Can Shrink property of the second text box to Yes. Also set the Can Shrink property of the Detail section to Yes.

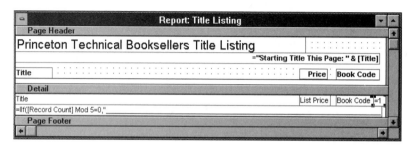

Figure 13.2 Controls to print a line every five records.

4. Since the line is created as a series of underline characters, the space above the line is determined by the font size of the control. To avoid a large space above the line, set the font size of the control to a small size, like 5 points.

Printing the Record Count at Intervals

You can use the technique described in the previous topic to print a count of records printed every n records.

If you want to print the record number every 10 records, you can use the same method:

1. Follow Step 1 from the previous topic to create a hidden running sum control named Record Count.

2. Make a text box in the Detail section that contains this expression:

    ```
    =IIf([Record Count] Mod 10=0, [Record Count], "")
    ```

3. If the text box is on a line by itself, set the Can Shrink property of the text box and the Detail section to Yes. If the text box is on a line with other controls, skip this step.

   Figure 13.3 shows a report with a line every five records (as described in the previous topic) and the record count every ten.

Report: Title Listing		
Princeton Technical Booksellers Title Listing		
	Starting Title This Page: 3 1/2 inch Disk for Complete Guide to PC-File	
Title	**Price**	**Book Code**
3 1/2 inch Disk for Complete Guide to PC-File	$7.00	CBP04-3
5 1/4 inch disk for The Complete Guide to PC-File	$7.00	CBP04-5
Adhesives in Manufacture	$185.00	MDP09
Adhesives Technology Handbook	$64.00	NYP08
Adhesives, Adherends, Adhesion	$31.50	KRP02
Advanced Ceramic Materials	$64.00	NYP04
Advanced Thermoset Composites: Industrial & Commercial Applications	$43.50	WDP02
AI and Expert Systems	$29.95	MCP33
An Encyclopedia of Metallurgy and Materials	$145.00	BRP07
Analysis of Distance Protection	$87.95	WIP54 10

Figure 13.3 Report with a line every five records and the record count every ten.

Summarizing the Records

You can create totals for any numeric field in a report or a count of any field. You can also count all records for which a condition is true, for example, all orders over $500.00.

To display a sum, count, average, or other summary of all or selected records in the report, create a text box control in the Report Header or Report Footer section. Enter an expression in the Control Source property of the text box, referring to one or more fields in the reports record source. The expression can use one of the *aggregate functions* listed in Table 13.1.

You must use these aggregate functions in the Report Header or Report Footer sections of the report if you want the functions to include all the records in the report. When you use them in the Group Header or Group Footer sections, they create subtotals rather than totals (see *Printing Subtotals,* later in this chapter). Don't use aggregate functions in the Page Header or Page footer sections. If you do, *#Error* appears on the report.

Table 13.1 Aggregate Functions

Function	Purpose
Sum()	Adds up the values of a field
Count()	Counts the number of values in a field
Avg()	Averages the values of a text box control in a field
Min()	Displays the minimum value of a field: For numeric values, the minimum value is the smallest number; for text values, the minimum value is the first in alphabetical order; for dates, the minimum value is the first date
Max()	Displays the maximum value of a field: For numeric values, the maximum value is the largest number; for text values, the maximum value is the last in alphabetical order; for dates, the maximum value is the last date
First()	Displays the value of a field for the first record in the report
Last()	Displays the value of a field for the last record in the report
StDev() and StDevP()	Calculates the standard deviation of a field: StDev() calculates the standard deviation for a population, and StDevP() calculates the standard deviation for a population sample
Var() and VarP()	Calculates the statistical variance of a field, for a population or population sample

This section describes some expressions you can use when summarizing the records in a report.

Printing the Number of Records in the Report

Use the Count( ) function to print the record count.

To print the number of records in a report, use this expression in a text box in the Report Header or Report Footer section:

```
= Count(*)
```

If you want to display the number of records that contain non-blank values in a text box, you can use the Count function like this:

```
= Count([fieldname])
```

The *fieldname* must be the name of a field in the record source of the report. It can't be the name of a text box control. For example, if you want to count a text box control named Field23 that displays a field named Tax Exempt?, use this expression:

```
= Count([Tax Exempt?])
```

Print Totals in the Report Header, Too

The report header can contain a text box that displays the total number of records in the report. Don't worry that Access hasn't "gotten to" the records yet when it prints the total. Access formats a report in two passes: In the first pass, Access calculates all expressions, including aggregate functions; in the second pass, Access determines where the information will appear on the page, including where pages will break.

Printing a Total of a Calculated Control

You cannot include the name of a control in a Sum( ) or other aggregate function.

To calculate the total of a calculated control, you must repeat the expression from the calculated control in the total expression. For example, in the Sales Ledger report in the bookseller database, the Profit text box control might calculate the estimated profit for each order using this expression:

```
=[Total Book Amt]*0.33
```

You might think that placing the expression

```
=Sum([Profit])
```

in the Report Header or Report Footer section will produce the total profit, but it won't. Because Profit is a calculated text box control on the report, not a field in the record source, Access can't perform aggregate functions using its value. Instead, use one of these two approaches:

- Incorporate the expression from the calculated control into the expression for the total. For example, you can use this expression to calculate the total profit for the report:

  ```
  =Sum([Total Book Amt]*.33)
  ```

- Add a calculated field to the record source of the report (see *Calculated Fields in Queries versus Calculations in Text Boxes* at the beginning of this chapter).

Using Subreports to Print Totals

Totals can include more than just the sums of the records in the report. You can include crosstabs and other summary information by using a subreport.

If you want to display more complex totals, such as ratios or other analyses, use a subreport that pulls data from a total or crosstab query, and create an unbound subreport control in the Report Header or Report Footer section. For example, at the end of the Sales Ledger report, rather than just totaling the various amounts in the report, you can include an analysis of sales by month or by book. You can even include two subreports to display both analyses!

To display summary information using a subreport:

1. Create a new report that displays the summary information you want to include at the end of your existing report. For example, make a report named Sales by Month that looks like Figure 13.4. The report has nothing in the Detail section, so no information is displayed for each record. It is grouped on the month of the sale date. Figure 13.5 shows the report in Design view.

2. Save and close the new report.

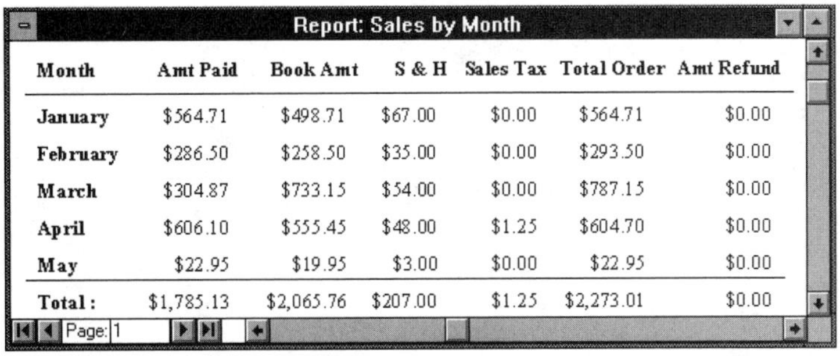

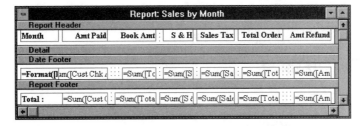

Figure 13.4 Report to be used as a subreport.

Figure 13.5 Design view of subreport.

3. Open the original report in Design view.

4. Select the new report from the Database window and drag it onto the original report, in the Report Header or Report Footer section. Access creates a new subreport control to contain the report.

5. Erase any entries that Access has made in the Link Child Fields and Link Master Fields of the subreport control. These properties should be blank so that the subreport is unbound and displays totals for the whole report.

6. Size the subreport control so that it is wide enough to display the full width of the report. Set the Can Grow property of the subreport control and of the Report Header or Report Footer section to Yes, so that the subreport control can grow to display the full length of the subreport. Figure 13.6 shows the Design view of the finished report, with the subreport control in the Report Footer section.

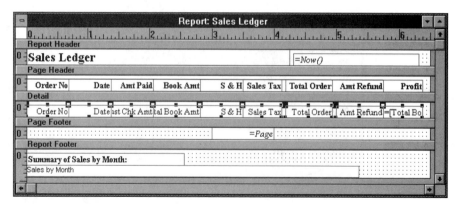

Figure 13.6   Summary of sales by month contained as a subreport in the Report Footer section.

Printing Subtotals

Access uses *groups* (also called *subtotal groups*) to create subtotals in reports. By selecting a field to group on, you tell Access to sort the records in the report by that field, to consider records that have the same value (or partial value) of the field as a group, and optionally to print a group header before each group and a group footer after each group. The field you group on is called the *group field* or *control break field.* You specify grouping for a report using the Sorting and Grouping dialog box.

The easiest way to create a report with subtotals is to use the Groups/ Totals ReportWizard. This ReportWizard makes a report with group headers and footers for each field you group on.

This section provides methods of creating subtotal groups manually, changing grouping specifications, and using group headers and footers to create a variety of reports.

Modifying Reports Created by the Groups/Totals ReportWizard

Once you have used the Groups/Totals ReportWizard to create a report with subtotals, you can make changes to the report in Design view.

The Groups/Totals ReportWizard creates reports that contain subtotals and totals for all Number and Currency fields in the report. You will need to delete the subtotals and totals for numeric fields that don't contain numbers to be totaled, like order numbers or check numbers. Delete unwanted total controls from both the Group Footer and Report Footer sections. You can also add other types of totals, like counts and averages, to the Group Header or Group Footer sections.

Creating and Changing Subtotal Groups

Use the Sorting and Grouping dialog box to control how a report is sorted and grouped.

To create subtotal groups manually, use the Sorting and Grouping dialog box, shown in Figure 13.7. To display the dialog box, choose View Sorting and Grouping from the menu, or click on the Sorting And Grouping button on the toolbar.

You can add a new group by filling in the Field/Expression column in the dialog box and choosing values for Sort Order, Group On, and Group Interval. You can delete a group by deleting a row from the table. You can also change the precedence of groups by changing their order in the dialog box—just select the row that describes the group and drag it up or down to its new position. A group's position in the table determines its precedence: The first group creates subtotals, the second group creates sub-subtotals, and so forth. For example, Figure 13.7 shows settings that create a group on the Book Code field, with a group header and group footer that prints for each book. Within the group for each book, records are sorted by the Order No field (the Group Header and Group Footer property are set to No for the Order No field). Figure 13.8 shows the resulting report in Design view.

To sort the records in the report by a field without grouping records by the field, set the Group Header and Group Footer properties, located in the lower part of the dialog box, to No.

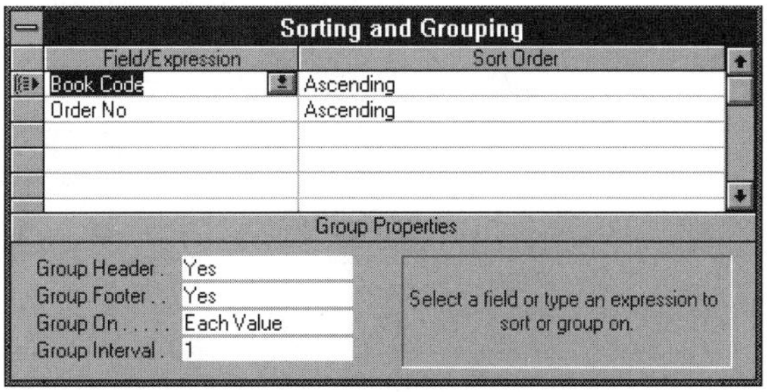

Figure 13.7 Creating or modifying sorting and grouping in a report.

Creating a Header for a Group

Include identifying information about the group in its header. You can also include counts, sums, and averages.

If you want to print information at the beginning of each group, follow these steps to create a Group Header section:

1. Display the Sorting and Grouping dialog box by choosing View Sorting and Grouping from the menu, or by clicking on the Sorting And Grouping button on the toolbar.

2. If you haven't already created a group, enter the field or expression on which you want to group in the Field/Expression column and choose a setting for Sort Order. Otherwise, select the row for the group for which you want a group header.

3. Choose Yes for the Group Header property.

4. Close the Sorting and Grouping dialog box by double-clicking on the Control-menu box. In Design view, the report now includes a Group Header section for the group.

5. In the Group Header section, create a text box control that displays the value of the field or expression on which you are grouping (the group field). For example, Figure 13.8 shows a text box in the Book Code Header section that displays the book code. You can also include labels or other controls. You may want to include a line control at the top of the Group Header section to divide one group from the next.

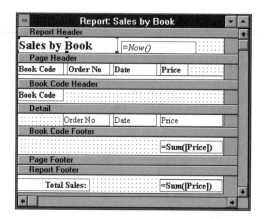

Figure 13.8 Design view of report with group header and footer.

Identify Each Group without a Group Header

You can also display the value of the group field at the beginning of each group without using a group header. Simply include a text box that displays the group field in the Detail section of the report. By default the text box will display the group value over and over for each record, as shown in Figure 13.9. However, you can set the text box's Hide Duplicates property to Yes to suppress the display of all but the first record in each group, as shown in Figure 13.10. This report contains no group header section.

Creating Subtotals for a Group

Include totals, counts, and other summary information about the records in a group in the Group Footer section of the report. If you think that the records will continue onto another page, repeat the identifying information from the header.

	Report: Sales by Book		
MDP19	4781	4/17/93	$228.00
			$228.00
PTP01-3	4739	1/1/93	$5.00
PTP01-3	4766	3/1/93	$4.00
PTP01-3	4779	4/6/93	$5.00
			$14.00
PTP01-5	4750	1/22/93	$5.00
PTP01-5	4777	4/6/93	$5.00
PTP01-5	4778	4/6/93	$5.00
			$15.00
Total Sales:			$2,083.96

Figure 13.9   Displaying the group field in the Detail section.

	Report: Sales by Book		
MDP19	4781	4/17/93	$228.00
			$228.00
PTP01-3	4739	1/1/93	$5.00
	4766	3/1/93	$4.00
	4779	4/6/93	$5.00
			$14.00
PTP01-5	4750	1/22/93	$5.00
	4777	4/6/93	$5.00
	4778	4/6/93	$5.00
			$15.00
Total Sales:			$2,083.96

Figure 13.10   Hiding all but the first value of the group field in each group.

If you want to print information at the end of each group, follow these steps to create a Group Footer section:

1. Display the Sorting and Grouping dialog box.

2. Select the row for the group for which you want a group footer.

3. Choose Yes for the Group Footer property.

4. Close the Sorting and Grouping dialog box by double-clicking on the Control-menu box. In Design view, the report now includes a Group Footer section for the group.

5. In the Group Footer section, create text box controls that display totals, counts, or other summaries of the records in the group. In the expression in the Control Source of the text box control, you can use the same aggregate functions described in Table 13.1: Sum(), Count(), Avg(), Min(), Max(), First(), Last(), StDev(), StDevP(), Var(), and VarP(). When Access calculates these functions in a group header or footer, it automatically restricts the records to those in the current group. For example, the Sum() function totals the values of a field for all the records in the current group. To subtotal the amount paid for each book in the current group, you would use this expression in the text box control:

   ```
   = Sum([Price])
   ```

   If you want the summary information to appear at the beginning of each group, place the text boxes in the Group Header section.

6. To leave some space between one group and the next, leave blank space at the bottom of the Group Footer section.

Starting Each Group on a New Page

Use the properties of the Group Header and Group Footer sections to control page breaks.

To start each group at the top of a new page, you can use the Force New Page property of the Group Header or Group Footer section. You can set this property in one of two ways:

• Set the Force New Page property of the group header to Before Section

• Set the Force New Page property of the group footer to After Section

It is better to use the first method, so that any controls in the page header that display information about the group, display information about the new group, not the previous group.

If you start a new page for each group, you may want to display information about the group in the Page Header section. By placing identifying information about the group in the page header, the identifying information will be repeated on each page if the group extends over multiple pages. For example, you can display the group field in the page header. Figure 13.11 shows the Sales by Book report, in which the Force New Page property of the Book Code Header is set to Before Section. The Page Header section contains text box controls to display both the Book Code, which is the group field, and the Title field. If there are several pages of sales for a book, the Book Code and Title fields for the book are repeated at the top of each page.

In multi-column reports, you can also start a new row or column for each group by using the New Row or Col property of the group header or footer (see *Creating Multiple Column Reports* in Chapter 14).

Grouping on the First Letter

You can make a telephone directory-style report with breaks for each letter.

In the Sorting and Grouping dialog box, Access provides the Group On and Group Interval properties that allow you to make more sophisticated types of groups. To print a heading every time the first letter of a field changes:

1. In the Sorting and Grouping dialog box, make a group for the field. For example, in a listing of book titles, make a group for the Title field.

2. Set the Group Header property to Yes and set the Group Footer property to No, unless you want to print summary information at the end of the entries for each letter.

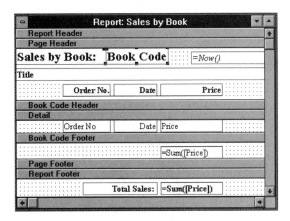

Figure 13.11   Displaying group information in the Page Header section.

3. Set the Group On property to Prefix Characters.

4. Set the Group Interval property to 1. For example, the Title Listing by Letter report in the bookseller database contains the group shown in Figure 13.12.

5. Close the Sorting and Grouping dialog box.

6. In the Group Header section of the report, create a text box with this expression in the Control Source property:

```
=Left([field], 1)
```

Use the name of the group field for the *field* portion of the entry. This expression displays the first letter of the group field (for example, the title) in the group heading. Figure 13.13 shows the Titles by Letter report in Design view. Figure 13.14 shows the same report in Print Preview.

You can use the same method to create subtotal groups based on the first few letters of a code. For example, if the first two letters of the book code indicate the publisher of the book, you can group on publisher by using the Book Code field as the group field, setting Group On to Prefix Characters and setting the Group Interval to 2. To print the publisher code in the group heading, use this expression in the Control Source of a text box control:

```
=Left([Book Code], 2)
```

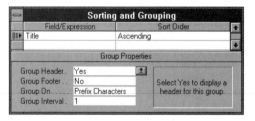

Figure 13.12 Grouping by the first letter of the book title.

Figure 13.13 The design of a report to print letter headings.

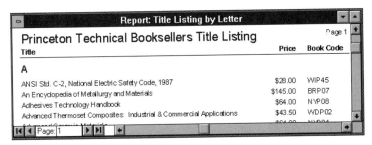

Figure 13.14 A report with letter headings.

You could also display the full name of the publisher by looking up the two-letter publisher code in the Publishers table (see *Printing a Field from Another Table,* earlier in this chapter).

Grouping on Weeks, Months, Quarters, or Years

When the group field is a date, you can set the Group On property to Each Value (so that there is a group for each separate value of the field), or to Year, Qtr, Month, Week, Day, Hour, or Minute.

To create a group based on a Date/Time field that groups entries by a time period:

1. In the Sorting and Grouping dialog box, make a group for the field. For example, in a listing of book sales, make a group for the Date field.
2. If you want to print a group header, set the Group Header property to Yes. If you want to print summary information at the end of the entries for each period, set the Group Footer property to Yes.
3. Set the Group On property to the time period, for example, Week.
4. Set the Group Interval property to 1.
5. Close the Sorting and Grouping dialog box.
6. In the Group Header or Detail section of the report, display the date formatted to match the period on which you are grouping. Create a text box with an expression in the Control Source property that uses the Format() function:

    ```
    =Format([field], "format")
    ```

For the *field*, use the name of the group field. For the *format*, use one of the custom formats listed in Table 13.2 to indicate what part of the date you want Access to display.

Table 13.2   Formats for Converting a Date to a Specified Period

Period Code	Meaning
yyyy	Year
q	Quarter number (1 to 4)
m	Month number (1 to 12)
mmmm	Month name (for instance, January)
ww	Week number (1 to 53)
d	Day number
h	Hour
n	Minute

The topic *Formatting Date/Time Values* in Chapter 5 contains additional date formats you can use. For example, if you are grouping by quarters, use this expression to display the quarter and the year (for example 2Q1994):

```
=Format([Date], "q") & "Q" & Format([Date], "yyyy")
```

To display the week and year (for example 16 Week 1995), use this expression:

```
=Format([Date], "ww") & " Week " & Format([Date], "yyyy")
```

If you place the text box control in the Detail section, set its Hide Duplicate property to Yes so that it is displayed only for the first record.

7. If you want subtotals for the section, enter them in the Group Header or Group Footer section of the report. Figure 13.15 shows the Sales by Week report in Design view, and Figure 13.16 shows the resulting report.

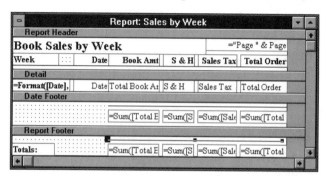

Figure 13.15   The design of a report that groups sales by week.

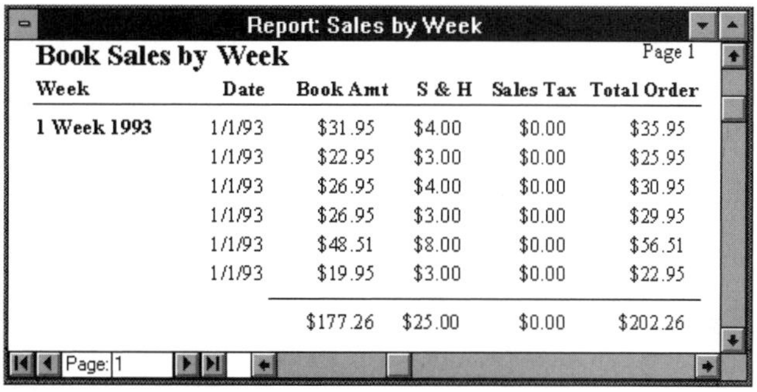

Report: Sales by Week					
Book Sales by Week					Page 1
Week	Date	Book Amt	S & H	Sales Tax	Total Order
1 Week 1993	1/1/93	$31.95	$4.00	$0.00	$35.95
	1/1/93	$22.95	$3.00	$0.00	$25.95
	1/1/93	$26.95	$4.00	$0.00	$30.95
	1/1/93	$26.95	$3.00	$0.00	$29.95
	1/1/93	$48.51	$8.00	$0.00	$56.51
	1/1/93	$19.95	$3.00	$0.00	$22.95
		$177.26	$25.00	$0.00	$202.26

Page: 1

Figure 13.16 A report that groups sales by week.

Numbering the Records in Each Group

On forms such as packing slips and invoices, you can number the items on each form.

To number the records in each group, starting over at 1 at the beginning of each group, make a text box in the Detail section of the report with this expression in the Control Source property:

=1

Set the Running Sum property to Over Groups to tell Access to reset the value for each group.

Printing Running Sums for Each Group

You can print running totals for each record that reset to zero at the beginning of each group.

To make a control that prints a running sum by group:

1. Create a text box in the Detail section of the report and select the name of the field for which you want a running sum. For example, in the Sales by Week report, you might want to make a running sum of sales for the week, so enter Total Order as the Control Source for the text box.

2. Set the Running Sum property to Over Groups.

Alternatively, you may want to create a running sum that is displayed just once for each group, not for each record. That is, you may want a running sum of group totals, accumulating over the whole report:

1. Create a text box in the Group Header or Group Footer section. For the Control Source property, enter the value for which you want a running sum. For example, in the Sales by Week report, you can enter this expression to make a running sum of the total sales for the week:

```
=Sum([Total Order])
```

2. Set the Running Sum property to Over Groups. Figure 13.17 shows the Design view of a report with a running sum for groups, and Figure 13.18 shows the resulting report.

You can make a running sum of a calculated amount as well as of a field—just enter an expression instead of a field name in the text box control. To create a running sum of the number of records in each group, use the Count() function in a text box control in the Group Header or Footer Section.

Printing a Subreport for Each Group

A subreport can contain totals and other summary information for each group.

You can place a bound subreport control in the Group Header or Group Footer section of a report. By linking the subreport based on the group field, the subreport displays information about that group. For example, if you add a subreport to the Sales by Book report, which is grouped by Book code, you can print additional information about each book.

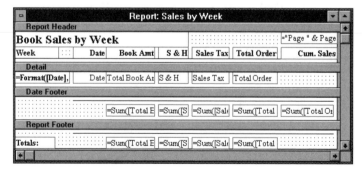

Figure 13.17 The design of a report with a running total of weekly sales.

Report: Sales by Week						
1 Week 1993	1/1/93	$31.95	$4.00	$0.00	$35.95	
	1/1/93	$22.95	$3.00	$0.00	$25.95	
	1/1/93	$26.95	$4.00	$0.00	$30.95	
	1/1/93	$26.95	$3.00	$0.00	$29.95	
	1/1/93	$48.51	$8.00	$0.00	$56.51	
	1/1/93	$19.95	$3.00	$0.00	$22.95	
		$177.26	$25.00	$0.00	$202.26	$202.26
3 Week 1993	1/11/93	$22.95	$4.00	$0.00	$26.95	
	1/11/93	$26.95	$3.00	$0.00	$29.95	
	1/13/93	$79.95	$4.00	$0.00	$83.95	
	1/13/93	$19.95	$3.00	$0.00	$22.95	
		$149.80	$14.00	$0.00	$163.80	$366.06

Page: 1

Figure 13.18 A report with a running total of weekly sales.

To print a subreport for each group:

1. Create a report to use as the subreport. For example, you can make a report that lists the company names and job titles of people who bought books, as shown in Figure 13.19.

2. In Design view, open the report you want to add the subreport to. For example, open the Sales by Book report.

3. Make the Group Header or Footer section large enough to fit the subreport (you can also adjust it later).

4. Select the subreport from the Database window and drag it to the Group Header or Group Footer section. For example, drag the Customer Companies report to the Book Code Footer section. Access creates a subreport control to contain the subreport.

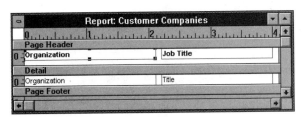

Figure 13.19 Report to use as a subreport.

5. Make the subreport control wide enough to display the full width of the subreport. Set the Can Grow property of both the control and the section to Yes, so that the subreport control can expand to display the full length of the subreport.

6. Enter the name of the group field in the Link Child Fields and Link Master Fields properties of the subreport control to tell Access to include only information about records in the group. Figure 13.20 shows the report in Design view, and Figure 13.21 shows the resulting report.

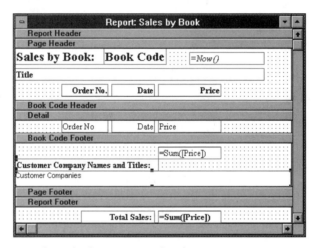

Figure 13.20 A bound subreport control in the Group Footer section.

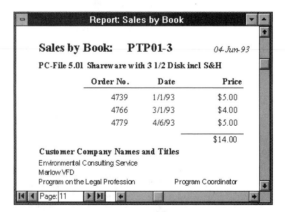

Figure 13.21 Printing additional information about each group in the Group Footer section.

Printing the Percentages of the Total

You can find out what percentage a group represents of the report total. For example, what percentage do the sales for each book represent of all sales?

To print the percentage that each group represents of the total for the report:

1. Create groups with subtotals, as described in *Creating Subtotals for a Group* earlier in this chapter. For example, in the Sales by Book report, the group field is Book Code, and the Book Code Footer section includes a text box that sums the sales for each book using this expression:

    ```
    =Sum([Price])
    ```

2. Enter a meaningful name in the Control Name property of the text box control that contains the quantity for which you want the percentage. For example, enter *Book Total* for the name of the control in the Book Code Footer section that sums the sales for each book.

3. Create a control in the Report Header or Report Footer section that calculates the grand total of the field. You can probably use the same expression as in Step 1: Since the control is in the Report Header or Report Footer section instead of the Group Header or Group Footer section, Access includes all the records in the report instead of just those in each group.

4. Enter a meaningful name as the Control Name of the grand total control. For example, enter *Total Sales* for the name of the control in the report footer.

5. In the Group Header or Group Footer section, create a text box control to calculate the percentage. Enter an expression that divides the group total by the grand total, for example:

    ```
    =[Book Total]/[Total Sales]
    ```

6. Choose Percent for the Format property of this control. Figure 13.22 shows the Sales by Book report in Design view, and Figure 13.23 shows the resulting report.

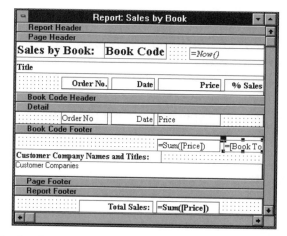

Figure 13.22   Displaying a percentage in the Group Footer section.

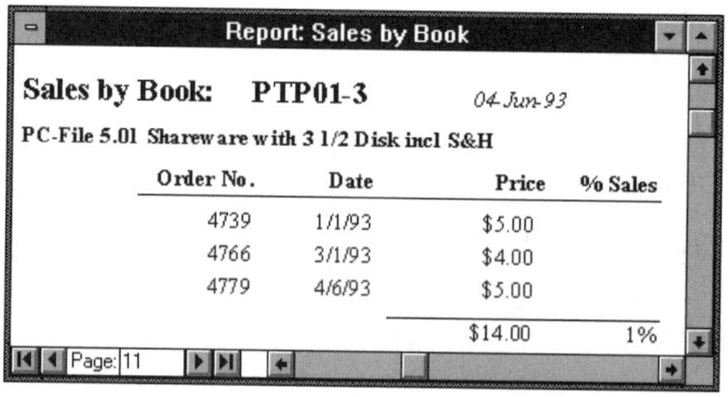

Figure 13.23   Printing the percentage each group represents of the whole report.

Printing a Summary Report

A summary report doesn't include information from individual records, only subtotals and totals.

There are two ways to create a summary report:

- Hide the Detail section by setting its Visible property to No.
- Leave the Detail section blank, and drag the bottom edge of the Detail section upward so that its length is zero.

Either way, Access will not print anything for each record. For example, if you want weekly sales data with no details of individual sales, you could modify the Sales by Week report, eliminating or hiding the Detail section.

Sample Report Formats

The last three chapters described tips and techniques for designing and printing reports. Now let's look at the most common types of reports: columnar reports, form letters, mailing labels, envelopes, invoices, membership lists, and transaction ledgers. This chapter contains guidelines for the best way to create and print each of these common report types.

Columnar Reports

Columnar reports can come in many formats: reports that look like spreadsheets (frequently based on crosstab queries) and reports with columns that snake like those of a newspaper. Here are ways to create each of these types of columnar reports.

Creating Reports That Look Like Spreadsheets

Start with the Groups/Total ReportWizard, then modify the report to add your own calculations.

The easiest way to create a columnar report is to use the Groups/Totals ReportWizard. This ReportWizard arranges the fields you select in rows, and sorts and groups them. Once the Goups/Teotals ReportWizard has completed your report, switch to Design view to modify its output:

- Eliminate the extra space between the rows of the report by closing up the blank space in the Detail section of the report
- Add row totals or other calculations to appear on each row of the report, by creating calculated text boxes in the Detail section of the report
- Delete column totals for numeric fields that shouldn't be totaled, like order numbers and ages
- Add counts, averages, ratios, and other information at the end of the report, by creating calculated text boxes in the Report Footer section

HOT TIP

Align Column Heads over Numeric Columns

In columnar reports, it is important to position the column headers (which are usually in the Page Header section) over the columns. For columns containing numeric values, place a label control above the text box control in the Detail section, and click on the Align-Right button on the toolbar to align the label to the right side of the control, to match the alignment of the numbers.

Hiding Repeating Values

You can suppress printing repeated values in a column.

If you sort the records in a report by a field, and many records contain the same value, the value is printed over and over for each record. To avoid this duplication, you can set the Hide Duplicates property of the text box control to Yes. With this modification, Access prints the value the first time it appears, then hides it for subsequent records.

For example, the Sales Ledger report in the mail-order booksellers database, shown in Figure 14.1, contains one line for each order. The report is sorted by date. To avoid repeating the same date over and over, the Hide Duplicates property of the Date field is set to Yes. Figure 14.2 shows the resulting report.

Suppressing Zero Values

In some reports, you may want zero values to appear blank, or as dashes.

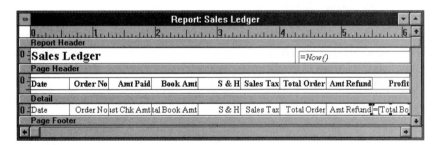

Figure 14.1 Design view of the Sales Ledger report.

Date	Order No	Amt Paid	Book Amt	S & H	Sales Tax	Total Order	Amt Refund	Profit
1/1/93	4738	$22.95	$19.95	$3.00	$0.00	$22.95	$0.00	$6.58
	4739	$35.95	$31.95	$4.00	$0.00	$35.95	$0.00	$10.54
	4740	$25.95	$22.95	$3.00	$0.00	$25.95	$0.00	$7.57
	4741	$30.95	$26.95	$4.00	$0.00	$30.95	$0.00	$8.89
	4742	$29.95	$26.95	$3.00	$0.00	$29.95	$0.00	$8.89
	4743	$56.51	$48.51	$8.00	$0.00	$56.51	$0.00	$16.01
1/11/93	4744	$26.95	$22.95	$4.00	$0.00	$26.95	$0.00	$7.57
	4745	$29.95	$26.95	$3.00	$0.00	$29.95	$0.00	$8.89
1/13/93	4746	$83.95	$79.95	$4.00	$0.00	$83.95	$0.00	$26.38

Sales Ledger — 05-Jun-93

Figure 14.2 Report with each date printed once.

You can instruct Access to print nothing when a field is zero by adding this expression to the Control Source field's text box:

```
=IIf([field]=0, "", [field])
```

For example, in Figure 14.2 the Sales Tax and Amt Refund columns contain mainly zeros. It would be easier to spot the occasional records for which these fields are non-zero if the zero values didn't print. To suppress zero printing for the Sales Tax field, change the Control Source of its text box to this expression:

```
=IIf([Sales Tax]=0, "", [Sales Tax])
```

If the Control Name of the control is Sales Tax, change it to another name to avoid an #Error value. (Remember, the Control Name of a text box containing an expression can't be the same as a field name in the expression.) For example, you can change it to Sales Tax2.

To print zeros as dashes or other characters, you can enclose the character in the quotes in the expression, like this:

```
=IIf([Sales Tax]=0, "—", [Sales Tax])
```

Creating Snaking-Column Reports

You can create newspaper-style multiple-column reports in Access by specifying the number of columns and the column type in the Print Setup dialog box.

In a two-column "snaking-column" report, you size the Detail section of the report to half the width of the page. When Access reaches the bottom of the page, it continues displaying records in the right half of the top of the page. You use the Print Setup dialog box to tell Access how many columns to create and how to fill the columns with information from the Detail section of the report. To print snaking-column reports with two or more columns:

1. Make the Detail section and any Group Header or Group Footer sections the width of one column. For example, if you want the column to be 3–1/2 inches wide, make the Detail section 3–1/2 inches wide. The Page and Report Header and Footer sections span the page normally. Access won't let you move the right edge of the Detail section leftward if other sections are wider, but don't worry. Just make sure that all the controls in the Detail section fall within the one-column width.

For example, Figure 14.3 shows the Brochure report from the bookseller database. This report will print a two-column brochure. Notice that the Report Header, Page Header, and Page Footer sections are the full width of a page, and that the Detail section is 3.8 inches wide.

2. To prevent the data in a record from being split across columns, set the Keep Together property for the Detail section to Yes.

3. Choose File Print Setup from the menu to display the Print Setup dialog box.

4. Click on the More button to display options for multi-column reports, shown in Figure 14.4.

5. Set the Items Across option to the number of columns you want on each page.

6. Set the Row Spacing option to the amount of space you want between each record in the Detail section. If you left space between the last control in the Detail section and the bottom edge of the Detail section, set this option to 0.

7. Set the Column Spacing options to the amount of space you want between the columns. This space is called the *gutter*.

8. Set the Item Size Width to the width of the Detail section, in this case, 3.8 inches.

9. Set the Item Size Height to the height of the Detail section. If you have set the Can Grow property of the Detail section to Yes, this height measurement won't prevent the section from growing.

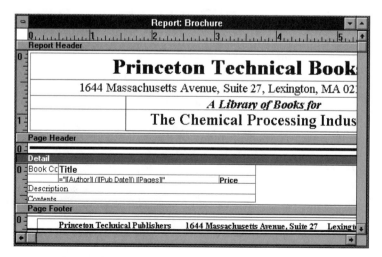

Figure 14.3 The Brochure report, set up for two-column printing.

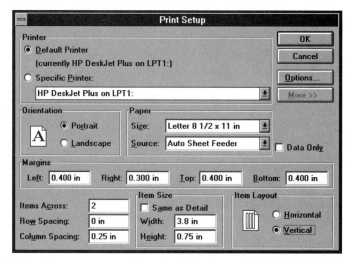

Figure 14.4   Setting up a two-column report.

10. Set the Item Layout box to Vertical, so Access fills up each column before starting the next. (If you choose Horizontal, Access prints a snaking-rows report, which is described in the next topic.)

11. Click on OK to exit from the Print Setup dialog box. Figure 14.5 shows the Brochure report in Print Preview.

Note: You can use this procedure to print multiple-column output from a form, as well as from a report.

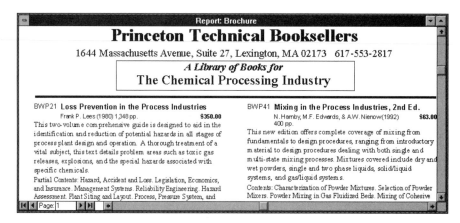

Figure 14.5   A two-column report.

Creating Snaking-Row Reports

Access can print records across the page, starting a new row when the previous row is full.

A snaking-row report is like a snaking-column report, except that Access fills each row before starting the next. For example, in a two-column, snaking-column report, Access prints the records in this order:

A F
B G
C H
D I
E J

In a two-column, snaking-row report, the records appear in this order:

A B
C D
E F
G H
I J

To create a snaking-row report, follow the steps in the previous topic to make a snaking-column reports, but in step 10, set the Item Layout option to Horizontal.

Starting a New Row or Column for Each Group

In snaking-column or snaking-row reports with groups, you can decide where to print the beginning of each group.

What if your snaking-column or snaking-row report contains group headers and footers? Access prints the Group Header and Group Footer sections in columns too, limiting their width to the width of one column. For example Figure 14.6 shows a two-column, snaking-row report listing book titles by publisher, and the resulting report is shown in Figure 14.7. It is hard to tell which publisher some titles are listed under.

Figure 14.6 Design view of a snaking-column report with groups.

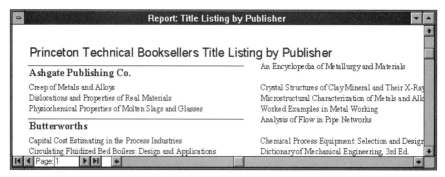

Figure 14.7 Two-column report of titles grouped by publisher.

To fix this problem, set the New Row Or Col property for the group header to Before & After. Now the Publisher Header section always prints in the left-hand column, as does the first title for each publisher. Figure 14.8 shows the report.

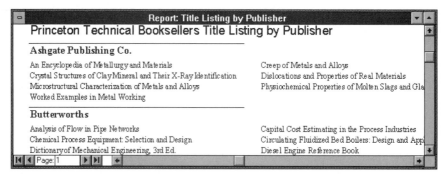

Figure 14.8 Snaking-rows report that starts a new row before and after each group header.

Creating a Crosstab Report

By creating a crosstab report, you can print the results of a crosstab query with row and column totals.

A crosstab report contains the results of a crosstab query, with row headings down the left side of the report and column headings across the top. In order to print the results of a crosstab query in a report, the crosstab query must use fixed headings, so that the names of the fields in the crosstab query's dynaset do not change. To create a crosstab report:

1. Create a crosstab query (see *Cross-Tabulating Records* in Chapter 10). For example, Figure 14.9 shows a crosstab query that totals book orders by month and by the brochure from which the order came.

2. Choose View Query Properties from the menu to display the Query Properties dialog box, shown in Figure 14.10.

3. Select Fixed Column Headings.

4. In the Fixed Column Headings text box, enter the column headings you want to appear in the report, separated by semicolons. For example, if the columns in the crosstab query represent the brochures you have mailed, enter the brochure codes as shown in Figure 14.9. (If column headings contain spaces or punctuation, make sure to enclose them in quotation marks.)

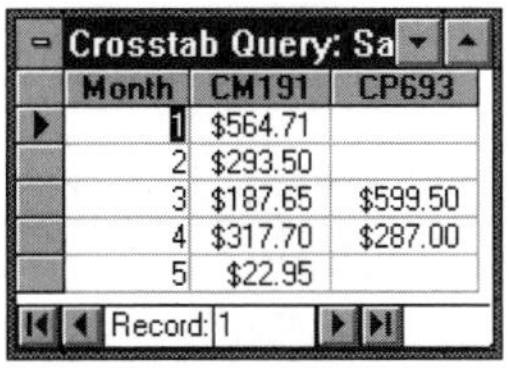

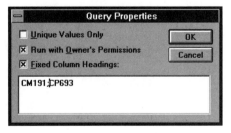

Figure 14.9 Crosstab query of sales by month and brochure.

Figure 14.10 Entering fixed headings for a crosstab query.

5. Save the crosstab query. You may want to leave the query open in Datasheet view to refer to as you create the report.

6. Create a blank report using the crosstab query as the record source. Choose Blank Report from the New Report dialog box, rather than using a ReportWizard.

7. In the Page Header section of the report, create label controls for the report title and the column headings. You may want to use the same headings that you entered in step 4, or you can use more descriptive ones. You may also want to create one or more line controls to separate the column headings from the Detail section.

8. In the Detail section of the report, create text boxes for the row headings and column values. The easiest way is to drag field names from the field list.

9. Add any calculated fields you may want. For example, you may want to total the values on each row. In Figure 14.11, the rightmost control in the Detail section totals the values in the row.

10. If you want column totals, add a Report Footer section and create calculated text boxes for the totals. Figure 14.12 shows the finished crosstab report.

Note: If the crosstab query tabulated three or more fields, the query will have multiple row headings. In this case, a text box for a row heading may contain duplicate values. You can set the Hide Duplicates property for the text box to Yes to display only the first instance of the value.

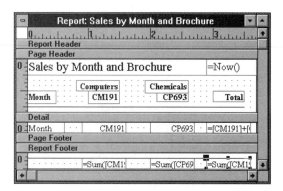

Figure 14.11   Design view of a crosstab report with row and column totals.

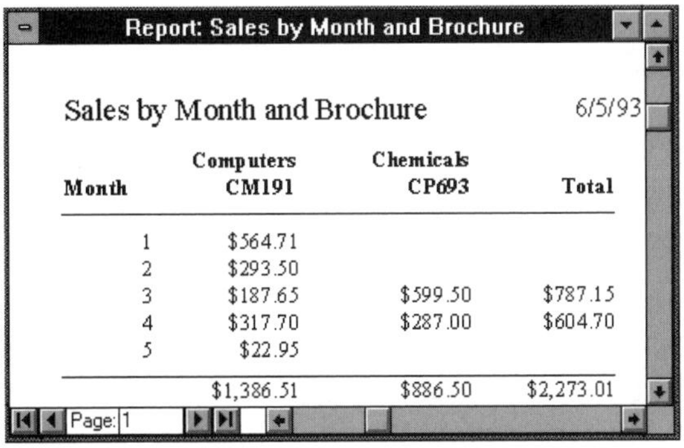

Figure 14.12 Crosstab report with row and column totals.

Form Letters

There are three ways to create a form letter using data in Access tables:

- Create a report in Access to print the letters
- Export the data for use as a merge file in a word-processing program, for example in Word for Windows merge format
- Buy a third-party, add-on software package that facilitates the use of Access data in Windows-based word processors

Let's look at the first two approaches. If neither one works for you, you may want to contact Kwery Corporation, which sells Access to Word (call 800-AT-KWERY), or Cary Prague, who has written a mail-merge ReportWizard (call 800-277-3117).

Printing One Letter for Each Record

If you create a report whose record source contains names and addresses, you can print one letter for each record.

You can create an Access report that looks like a form letter. To print one letter for each record in the record source of the report:

1. Create a query that includes the records and fields you want to include in the letter. For example, the bookseller database contains a query called One Order that includes all the fields from the Orders table, and prompts for an order number.

2. Create a new report. In the New Order dialog box, choose Blank Report—there is no ReportWizard for form letters.

3. Make the report the width you want the letter to be, not including the margins. For example, if you use 8–1/2-inch-wide paper with one-inch margins, make the report 6–1/2 inches wide. You can set the width by entering a value in the Width setting on the property sheet for the report, or by dragging the right edge of the report to the desired position.

4. Set the font for the default label control and the default text box control on the property sheet. Use the same font for both types of controls, because you will intermix them on the report. Also choose No for the Auto Label property of the default text box control.

5. Set the Force New Page property of the Detail section of the report to Before Section, so that the letter for each record prints on a separate page.

6. If the form letter will be one page long, you don't need to use page headers or footers. If the letter will be more than one page long, create controls in the Page Header or Page Footer sections for page numbers.

7. If you plan to print the letters on blank paper, create controls for the return address, logo, and other information to appear at the top of each page. Place them in the Page Header section, if you use one, or at the top of the Detail section. If you plan to print on letterhead, leave blank space at the top of the Page Header or Detail section of the report to avoid printing on top of the preprinted text.

8. Create a text box to print today's date, using this expression:

   ```
   =Now()
   ```

   Then, format the date.

9. Create text boxes to display the name and address of the addressee. Concatenate fields as needed using either ampersands or vertical bars (as described in *Combining Values* in Chapter 13). Also create a salutation, like this:

   ```
   ="Dear |[First Name]|,"
   ```

   or

   ```
   ="Dear |[MrMs]|. |[Last Name]|,"
   ```

   If there is a chance that any of the text boxes may be blank, set their Can Shrink property to Yes to eliminate the blank space occupied by the control.

10. Now you are ready for the body of the letter. For paragraphs that do not contain any variable information—no fields from the record source of the report—you can create either a label or a text box control to display the text. It is a good idea to use text boxes so that if you decide to add variable information later, you can just edit the expression in the Control Source property of the text box. For example, you might create a text box with this expression:

```
="It is always a pleasure doing business with you, and we
    look forward to future orders."
```

Make the text box control the full width of the page, and long enough to accommodate the text.

11. For paragraphs in which you want to include information from records, include the fixed text with the variable information, using an expression like this:

```
="Thank you for ordering the new book, '|[Books.Title]|,'
    by |[Author]|. We are sorry to report that the publication of
    this book has been delayed."
```

Set the Can Grow property of the text box to Yes, so that if the field information is long, the control can expand to fit extra lines.

If you want to include a numeric or date field in the letter, use the Format() function to control its format (see Chapter 5 for information on formatting values). For example, this expression formats the Date field as a Long Date and the Cust Chk Amt field as Currency:

```
="We are holding your order, dated |Format([Date],"Long Date")|,
    until we hear from you. Please tell us whether to refund your
    payment of |Format([Cust Chk Amt],"$0.00")| or to backorder the
    book for you."
```

12. Use the IIf() function to display text conditionally. For example, this expression displays one phrase if the customer has already paid for the order and another phrase if the order is not yet paid:

```
="We will hold your order, dated |Format([Date],"Long Date")|,
    until we hear from you. Please tell us " & IIf([Cust Chk
    Amt]>0,"whether to refund your payment of |Format([Cust Chk
    Amt],"$0.00")|","whether to cancel the order") & " or to
    backorder the book for you."
```

The IIf() function tends to create very long expressions; the text that prints in the letter is usually shorter than the expression in the control—in this example, one of the phrases in the IIf() function is printed, but not both. As a result, if you make the text box control long enough to display the whole expression in Design view, it will probably be too long when the report is printed. Be sure to set the Can Shrink property of the text box control to Yes so that Access can eliminate the extra space.

13. Create text boxes for the closing and signature lines. If you have a scanned signature, you can include it in the letter in an unbound object frame.

Figure 14.13 shows a form letter in Design view and Figure 14.14 shows the resulting report.

Printing One Letter for Each Group

A form letter can include a list of detail information—just put the text of the letter in the Group Header and Group Footer sections.

You may want your form letter to list one or more records in the letter. For example, you may want a letter to a customer to contain a list of the

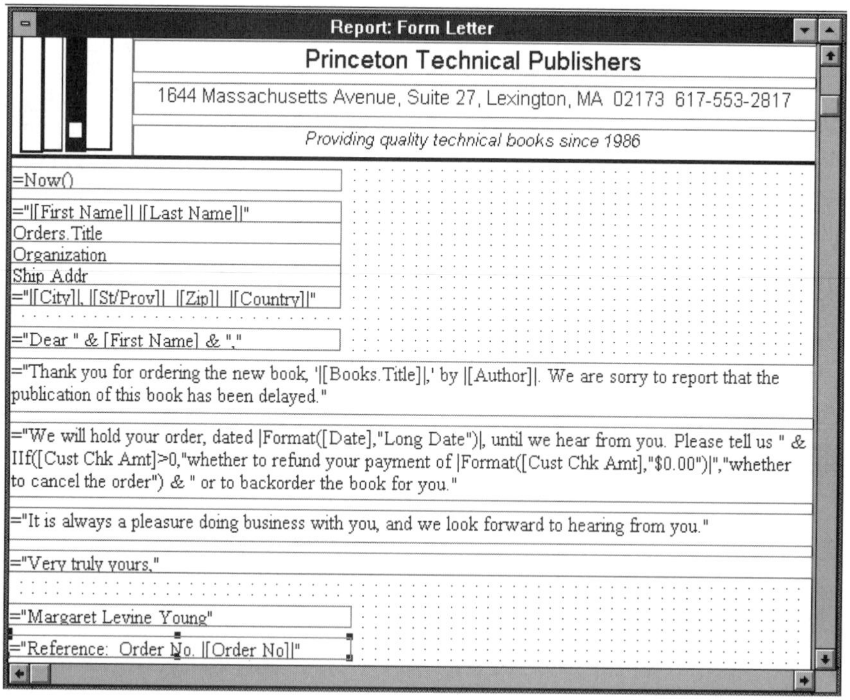

Figure 14.13 Design view of a form letter.

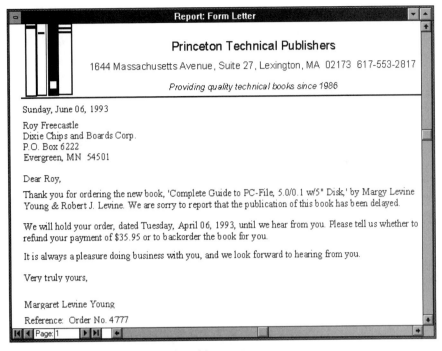

Figure 14.14 Form letter produced by an Access report.

books ordered. To print a letter like this, create a subtotal group in the report, as described in *Creating and Changing Subtotal Groups* in Chapter 13, and print one letter per group.

For example, to print one letter per order, listing the books included in the order:

1. Create a query that includes the records and fields you want to include in the letter.

2. Create a new, blank report.

3. Make the report the width you want the letter to be.

4. Set the font for default label control and the default text box control.

5. Create a group, using the Sorting and Grouping dialog box. For example, enter Order No in the Field/Expression column of the dialog box. Select Yes for Group Header and Group Footer, so that you can print text above and below the listing of books ordered. Close the dialog box.

6. Set the Force New Page property of the Group Header section of the report to Before Section, so that the letter for each group prints on a separate page.

7. If the form letter will be one page long, you don't need to use page headers or footers. If the letter will be more than one page long, create controls in the Page Header or Page Footer sections.

8. If you plan to print the letters on blank paper, create controls for the return address, logo, and other information to appear at the top of each page. Place them in the Page Header section, if you use one, or in the Group Header section.

9. In the Group Header section, create text boxes to print today's date, the name and address of the addressee, a salutation, and the first part of the body of the letter. Include the part of the letter that you want to appear above the listing of detail records.

10. In the Detail section of the report, create text boxes to print information for each record. For example, the Detail section can include text boxes for the Title, Author, and Price fields for each book order.

11. In the Group Footer section, create text boxes for the remainder of the letter, the closing, and the signature line. Figure 14.15 shows this form letter in Design view and Figure 14.16 shows the resulting report.

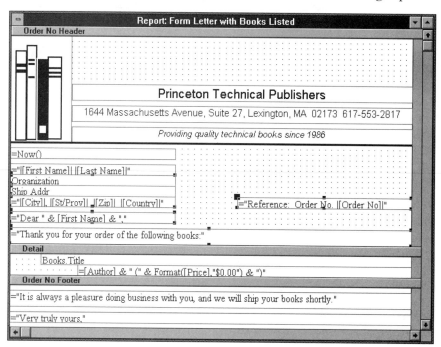

Figure 14.15 Design view of a form letter by group.

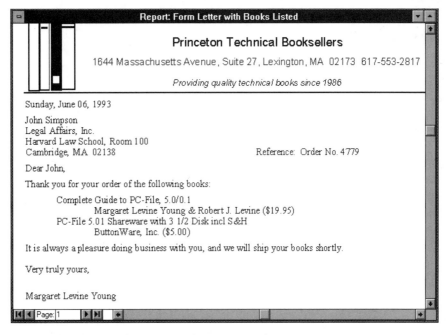

Figure 14.16   Form letter report that prints one letter per group.

Creating Merge Files for Use with a Word Processor

You may prefer to use your word processor to print form letters, since word processors have better formatting capabilities than Access.

You can export Access tables in a variety of formats that word processors can read. For example, WordPerfect for Windows can accept a delimited text file as the secondary file (the file that contains the list of addresses). You can use the Word for Windows merge format to export a table for use in a mail merge operation in Word for Windows. You can, however, encounter limitations when working with a word processor—for example, Word limits its data files to 32 fields.

To export your information to be used for printing form letters from a word processor:

1. Create a query that contains the fields and records you want to include in the form letter. For example, the booksellers database contains addresses of past customers to which promotional letters could be sent. You could create a query that would contain just the name and address information for all purchasers of books in a certain interest area.

You must now change the query to a make-table query.

2. In the Query window, choose Query Make Table from the menu to display the Query Properties dialog box for make-table queries, shown in Figure 14.17.

3. Enter a new table name in the Table Name text box.

4. To avoid duplicate addresses, select Unique Values Only. (If your query contains more than ten fields, don't select Unique Values Only—Access will refuse to run the query.)

5. Click on OK to exit from the dialog box.

6. Click on the Run button on the toolbar. Access runs the query, and tells you how many records (rows) it will add to the new table. If the table you selected in step 3 already contains records, Access warns you that it will delete them.

7. Close the Query window and open the new table in Datasheet view to make sure that the query selected the fields and records you wanted.

8. Export the new table by selecting it in the Database window and choosing File Export from the menu. Access displays the Export dialog box, shown in Figure 14.18.

9. Select the format in which to write the exported file. Choose a format that your word processor can read directly, or one that it can convert

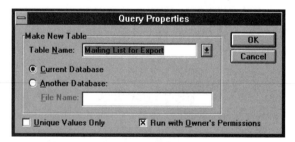

Figure 14.17 Setting the properties of a make-table query.

Figure 14.18 Selecting the format for the output file.

to its format. Click on OK. Access displays the Select Microsoft Access Object dialog box, shown in Figure 14.19.

10. Select the table you created with the make-table query in steps 1 through 6. Click on OK. Access displays the Export to File dialog box, shown in Figure 14.20.

11. Enter a filename for the exported file. Access suggests a name using the first word of the table name with the extension .TXT. Click on OK.

12. If you are exporting to a text file, Access displays the Export Text Options dialog box. Click on the Options button to see the expanded dialog box, shown in Figure 14.21.

    You use this dialog box to specify whether to include a record at the beginning of the file containing the field names (some applications require this), the text delimiter in which text values will be enclosed, the field separator that Access will place between each field, and the format in which you want dates and times to appear. Click on OK after making your selections.

13. Access creates the file. Refer to your word processor's documentation to read the file and create form letters.

Note: To export a table to a fixed-width text file, you must first create an import/export specification. See *Importing a Fixed-Width File* in Chapter 2 for information about import/export specifications.

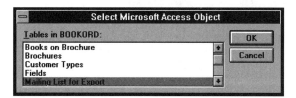

Figure 14.19   Selecting the table to export.

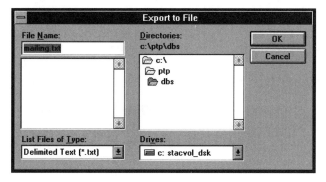

Figure 14.20   Entering the filename for the exported file.

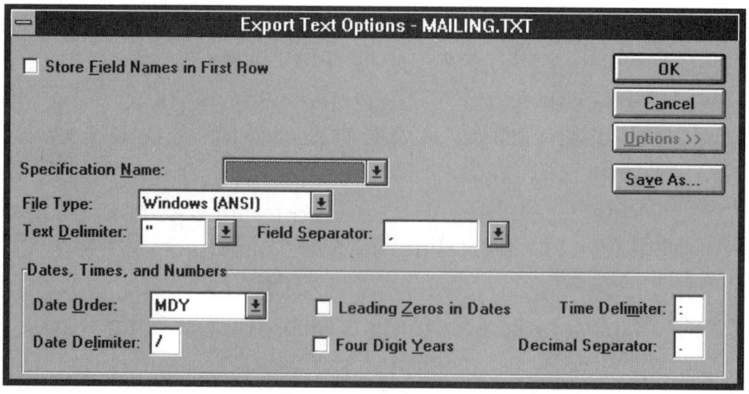

Figure 14.21 Specifying options for a text file.

Mailing Labels and Envelopes

If you maintain a list of names and addresses in an Access table, you will probably want to print mailing labels. Mailing labels come in an amazing variety of sizes, on sheets or on continuous paper, ranging from one to four labels across the page. Labels that are one across are called *one-up*, those that are two across are *two-up*, and so on.

The easiest way to create a report that prints mailing labels is to use the Mailing Label ReportWizard, which contains a long list of settings for all standard Avery brand labels and compatible labels. Many brands of labels now include an *Avery number* on the package, which is the product number of the equivalent Avery brand label.

Once you have used the ReportWizard to create the mailing label report, you can make further changes in Design view. This section describes how to use the Mailing Label ReportWizard and how to customize the labels it creates, as well as how to create reports for printing envelopes.

You can also export address information to a word processor to print mailing labels and envelopes. If you are exporting the address list to print form letters as described in the previous topic, you might find it more convenient to print the labels or envelopes from the word processor, too.

Using the Mailing Label ReportWizard

The Mailing Label ReportWizard has more options than the other ReportWizards, because it allows you to specify not only fields to appear on the labels, but also punctuation and fixed text that you enter.

To run the Mailing Label ReportWizard:

1. To start the ReportWizard, select the table or query containing the addresses, click on the New Report button on the toolbar, select ReportWizards from the New Report dialog box, select Mailing Label from the menu of ReportWizards, and click on OK. The Microsoft Access ReportWizard dialog box, shown in Figure 14.22, appears.

2. Before beginning to lay out the label, figure out how many lines of text can fit. Using 10-point type, you can print six lines per inch. Using 11-point or 12-point type, you can print about five lines per inch. Measure the height of your mailing labels, omitting the non-printable space between the labels, and allowing extra margins in case the labels don't feed squarely. For example, if your labels are one inch high and you plan to use 10-point type, don't print more than five lines on each label. Four lines would be a safer bet unless your printer feeds labels very precisely, because you must leave at least a little blank space at the top and bottom of each label to allow for the gap between labels on the page.

3. Choose what information to display on each line of the label. You can display these three types of information:

   - Fields from the record source, like First Name; choose the field name from the list of available fields and click on the Right Arrow button (>)

   - Punctuation, like a comma or a space; select one of the punctuation buttons

   - Text, like *First Class Mail*; type the text into the text box and click on the Text-> button

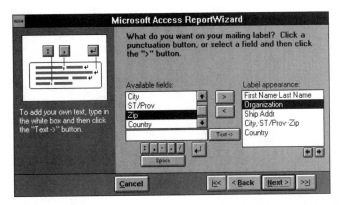

Figure 14.22 Use this dialog box to choose what to display on mailing labels.

If you make a mistake and want to undo your last choice, click on the Left Arrow button (<). This undoes the last field, punctuation, or text you selected.

When you have selected the fields to appear on one line of the label, press the Enter button (the bent arrow) to move to the next line of the label. To move to a previous line of the label to make changes, click on the line in the Label appearance text box.

4. When you have finished selecting the items for the label, click on the Next button.

5. Select one or more fields to sort by when printing the labels. Then click on the Next button again to display the dialog box shown in Figure 14.23.

6. Find your mailing labels on the list of label sizes. If your labels do not have an Avery number on the box, look for the type of label with measurements that are similar to yours. If you see a label that is the right size, but the wrong number of labels across the page, choose it anyway—you can change the number of labels across the page later in Design view. For Cheshire labels, choose any label that is 1 inch high and about 3–1/2 inches wide (see *Printing Cheshire Labels* later in this chapter for more information). Highlight the type of label and click on the Next button.

7. You are done telling the ReportWizard how to design the mailing label. Click on the Print Preview button on the dialog box to see the first draft of the labels. The ReportWizard creates the new report. If you have entered too many lines of information to fit on the mailing label, Access warns you that it will omit them. (You can fix the problem later in Design view.)

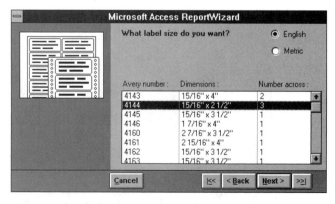

Figure 14.23 Use this dialog box to choose the types of mailing labels.

Modifying the Mailing Label ReportWizard Output

You can add lines, boxes, and graphics to mailing labels, and correct flaws in the ReportWizard's design.

To make further changes in your mailing label report, view the report in Design view. Figure 14.24 shows a mailing label report created by the Mailing Label ReportWizard. Access uses the ampersand concatenation operators to combine the values for each line. The report shows just one mailing label—the report uses the Print Setup dialog box settings to create a multiple-column report.

You may want to make the following kinds of changes:

- If you couldn't find the right label size in the ReportWizard list, change the size of the Detail section of the report to match your label size. Make the height of the Detail section equal to the distance from the top of one label to the top of the next, including the non-printable region between the labels (note this height for entry in the Print Setup dialog box). Make the width of the Detail section equal to the distance from the left edge of one label to the left edge of the next—for one-up labels, make the Detail section the width of the label. (Note the width.) Then choose File Print Setup from the menu, click on the More button to see the multi-column settings, and change the Item Size Width and Height measurements to the width and height of one label.

- To change the number of labels that print across the page, choose File Print Setup from the menu, click on the More button to see the multi-column settings, and change the Items Across setting.

- To change the order in which Access prints the labels on the page—to fill each column before starting the next column rather than filling each row before filling the next row—choose File Print Setup from the

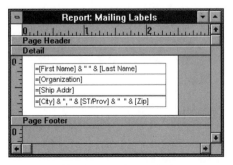

Figure 14.24 Report created by the Mailing Label ReportWizard.

menu, click on the More button to see the multi-column settings, and change the Item Layout setting from Horizontal to Vertical.

- To change the font used on the labels, choose Edit Select All from the menu to choose all the controls on the label. Then choose the font from the Font name box on the toolbar and choose the size from the Font Size box. It is a good idea to change the font size to at least 10 points so that the postal service can read the addresses easily.

- If you choose too many fields to fit on the label, Access omits the extra lines when it creates the reports. You can move fields around on the report and create text box controls for the omitted fields.

- The ReportWizard sets the Can Grow property of each control to Yes, and the Can Grow property of the Detail section to No. This allows each line of the label to wrap to additional lines as needed, but it doesn't allow the Detail section to expand beyond the size of one label. If you have long address lines and the label doesn't have extra blank space at the bottom, the last line of the address may be omitted on some labels. Check for missing lines in Print Preview.

- You can add lines, boxes, and graphics to the labels by creating line, rectangle, and unbound object frame controls on the labels. Just be careful not to change the length and width of the Detail section or you will need to change the label size!

Avoiding Blank Lines

Use the Can Shrink property of text boxes to avoid leaving blank lines when fields are blank.

If your mailing list table contains two fields for the street address or a field for company or organization, one or more of these fields may be blank for some addresses. To avoid leaving blank lines when a field is blank, set the Can Shrink property of the text box to Yes. When printing the report, Access omits the control if the field value is blank (null).

When you set the Can Shrink property of a control to Yes, Access does not automatically change the Can Shrink property of the section that contains the control. Leave the Can Shrink (and Can Grow) properties of the Detail section of the report set to No so that Access prints the same number of lines for each mailing label.

The Mailing Label ReportWizard automatically sets the Can Shrink property of all controls to Yes and the Can Shrink property of the Detail section to No. If you create a mailing label report without using the ReportWizard, or if you create additional text boxes on a mailing label report, be sure to set the Can Shrink property of all controls.

Printing Tightly Spaced Address Lines

By printing the whole address in one multi-line text box control,
you can space the lines more closely.

When you print each line of the address using a separate control, the lines
are more widely spaced than if you create one multi-line text box control.
To make a label with more tightly spaced lines, use only the first text box
control in the Detail section. Concatenate all the information in the report into
one long expression in the Control Source of the first text box. You can copy
the field names from the control source properties of the other text boxes on
the label. To avoid blank lines, you can use the IIf() function to skip blank
fields. To separate one line of the address from the next, use the Chr()
function to provide carriage return and line feed characters like this:

```
Chr(13) & Chr(10)
```

Here is a sample Control Source expression:

```
=[First Name] & " " & [Last Name] & Chr(13) & Chr(10) &
   IIf(IsNull([Organization]),"",[Organization] & Chr(13) & Chr(10)) &
   IIf(IsNull([Ship Addr]),"",[Ship Addr] & Chr(13) & Chr(10)) & [City]
   & ", " & [St/Prov] & " " & [Zip]
```

Alternatively, you can write an Access Basic function to combine the
values. See *Printing Closely Spaced Lines on Mailing Labels* in Chapter 17.
Make sure to set the Can Grow property for the control to Yes, so it can
expand to print all the address lines!

Once you have concatenated the address, delete all but the first text
box on the label.

Using Continuous-Feed Labels

If you have a dot-matrix or other pin-feed printer, you will use
continuous-feed labels, which Access wasn't designed to handle.

Access always prints an entire page whenever it prints a report—it won't stop
in the middle of a page if the rest of the page is blank. This can be annoying
when you want to print just a few mailing labels on continuous-feed labels—
Access spits out many extra blank labels after the ones it prints.

The solution is to tell Access (and Windows) that your pages are very
small—the size of one label. To create a user-defined page size:

1. In the Windows Program Manager, open the Main group window
   and double-click on the Control Panel icon.

2. Double-click on the Printers program.

3. Select the printer driver for the printer you will use to print the labels.

4. Click on Setup.

5. For the Paper Size setting, select User Defined Size. Control Panel displays the User Defined Size dialog box, shown in Figure 14.25.

6. Set the width and length (height) of the paper to be the size of one label. Choose the units in which you want to enter the measurements, either 0.1 mm or 0.01 inch. For example, if you choose 0.01 inch as the unit and your labels are one inch high (from the top of one label to the top of the next), enter 100 for the length.

7. Click on OK to save the user-defined size.

8. The Printers utility remembers the values you entered for the User Defined Size regardless of the current Paper Size setting. So, if you use regular paper as well as mailing labels in the same printer, you probably want to set the default paper size back to full sheets. The Paper Size setting is used not only by Access for printing reports, but also by other applications on your computer.

9. Click on OK to exit from the dialog box for the printer driver.

10. Click on Close to exit from the Printers dialog box.

11. Double-click on the Control-menu box to exit the Control Panel application. You may want to leave it open until you are sure that you have set the user-defined paper size correctly.

12. In Access, view the mailing label report in Print Preview.

13. Choose File Print Setup from the menu to display the Print Setup dialog box.

14. Select User Defined Size for the Paper Size. Set the margins to zero.

15. Click on OK to exit from the Print Setup dialog box. Print Preview shows the report as it will print on a single label.

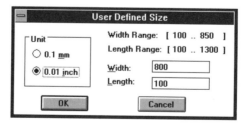

Figure 14.25 Creating a user-defined paper size for continuous-feed labels.

This procedure should not change the paper size for other reports in your Access database, or printing from other applications, unless these items also make use of a user-defined paper size.

You may still have trouble with the alignment of continuous-feed labels "creeping" upward or downward after you have printed a number of labels. To solve the "creep" problem, try these techniques:

- Don't use page or report headers or footers in the mailing label report.

- Make sure that the height of the Detail section is exactly the size of your label, measuring from the top edge of one label to the top edge of the next.

- Make sure the Item Size in the Print Setup dialog box is either set to Same as Detail or that the Item Size Height setting is correct. Set the margins to zero.

- On the property sheet for the report, set Grid X to 12 and Grid Y to 10. Align all controls to the grid.

- Make sure that no controls overlap.

Using Sheets of Labels

You may need to skip the first and last rows of labels if your printer can't print near enough to the edge of the label sheet.

If the text at the edge of your labels is cut off, your printer may not be able to print near enough to the edge of the sheet of labels. The Mailing Label Report Wizard assumes that your printer can print to within 1/4 inch of the paper. If the edges of your text are cut off, move the controls in the report until they print correctly.

If your printer requires a large top or bottom margin, printing correctly may be impossible, or it may require you to crowd the controls into the middle part of each label. Instead, you can tell Access to skip the first and/or last row of labels on each page. For example, if your sheets of labels are one inch high, there are 11 rows of labels on the page, and your printer can print to within 1/4 inch of the edge, you can only print on the middle 1/2 inch of each label to avoid cutting off information on the top and bottom row of labels. This isn't enough space to fit most addresses. Instead, you can skip the top and bottom rows of labels—wasteful, but necessary.

To skip these rows, choose File Print Setup from the menu. In the Print Setup dialog box, increase the Top Margin and Bottom Margin settings by the height of one label. For example, if the top and bottom margins are .25 inch and your labels are one inch high, increase the top and bottom margins to 1.25.

If you use sheets of labels and print only a few labels at a time, you may want to tell Access to start printing on a label other than the first label on the page. To starting printing on a label other than the first one requires writing an Access Basic function. See the topic *Printing Sheets of Mailing Labels* in Chapter 17. Before going to the trouble, make sure that after you have peeled off and used the first few labels on the page, the page will feed properly through the printer!

Printing Many Copies of One Label

It is easy to print multiple copies of a one-up, continuous-feed label. For other label types, however, you'll need to write Access Basic functions.

Access prints each copy of a report starting at the top of a new page. If you want to print many copies of a set of labels and you enter the number of copies in the Copies setting in the Print dialog box, Access prints each set starting on a new page. How can you avoid wasting the rest of the labels?

If you use one-up continuous-feed labels (not sheets of labels), set the page size to the size of one label, as described earlier in *Using Continuous-Feed Labels*. Then, when you print the mailing label report, enter the number of labels to print in the Print dialog box. Since each label is a separate "page" to Access, no labels are wasted.

If you use sheets of labels, or if you use labels with more than one across (*multi-up* labels), you can write Access Basic functions to avoid waste when printing multiple copies. See *Printing Sheets of Mailing Labels* in Chapter 17 for information on writing these Access Basic functions.

Printing Multiple Copies Based on a Field

What if you want to print different numbers of labels for each record depending on the information in the record?

For example, what if you are printing labels to be placed on items in inventory, and your table contains the number of each item you have? You would like to print the same number of each label as there are items in inventory. You can print variable numbers of labels by using a clever query trick invented by Microsoft Technical Support personnel:

1. Make a new table named Label Counts to contain one record for each number of labels you might want to print. The table has one field,

a Number field named LabelCount with size Byte. Figure 14.26 shows the new table, with records for each quantity that might be in stock.

2. Make a query that includes the information you want printed on the label, as well as the number you want to print of each label. For example, the Inventory table in the bookseller database contains the count of each book in stock, by Book Code. The query in Figure 14.27 contains the information to print on the inventory labels.

3. Add the Label Counts table to the query you made in step 2. There is no join line between the Label Counts table and any other table.

4. In the column of the query grid that contains the quantity of labels to print, enter this expression in the Criteria row:

```
> [LabelCount]
```

The finished query looks like Figure 14.28.

5. When you switch to Datasheet view, the query contains the same number of duplicate records as you want duplicate labels, as shown in Figure 14.29. Now you can use a mailing label report to print labels using this query as the record source.

Figure 14.26 Label Counts table to store potential counts of labels.

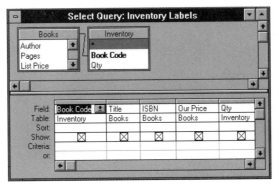

Figure 14.27 Query containing information for inventory labels, with quantities to print.

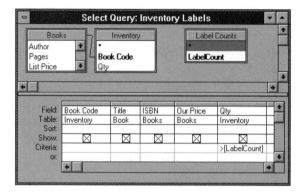

Figure 14.28   Query to create duplicate records for multiple label printing.

Book Co	Title	ISBN	Ou
BW004	J & P Transformer Book, 11th Ed., Completel	0-408-00494-0	
CB002	Complete Guide to PC-File, 5.0/0.1	0-944954-01-4	
CB002	Complete Guide to PC-File, 5.0/0.1	0-944954-01-4	
CB002	Complete Guide to PC-File, 5.0/0.1	0-944954-01-4	
CB002	Complete Guide to PC-File, 5.0/0.1	0-944954-01-4	
CB002	Complete Guide to PC-File, 5.0/0.1	0-944954-01-4	
CB002	Complete Guide to PC-File, 5.0/0.1	0-944954-01-4	
CB003	Complete Guide to PC-File, 5.0/0.1 w/3" Disl	0-944954-01-4	
CB003	Complete Guide to PC-File, 5.0/0.1 w/3" Disl	0-944954-01-4	

Figure 14.29   Query with duplicate records.

Printing Cheshire Labels

Cheshire labels—labels printed on plain paper—are used for large-scale mailings.

Cheshire labels are printed on plain 14 inch-wide continuous paper and are sliced up by a Cheshire machine and glued onto envelopes. The addresses must be printed in exactly the right positions on the paper so that the cutter in the machine doesn't slice them into pieces. To print Cheshire labels, make sure that your mailing label report uses these specifications:

- Make the report 3.38 inches wide. Enter this measurement into the Width property on the property sheet for the report.

- Make the Detail section 1 inch high. Enter this measurement into the Height property on the property sheet for the Detail section.

- Don't use a Page Header or Page Footer section.
- Print four addresses across the page with no space between the items. To specify this setting, choose File Print Setup and click on More in the Print Setup dialog box. In the Items Across box, enter **4**. In the Row Spacing and Column Spacing box, enter **0** (zero). For the item Size, select Same as Detail, or enter **3.38** inches for the Item Width and **1** inch for the Item Height. When you print the report, be sure to leave a few pages of blank paper attached at the beginning and end of the report so the Cheshire machine can start cutting the first row of addresses.

Print Labels Faster Using Text Mode

It is faster to print labels in text mode, rather than graphics mode. To print in text mode, either use the Generic/Text Only printer driver (see *Printing ASCII Text* in Chapter 12), or choose a font that matches a built-in font in your printer. Try Courier or Roman 10 pitch.

Printing Envelopes

For classier-looking mail, you may want to print addresses directly onto envelopes using information from Access tables.

Almost all laser printers can accept envelopes fed by hand, as can most dot matrix printers. If you need to print a lot of envelopes, you may be able to add an envelope feeder to your printer.

The information on an envelope is similar to that on a mailing label, so an envelope report is similar to a mailing label report for one-up labels. To print addresses on envelopes:

1. Create a report for printing envelopes, in one of three ways:

   - Start with a new, blank report
   - Copy a mailing label report
   - Use the Mailing Label ReportWizard to create a report, choosing a one-up label from the list of label sizes necessary.

2. Set the Force New Page property of the Detail section to Before Section or After Section. Either setting works—Access can skip to a new envelope before or after printing each envelope.

3. Create (or move) the controls that display the name and address in the Detail section of the report. Place the first control about two inches from the top of the envelope and about three inches from the left edge of the envelope, depending on the size of your envelopes, as shown in Figure 14.30.

4. If you want to print a return address, create label controls to display the text in the upper-left corner of the Detail section. You can even create an unbound object frame control to display a picture, like your organization's logo.

5. Set the Can Shrink property for each line of the address to Yes.

6. Choose File Print Setup to display the Print Setup dialog box.

7. For Paper Size, select an envelope size. The envelopes listed will depend on your printer. For Paper Source, choose the envelope feeder, or manually feeding envelopes.

8. Set the top and left margins to .25 inch, so that you can print a return address close to the edge of the envelope.

9. If the report was created by the Mailing Label ReportWizard, you will need to make sure that only one address will print across the page. Click on the More button to display the multi-column part of the dialog box. Set Items Across to 1 and Item Size to Same as Detail.

10. Click on OK to exit from the Print Setup dialog box.

You will probably need to print the envelope report a number of times to position the controls just where you want them and to learn how and where to feed the envelopes into the printer.

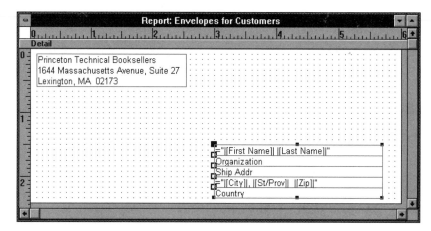

Figure 14.30 Design view of an envelope report.

Other Types of Reports

Finally, here are techniques for printing other standard reports: a membership roster for an organization, a check register, and a packing slip or invoice.

Membership Roster

Use a report with groups to print a membership roster by family.

A common database application is maintaining a membership list of families and individuals, for example, for a church. It is a good idea to store family and individual information separately: Since some information is the same for all members of a family, it is inefficient and redundant to store all the information in one table.

ON DISK

The CHURCH Database

In the CHURCH database on the Companion Disk, the membership list is stored in two tables: Families and Individuals. The Families table, shown in Figure 14.31, contains information that is the same for all the members in a family. The Individuals table, shown in Figure 14.32, contains information that is different for each person. The two tables are related by a Family Code field, which is the primary key field of the Families table and a foreign key field in the Individuals table. The Individuals table has a two-field primary key, Family Code and First Name, which assumes that people within a family have unique names or nicknames. Figures 14.33 and 14.34 show the records in the two tables.

Table: Families		
Field Name	**Data Type**	**Description**
Family Code	Text	Unique code for each family, related to Individu
Family Name	Text	Last name of majority of family members
Address	Text	Street address
City	Text	City or town
State	Text	State or province (standard two-letter code)
ZIP	Text	ZIP or postal code
Phone	Text	Home phone number

Field Properties

Field Size	15
Format	
Caption	
Default Value	
Validation Rule	
Validation Text	
Indexed	Yes (No Duplicates)

The field description is optional. It helps you describe the field and is also displayed in the status bar when you select this field on a form. Press F1 for help on descriptions.

Figure 14.31 Families table design.

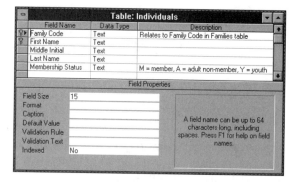

Figure 14.32   Individuals table design.

Family Code	Family Name	Address	City	State	ZIP	Phone
CHANNING	Channing	12 Adams Street	Lexington	MA	02173	617-552-4567
COHEN	Cohen	18 Mass. Ave.	Lexington	MA	02173	617-556-7890
EMERSON	Emerson	23 Thoreau Street	Concord	MA	01720	508-554-2345
PARKER	Parker	6 Harrington Road	Lexington	MA	02173	617-553-0123

Figure 14.33   Families table records.

Family Code	First Name	Middle	Last Name	Membership Status
CHANNING	William	E	Channing	M
COHEN	Donald	R	Cohen	M
COHEN	Helen	L	Cohen	M
COHEN	Margaret	L	Cohen	Y
EMERSON	Donald	G	Smith	Y
EMERSON	Helen	H	Emerson	Y
EMERSON	Henry	T	Emerson	Y
EMERSON	Martha	W	Smith	A
EMERSON	Ralph	W	Emerson	M
PARKER	Sarah		Parker	M
PARKER	Sarah Jr.	R	Parker	Y
PARKER	Theodore	S	Parker	M

Figure 14.34   Individuals table records.

To produce a membership roster like the one shown in Figure 14.35:

1. Create a query that includes the fields in Table 14.1.
2. Save the query.
3. Create a report that uses the query as its record source.
4. In the Page Header section, create label controls for the name of the organization, date, and other information. In the Page Footer section, create a label control for the page number.
5. Display the Sorting and Grouping dialog box. For the first group, choose the Family Code field, so members of the same family are

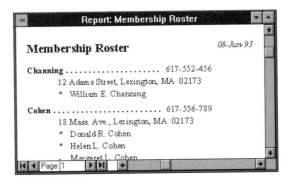

Figure 14.35 Membership roster report.

Table 14.1 Fields for the Membership Roster

Field Name	Table
Family Number	Families
Family Name	Families
Address	Families
City	Families
State	Families
ZIP	Families
Phone	Families
First Name	Individuals
Middle Initial	Individuals
Last Name	Individuals
Membership Status	Individuals

listed together. Choose Yes for the Group Header so the report can print the family name, address, and phone at the beginning of the list of people in the family. For the second group choose the field by which you want to sort people within a family. In Figure 14.36, family members are sorted by Membership Code, then by First Name. Close the dialog box.

6. In the Family Code Header section, create controls to display the Family Name, Address, City, State, ZIP, and Phone fields, which come from the Families table. In Figure 14.37 the Family Name field is shown with a series of dots concatenated after it in the control, to create a dot leader between the Family Name and Phone fields.

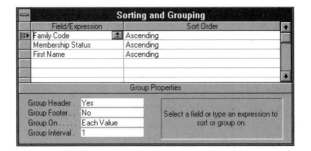

Figure 14.36 Sorting and grouping for the membership roster.

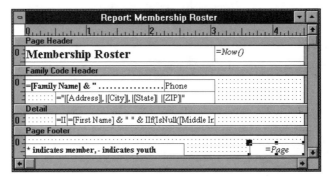

Figure 14.37 Design view of the membership roster.

7. In the Detail section of the report, create a control to display the First Name, Middle Initial, and Last Name for a family member; for example:

```
=[First Name] & " " & IIf(IsNull([Middle Initial]),"",[Middle
    Initial] & ". ") & [Last Name]
```

You may also want to display a symbol to indicate the person's membership status. In this example, the status codes are M (member), A (adult non-member), and Y (youth). You can use this expression to display an asterisk for members and a dash for children:

```
=IIf([Membership Status]="M","*",IIf([Membership Status]="Y","-",""))
```

The finished report is shown in Figure 14.35. If you're feeling confident, you can even format it as a two-column report (see *Creating Snaking-Column Reports* earlier in this chapter).

Invoices, Order Confirmations, and Packing Slips

Invoices, order confirmations, and packing slips are similar report types, containing information from many tables, as well as calculated values.

Invoices usually require combining fields from a number of tables. For example, the Invoice to Customer report in the bookseller database is based on a query containing fields from the Orders, Order Details, and Books tables. To create an invoice that looks like Figure 14.38:

1. Create a query that combines all the fields that appear on the invoice, as well as the fields that are required for calculating values to appear on the invoice. The Invoice to Customer query in the bookseller database contains the fields in Table 14.2.

2. To select which invoices to print in the query, enter an expression with parameters in the Criteria row for the Order No, like this:

```
Between [Starting order for invoices] And [Ending order for
    invoices]
```

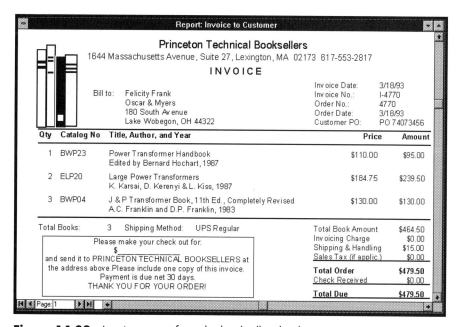

Figure 14.38 Invoice report from the bookseller database.

Table 14.2   Fields for the Customer Invoice

Field Name	Table
Order No	Orders
Cust PO	Orders
Date	Orders
Organization	Orders
Bill to F&LName	Orders
Bill Addr	Orders
Bill CityStZIP	Orders
Ship Addr	Orders
City	Orders
St/Prov	Orders
Zip	Orders
Country	Orders
Cust Chk Amt	Orders
Total Book Amt	Orders
Ship Via	Orders
S & H	Orders
Invoice Chg	Orders
Sales Tax	Orders
Total Order	Orders
Invoice Date	Orders
Book Code	Order Details
Price	Order Details
Qty	Order Details
Title	Books
Author	Books
Pub Date	Books

3. Add a calculated field to the query for the extended price for each item ordered, since this appears on the invoice in several places:

```
Extended Price: [Price] * [Qty]
```

4. Save the query.

5. Create a new report based on the query.

6. In the Sorting and Grouping dialog box, create a group for Order No, so there is one invoice for each order. Choose Yes for Group Header and Group Footer.

7. In the Order No Header section, create controls for the information you want to print at the top of the invoice, including your company name and address, the customer's billing address, the order number, and order date, and the customer purchase order or check number. If invoices may be more than one page long, you might want to put some of this information in the Page Header section so that it will print on the top of the second page of two-page invoices. Figure 14.39 shows the Invoice to Customer report in Design view.

8. In the Detail section of the report, create controls for each item ordered. Include the fields for the quantity ordered, the item code, the item description, the price, and extended price (calculated in the query).

9. In the Order No Footer section, create controls for the totals. In Figure 14.39, the Total Books control contains this expression:

```
= Sum([Qty])
```

The Shipping Method control uses a combo box to look up the description of the shipping code from the Ship Via field (see *Printing a Field from Another Table* in Chapter 13).

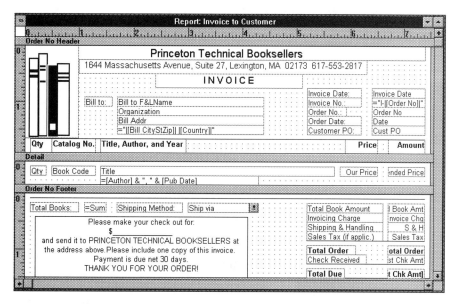

Figure 14.39 Invoice report in Design view.

Total Book Amt, Invoice Charge, Shipping & Handing, Sales Tax, Total Order, and Check Received controls display fields from the query. Rather than calculating these amounts as part of the report, they are calculated by macros in the form in which orders are entered and stored in the Orders table. Using macros allows the amounts to appear in many forms and reports.

The Total Due control contains this expression:

```
=[Total Order]-[Cust Chk Amt]
```

Figure 14.39 shows the report in Design view and Figure 14.38 shows the finished report.

Packing slips are similar to invoices, except that they omit all pricing information. Order confirmations are also similar to invoices, but you can include controls that print different messages depending on whether the order was prepaid, based on a purchase order, or charged to a credit card (this information is stored in the Payment Method field of the Orders table).

Note: If you have a fax board and Windows fax software, you may also want to make invoice and order confirmation reports that are designed for faxing to customers. For example, you can add a report header like the one shown in Figure 14.40 to the beginning of the report (see *Faxing Access Reports* in Chapter 12).

Check Register

You can use Access to store your checkbook and print a ledger of checks and deposits.

The CHECKBK database on the Companion Disk contains a simple checkbook application. The Transactions table contains checks, deposits, interest, and bank charges, as shown in Figures 14.41 and 14.42.

The Types table shown in Figure 14.43 contains descriptions of the types of transactions, and relates to the Type field in the Transactions table. The Sign field indicates whether this type of transaction is a credit (1) or a debit (-1). There is also a Categories table containing budget categories, so you can categorize each transaction.

To make a transaction ledger with a running balance:

1. Create a query in which the amounts of debits (checks and bank charges) are negative and the amounts of credits (deposits and interest) are positive. Enter this expression in the Field row of the query grid to create a field in which debits are negative and credits are positive:

    ```
    Amt: [Amount] * [Sign]
    ```

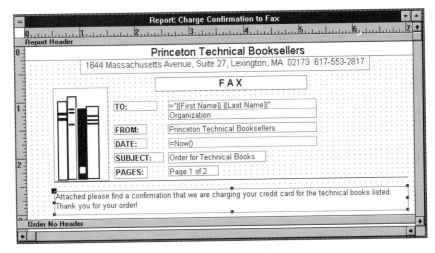

Figure 14.40 Fax cover page for an order confirmation report.

Field Name	Data Type	Description
Trans No	Number	Transaction number (check number for checks, depos
Type	Text	Relates to Types table
Date	Date/Time	
Amount	Currency	Always positive
ToFrom	Text	Payee for checks, payer for deposits
Category	Text	Budget category, relates to Categories table
Description	Text	

Field Properties

Field Size	Integer
Format	
Decimal Places	Auto
Caption	
Default Value	0
Validation Rule	
Validation Text	
Indexed	Yes (No Duplicates)

A field name can be up to 64 characters long, including spaces. Press F1 for help on field names.

Figure 14.41 Design of the Transactions table.

Trans No	Type	Date	Amount	ToFrom	Category	Description
101	D	4/1/93	$500.00	Savings	SAVINGS	Starting deposit
102	D	4/4/93	$108.00	3M	SALE	first order! for book MCP4
1001	C	4/2/93	$7.66	Checks in the Mail	OFFICE	Checks
1002	C	4/2/93	$97.68	New England Telep	OFFICE	Phone installation
1003	C	4/3/93	$45.23	Staples	OFFICE	Supplies
1004	C	4/10/93	$29.00	Postmaster Boston	OFFICE	stamps
0			$0.00			

Record: 1

Figure 14.42 Transactions table.

Figure 14.43   Types of transactions.

For each transaction, Access looks up the transaction type in the Types field, finds the Sign amount, and multiplies it by the Amount. The query is shown in Figure 14.44.

2.   Create a report based on the query to print the running balance. The report is shown in Figure 14.45. To print the transactions in chronological order, display the Sorting and Grouping dialog box and select Date as the field to sort by. Select No for Group Header and Group Footer. Close the dialog box.

To calculate the running balance, create a control that displays the Amt field, which is the field containing transaction amounts that are positive

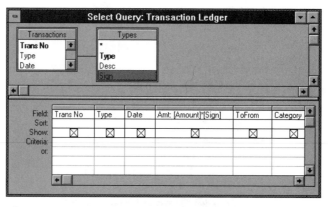

Figure 14.44   Query to calculate signs of transactions.

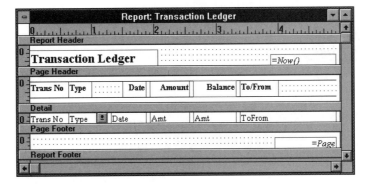

Figure 14.45 Transaction ledger report in Design view.

for credits and negative for debits. Set its Running Sum property to Yes to see the running balance. If you want negative numbers to appear in red, enter this custom format in the Format property (see *Formatting in Color* in Chapter 5):

```
$#,##0.00; ($#,##0.00) [Red]
```

Figure 14.46 shows the transaction ledger report.

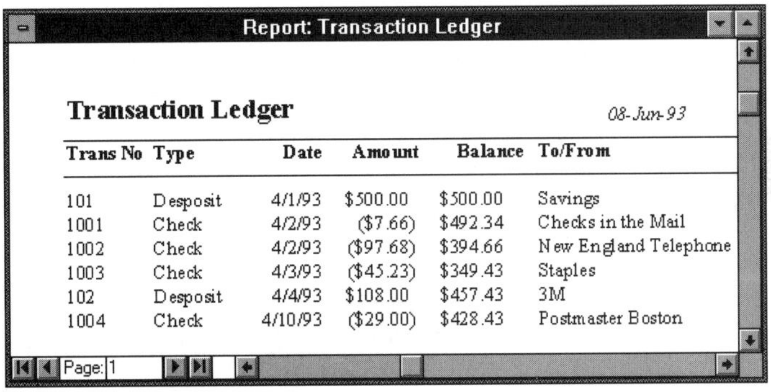

Figure 14.46 Transaction ledger report.

Part Overview

15 Customizing Access 425

Access is a malleable program that can be modified to suit your work habits. This chapter will teach you how to customize the Access startup, how to change the initialization settings in your MSACCESS.INI file, and how to customize your Access toolbar.

16 Access Macro Tips 449

Macros can increase you productivity and save you time. In this chapter, you will find out how to create, edit, and test macros, with an overview of all the macro actions you'll usually need. In addition to learning useful macros for forms and reports, you'll find out how to create complete turn-key applications with macros.

17 An Introduction to Access Basic 487

This chapter shows you how to write Access Basic procedures for creating a wide variety of transformation functions—functions that validate, format, or calculate new values based on information in your tables. You can enter these ready-to-run procedures in your own databases—or copy them from databases on the Companion Disk.

PART 5

Customizing Access

Access is a rich and complex program—sometimes the features can be overwhelming. To make Access work for you, this final part of the book shows how to customize many aspects of the program, including what libraries are loaded, how Access attaches to external databases, what the Access window displays, how keys act, and how the Zoom box looks. A crucial part of your Access environment is its security system, which you can customize to match the way members of your workgroup will share databases. By creating macros and modules in your Access databases, you can create custom functions, commands, menus, and entire applications.

Chapter 15 describes how to load databases and run macros automatically when you load Access, how to modify the initialization settings in the MSACCESS.INI file, and how to customize your keyboard and screen in Access. Chapter 16 helps you create and test macros as well as showing you how to create turn-key applications in Access. Chapter 17 reveals the world of Access Basic programming, and contains a wealth of ready-to-run functions.

423

CHAPTER

15

Customizing Access

O nce you have used Access for a few weeks, there may be ways you wish it worked differently. Wouldn't it be nice if you could get rid of the status bar to make more space in the Access window, or wouldn't it be convenient if Access would automatically display the Macro Name and Condition columns when you work in the Macro window? Streamlining Acces even in minor ways can save many hours over the long term—every keystroke counts, especially during data entry.

Good news! There are many configuration options you can set in Access to customize the application to meet your specific needs and work habits. You can also make changes to MSACCESS.INI, the Access initialization file, and to UTILITY.MDA, the database that contains many Access settings. This chapter describes these and other methods of customizing Access. Because each user's hardware and software environment is different, you should experiment with Access' configuration options. Just be sure to make backups before making changes!

Using Command-Line Options

When you run Access, you can tell it to open a database or run a macro as soon as it is loaded. For example, Access can automatically open your most frequently used database and run a macro that opens a form. Here is information on using command-line options.

Entering Command-Line Options

A command-line option supplies additional information when you tell Windows to run Access.

The Access program item in the Windows Program Manager contains the *command line* that runs Access. Usually, this command line contains the path and the executable filename for the Access program (for example, C:\ACCESS\MSACCESS.EXE). However, you can supply additional information by adding *command-line options*—such as the option to start up Access and a database file simultaneously—to the end of the command line.

To enter command-line options in the Access program item:

1. Exit Access.
2. In the Windows Program Manager, highlight the Access icon (the program item).
3. Choose File Properties from the menu, or press **Alt+Enter** to display the Program Item Properties dialog box, shown in Figure 15.1.

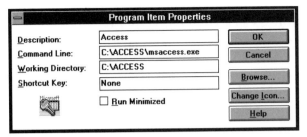

Figure 15.1 Adding command-line options to the Access program item.

4. The Command Line box contains the command that runs Access, which is usually:

```
C:\ACCESS\msaccess.exe
```

To the end of this command line, add the command-line option(s) you want to use. The available options are listed in Table 15.1.

5. Click on OK to exit the Program Item Properties dialog box.
6. To run Access, double-click the Access icon.

Table 15.1   Access Command-Line Options

Option	Purpose
database name	Opens the specified database as soon as Access is loaded; If the database isn't stored in Access' default database directory, include the full pathname.
/Excl	Opens a database for exclusive (not sharable) access; to open the database for shared access, don't use this option.
/Ro	Opens a database for read-only access.
/User *user name*	Runs Access with the specified user name.
/Pwd *password*	Runs Access with the specified password.
/X *macro*	Runs the specified macro as soon as Access is loaded; you can also create an AutoExec macro for the same result.
/Cmd or ;	Specifies text, which is stored by Access and used whenever a macro or module uses Command(), to be returned by the Command() function; this option must be the last option on the command line.

Note: Because the slash (/) is used to begin command-line options and the semicolon (;) is used as a synonym for the /Cmd option, if you want to include either character in command-line options, type the character twice. For example, to specify the password *meg/baby;* on the command line, type the option like this:

```
/Pwd meg//baby;;
```

Making an Icon for a Database

You can make a separate icon in the Windows Program Manager for databases you use often.

Rather than double-clicking the Access icon to run Access and then opening a database, or altering the command line for a single database file, you can make a special icon for each database you use on a regular basis. When you double-click on the database icon, the Program Manager runs Access and opens your database automatically.

To make a database icon:

1. Exit Access.
2. In the Windows Program Manager, open the program group in which you want to place the new database icon.
3. Choose File New from the menu. You'll see the New Program Object dialog box, shown in Figure 15.2.
4. Make sure the Program Item option is selected and click on OK to display the Program Item Properties dialog box (Figure 15.1).
5. In the Description text box, enter the database name or whatever you want to appear as the label for the icon.
6. In the Command Line text box, enter the path and filename of your Access program, followed by a space and the path and filename of your database. For example, this entry runs Access and opens the MAILLIST.MDB database located in the C:\ADDRESS directory:

   ```
   c:\access\msaccess.exe  c:\address\maillist.mdb
   ```

Figure 15.2 Creating a new database icon.

If you are not sure of the path and filename of your Access program, click on Cancel to exit the dialog box, and copy the information from your existing Access program icon (select the icon, press **Alt+Enter** to see its Program Item Properties dialog box, copy the command line to the Clipboard, and click on Cancel).

7. In the Working Directory text box, enter the Access program directory, which is usually C:\ACCESS.

8. If you want to be able to press a combination of keys to activate this icon, move your cursor to the Shortcut Key text box and press the keys. The key combination must be Ctrl+Alt+*key*, Ctrl+Shift+*key*, Ctrl+Alt+Shift+*key*, or Ctrl+Shift+Alt+*key*. The key can be any letter, number, or punctuation.

9. Choose an icon to appear in the Program Manager by clicking on Change Icon and selecting an image from the Change Icon dialog box, shown in Figure 15.3.

If you want more icons to choose from, you need to specify another icon file.

10. In the File Name text box, type:

```
c:\windows\progman.exe
```

then press **Enter** to see the icons that come with the Program Manager. When you have chosen an icon, click on OK to exit the Change Icon dialog box.

11. Click on OK to exit the Program Item Properties dialog box. The new database icon now appears in the Program Manager. Figure 15.4 shows a program group window with one Windows Terminal icon (Call John) and two database icons (PTB Order Entry and Mailing List).

12. Double-click on the database icon, or use the shortcut key if you assigned one. The Program Manager should run Access and load the database you named.

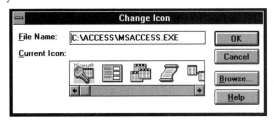

Figure 15.3 Choosing an icon for a database.

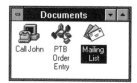

Figure 15.4 Database icons in Program Manager.

Note: If you are already running Access and you double-click on a database icon, the Program Manager runs another copy of Access. The existing Access program remains open, and the second copy of Access opens the database. Unless your computer has *a lot* of memory (at least 12Mb), it isn't very efficient to run two or more copies of Access at the same time. Instead, close one database and open another in one copy of Access.

Customizing Initialization Settings in MSACCESS.INI

Your Windows program directory contains an initialization file for each Windows program you run. The Access initialization file is called MSACCESS.INI. It is a text file that contains a long list of settings that Access reads when it loads. You can change these initalization settings—just be sure to make a backup copy of your MSACCESS.INI file first!

The settings are divided into sections, as shown in Table 15.2. Some sections should not be modified unless you plan to perform lots of experimentation, because changes may produce unexpected results.

Table 15.2   MSACCESS.INI Sections

Section Name	Safe to Modify?	Purpose
Paradox 3.X	No	Specifies how to attach to or import from Paradox 3.X tables.
dBASE III	No	Specifies how to attach to or import from dBASE III databases.
dBASE IV	No	Specifies how to attach to or import from dBASE IV databases.
FoxPro 2.0	No	Specifies how to attach to or import from FoxPro 2.0 databases.
Btrieve	No	Specifies how to attach to or import from Btrieve databases.
Microsoft Access	No	Specifies how to attach to or import from other Access databases.

Table 15.2   MSACCESS.INI Sections (continued)

Section Name	Safe to Modify?	Purpose
Delimited Text	No	Specifies how to import from delimited text files.
Fixed Width Text	No	Specifies how to import from fixed width text files.
Microsoft Excel	No	Specifies how to import from Excel spreadsheet files.
Lotus WKS	No	Specifies how to import from 1-2-3 .WKS spreadsheet files.
Lotus WK1	No	Specifies how to import from 1-2-3 .WK1 spreadsheet files.
Lotus WK3	No	Specifies how to import from 1-2-3 .WK3 spreadsheet files.
Options	Yes	Specifies the names of Access databases that contain system options, usually SYSTEM.MDA and UTILITY.MDA.
Libraries	Yes	Specifies the names of Access databases to load as libraries (see Chapter 17).
ODBC	Yes	Specifies information about Open Database Connectivity links.
ISAM	Yes	Contains settings regarding input and output to the Access database on disk.
Installable ISAMs	No	Contains settings for attaching to external database tables.
Paradox ISAM	Yes	Specifies settings for attaching to Paradox databases (see *Changing How Access Attaches to Paradox Databases,* later in this chapter).
dBASE ISAM	Yes	Specifies settings for attaching to dBASE databases (see *Changing How Access Attaches to dBASE Databases,* later in this chapter).
Word for Windows Merge	No	Specifies how to export to a merge file readable by Word for Windows and compatible word processors.
FoxPro 2.5	No	Specifies how to import from or export to FoxPro 2.5 databases.
FormWizards	No	Specifies which Access Basic procedure is called by each FormWizard.
ReportWizards	No	Same as FormWizard.
Menu Add-ins	Yes	Specifies commands to add to the Help menu.

Changing MSACCESS.INI Settings

You can change some settings in the Access initialization file.

You can add library databases to make other Access Basic modules available (see Chapter 17 for how to create a library database). To change the settings in MSACCESS.INI:

1. If you have not made a backup copy of your MSACCESS.INI file, do so now. Use the Windows File Manager to copy MSACCESS.INI to another name, perhaps MSACCINI.BAK. MSACCESS.INI is in your Windows program directory, usually C:\WINDOWS. If you can't find MSACCESS.INI, use File Manager to search for it.

2. Using a text editor like the Windows Notepad, open the MSACCESS.INI file.

3. Find the section that contains the setting you want to change. Section names are enclosed in square brackets, like this:

    ```
    [Libraries]
    ```

    The lines below the section name are the settings for that section. You can also add section names—for example, the [Menu Add-ins] section doesn't exist in your MSACCESS.INI file until you add it. To add a new section, move to the last line of the file, add a new line, and type the section name enclosed in square brackets.

4. Modify or add settings as described in the following topics in this chapter.

5. Save the MSACCESS.INI file.

6. If you are running Access, exit, then restart the program. Access reads the MSACCESS.INI file only when it loads.

Document MSACCESS.INI Changes

Changes to your MSACCESS.INI file must be correct or Access won't run properly. It is a good idea to document the changes you make, in case you need to undo or fix them later.

The easiest way to document your changes is to add comments to the MSACCESS.INI file. To add a comment line, begin the line with a semicolon (;). Access ignores lines that begin with semicolons. For example, you could add these lines to the beginning of the file:

```
;  MSACCESS.INI last modified 6/14/94
;  added analyzer.mda to Libraries section 4/11/93
;  added menu.mda to Libraries section 7/7/93
;  changed ODBC settings 6/14/94
```

Adding Libraries to Access

A library database contains Access Basic modules you can run from within any open database.

You may get library databases from various sources:

- You may want to use the Database Analyzer library that comes with Access (see *What Is the Database Analyzer?* in Chapter 3).

- You may download a library database from the MSACCESS forum on CompuServe, like the OutputAs library described in *Printing to File* in Chapter 12.

- You or someone in your organization may write a library of Access Basic modules and functions to be used in your organization's databases (see *Creating Library Databases* in Chapter 17).

To use a library database, you add a line to the [Libraries] section of MSACCESS.INI to tell Access to load this library database when you run Access. Following the steps in *Changing MSACCESS.INI Settings* earlier in this chapter, add an entry to the [Libraries] section that contains the name of the database, followed by an equal sign. If the database *is not* stored in the Access program directory, make sure to include its path and filename. For example, to use the Database Analyzer, which is stored in the ANALYZER.MDA file in the Access program directory, enter this line:

```
analyzer.mda=
```

If you want to load the database for read-only access, type **ro** after the equal sign. For example, the [Libraries] section of MSACCESS.INI already contains this line, which installs the FormWizards and ReportWizards contained in the WIZARD.MDA file:

```
wizard.mda=ro
```

Once you have installed a library database, whenever you open a database, Access automatically includes the objects from the library database. For example, you can load a library database containing commonly used queries, forms, reports, or modules. You can then use these objects when you work with any database.

Using the Default Windows Print Setup

You can add a line to your MSACCESS.INI file to tell Access to ignore your Print Setup settings.

If you are using a database that was designed to work with a different printer than the one that is available, you may have problems printing reports and forms. The print setup, which is saved with each report and form, refers to a printer driver you may not want to use.

Instead, you can tell Access to use the default Windows print options and to ignore the settings in the Access Print Setup command. Add the following entry to the [Microsoft Access] section of MSACCESS.INI:

```
UseDefaultPrSetup=1
```

You must restart Access before this setting takes effect.

Changing How Access Attaches to Paradox Databases

You can specify your user name, the location of the PARADOX.NET file, and how records are sorted in attached Paradox tables.

The [Paradox ISAM] section of MSACCESS.INI contains the options shown in Table 15.3. To change these settings, follow the steps in *Changing MSACCESS.INI Settings* earlier in this chapter. Do not add any new settings to this section or change the names of existing settings. Just change the value of the setting that appears after the equal sign. Be sure to make a backup copy of your MSACCESS.INI file in case your changes don't have the effect you intended.

Changing How Access Attaches to dBASE Databases

You can select how Access displays dates, sorts records, and whether records marked for deletion are displayed.

The [dBASE ISAM] section of MSACCESS.INI contains the options shown in Table 15.4. To change these settings, follow the steps in *Changing MSACCESS.INI Settings* earlier in this chapter.

Table 15.3   Initialization Settings for Attaching to Paradox Databases

Option	Description	Example
ParadoxUserName	Specifies the user name Paradox uses to alert other users if there is a locking conflict.	ParadoxUserName =Margy
ParadoxNetPath	Specifies the directory containing your PARADOX.NET file.	ParadoxNetPath=J: \WRKGRP\
CollatingSequence	Specifies the sort sequence to use with Paradox databases (ASCII, International, Norwegian-Dutch, or Swedish-Finnish).	CollatingSequence =ASCII

Table 15.4   Initialization Settings for Attaching to dBASE Databases

Option	Description	Example
CollatingSequence	Specifies the sort sequence to use with dBASE databases, either ASCII or International.	CollatingSequence =ASCII
Century	Controls whether Access displays four-digit years from attached dBASE databases (On or Off).	Century=On
Date	Specifies how Access displays dates from attached dBASE databases.	Date=American
Mark	Specifies the ASCII character code of the date separator; ASCII 47 is the slash character.	Mark=47
Deleted	Controls whether Access displays records that are marked for deletion in attached dBASE databases (On or Off).	Deleted=Off

Customizing Access for the ODBC Driver and SQL Server

If your network is unusually slow, you can increase the time Access will wait to get a response from the SQL Server.

If you use the Microsoft SQL Server to attach, import from, or export to SQL databases, you use the Microsoft ODBC driver. The [ODBC] section of MSACCESS.INI contains settings that control how long the ODBC driver waits for a response:

- **QueryTimeout**: Specifies how many seconds before ODBC stops trying to process query results; the default is 5 seconds
- **LoginTimeout**: Specifies how many seconds before ODBC stops trying to connect to a server; the default setting is 20

To increase these time-out settings, follow the steps in *Changing MSACCESS.INI Settings,* earlier in this chapter.

Trace ODBC Communication with the SQL Server

If your system is acting unpredictably and you want to know exactly what commands Access sends to the ODBC driver for transmission to the SQL Server, you can tell Access to store the commands for your review. In the [ODBC] section of the MSACCESS file, you can add this line:

```
TraceSQLMode=1
```

This line tells Access to create a file called SQLOUT.TXT in the database directory that will list the commands that are sent to the ODBC driver. When you have diagnosed the problem, be sure to remove this line (or precede it with a semicolon so that Access ignores it as a comment), or the SQLOUT.TXT file will grow larger and larger.

Speeding Up Access

You can change the size of the buffer Access uses to cache data and other database objects.

In the [ISAM] section of MSACCESS.INI, you can insert the following line:

```
MaxBufferSize=xxx
```

Replace *xxx* with a number between 128 and 4096, representing Access' buffer size in kilobytes. To speed up Access, you can try increasing or decreasing the buffer size.

If you have a large disk cache (using SMARTDrive) or a RAM drive, these require large buffers, too. By occupying so much of the computer's memory with buffers, you may be restricting the amount of memory available to Access. You may want to try reducing the size of these buffers, or eliminating the RAM drive.

Changing the Default Configuration Options

Access has many configuration options that you can change to fit your work habits. Unfortunately, these options aren't mentioned in the documentation! To view and change your configuration options, choose View Options from the menu to display the Options dialog box, shown in Figure 15.5.

The options displayed in the Options dialog box are stored in SYSTEM.MDA, which affects all databases you open in Access, not just the current database.

Customizing Your Screen

You can choose whether to display the toolbar and status bar.

Although the toolbar is very useful, it takes up space on your screen. If you would rather have extra space for viewing Access objects, choose View Options from the menu, choose the General category, and set the Show Tool Bar option to No.

The status bar is the gray bar at the bottom of the Access window that shows status messages, modes, and the status of the locking keys. If you

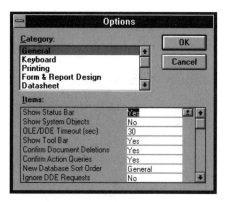

Figure 15.5 Changing your Access configuration options.

don't want Access to display the status bar, choose View Options from the menu, choose the General category, and set the Show Status Bar option to No.

Requiring Confirmation for Changes

Access provides several confirmation options that specify whether or not to notify the user before performing certain edits.

Access usually asks you for confirmation before performing operations that might delete information or make changes to large number of records. You can confirm three types of edits:

- Received changes: When deleting a record in a table, pasting a new record into a table, or running the Edit Replace command
- Document deletors: When deleting an object, like a table or a form
- Action queries

These three settings in the General category of the Options dialog box control whether Access asks for confirmation in these situations, or whether Access performs the operation without asking:

- Confirm Record Changes
- Confirm Document Deletions (for deleting objects)
- Confirm Action Queries

When you install Access, these options are set to Yes for your own protection. To perform editing tasks without having Access ask for confirmation, you can change one or all of these options to No. But remember: It is easy to press the Del key by mistake, so it might be more convenient, not to mention less frustrating, to respond to a confirmation request from Access than to retype a record!

Telling Access where Your Databases Are

You can enter a default database directory path name, so Access knows where to look for your database files.

If you keep most or all of your Access database files in the same directory, it would be convenient for Access to display the files in that directory automatically when you use the File Open Database command. To tell Access where your databases are stored, choose View Options from the menu, choose the General category, and set the Default Database Directory option to the full path name of the directory that contains your database files. For example, you might enter:

```
c:\bookstor\dbs
```

You can still open databases in other directories, using the Open Database dialog box.

Customizing the Keyboard

You can control the way the Arrow and Enter keys work in forms and datasheets.

Three configuration options control how the Arrow and Enter keys move during data entry:

- **Arrow Key Behavior**: Next Field or Next Character
- **Move After Enter**: No, Next Field, or Next Record
- **Cursor Stops at First/Last Field**: Yes or No

When you edit fields in a datasheet or form, when the Arrow Key Behavior is set to Next Field, the cursor moves from field to field, selecting each field as it moves. To edit the contents of a field, you press **F2** to switch to edit mode. If you set the Arrow Key Behavior to Next Character, you remain in edit mode all the time. The Arrow keys move from character to character within the current field, then move to the first character of the next field. If you find yourself pressing F2 constantly, or accidentally deleting data when you try to edit values, you may want to use the Next Character setting.

When you are editing records in a form, it can be annoying when you accidentally press the Right Arrow or Down Arrow key in the last field and move to the first field of the next record. If you work on one record at a time and don't want to move from record to record by accident, you can set the Cursor Stops at First/Last Record option to Yes.

Customizing the Toolbar and Other Windows

The UTILITY.MDA database contains the specifications for the toolbar as it appears when different windows are active. It also contains the specifications for the toolbox, palette, and Zoom box. By modifying the UTILITY.MDA database, you can customize these features of Access.

Changing Your UTILITY.MDA Database

Make changes to a copy of the database, then edit your MSACCESS.INI file to refer to the copy.

Access uses the UTILITY.MDA database as a library database, containing tables, forms, and modules that Access uses when displaying the toolbar, toolbox, palette, and other windows. Because UTILITY.MDA is already open when you run Access, you cannot modify it. If you try to open UTILITY.MDA, you see the message, "The database "C:\MSACCESS\ UTILITY.MDA" is already open as a library database."

Rather than changing your UTILITY.MDA file, it is a good idea to make a copy of it, then modify the copy. You can then tell Access to use the new, modified database by editing your MSACCESS.INI file:

1. Use Windows File Manager to copy the UTILITY.MDA file, which is stored in your Access program directory, to the same directory, but with a new name. For example, you might call your copy UTIL.MDA.

2. In Access, open the copy. Access usually displays only databases with the extension .MDB. To open a database that has the extension .MDA, edit the contents of the File Name text box in the Open Database dialog box to read:

    ```
    *.MDA
    ```

    When you press **Enter**, Access displays all the files with the extension .MDA, including your database.

3. As Access loads the database, it displays two warning boxes, saying that it tried to load a module with a duplicate procedure definition. Click on OK on each of these boxes.

4. Make changes to the UTIL.MDA database as described in the following topics.

5. Save the updated UTIL.MDA database and exit Access.

6. Using a text editor like the Windows Notepad, modify your MSACCESS.INI file to refer to the copied .MDA file (as described in *Changing MSACCESS.INI Settings* earlier in this chapter). In the [Options] section, change this line:

    ```
    UtilityDB=C:\SW\ACCESS\UTILITY.MDA
    ```

    to this:

    ```
    UtilityDB=C:\SW\ACCESS\UTIL.MDA
    ```

(Make sure to use the name you gave your modified copy of the UTILITY.MDA file.)

7. Restart Access.

If you want to make further changes:

1. Use a text editor to change the UtilityDB line in your MSACCESS.INI file to refer to the original UTILITY.MDA database.

2. Run Access.

3. Open your modified database (UTIL.MDA).

4. Make your changes.

5. Exit Access.

6. Use the text editor to edit the MSACCESS.INI file to refer to your database again.

Note: The easiest way to switch back and forth in your MSACCESS.INI file is to open the file in Windows Notepad and leave it open while you work. Leave lines in that refer to both the original UTILITY.MDA and your modified UTIL.MDA, but "comment one out" by preceding it with a semicolon. For example, to use the original UTILITY.MDA, the [Options] section of MSACCESS.INI looks like this:

```
[Options]
SystemDB=C:\ACCESS\SYSTEM.MDA
UtilityDB=C:\ACCESS\UTILITY.MDA
;  UtilityDB=C:\ACESS\UTIL.MDA
```

To switch to using your modified UTIL.MDA, delete the semicolon on the line that refers to the UTIL.MDA file and insert a semicolon on the preceding line that refers to UTILITY.MDA.

Hot Tip

Get Replacement UTILITY.MDA Files

Access users have created replacement UTILITY.MDA files that you can download from the CompuServe MSACCESS Forum. One useful file, written by Helen Feddema, is called NEWUTIL.MDA and is contained in NEWUTL.ZIP.

Enlarging Text in the Zoom Box

You can change the font and font size used in the Zoom box.

To edit long values, you can press **Shift+F2** to display the Zoom box. Many users find the type in the Zoom box too small. To make the text bigger, open your copy of the UTILITY.MDA database and then follow these steps:

1. Open the ZoomForm form in Design view. The form, shown in Figure 15.6, contains a text box and two command buttons. Don't resize the Design view window.

2. Select the text box.

3. On the toolbar, select a larger font size from the Font size list.

4. You can also change the font by choosing a different font from the Font list.

5. Close and save the form.

6. Exit Access.

When you reload Access, the change will take effect.

Customizing the Toolbar

It is easy to change the appearance and location of buttons on the toolbar. However, to create your own buttons, you must write Access Basic functions.

The Access toolbar changes depending on which window you are using. Different buttons appear when you use the Database window, the Design window, the Form window, the Macro window, the Module window, and others. Each toolbar is stored in UTILITY.MDA as a separate form—they look just like regular Access forms. Each button on the toolbar is a command button control on the form. Figure 15.7 shows the toolbar that appears when the Database window is active.

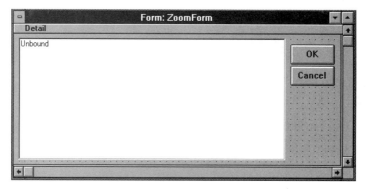

Figure 15.6 ZoomForm in Design view.

Figure 15.7 Toolbar form in Design view.

The toolbar forms in UTILITY.MDA are:

- DBTB: Database window toolbar
- FBTB: Form window toolbar
- FDTB: Form Design window toolbar
- METB: Module window toolbar
- NOTB: Toolbar when no database is loaded
- PPTB: Print Preview toolbar
- QDTB: Query Design window toolbar
- RDTB: Report Design window toolbar
- SDTB: Macro window toolbar
- TBTB: Datasheet window toolbar
- TDTB1: Table Design window toolbar

You can open these forms in Design view and make changes to the forms. Don't change the size of the toolbar form, and don't rename any of the existing controls on the toolbars. The remaining topics in this section describe how to change the appearance of existing buttons and how to make new buttons.

Changing the Appearance of Toolbar Buttons

You can display different pictures or captions on toolbar buttons.

If it is hard to remember what a toolbar button does, you can change the picture on the button. To make a new icon, you can use a screen capture program to copy an icon you like from any Windows application. For example, if you prefer the Find toolbar button in Word for Windows to the one Access uses, capture the Find button icon in Word, but don't include the edges of the button. Be sure to capture it as a Windows Bitmap (.BMP) file.

Alternatively, you can draw your own icon, or enhance an icon you have captured. Use Windows Paintbrush or any draw program that can save pictures in .BMP format. Make the background of the icon gray to match the other toolbar buttons, and don't enclose it in a box.

To change the icon on a toolbar button:

1. Using your copy of the UTILITY.MDA database (described in *Changing Your UTILITY.MDA Database* earlier in this chapter), open the toolbar form in Design view.

2. Turn off Snap to Grid, to avoid moving buttons on the toolbar by accident. (If Snap to Grid is on, a check mark appears by it on the Layout menu. To turn it off, choose Layout Snap to Grid.)

3. Display the property sheet.

4. Select the button you want to modify, being careful not to move it.

5. To change the picture that is displayed, enter the full path and filename of the Windows Bitmap (.BMP) file in the Picture property.

6. So that you can tell which file contains the bitmap, enter the same path and filename in the Caption property. Access ignores the caption if there is a picture.

7. Save and close the toolbar form.

8. Exit Access and follow the steps in *Changing Your UTILITY.MDA Database* earlier in this chapter to use your newly modified UTIL.MDA database.

Adding Buttons to the Toolbar

You can create your own toolbar buttons to call Access Basic functions.

You can add new buttons to the toolbar by creating command button controls. The buttons must run Access Basic functions, not macros, because macros don't work in library databases.

For example, you can add a button to the Form Design or Report Design window toolbar to display or hide the toolbox (this example comes from a Microsoft technical note):

1. In your copy of the UTILITY.MDA database, open the FDTB form in Design view.

2. Create a new command button control in a blank space on the form, perhaps to the right of the Palette button. Make sure the new button

control does not overlap any other controls and that it does not alter the height of the form. You can move other buttons closer together to make room for the new button.

3. For the button's On Push property, enter this expression:

```
=ToggleToolBox()
```

This calls an Access Basic function, which you will create in a later step.

4. For the button's Picture property, enter the full path and filename of a Windows Bitmap (.BMP) that contains the icon you want to use on the button. Alternatively, enter text in the Caption property and Access will display the first letter of the text on the button. For example, enter *T* or *Toolbox* as the caption. Figure 15.8 shows the left part of the toolbar form, with the new button to the right of the Palette button.

5. Save and close the form.

To create a new Access Basic module to contain the Access Basic function called by this button:

1. View the list of modules in the Database window and click on New.

2. The Module window contains one declaration. (See Chapter 17 for what this means, and how to use the Module window.) On the next (blank) line, type the first line of your new function:

```
Function ToggleToolBox ()
```

Access recognizes that you are writing a new function, creates a new function, and types the End Function command that will appear as the last line of the function.

3. Between the Function and End Function lines, type this command:

```
DoCmd DoMenuItem 3, 2, 8
```

The DoCmd command chooses View Toolbox from the menu. The finished function appears in Figure 15.9.

Figure 15.8 Adding a button to toggle the toolbox.

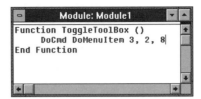

Figure 15.9 Access Basic function to toggle the toolbox on and off.

4. Close and save the module with the name NewToolBarFunctions.

5. Exit Access.

When you edit your MSACCESS.INI file to use your copy of the UTILITY.MDA database and run Access, you will see the new button on the toolbar when you edit a form. For more information on writing Access Basic functions, see Chapter 17.

Optimizing Access' Environment

Access is a large program, taking up lots of both disk space and memory. Although you can run Access on a computer with 4Mb of RAM, Microsoft recommends at least 8Mb. If you have only 4Mb, the first topic in this section describes ways to improve your performance. In fact, these suggestions are useful no matter how much memory your computer has! This section also describes how to tell Access where to store its temporary files.

Running Access with 4Mb of RAM

Leave as much RAM a possible free for Access to use.

Microsoft offers the following suggestions if you must run Access on a computer with only 4Mb of RAM:

- Don't use a RAM disk, because this restricts the amount of RAM Access can use. Don't use the RAMDrive utility that comes with Windows.
- If you use SMARTDrive to make a disk cache in RAM, don't make it large. Use at most 512K for a disk cache.
- If you use a network, install the minimum network drivers.
- Run Windows in standard mode.
- Load as few device drivers as possible.

- If you use "wallpaper" as the background of your screen, remove it. From the Windows Program Manager, run Control Panel, double-click on the Desktop icon to display the Desktop dialog box shown in Figure 15.10, and set Wallpaper to (None). This change can save from 256K to 768K of RAM, depending on your screen resolution and the size of the bitmap file.

- Don't run other large applications at the same time that you run Access—even desktop managers can take enough memory to slow Access down. Run as few small applications (Windows File Manager, Windows Clock, etc.) as possible.

- Access uses its own buffer for reading and writing database information on disk. The size of the buffer is specified by the MaxBufferSize entry in your MSACCESS.INI file (see *Speeding Up Access* earlier in this chapter). If your memory is limited, set this initialization setting to no more than 512 (that is, 512K).

- If you do not plan to create new reports and forms, disable ReportWizards and FormWizards. In your MSACCESS.INI file (described in *Customizing Initialization Settings in MSACCESS.INI* earlier in this chapter), find the line in the [Libraries] section that lists the WIZARD.MDA file. Insert a semicolon at the beginning of the line to turn the line into a comment, which Access then ignores. When you exit and restart Access, the WIZARD.MDA database will not be loaded as a library file, saving 300K of RAM. If you want to use ReportWizards or FormWizards later, you can easily remove the semicolon from your MSACCESS.INI file.

Figure 15.10 Don't use wallpaper if you have limited memory.

- When you open a database, select the Exclusive box in the Open Database dialog box. This means that only you can use the database. It requires extra memory to share databases.

- If possible, open databases in read-only mode by selecting the Read Only box in the Open Database dialog box. If you plan to look at the contents of the database without making changes, read-only access is faster than read-write access.

Selecting where Access Stores Temporary Files

You can specify the directory name by including a line in your AUTOEXEC.BAT file.

Many programs, including Access, create temporary files while they are running, and delete these temporary files automatically when the work session is over. Many Windows programs, including Access, store these temporary files in the Windows TEMP directory.

To specify the Windows TEMP directory, you use the DOS SET command to create this line in your AUTOEXEC.BAT file:

```
set temp=c:\tempfile
```

This command creates a DOS variable named temp and sets it equal to the directory name you specify. Because this line is included in your AUTOEXEC.BAT file, it is run automatically every time you start your computer. You can use a text editor like Windows Notepad to add this line to your AUTOEXEC.BAT file, which is stored in the root directory of your startup disk, usually in C:\.

When you choose the directory in which to store temporary files, don't use the root directory (C:\) or a directory on a disk that is almost full. Make a directory named something like C:\TEMP or C:\WINDOWS\TEMP. Alternatively you can store your temporary files on a RAM disk, which requires extra memory but can speed up Access operations. (Refer to your Microsoft Windows *User's Guide* on using the RAMDrive utility.)

Deleting Unnecessary Setup Files

Early versions of the Setup program sometimes left unneeded files on your hard disk.

The Access 1.0 Setup program may have left unnecessary files on your hard disk. If you see a directory named MS-SETUP.T on your hard disk, containing five files (STFSETUP.EXE, STFSETUP.INF, DETCMD.DLL, VER.DLL, and COMMDLG.DLL), you can delete the files and the directory. This can save you 656K of disk space!

CHAPTER

16

ccess Macro Tips

Throughout this book, I have touched on how macros can make your Access database smarter. Chapter 8 contains macros for use with forms, both to be run by command buttons and to be triggered by form events. In this chapter, I'll describe general techniques for creating, modifying, and testing macros, actions you can include in macros, and techniques for creating turn-key applications with macros.

Access automates many tasks that require programming in other database programs. For example, Access automates the following procedures:

- Copying values from the previous record into the current record—just press **Ctrl+"**

- Entering today's date—just press **Ctrl+;**

- Validating entries—just enter an expression in the Validation Rule property of the field when you design the table, or of the control when you design a form that displays the field

- Displaying a linked subform—just enter the names of linking fields in the Link Child Fields and Link Master Fields properties of the subform control

- Requiring that an entry in the key field of a detail table correspond to an existing entry in the master table—just define a relationship and select the Enforce Referential Integrity option on the Relationships dialog box

If you have used less advanced database programs, you know how much work it can be to program these tasks yourself—it's great that Access built them in!

The examples in this chapter are based on the church membership database (CHURCH) described in the *Membership Roster* topic in Chapter 14.

Creating and Editing Macros

Creating a new macro is easy—just click on the Macro button in the Database window, then click on New. Access displays the Macro window, in which you enter the actions that make up the macro. This section contains tips for creating new macros and editing existing ones, as well as a list of the actions you can include in macros.

Storing Related Macros in Groups

Just as with all other aspects of the Access environment, organization is of the utmost importance. You'll find it more efficient—not to mention less confusing—to organize related macros into groups.

Because most macros are very short—frequently only one or two rows—it is more efficient to store macros in groups; efficiency comes both in terms of Access storage and in terms of organizing macros for easy maintainence. Here are examples of macros that should be stored in macro groups:

- All macros used on one form
- All macros used with one report
- All macros for one drop-down menu on a custom menu for a form (described in *Creating Custom Menus for a Form* at the end of this chapter)

To create a macro group:

1. Create a new macro by clicking on Macro, then New, in the Database window.
2. Display the Macro Name column. If it is not already displayed, choose View Macro Names from the menu.
3. For each macro you want to store in the group, enter the name in the Macro Name column.

Running Macros from Macro Groups

There are two ways to run a macro: by entering its name in the property of a form or report, or by clicking on the Run button in the Database window.

To run a macro from a form or report, set the property to the name of the macro group, followed by a period, followed by the name you entered in the Macro Name column. For example, if the macro group is named Families Form and the macro name is Print, set a form, report, or control property to

```
Families Form.Print
```

If you use the Run button in the Database window to run a macro, Access runs only the first macro in the group.

Note: If you have two macros with the same name in a group, and they are stored consecutively (without another macro in between), Access will run both of them even though you intended to run only one. That is, a macro continues running until Access encounters a *different* name in the Macro Name column.

Prevent Macros from Running Directly

If a macro group contains macros to be run from a form or report, and not directly from the File Run Macro command or Run button, enter a comment on the first row of the macro group. Usually, the File Run Macro command runs the first macro in the macro group. If the first row of the macro is a comment, the command or button won't run anything.

Copying a Macro or Macro Group

If you want to create a new macro that is similar to an existing one, it is more efficient to modify a copy of the existing macro rather than starting from scratch.

There are two ways to copy a macro group:

- Open the macro group in the Macro window and save it with a different name by choosing the File Save As command
- In the Database window, highlight the macro group, copy it to the Clipboard by pressing **Ctrl+C**, then paste a copy of it back into the database by pressing **Ctrl+V**

You can use the second method to copy a macro group from one database into another.

Copy a Macro in a Macro Group

If you use a macro group to store several macros, you can make a copy of a single macro within the group by copying the lines that contain the macro. When you copy a line of a macro, Access copies all the associated arguments, too.

Printing a Macro Using the Database Analyzer

If you are creating a database that contains many macros, you may want to print the macros out for reference, or as part of the technical documentation for the database.

Because there is no File Print command in the Macro window, you must use the Database Analyzer that comes with Access. Refer to *Documenting Your Database* in Chapter 3 for instructions on installing the Database Analyzer.

To use the Database Analyzer to print out a macro:

1. Run the Analyzer macro you created during installation of the Database Analyzer.

2. Click on the Macro button to display a list of macros in the Items Available list.

3. Select the macro or macros you want to print.

4. Click on the Analyze button.

5. Choose a database to contain the resulting @MacroDetails table. You can choose the current database (which contains the macro) or another database, but the database must already exist. Click on OK to begin the analysis.

6. Access analyzes the macro(s) and displays the message "Process Completed." Click on OK.

7. Click on Close to exit from the Analyzer. Now there is a table named @MacroDetails in the database you selected in step 5.

8. View the @MacroDetails table in Datasheet view, as shown in Figure 16.1. You can either print the Datasheet view or create a report based on the table. Figure 16.2 shows a report to print macros.

MacroGroup	Action	Condition	Argument1	Argument2	Argument3	Ar
	OpenForm		Main Menu	0		
View Publishers	OpenForm		Publishers	0		[P
By Title	ApplyFilter		Books By Title			
	GoToControl		Title			
By Code	ApplyFilter		Books by Cod			
	GoToControl		Bk Code			
Publisher	SetValue		Forms![Books	Left(Forms![Bo		
	GoToControl		Available?			
NewCode	SetValue	([Publisher] I	[Bk Code]	[Publisher] & "		
	SetValue	Len([Bk Cod	[Bk Code]	[Publisher] & "		

Record: 7

Figure 16.1 Printing a macro from the @MacroDetails table.

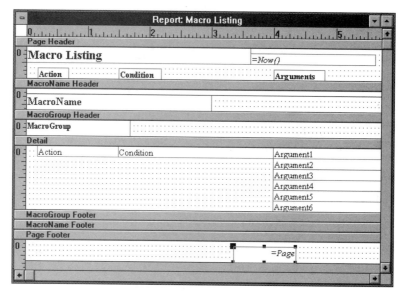

Figure 16.2　Report design for printing macros.

Choosing Macro Actions

Access contains 42 actions that you can use in your macros. This section contains suggestions for choosing and entering macro actions.

Using Actions That Give Commands

Most Access commands have a macro action equivalent.

Table 16.1 shows Access commands and their equivalent macro actions. To execute other commands from macros, use the DoMenuItem action.

Opening Objects in a Macro

You can drag objects from the Database window to a macro.

If you drag a table to a row of your macro, Access inserts an OpenTable action in the macro, enters the table name as the Table Name argument, and enters the default values for the other arguments. You can also drag queries, forms, reports, and macros from the Database window to create OpenQuery, OpenForm, OpenReport, and RunMacro actions, respectively.

If you have already selected an action for a line of a macro, you can also drag objects to the arguments of the action. For example, if you have

Table 16.1 Access Commands and Macro Action Equivalents

Access Command	Macro Action	Comments
Edit Find (or Find button on toolbar)	FindRecord and FindNext	FindRecord tells Access what to search for, and is equivalent to filling in the text boxes of the Find dialog box; FindNext repeats the search.
File Attach Table	TransferDatabase	Select Attach Table for the Transfer Type argument.
File Close	Close	Closes the object you specify. You can use it to close any type of Access window.
File Exit	Quit	Set the Options argument to tell Access whether to save any unsaved objects before quitting.
File Export	TransferDatabase, TransferSpreadsheet, or TransferText	Select Export for the Transfer Type argument.
File Import	TransferDatabase, TransferSpreadsheet, or TransferText	Select Import for the Transfer Type argument.
File Print	Print	Specifies which pages and how many copies to print.
File Rename	Rename	Use the SelectObject action first to select the object to rename.
Edit Copy and Edit Paste	CopyObject	Copies the object to specify; you can even copy it to another Access database.
Records Apply Filter/Sort (in forms)	ApplyFilter	Set the Filter Name argument to the name of an existing query to use as a filter, or enter an SQL WHERE statement as the Where Condition argument.
Records Go To	GoToRecord	Choose First, Last, Previous, Next, or New for the Record argument.
Records Show All Records (in forms)	ShowAllRecords	
Open button in Database window	OpenForm, OpenQuery, or OpenTable	

Table 16.1 Access Commands and Macro Action Equivalents (continued)

Access Command	Macro Action	Comments
Preview button in Database window	OpenReport	
Shift+F9	Requery	Reruns the query that is the record source of a form, subform, or object.

already entered ApplyFilter as the action, you can drag a query from the Database window to the Filter Name argument of the action. Access will then enter the name of the query in the Filter Name argument.

Entering Information in Dialog Boxes

If your macro displays a dialog box, use the SendKeys action to fill it in.

To include most Access commands in a macro, you can use the equivalent macro action used in Table 16.1. However, for commands that do not have a macro equivalent, you may need to have your macro run a command that displays a dialog box. For example, there is no macro action that changes options on the Options dialog box; instead, you can use the DoMenuItem action to choose View Options from the menu and view the Options dialog box.

To enter information in the dialog box, you use the SendKeys action. However, instead of putting the SendKeys action *after* the DoMenuItem action in your macro as you would expect, you must position it just *before* the DoMenuItem action. When a DoMenuItem action displays a dialog box, the macro is suspended. To prevent the macro from stopping at this point, you must already have told Access what to type in the dialog box, using a SendKeys action.

The SendKeys action uses two arguments: Keystrokes and Wait. The Keystrokes argument contains *keystroke codes*—the letters, numbers, spaces, and punctuation you want Access to type. Table 16.2 shows how to enter special keys. To press a function key, enclose the key name in curly braces (for example, enter {**F2**} to tell the macro to press **F2**). To hold down the Shift, Alt, or Ctrl key while another key is pressed, precede the key name with + for Shift, ^ for Ctrl, and % for Alt. For example, enter **%V** to tell the macro to press **Alt+V**.

Table 16.2   Keystroke Codes for SendKeys Action

Key	Keystroke Code
Enter	{ENTER} or ~
Esc	{ESC}
Up Arrow	{UP}
Down Arrow	{DOWN}
Left Arrow	{LEFT}
Right Arrow	{RIGHT}
Backspace	{BKSP} or {BS}
Tab	{TAB}
Insert	{INSERT}
Delete	{DEL}
Home	{HOME}
End	{END}
PgUp	{PGUP}
PgDn	{PGDN}
Num Lock	{NUMLOCK}
Scroll Lock	{SCROLLLOCK}
Break	{BREAK}
Print Screen	{PRTSC}
Caps Lock	{CAPSLOCK}

For example, in the Options dialog box, if you want to set the Show System Objects option to Yes, you would enter these keystroke codes:

- **{DOWN}** (to move down one option to the Show System Objects option)
- **Yes** (to enter the setting)
- **{ENTER}** or ~ (to exit from the dialog box)

The Wait argument tells Access whether the macro should wait until the keystrokes have been processed before continuing to run the macro (Yes) or to continue running the macro (No).

Here's a sample macro that displays a dialog box and enters information. To set configuration options from within a macro:

1. In one row of a macro, choose the SendKeys action.

2. In the Keystrokes argument, enter the keys you want the macro to press in the Options dialog box. For example, to show system objects, enter this text in the Keystrokes argument:

   `{DOWN}Yes~`

3. Leave the Wait argument set to No. This setting is required when using SendKeys to enter information in a dialog box.

4. In the next row of the macro, choose the DoMenuItem action.

5. For the arguments, enter information about the command you want to choose. The Access menu contains different commands, depending on which window you are using, so you must tell Access which menu to use. To set configuration options, you can use the Database menu, that is, the menu that appears when you are using the Database window—choose Database for the Menu Bar argument.

6. For the Menu Name argument, choose the menu name you want the macro to choose from the menu. For example, choose View.

7. For the Command argument, choose the command you want the macro to choose from the drop-down menu you specified in the Menu Name argument. For example, select Options.

8. If the command you want to choose has a subcommand (that is, a third choice), choose it for the Subcommand argument. The View Options command doesn't have a subcommand, so in our example, leave it blank.

Note: The SendKeys action can send up to 255 keystrokes. If you need to type more than 255 keystrokes, you'll need to use more than one SendKeys action.

Hide the Toolbar or Status Bar

While your macro is running, you may not want the toolbar to appear. To turn it off, use the SendKeys and DoMenuItem actions to set the Show Tool Bar option to No. You can also suppress the status bar by setting the Show Status Bar option to No.

Dealing with Warnings and Message Boxes

You usually don't want to see Access' routine warning boxes while a macro is running.

To suppress warning boxes while a macro is running, use the SetWarnings action with the Warnings On argument set to No. Using this action is like telling Access to press **Enter** whenever a warning or message box appears. It doesn't affect error boxes, which still appear and cause the macro to stop.

To turn warnings back on, repeat the SetWarnings action with the Warnings On argument set to Yes.

Displaying Multiple-Line Messages

When you use the MsgBox action in a macro, Access displays a message box with the text you enter in the Message argument.

To tell Access to split the message into several lines, enter the message as a text expression and concatenate a carriage return character and a line feed character where you want the line break to appear. To include these characters in the expression, use the Chr() function and the ASCII character codes of the characters (Chr(13) for a carriage return and Chr(10) for a line feed).

For example, you could enter this expression in the Message argument for the MsgBox action in a macro:

```
"Attention New Users:" & Chr(13) & Chr(10) & "You must enter a Family
   Name."
```

The message would appear like this:

```
Attention New Users:
You must enter a Family Name.
```

Handling Errors

Access doesn't include true error-handling actions for macros, but you can make your own for some errors.

Access doesn't provide a way to "trap" errors when they occur in your macros. However, by using conditions you can prevent some errors, display a message to the user, and either cancel the task that would have caused the error or stop the macro.

For example, if you write a macro that prints the current record in a form, you may want to prevent the macro from printing if the form is blank. Include these actions before the Print action that prints the form:

- Enter a condition that detects a potential error, for example:

```
[Family Name] Is Null
```

- On the same row of the macro, enter a MsgBox action that displays a message box that tells the user to display a record and try printing again.

- On the next row of the macro, enter an ellipsis (...) in the Condition column to repeat the preceding condition.

- On the same row as the ellipsis, enter a StopMacro action to stop processing.

In some macros, if your condition detects an error, you'll want to cancel the event that triggered the macro. For example, a macro that is called by the Before Update property of a control on a form is used to validate the value of the control. If the condition detects an error, use the CancelEvent action to cancel the update that triggered the macro. For examples of using the CancelEvent action, see *Requiring an Entry, Avoiding Acciden-tal Deletions,* and *Checking for Duplicates* in Chapter 8.

Selecting the Object to Use

Some macro actions affect the currently selected object.

To choose an object on which you want the action to work, use the SelectObject action first. Set the Object Type argument to the type of object to select, and the Object Name argument to its name.

If you set the In Database Window argument to No, Access looks among the open objects in the Access window and makes the one you specified active. If the object isn't open, it causes an error.

If you set the In Database Window argument to Yes, Access selects the object's name in the Database window. You can then copy or rename it by using the CopyObject or Rename actions.

Running Action Queries

It is always more efficient to store an SQL statement than an Access query.

In previous chapters, I have described how to use an SQL statement instead of a query for the record source of a form or report or as the source of a combo box control on a form. You can use the same method to include an SQL statement in a macro, although in macros you can only use SQL statements for action queries, not for select or crosstab queries.

To run an action query in a macro as an SQL statement:

1. View the action query in Design view.
2. Choose View SQL from the menu to display the SQL dialog box.
3. In the SQL dialog box, select the entire SQL statement, then press **Ctrl+C** to copy it to the Clipboard.
4. Switch to the Macro window.
5. Choose RunSQL as the action for a row in the macro.
6. Move to the SQL Statement argument for the row.
7. Press **Ctrl+V** to paste the SQL statement into the argument text box. You can then press **Shift+F2** to view the entire SQL statement.
8. Unless you need the action query for other purposes, delete the query.

Running an Access Basic Function from a Macro

If you have written functions in Access Basic, you can use them in macros.

To run an Access Basic function in a macro, use the RunCode action and enter the name of the function in the Function Name argument. However, you can't run an Access Basic subroutine (sub) this way. To run an Access Basic subroutine, create a function that calls the sub (see Chapter 17).

Running Another Windows Application

You can even run another application while Access remains loaded and the database remains open.

To run a Windows or non-Windows program, use the RunApp action in your macro. For the Command Line argument, enter the command that runs the program. If the program has an icon in the Windows Program Manager, you can copy the command line from the icon by highlighting the icon in Program Manager, choosing File Properties from the menu, and copying the contents of the Command Line text box.

When Access executes the RunApp action in a macro, it runs the application. Access remains loaded as well. You can issue commands or type in the other program, switch between it and Access, use Access, switch to and exit from the other program, or exit from Access—it is just the same as running the program by double-clicking on its icon in Program Manager.

You can also tell Access to type commands in the other program. By using a SendKeys action before the RunApp action, you can give Access a series of keys to press. The SendKeys keystroke codes are described in *Entering Information in Dialog Boxes* earlier in this chapter.

For example, you might want to save information from your database in a text file. The macro in Table 16.3 runs the Windows Notepad, pastes the contents of the Clipboard at the end of a file called DATA.TXT (assuming that this file exists), saves the file, and exits from Notepad.

The Keystrokes argument translates like this:

- %FOC:\DBS\DATA.TXT~: Chooses File Open from the menu in Notepad and opens the file C:\DBS\DATA.TXT

- ^{END}: Moves to the end of the file

- ^V~: Pastes the contents of the Clipboard into the file, followed by a carriage return

- %FS: Chooses File Save

- %FX: Chooses File Exit to exit from Notepad

To use the macro, create an empty file called DATA.TXT in the C:\DBS directory (you can change the path and filename in the macro if you want the file to have a different path and name). Copy information from the database onto the Clipboard by selecting it and presing **Ctrl+C**. Then run the macro to copy the information into the file.

You can use RunApp to run any Windows or non-Windows program. However, you can only use the SendKeys action with Windows programs—non-Windows programs won't receive the keystrokes it sends.

Table 16.3   Macro to Copy Text to a Text File

Macro Name	Condition	Action	Arguments
Copy Text		SendKeys	Keystrokes: %FOC:\DBS\DATA.TXT ~^{END}^V~%FS%FX Wait: No
		RunApp	Command Line: NOTEPAD.EXE

Running Macros

You can run a macro directly by using the File Run Macro command, by clicking on the Run button, by attaching it to the property of a form or report, or by running it from another macro or module. You can also tell Access to run the macro automatically when Access loads or when you open a database.

Running a Macro When You Open a Database

You can automatically run a macro that displays a main menu form.

To run a macro automatically whenever you open a database, name the macro group AutoExec. When Access opens a database, it looks in the database for a macro named AutoExec and runs it. Access won't run the AutoExec macro when you restore Access from an icon, only when you start the program.

HOT TIP

Skip the AutoExec Macro

What if you want to open a database without running its AutoExec macro? Hold down the **Shift** key while the database is loading.

Running a Macro When You Run Access

You can also specify a macro to run on the Access command line.

Access has a command-line option for running a macro automatically when Access loads. If you include a database name on the command line, you can use the /X command-line option to specify a macro in that database. Access opens the database you name and then runs the macro.

For example, this Access command line opens the CHURCH database and runs the MainMenu macro:

```
c:\access\msaccess.exe c:\church\church /x mainmenu
```

Running Long Macros

While a macro is running, you may not want Access to update the screen.

If a macro takes a long time to run—perhaps it imports a large file—it will run faster if Access doesn't have to update the screen. You can use the Echo action to tell Access not to update the screen by entering No for the Echo On argument. However, if the screen doesn't update, the user may not know what's going on—it may appear that Access has hung. To keep the user informed, enter a message in the Status Bar Text argument of the Echo command. You can also use the hourglass mouse pointer to tell the user that the macro will take a while by using the Hourglass action with Yes for the Hourglass On argument.

At the end of the macro (or of the time-consuming part of the macro), be sure to turn echoing back on and turn the mouse pointer back into an arrow by using the Echo action with Yes for the Echo On argument and the Hourglass action with No for the Hourglass On argument.

Include an Audible Signal

If a macro takes a long time to run, you can tell Access to beep when it is done. Include a Beep action after the actions that take a long time to process.

Running Another Macro

You can run another macro as a subroutine of the macro that is running.

A *subroutine* is a program that is run from another program. To run one macro as a subroutine from another macro, use the RunMacro action. Access stops running the current macro and runs the subroutine macro you name. When the subroutine macro is done, Access resumes running the original macro.

You can run a subroutine macro more than one time. Simply enter a number in the Repeat Count argument to run it a fixed number of times. By using the RunMacro action and the Repeat Count argument, you can make a macro loop like a For/Next loop in Access Basic or other languages.

You can also keep running the macro over and over until a condition becomes true by entering the condition in the Repeat Expression argument. Be sure that the Repeat Expression will eventually come true, or the macro will repeat *forever*! Using the Repeat Expression makes a macro loop like a While/Wend loop in Access Basic.

Assigning Macros to Keys

You can create your own keyboard macros by assigning macros to keys on the keyboard.

Your database can contain a *key-assignment* macro—a macro that assigns keys on the keyboard to run macros. This macro is usually the AutoKeys macro, although you can change this name by choosing View Options Keyboard and entering a different name for the Key Assignment Macro option.

In the AutoKeys macro, your entry in the Macro Name column tells Access what key you want to assign each macro to. You enter the keys the same way you enter the Keystrokes argument for the SendKeys action (see *Entering Information in Dialog Boxes* earlier in this chapter). For example, if you find that you have to type the name of a nearby town in many entries in a table (but you don't want to make it the default value), you can assign it to a key. The ^A macro in Table 16.4 assigns the text "Arlington" to the Ctrl+A key combination.

You can also assign macros that give other macro commands—for example, the macro in Table 16.5 assigns the Ctrl+P key combination to print a report.

Users Can Have Their Own Key Assignments

If several people use the same database, they may want different key assignments. For example, one may spend most of his time entering data, and want text assigned to several keys. Another user may print reports, and she may want each key to print a different report.

Table 16.4   AutoKeys Macro

Macro Name	Condition	Action	Arguments
^A		SendKeys	Keystrokes: Arlington Wait: No

Table 16.5   AutoKeys Macro to Print a Report

Macro Name	Condition	Action	Arguments
^P		OpenReport	Report Name: Membership Roster View: Print Preview Filter Name: Where Condition:

You can make a key-assignment macro for each person, and each user can use the View Options Keyboard command to enter a different name for the Key Assignment Macro option

Disable Keys

You can also use the AutoKeys macro to disable keys that you don't want to press by accident, or that you don't want other people to use. In the AutoKeys macro, assign the key to a macro that does nothing, or that displays a message box explaining that the key has been disabled.

Testing Macros

Few macros run correctly the first time. When a macro doesn't work the way you want, Access provides several tools to find the problem.

Stepping through a Macro

Single-stepping runs the macro one action at a time with a pause between each action.

Single-step mode lets you see what each action in your macro does and makes it easy to see if you have chosen the right actions and arguments and if they are in the right order. To turn on single-step mode, click on the Single Step button on the toolbar or choose Macro Single Step from the menu.

While single-step mode is on, all macros run one action at a time, including macros that are run from form or report properties. When you run a macro, Access displays the Macro Single Step dialog box, shown in Figure 16.3. The dialog box shows the next action in the macro—Access has not yet performed the action. To continue macro execution, you can choose one of the three buttons in the dialog box:

```
┌─────────────────────────────────────────────┐
│            Macro Single Step                 │
│ Macro Name:                    ┌──────────┐  │
│ SetConfigOptions               │  Step    │  │
│                                └──────────┘  │
│ Action Name:                   ┌──────────┐  │
│ SendKeys                       │  Halt    │  │
│                                └──────────┘  │
│ Arguments:                     ┌──────────┐  │
│ {DOWN}Yes~, No                 │ Continue │  │
│                                └──────────┘  │
└─────────────────────────────────────────────┘
```

Figure 16.3 Single-stepping through a macro.

- Choosing Step performs the action shown in the Macro Single Step dialog box and continues running the macro in single-step mode
- Choosing Halt stops running the macro
- Choosing Continue turns off single-step mode and continues running the macro.

To turn off single-step mode, click on the Single Step button on the toolbar or choose Macro Single Step from the menu.

Note: The Macro Single Step dialog box shows an action even if its condition is false and the macro won't perform the action.

Single-Step Macros in a Macro Group

To test a macro that is located in the middle of a macro group, move it to the top. Then, you can use the Run button on the toolbar or the Macro Run command to test the macro.

Turn On Single-Step while a Macro Is Running

Press **Ctrl+Break** while a macro is running to switch to single-step mode.

When Actions Fail

Access displays the Action Failed dialog box to tell you what action it couldn't perform.

When a macro causes an error, Access displays a message box explaining the error. When you click on OK, Access then displays the Action Failed dialog box, shown in Figure 16.4, which looks just like the Macro Single Step dialog box except that the Step and Continue buttons aren't available—they are grayed out.

To return to the Macro window to fix the problem, click on the Halt button.

Figure 16.4 Access tells you what went wrong when a macro fails.

Displaying the Status of a Macro

While you are testing a macro, add MsgBox actions to display information to help in testing.

For example, you can use a MsgBox action to display the value of a control in a form. In the Message argument, enter the name of the control. For example, to display the value of a control named Family Code in the Families form, enter this expression as the Message argument:

```
=Forms!Families![Family Code]
```

Don't enclose the control name in quotes. To make the message clearer, you can concatenate text with the value of the control, like this:

```
="Family code is " & Forms![Families]![Family Code]
```

Access displays a message box like the one shown in Figure 16.5.

Stop a Macro during Testing

When testing a long macro, you may want to test it in parts. You can test just the beginning by adding a StopMacro action at the end of the section you are testing. Then you can look at the results of the macro so far.

Using the Immediate Window

You can use the Immediate window to view the values of controls and to test expressions you plan to use in your macros.

The Immediate window is a window you can display while working on Access Basic modules in the Module window. I'll describe the Module window and Access Basic in the next chapter, but the Immediate window is useful when testing macros, too. Microsoft suggests using the Immediate window for these tasks:

- Testing a form expression such as Forms!Families![Family Code] to see if it returns the value you want

Figure 16.5 Displaying a message for testing only.

- Trying out a query expression using aggregate functions like DSum()
- Testing a macro action

To display the Immediate window:

1. Open an existing module. If your database has no modules, click on the Module button in the Database window and choose New to create a new one.

2. Choose View Immediate Window from the menu to display the Immediate window shown in Figure 16.6 (except when it first appears, it is blank).

In the Immediate window you can view the values of controls in open forms. To display the value of a control or expression, type a question mark, then the complete control name or expression as shown in Figure 16.7. When you press **Enter**, Access displays the value.

Access displays the Immediate window only when the Module window is selected. However, you can display the Immediate window quickly by using the AutoKeys macro:

1. Open the AutoKeys macro, or create a new, blank one.

2. If the Macro Name and Conditions columns are not displayed in the Macros window, choose View Macro Names and View Conditions from the menu.

3. Enter the macro shown in Table 16.6. This macro, assigned to Ctrl+I, opens a new, blank module. Then it displays a message box asking if the Immediate window is already on screen. If the answer is No, it displays the Immediate window.

4. Save the macro as AutoKeys.

5. Close the Immediate window if it is open.

6. Press **Ctrl+I** to run the macro once. A Module window appears, then a message box asking, "Is the Immediate window already on the screen?"

7. Click on No.

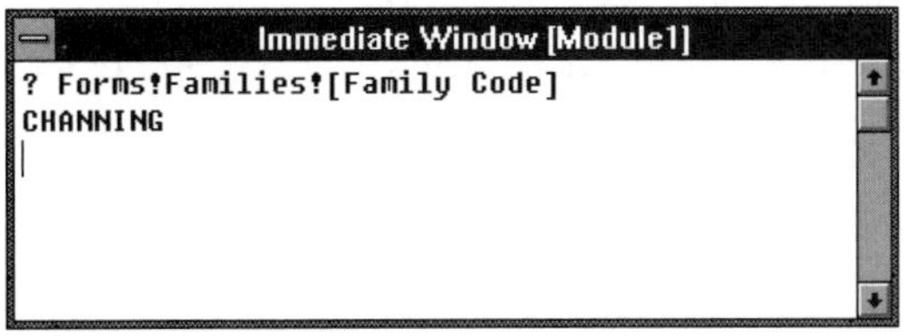

```
Immediate Window [Module1]
? Forms!Families![Family Code]
CHANNING
|
```

Figure 16.6 Viewing the Immediate window.

Table 16.6   AutoKeys Macro to Display Immediate Window

Macro Name	Condition	Action	Arguments
^I		SendKeys	KeyStrokes: {F11} Wait: Yes
		DoMenuItem	Menu Bar: Database Menu Name: View Command: Modules
		SendKeys	KeyStrokes: %N Wait: Yes
	MsgBox ("Is the Immediate window already on the screen?", 4)=7	DoMenuItem	Menu Bar: Module Menu Name: View Command: Immediate Window

8. The macro displays the Immediate window. The Module window is also still on screen.

9. Make the Module window small, perhaps one inch square, but don't iconize it. Move it to an out-of-the way part of the Access window, like the lower-right corner.

10. Size and position the Immediate window as you want it to be displayed.

Now you can use the Immediate window. You need to press **Ctrl+I** only once to open the Immediate window and the small Module window. When you select a window other than the Immediate or Module window, it disappears. To display it again, click on the Module window.

Skipping Macro Commands Temporarily

If you want to skip an action in a macro, but you might want to use it in the future, don't delete it.

Instead of deleting the action, "comment it out!" In the Condition column of the Macro window, enter **False** as the condition for the action. If there is already a condition, add **False And** to the beginning of the condition. Because the condition is always false, Access never runs the action.

Add Rows for Extra Comments

If you want to include a lot of comments in your macros, you can insert extra rows to contain the comments. To add a row for an extra comment, insert a new row in the macro by choosing Edit Insert Row from the menu. Leave the Macro Name, Condition, and Action columns blank, and enter the comment in the Comment column. Access skips the row when the Action column is blank.

Using Macros with Forms

In Chapter 8 you saw how to use macros with form properties and command buttons to make "smart forms." This section contains more macros to make your forms even more powerful.

Deleting One Master Record and Its Related Detail Records

When you define a relationship between two tables with referential integrity enforced, Access won't let you delete a record in the master table if the detail table contains related records. Instead, you must write a macro.

A *cascading delete* is the deletion of the records in the detail table that relate to the current record in the master table. Access doesn't do this automatically.

You can create a macro that deletes the detail records that are related to the current record in the master table. For example, in the church membership database, when you want to delete a record in the Families table, the macro could delete all the family members in the Individuals table. Follow these steps:

1. In the macro group that contains macros for the Families form, or in a new macro group, create the macro shown in Table 16.7.

    Note: Don't forget the semicolon at the end of the SQL Statement argument for the RunSQL action.

    The MsgBox function displays a message box that asks the user to confirm the deletion. The 33 argument produces a Warning message box with two buttons: OK and Cancel. If the user clicks on OK, the MsgBox ( ) function returns 1. If cancel is checked, MsgBox( ) returns 2. If the result isn't OK (1), the message box is canceled and the macro stops. Otherwise, the macro suppresses warnings regarding the upcoming deletions, and runs an SQL statement that deletes the records from the Individuals table.

Table 16.7 Cascading Delete Macro

Macro Name	Condition	Action	Arguments
Cascade	MsgBox("Delete all members of this family?", 33)<>1	CancelEvent	
	...	StopMacro	
		SetWarnings	Warnings On: No
		RunSQL	SQL Statement: DELETE * FROM Individuals WHERE [Family Code] = Forms!Families![Family Code];

2. Save the macro.

3. In Design view, open the form to which you want to attach the macro. For example, open the Families form.

4. In the property sheet for the form, enter the macro name in the On Delete property of the form.

5. Save the form.

Now when you delete the record from the master table using the form, you can delete all its related detail records, too.

Displaying the Related Master Record in a Form

When you are editing a form that contains codes, like the Membership Status code in the Individuals table, you may want to display the full list of codes to add new ones or change existing ones.

You can make a macro that displays a related table and attach the macro to a control on the form. For example, the Individuals form allows you to enter individual members of the church, including each person's membership status. You can attach the macro shown in Table 16.8 to the On Dbl Click property of the Membership Status control, so that double-clicking on the control displays the related table.

Creating Custom Counter Fields

For some operations, you need a place to store a value for a while—a variable.

Table 16.8   Macro to Display Related Table

Macro Name	Condition	Action	Arguments
Status		OpenForm	Form Name: Membership Status
			View: Form
			Filter Name:
			Where Condition:
			Data Mode: Edit
			Window Mode: Normal

A *variable* is a storage location in which you can store information temporarily. Modules written in Access Basic can use variables, but macros can't. To simulate a variable in a macro, make a text box control on a form and set its Visible property to No. Then create a macro attached to the form that copies values to the control by using the SetValue action.

Here's a reason to use this trick: You may not want to use Access' Counter fields to number your records, because you want to reuse record numbers when records are deleted—Counter fields never reuse the number of deleted records. You may also want to be able to skip numbers or start numbering any time to match the number on preprinted forms. Rather than using a Counter field, use a Number field and write a macro to assign record numbers.

For example, if the church membership committee wants to assign unique numbers to each member, it can add a Member Number to the Individuals table, using a Number field of size Integer (assuming that this organization won't have more than 32,000 members!).

To find the highest existing Member Number, you can use this expression:

```
DMax("[Member Number]", "Individuals")
```

As the Individuals table gets bigger, this expression will take longer and longer to run. Rather than using the DMax() function every time you want to add a new member, you can store it in a hidden control on the form. Follow these steps:

1. On the form you plan to use for entering records, create a new unbound text box. For example, create a text box on the Individuals form.

2. Enter a Control Name for the text box, to be used for accessing its value. For example, name the text box MNumber.

3. Create a bound text box to display the Number field you plan to number automatically, in this example, Member Number.

4. "Seed" the Number field by entering the starting number in the first record (or any record). For example, enter **100** as the Member Number for one individual. You can use the form to enter the number, or enter it in the Datasheet view of the table.

5. Create the macro shown in Table 16.9. In the first row, the macro finds the highest existing Member Number and stores it in the MNumber control. In the second row, it sets the Member Number (if blank) to MNumber+1. Finally, it increments MNumber.

6. Enter the macro name in the On Enter property of the Number field that the macro fills, in this case, the Member Number field.

7. Test the macro by moving from field to field in the form, watching that the macro fills in increasing Member Numbers.

8. Hide the unbound text box you are using as a variable, in this case the MNumber control, by setting its Visible property to No.

Note: Using a form control as a variable works well if only one person uses the database at a time. If the database is shared and more than one person adds records, this method won't work because the hidden controls on the forms for each user aren't updated when other users enter records. Instead, you can store the highest existing record number in a one-record, one-field table, since tables are updated by Access when multiple users share a database.

Using Macros with Reports

You can use macros to print reports, to display controls on a report, and to print a report for each new record you enter in a form. This section tells you how.

Table 16.9   Macro to Assign Record Numbers

Macro Name	Condition	Action	Arguments
NewNumber	[MNumber] Is Null	SetValue	Item: [MNumber] Expression: DMax("[Member Number]","Individuals")
	[Member Number] Is Null	SetValue	Item: [Member Number] Expression: Val([MNumber]) + 1
	...	SetValue	Item: [MNumber] Expression: Val([MNumber]) + 1

Printing a Report Showing the Current Record in a Form

Rather than printing the current record in the current form, you can print it in a report.

To print a report for the current record, use the OpenReport action in the macro to open the report. Enter an expression in the Where Condition argument to select only records that match the current record in the form. Table 16.10 shows the macro.

Automatically Printing New Records

You can create a macro that automatically prints a report for each new record you add.

By attaching a macro to the On Insert property of the form, you can tell Access that this new record should be printed. However, the On Insert property runs the macro when the user presses the first key to enter a new record. This is too early to print the new record, since the information hasn't been entered yet. To store the fact that this is a new record, you can use a hidden control as a variable. When the user has entered information into the record and moves to another record or closes the form, a macro attached to the After Update property of the form can print a report for the new record. When you use an unbound control as a variable to indicate that a macro should be run, it is called a *flag*.

For example, you can create a macro attached to the Families form that prints a report showing each family as you enter it in the form:

1. Open the form in Design view. In this example, open the Families form.

2. Create an unbound text box to use as the "flag." Name the control ToPrint.

3. Create the SetFlag macro shown in Table 16.11 to set the flag control to True.

4. Attach the SetFlag macro to the On Insert property of the form, so it runs when a new record is inserted.

Table 16.10 **Print Macro to Print a Report**

Macro Name	Condition	Action	Arguments
PrintRec		OpenReport	Report Name: Families View: Print Filter Name: Where Condition:[Family Code]=Forms![Families]![Family Code]

Table 16.11   Macros to Print New Records

Macro Name	Condition	Action	Arguments
SetFlag		SetValue	Item: Forms![Families]![ToPrint] Expression: True
PrintNew	Forms![Families]![ToPrint] Is Not Null	OpenReport	Report Name: Families View: Print Filter Name: Where Condition: [Family Code]=Forms![Families]![Family Code]
	...	SetValue	Item: Forms![Families]![ToPrint] Expression: Null

5. Create the PrintNew macro shown in Table 16.11 to print the current record when the flag is not blank, then to clear the flag.

6. Attach the PrintNew macro to the After Update property of the form.

In the PrintNew macro, you must check that the flag isn't null. However, you can't check for a particular value, using a condition like this:

```
Forms![Families]![ToPrint] = True
```

This condition won't work because when Access compares a null value to any other value, the result is null rather than false, and the action is performed when you don't want it to be. Instead, use the condition shown in Table 16.11.

Printing Multiple Copies of a Report

What if you always want to print multiple copies of a report, for example, three copies of all invoices?

If you use the Print action to print a report, you can specify the pages and number of copies to print. You may want a macro to print multiple copies of a report—for example, when you print a customer invoice, you usually want three copies: two for the customer and one for your files.

To print multiple copies of a report in a macro, first open the report using the OpenReport action, and set the View argument to Print Preview rather than to Print. Then use the Print action to print the report, setting the Copies argument to the number you want. Finally, use the Close action to close the Print Preview of the report.

Printing "Continued" on Grouped Reports

When you create a report with groups, long groups may spill onto additional pages. Access doesn't have a feature to print the group name and "continued" at the top of the second page for each group, but you can write a macro to do so.

For example, when you print a membership roster, families with many members may run off the bottom of one page and continue on the next page. Microsoft figured out a way to print the group name and "continued" at the top of the column when groups continue in another column or page.

This method uses a hidden text box control called TopPos on the report to contain the vertical position on the page (the distance from the top of the page) of the end of the Page Header. Two macros use the Top property of reports to find this vertical position (measured in twips, or 1/1440ths of an inch) and store it in the TopPos control. Another text box called Continued contains the continuation message you want to display at the tops of pages or columns in which groups continue.

The system works like this:

- When Access starts formatting the page, TopPos is set to zero (by the PageReset macro).

- When Access gets to the first Group Header, Group Footer, or Detail section in the report, a macro (SetTopPos or Print) sets TopPos to the current vertical position on the page, that is, just below the Page Header.

- If the first section to print after the Page Header is a Detail section, then the group is continued from the previous page. Access can tell when the first section prints because TopPos is still zero; the Print macro prints the continuation message and tells Access not to advance to the next record.

- Access then processes the same record again, since the Print macro told it not to advance to the next record, and prints it normally. Because the Print macro set TopPos to the current vertical position, the rest of the records on the page print normally, hiding the continuation message.

This system is confusing, but it works! To modify a grouped report to print continuation messages:

1. Create a new macro group and enter the macros in Table 16.12.

The PageReset macro sets the TopPos control on the report to zero at the top of each page when the Page Header is formatted.

Table 16.12   Macros to Print "Continued" on Subsequent Pages

Macro Name	Condition	Action	Arguments	Row
PageReset		SetValue	Item: [TopPos] Expression: 0	1
SetTopPos	[TopPos]=0	SetValue	Item: [TopPos] Expression: Top	2
Print	[TopPos]=0	SetValue	Item: [TopPos] Expression: Top	3
	[TopPos]=Top	SetValue	Item: [Continued]. Visible Expression: Yes	4
	...	SetValue	Item: [Name].Visible Expression: No	5
	...	SetValue	Item: [MS].Visible Expression: No	6
	...	SetValue	Item: NextRecord Expression: False	7
	...	StopMacro		8
		SetValue	Item: [Continued]. Visible Expression: No	9
		SetValue	Item: [Name].Visible Expression: Yes	10
		SetValue	Item: [MS].Visible Expression: Yes	11

The SetTopPos macro sets the TopPos control to the current vertical position on the page, using the Top report property, when the Group Header or Group Footer section is formatted.

The Print macro prints either the continuation message or the regular Detail section, depending on whether TopPos is zero or a different value. If TopPos is zero, meaning that no Group Header has printed and a group is continued from the previous page, the action in row 3 of Table 16.12 sets TopPos to the vertical position on the page, so that the continuation message won't print a second time. Rows 4 through 8 are executed if Access is printing the continuation message. Rows 9 through 11 are executed for the rest of the records of the page, and print the regular Detail section information.

In this example, the Detail section of the report contains two controls: Name (which displays the full name) and MS (which displays the

Membership Status). Rows 5 and 6 hide them when printing the continuation message, and rows 10 and 11 display them when printing the regular Detail section. When using this method for other reports, you must replace rows 5, 6, 10, and 11 with SetValue actions to hide and display each control in the Detail section of your report.

2. Save the macro group as Continued.

3. Open the report in Design view.

4. For the Page Header section, set the On Format property to the Continued.PageReset macro, so that at the top of each page, the TopPos control is set to zero.

5. For the Group Header and Group Footer sections, set the On Format property to the Continued.SetTopPos macro, so that when a group header or footer is printed, the TopPos control no longer contains zero.

6. For the Detail section, set the On Format property to the Continued.Print macro, to print the continuation message if you are at the top of the page and no group header has printed, and to print the usual Detail section controls otherwise.

7. Create an unbound text box in the Detail section to display the continuation message. Make the Detail section of the report longer, and place the new control at the bottom. Format it to match the controls in the Group Header, for example, boldface and large.

8. Set these properties of the new control:
   - Control Name: Continued
   - Control Source: =[Family Name] & ", continued"
   - Visible: No
   - Can Shrink: Yes

   For the Control Source, use an expression that displays the field name on which the report is grouped, in this example, Family Name.

9. Create another unbound text box in the Group Header section. Set these properties:
   - Control Name: TopPos
   - Visible: No

   It doesn't matter exactly where this control is or how it is formatted, since it remains hidden.

10. Set the Can Shrink properties of all the controls in the Detail section to Yes, to avoid a blank space above the continuation message.

11. Save the report and run it.

This method also works if your grouped report has snaking columns. The macros display a continuation message at the top of columns that contain a continuation of a group.

Using Forms to Prompt for Parameters

Rather than letting Access pop up a bunch of parameter boxes when a user views a parameter query, create a form that collects the information and contains a button to view the query.

For example, in the church database, you might want to see the donations for one quarter. You can make a query called Donations for One Quarter that selects the donations based on a criterion like this:

```
Between FirstOfQtr([Enter date]) And LastOfQtr([Enter date])
```

This expression uses the FirstOfQtr( ) and LastOfQtr( ) functions we will create in Chapter 17 to find the first and last day of the quarter that contains the date entered.

Rather than letting Access display a popup parameter box when the query is run, create a form called Donations for Quarter to collect the information. The text box on this form is called QtrDate.

When the user fills in the date on the form and presses the View command button, a macro uses the OpenQuery action to display the results of the Donations for One Quarter query in Datasheet view. For the query to use the date the person entered on the Donations for Quarter form, you must change the criterion to refer to the control on the form:

```
Between FirstOfQtr([Forms]![Donations for Quarter]![QtrDate]) And
   LastOfQtr([Forms]![Donations for Quarter]![QtrDate])
```

You can make your database much friendlier by creating forms for entering parameters rather than letting Access prompt for parameters one at a time. Command buttons on the form can then display query dynasets (using the OpenQuery action), display information on forms (using the OpenForm action), or print reports (using the Print or OpenReport action) that select information based on the values the user entered on the form. Some advantages are:

- If a query has several parameters, the user can enter them all on the form, editing and correcting all the entries before pressing the command button that views the query or form or prints the report

- If several different forms or reports use the same selection of information, the user can enter the information once, then press different command buttons to view the forms or print the reports

- You can include instructions on the form to explain exactly what information is needed

- You can use combo boxes to allow the user to choose a value from a list, a toggle, an option, or checkboxes to specify Yes/No information

The only disadvantage to this system is that your queries will only work when the appropriate form is displayed. In a turn-key application, this restriction is no problem—you have control over which forms are displayed when, and your macros can always display the form into which the user enters the parameters before using any forms or reports that depend on that form.

Creating Turn-Key Applications

Once you have created the tables, queries, forms, and reports that make up a database, and the macros that are used in form and report properties, you can take your database design one step further. To streamline database operations, you can create macros and forms that display menus of your frequently performed tasks.

When your macros and forms provide menus, accept input into tables, and prompt for information for queries and reports, the user never needs to use Access' menus and tools. A database in which the user is always interacting with your forms and menus rather than with Access' is called a *turn-key application* (or just *application*); in fact, the user never needs to know that your program is based on Access.

Converting a Database into an Application

In a turn-key application it is important to prevent users from making changes to tables except through the forms that you provide. If users can enter information directly into tables using the Datasheet view, they will be able to bypass the validations you build into your forms.

To turn a database into a turn-key application, you must design your forms and macros so that the user is *always* in a form. Then you can control what the user can do by hiding the toolbar and replacing the Access menu with your own menus.

Use these general steps as a guide for turning an Access database into a turn-key application:

1. Create a program item icon for the database in the Windows Program Manager (see *Making an Icon for a Database* in Chapter 15). Include the database name in the Command Line text box so that Access opens the database automatically.

2. If you want the database to open when Windows starts, copy the database icon into the Windows Startup program group. Open the Startup program group window, hold down **Ctrl**, and drag your database icon into the Startup group. Then minimize the Startup program group by clicking on the Minimize button, located on the title bar.

3. Determine whether you want to use Access security to prevent other users from changing objects in the database. As you make further changes in the database, be sure to log in using your user account, not as Admin!

4. In Access, create a macro named AutoExec in your database. The AutoExec macro should do the following:

   • Set the title bar caption for the Access window to display the name of your application

   • Hide the toolbar (see *Hide the Toolbar or Status Bar* earlier in this chapter) so that users can't use buttons on the toolbar to modify forms or reports in Design view

   • Hide the Database window (by using the DoMenuItem action to give the Window Hide command) so that users can't open, design, or run database objects except by using your menus

   • Display a form that contains the main menu for the application

   Table 16.13 shows the AutoExec macro from the church membership database. The first row of the macro changes the title bar caption of the Access window. The second and third rows hide the toolbar by setting the Show Tool Bar option to No on the Options dialog box. The fourth and fifth rows hide the Database window. The last row displays a form named Main Menu.

5. Create the AutoKeys macro that contains a macro named {F11} with no macro action. This macro redefines the F11 key not to display the Database window (see *Assigning Macros to Keys* in Chapter 16). When you redefine F11, Access redefines Alt+F1, too.

6. Create a Main Menu form. Create a menu either using form menus (described later in this chapter) or a group of command buttons.

7. For complex applications with many forms and tables, create additional forms to act as submenus for each major activity, for example for order entry, order processing, and sales reports. For the church membership database, there might be additional forms

Table 16.13 AutoExec Macro for a Turn-Key Application

Action	Arguments
RunCode	FunctionName: SetAccessCaption("Church Membership Database: " & User())
SendKeys	Keystrokes: {DOWN}{DOWN}{DOWN}No~ Wait: No
DoMenuItem	Menu Bar: Form Menu Name: View Command: Options Subcommand:
SelectObject	Object Type: Macro Object Name: AutoExec In Database Window: Yes
DoMenuItem	Menu Bar: Database Menu Name: Window Command: Hide Subcommand:
OpenForm	Form Name: Main Menu View: Form Filter Name: Where Condition: Data Mode: Edit Window Mode: Normal;

named Members, Donations and Donations and Pledges, and Miscellaneous. On each of these forms, create a menu using command buttons or form menus. For example, the Pledges form might contain a menu of command buttons for related tasks like entering pledges, entering donations printing pledge invoices, and printing pledge reports. Make sure that each form contains a button or menu choice to close the form and return to the main menu. Alternatively, you can display the main menu form all the time, and provide buttons or menu choices that close the other forms.

8. Include a command button or menu choice on the main menu to exit from Access.

Making Menus

Access provides two ways of presenting a user with a menu of options: display a group of command buttons on a form, or create a custom menu bar for a form. The advantage of using command buttons as a menu is that the regular Access menus are still accessible. For databases that do not contain turn-key applications, this is the easiest method to use. However, if you are creating a turn-key application in which you do not want users to be able to choose commands from the Access menu, you must create custom menu bars for all the forms in the database so that users never see the Access menu.

Making a Menu of Command Buttons

You can use a form to display a menu of commands, each in the form of a command button on the form.

To create a form that will contain a menu of command buttons:

1. Create an unbound form, that is, a form for which the Record Source property is blank.

2. On the property sheet for the form, set the Default View property of the form to Single Form.

3. Set the Scroll Bars property to Neither, since the form doesn't display records to scroll among.

4. Set the Views Allowed property to Form, since there is no Datasheet to view for this form.

5. Set the Popup and Modal properties to No, so that the user can view other forms at the same time.

6. Set the Record Selectors property to No, since no records are displayed in the form, record selectors are useless.

7. Create the buttons that make up the menu by following the instructions in the section *Creating Command Buttons on Forms* in Chapter 8.

Creating Custom Menus for a Form

To define your own menus, you write macros that define each menu and the commands on it. The menus you create replace the Access menu bar, so be sure to include all the commands a user might need.

Microsoft uses these terms for the parts of a custom menu for a form:

- The *menu bar* is the bar that appears just below the title bar of the Access window. When you create custom menus for a form, the menus don't appear inside the form they appear in the menu bar, replacing Access' usual menu.

- A *drop-down menu* is displayed when you choose a command from the menu bar. For example, the File command on the menu bar displays the File drop-down menu.
- A *command* is a choice on a drop-down menu.

To create a menu bar that replaces the Access menu bar whenever you are in a particular form:

1. Create a macro group for each drop-down menu on the menu bar. For example, if the menu bar will have three drop-down menus named File, Edit, and Help, create three macro groups, perhaps named File Menu, Edit Menu, and Help Menu.

2. In each macro group you created in step 1, create one macro for each command. Name each macro with the command you want to appear on the drop-down menu. For example, the Edit Menu macro group might contain macros named Families, Pledges, and Donations, as shown in Table 16.14.

3. Create a menu bar macro that defines the entire menu bar. For each drop-down menu on the menu bar, you use the AddMenu action to tell Access the name of the macro that contains the commands for that drop-down menu. Table 16.15 contains a menu bar macro defining a menu bar with three drop-down menus: File, Edit, and Help. Use only AddMenu actions in menu bar macros—don't mix in any other actions!

4. Open the form to which you want to attach the menu bar. In the On Menu property of the form, enter the name of the menu bar macro.

Table 16.14 Edit Menu Macro

Macro Name	Condition	Action	Arguments
Families		OpenForm	Form Name: Families View: Form Data Mode: Edit
Pledges		OpenForm	Form Name: Pledges View: Form Data Mode: Edit
Donations		OpenForm	Form Name: Families with Donations View: Form Data Mode: Edit

Designing Menus

Here are some tips for good menu design.

To make your users comfortable with your custom menus and match the menu bars of other Windows applications, keep the following guidelines in mind:

- Always include a File menu that contains a Close or Exit command. You can run a macro to exit from Access or just from the form.

- Include status bar text for each command by entering the text in the Comment column of the Macro window.

- Include any Access commands the user might need—remember, your custom menu replaces the Access menu. Use DoMenuItem actions to run commands.

- Provide access keys (Alt+key combinations that allow users to choose commands from the keyboard) by preceding one letter in each menu and command name with an ampersand (&).

- If there are more than four or five commands on a menu, separate them into groups. Separate the groups with a horizontal line by entering a hyphen (-) in the Macro Name column between the macros for two commands.

- To keep the macro groups that define your drop-down menus simple, don't include any macros that perform more than one action—instead, use the RunMacro action to run a macro in another macro group. Keeping your drop-down menu macros short makes it easier to maintain them. Also, macros called from menu macros may be useful elsewhere.

Table 16.15   Menu Bar Macro

Action	Arguments
AddMenu	Menu Name: File Menu Macro Name: File Menu Status Bar Text: Close database or exit
AddMenu	Menu Name: Edit Menu Macro Name: Edit Menu Status Bar Text: Edit families, pledges, or donations
AddMenu	Menu Name: Help Menu Macro Name: Help Menu Status Bar Text: Get more information

CHAPTER

17

An Introduction to Access Basic

T he great thing about Access is that you don't have to learn Access Basic to create complex and useful database applications. But if you run into something you can't do with Access' other features, including macros, you can jump into the world of programming.

Access Basic is a full-featured programming language and entire books have been written about it. In this chapter, I'll describe the fundamentals of creating and running functions written in Access Basic, with some sample functions you can use in your databases. I'll also describe how to create your own library database of Access Basic functions.

The examples in this chapter are included in the CHURCH database on the Companion Diskette.

Module Concepts

A *module* is a set of programs written in Access Basic. Each program is called a *procedure*. There are two kinds of procedures: *functions* and *subs*.

A *function* is an Access Basic program that returns a value—that is, Access uses the result of the function at the location that the function was called. Like Access' built-in functions, you can use functions in properties and expressions throughout Access. For example, you can write a ProperCase( ) function to capitalize the first letter of each word in a text value (in fact, you'll do so later in this chapter). The function returns a text value with first letters capitalized.

A *sub* (short for *subroutine*) is an Access Basic program that doesn't return a value. For example, you can write a sub that sets the size of a window. The sub doesn't produce any resulting value, it simply changes the attributes of an object.

As with Access' built-in functions, when you use a function or sub, you frequently give it information in the form of *arguments*. Arguments follow the function or sub name and are enclosed in parentheses.

A procedure (function or sub) is made up of *statements*, that is, lines of Access Basic code. Statements that operate on database objects are called *methods* (not a particularly intuitive name). For example, you can use the Print method in an Access Basic procedure to print a report.

At the beginning of each module is the *Declarations section,* which contains the Access Basic statements that apply to all the procedures in the module. A *declaration* tells Access about a variable you plan to use. A *variable* is a named location in memory for you to store information temporarily.

Creating Modules and Procedures

It is easy to create a new module—you click on the Module button in the Database window and then click on the New button to display a new, empty module in the Module window, shown in Figure 17.1.

This section contains information about what modules contain and how to create procedures.

Setting Module Options

A module consists of a Declarations section followed by a series of procedures.

You can use two kinds of statements in the Declarations section:

- Option statements, which set Access Basic options for all the procedures in the module

- Declarations, which are described in the topic *Declaring Variables* later in this chapter

New modules automatically contain one Option statement:

```
Option Compare Database
```

The Option Compare statement tells Access how you want to compare text: By setting the option to Database, Access will perform text comparisons based on the sort order of your database, which is specified in the Options dialog box (choose View Options General to see the New Database Sort Order setting). Since Access puts the Option Compare statement into every new module, one wonders why Microsoft didn't make Database the default comparison option so this statement wouldn't be necessary!

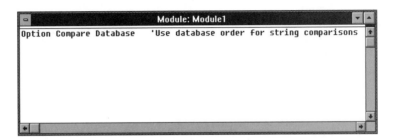

Figure 17.1 A new module in the Module window.

Creating Functions

To create a new function simply type the first line of the function.

The first statement of a function looks like this:

```
Function functionname (arguments)
```

For example, you can create the function called Dollars by typing this statement in a module:

```
Function Dollars(Amount)
```

Dollars() is the name of the new function. The function will accept one argument, a variable named *Amount*. If you want to make a function that doesn't need any input to do its work, you can omit the arguments, but you have to include the parentheses, like this:

```
Function CurrentMonth()
```

When you enter a function statement, Access creates the new procedure. It creates a new page in the module for the procedure and it enters the statement that ends the procedure, as shown in Figure 17.2. For functions, the ending statement is:

```
End Function
```

You enter the statements that make up the function between the Function statement and the End Function statement.

Another way to create a new function is to choose Edit New Procedure from the menu to display the New Procedure dialog box, shown in Figure 17.3. Choose Function for the Type, enter a name, and click on OK.

Spaces after Function Names

It doesn't matter whether you type a space before the parentheses—Access sticks one in for you. However, when you use functions in properties or expressions, never type a space between the function name and the parentheses.

Creating Subs

You create a sub just as you create a function, but you use the Sub statement.

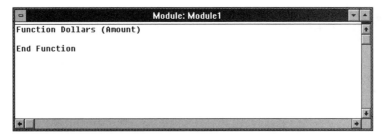

Figure 17.2 A new function.

To create a sub, you type a statement starting with Sub instead of Function, like this:

```
Sub subname ()
```

Access creates a new procedure and adds this statement:

```
End Sub
```

You enter the statements that make up the function between the Sub statement and the End Sub statement.

You can also create a sub by choosing Edit New Procedure and then choosing Sub for the Type in the New Procedure dialog box (Figure 17.3).

Most Access Basic programmers use functions for almost all their programming and don't often create subs, because you can't use subs in expressions, in properties, or from macros using the RunCode action.

Entering Statements in a Procedure

A tremendous advantage of systems like Access, where you enter your programs in a window designed specifically for programming, is that the syntax of each statement is verified as you enter it.

Access can't spot all programming errors, but it can catch spelling and punctuation errors. Access also formats each statement using standard capitalization and spacing. This reformatting makes your procedures

Figure 17.3 Using the New Procedure dialog box to create a new function.

easier to read and debug. For example, you can enter this Dollars() function:

```
Function Dollars (Amount)
  Dollars = CInt(Amount * 100) / 100
End Function
```

This function rounds numbers off to two decimal places and is very useful in reports that do calculations with Currency values, so that rounding errors don't produce errors in your totals. The function accepts one argument, called *Amount*, and returns one value, the rounded-off amount. To tell Access what to return, you assign a value to a variable with the same name as the function.

If you enter an incorrect statement, Access displays a message box like the one in Figure 17.4 and highlights the part of the statement it didn't understand. After you click OK to clear the message box, you can fix the statement.

To use the function, save the module by choosing File Save from the menu. Then enter the function name in any expression or property in your Access database. For example, you can use the Dollars() function in the expression that creates a calculated field in a query, like this:

```
Dollars([List  Price]*[Discount])
```

Moving within the Module Window

In addition to using the cursor keys to move within a procedure, you can quickly move from procedure to procedure.

A module can contain many procedures. To move quickly to the procedure you want to work on, you can use the Next Procedure and Previous Procedure buttons on the toolbar, shown in Figure 17.5. Or you can choose the procedure name from the Procedure list on the toolbar.

If you want to view two procedures at the same time, or two parts of a long procedure, you can split the Module window. Choose View Split Window from the menu. Access splits the Module window horizontally

Figure 17.4   A message box alerting you to an error.

Figure 17.5 Procedure list, Previous Procedure button, and Next Procedure button on the Module window toolbar.

into two smaller windows. Figure 17.6 shows two procedures in the same module, allowing the programmer to compare the code. To return to a single window, choose View Split Window again.

Trying Out a Function

The easiest way to test most functions is in the Immediate window.

Access provides a way to test functions and subs, without using them in any other object in the database. The Immediate window, shown in Figure 17.7, lets you execute any Access Basic statement. To view the Immediate window, choose View Immediate Window from the menu (this command is only available in the Module window).

To test a function in the Immediate window, use the Print method (that is, the Access Basic statement named Print), or its abbreviation, a question mark (?). Figure 17.7 shows how you can try out the Dollars() function. Access prints the result on the next line of the window.

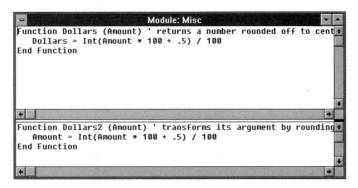

Figure 17.6 Viewing two procedures at the same time.

```
Immediate Window [Misc]
? Dollars(1.2345)
 1.23
? Dollars(1.236)
 1.24
```

Figure 17.7 Testing a function in the Immediate window.

Using a Text Editor to Write Procedures

If you would prefer to write procedures using your favorite text editor or word processor, you can!

Access lets you write or edit modules in any text editor or word processor that can create ASCII text files. Once you have written a module and saved it in a text file, create a new module or open an existing module in Access to contain the code you have written. Choose File Load Text from the menu to display the Load Text dialog box, shown in Figure 17.8.

Choose the file containing the text, and then choose one of these buttons:

- Replace: Replaces all the procedures in this module with the text from the file

- Merge: Adds the text from the file to this module at the cursor location without deleting any procedures

- New: Creates a new module to contain the text from the file

You may want to name your text files that contain Access Basic programs using the file extension .BAS. To see only your Access Basic programs in the Load Text dialog box, choose Basic Files (*.BAS) from the List Files of Type combo box.

When you use a text editor or word processor to write Access Basic programs, make sure that it doesn't break long lines of code by adding line-ending characters to create additional lines. In Access Basic, statements can't wrap to additional lines. Also, don't use any non-ASCII characters, such as line-drawing characters or international characters, that might not load properly.

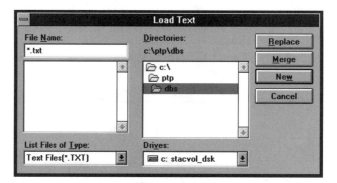

Figure 17.8   Loading text into a module.

Printing Modules

To print the whole module, view it in the Module window and choose File Print from the menu.

When Access prints a module, it doesn't include the module name (a silly omission, I think!). However, you can enter comments at the beginning of the Declaration section of the module that include the database name, module name, your name, the date the module was last updated, and any other documentation you think would be useful.

Print One Procedure

The easiest way to print a single procedure from a module is to copy it to the Windows Notepad:

1. Highlight the procedure in the Module window.
2. Press **Ctrl+C** to copy it to the Clipboard.
3. Press **Alt+Tab** until the Program Manager is active.
4. Open the Accessories program group window and double-click on the Notepad icon.
5. In Notepad, press **Ctrl+V** to paste the procedure from the Clipboard.
6. Choose File Print from Notepad.
7. Exit from Notepad without saving the document, or leave it running so you can quickly print another procedure.

Programming Basics

Each Access Basic procedure consists of optional declarations followed by a list of statements. This section describes how and why to declare variables and explains some common Access Basic statements. You've already seen the most common statement—the assignment statement, which uses an equal sign to assign a value to a variable, like this:

```
Dollars = CInt(Amount * 100) / 100
```

Other common statements will be detailed later in this chapter as they appear in examples.

Declaring Variables

If you tell Access that you will declare all the variables you use, Access can tell you when you have spelled a variable name wrong.

You don't have to declare variables before you use them. However, declaring variables has several advantages:

- You can tell Access what kind of data the variable should contain, so Access can issue an error message if the wrong type of data is stored in the variable

- You can include a comment on the declaration line explaining what the variable is for

- You can tell Access that you will declare all the variables you use; if you spell a variable name wrong in a statement, Access knows that you aren't creating a new variable and alerts you

You can declare variables in two places:

- At the beginning of the procedure, for variables used only within the procedure

- In the Declarations section at the beginning of the module, for variables used by more than one procedure in the module

Generally, unless you know you will be using the same variables in several procedures, it is easier to declare variables in the procedure in which they are used.

To declare a variable, you use the Dim statement (which stands for Dimension), like this:

```
Dim Amount
```

Variables can be one of the following types:

- String, like a Text field

- Currency, like a Currency field

- Integer, like a Number field of size Integer, for integers from approximately -32,000 to approximately 32,000

- Long, like a Number field of size Long, for integers that don't fit in an Integer variable

- Single, like a Number field of size Single, for numbers with six digits of precision

- Double, like a Number field of size Double, for numbers with ten digits of precision

- Variant (the default type), which can contain any type of information

To tell Access what kind of information the variable should contain, add the information onto the end of the declaration like this:

```
Dim Amount As Currency
```

If you don't tell Access what kind of variable to create, it makes a variable of type Variant, which can contain any type of data.

You can't declare a variable that has the same name as the function, for example, the *Dollars* variable in the Dollars function. You also can't declare variables used as arguments, like the *Amount* variable in the Dollars function, inside the function.

Indicate Variable Types Automatically

When you name your variables, you can tell Access what type of data they will contain by adding a special character to the end of the variable name. The special characters Access recognizes are:

- String $
- Currency   @
- Integer   %
- Long   &
- Single   !
- Double   #

For example, if you name a variable *Price@*, this variable will contain Currency data.

Declare the Type of Data a Function Returns

You can specify what type of information a function returns by adding this information to the end of the Function statement. For example, to tell Access that the Dollars() function should return Currency data, begin the function with this statement:

```
Function Dollars (Amount) As Currency
```

Documenting Your Procedures

Include comments to describe what each variable is for and what each section of code does.

To include a comment in your Access Basic programs, begin the comment with an apostrophe ('). Access ignores everything on the line following the apostrophe. You can enter comments on lines by themselves, or you can add them to the end of statements.

For example, you can comment the Dollars function like this:

```
Function Dollars (Amount) As Currency 'Rounds to cents
'Using CInt rounds to nearest integer
  Dollars = CInt(Amount * 100) / 100
End Function
```

Running Macro Actions or Macros from a Procedure

You can execute macro actions or entire macros from within a procedure.

You use the Access Basic DoCmd statement to execute either a single macro action or an entire macro. To run a macro action, use DoCmd followed by the macro action you want to perform. For example, to turn the mouse pointer into an hourglass, you can use the Hourglass action like this:

```
DoCmd Hourglass "Yes"
```

Most macro actions require arguments, and you include them after the action name, enclosed in quotes. In the Hourglass action, the first and only argument is Hourglass On, and this DoCmd statement sets this argument to Yes.

If the action requires more than one argument, you list them separated by commas. For example, if you want to execute the Echo action in your function so that Access doesn't update the screen while the function runs, you can use this statement:

```
DoCmd Echo "Yes", "The function is running!"
```

The Echo action has two arguments, Echo On and Status Bar Text. This DoCmd statement sets the Echo On argument to Yes and the Status Bar Text argument to "The function is running!"

To run a whole macro from a procedure, you can use the DoCmd statement to run the RunMacro action, like this:

```
DoCmd RunMacro "macroname"
```

For example, to run a macro named Update, use this statement:

```
DoCmd RunMacro "Update"
```

Writing Transformation Functions

You can write functions that transform text, date, or numeric data in ways that the Access built-in functions can't do. For example, although Access has the LCase() and UCase() functions for converting text to all uppercase or all lowercase letters, there is no function to capitalize only the first letter of each word; you must write this function.

There are three ways to write this type of "transformation" function:

- The function accepts an argument, transforms it, and returns the result
- The function accepts an argument and changes that argument; the argument must be a field in a table or a control on a form or report
- The function accepts an argument, changes the argument, and also returns a result

The first method works like Access' built-in functions, and you can use functions written this way in expressions anywhere in Access. However, you can't enter these functions directly in the After Update property of forms to change the values of controls. If you enter a function that returns a value into a property, Access executes the function but throws away the result!

The second method works perfectly in the After Update property of a form. However, since it doesn't return any value, it won't work as a part of an expression.

The third method works in both expressions and After Update properties.

For example, the Dollars() function described earlier in this chapter rounds off an amount to dollars and cents. The following version, using the third method, changes the value of its argument *and* returns a value:

```
Function Dollars (Amount) As Currency
   Amount = CInt(Amount * 100) / 100
   Dollars = Amount
End Function
```

Here's how the function works: Because the rounded-off amount is stored back in the argument (Amount), Access changes the value of the argument. If the argument is a control on a form or report, Access changes the value of the currently displayed record. Since the rounded off amount is also stored in a variable with the same name as the function (*Dollars*), Access returns that value when the function is executed.

When you write a function that transforms one value into another, think about where you plan to use it—in expressions, in the After Update property of controls, or both—and choose your method of transformation accordingly. To avoid confusion, I try to write all my functions using the third method, so that I can use them in either properties or expressions. However, some programmers prefer to use only the first method, in which the function returns the result, to avoid having functions change the values of arguments unexpectedly.

Don't Use the Wrong Type of Data

If the data type of the result of a transformation function is different from the type of the argument, don't change the value of the argument. For example, the CHURCH database on the optional companion diskette contains an Age() function, which takes a date as the argument (birthday) and returns a number (the age in years). Functions like this one shouldn't change the value of their argument, since the argument may not be defined to accept the data type of the result.

Capitalizing the First Letters of Words

To properly capitalize most names and addresses, the first letter of each word should be uppercase and other letters should be lowercase.

A common complaint about Access is its lack of a function to capitalize the first letter of every word. Access users around the world have written their own functions to do this, and Microsoft includes a version in their Access technical notes.

To capitalize text correctly is actually a complex, language-specific task. Also, the capitalization of names varies from family to family (for example, Van Kamp or van Kamp may be correct) so no function will handle them all correctly. However, a function can do an acceptable job on English text if it uses the following rule: capitalize every letter that follows a space or word-separating punctuation, and convert all other letters to lowercase. Word-separating punctuation includes these characters:

```
. , ; : ! ? ( ) [ ] { } - + = / "
```

Don't include an apostrophe among these characters, or your function will change the text value *Don't* to *Don'T*. Our rule still gets some things wrong—for example, the name *John van Nuys III* will be changed to *John Van Nuys Iii.*

The following ProperCase( ) function returns the "proper-cased" result:

```
Function ProperCase (Text)
    '1. Declarations
    Dim Temp As String      'holds text during processing
    Dim Char As String      'next character to process
    Dim OldChar As String   'previous character processed
    Dim Sep As String       'list of punctuation
    Dim i As Integer        'counter for loop
    'list of space and word-separating punctuation
    Sep = " .,;:!?()[]{}-+=/" & Chr$(34) '(double quote)

    '2. If Text is blank, return blank
    If IsNull(Text) Then
     ProperCase = Null
     Exit Function
    End If

    '3. Convert to lowercase
    'convert to lowercase string, store in Temp
    Temp = LCase$(Text)
    'Set OldChar to space, so the first letter
    'is capitalized
    OldChar = " "

    '4. Loop to examine each character of Temp
    For i = 1 To Len(Temp)
     'isolate current character as Char
     Char = Mid$(Temp, i, 1)
     'if previous character (OldChar) is in Sep
     If InStr(Sep, OldChar) <> 0 Then
      'then capitalize the current character
      Mid$(Temp, i, 1) = UCase$(Char)
     End If
     'set OldChar to the current character to
     'prepare to examine the next character
     OldChar = Char
    Next i

    '5. Return the value of Temp
    ProperCase = Temp
    Text = Temp
End Function
```

As indicated in the comments, the function has five sections. Here's how each section works:

1. The *Temp* variable will hold a copy of the argument during processing. While the function processes the text one character at a time, the *Char* variable holds the current character from the argument and *OldChar* holds the previous character. The *Sep*

variable holds a list of word-separating punctuation as well as a space—all the characters after which a letter should be capitalized. The *i* variable is a counter used to process each character (see section 3 of the function).

2. If the input string is blank (null), return a null value. This section uses the If/Then/EndIf statement to perform the conditional processing.

3. Use the LCase$() built-in function to convert the entire string into lowercase. If the argument contains a number or a date, this function converts it to a string at the same time.

    OldChar is the previous character in the text, for use in determining whether to capitalize the current character. Set it to a space character to start out, so that the first character is capitalized.

4. Use a For/Next statement to perform the same set of statements over and over for each character in the string. Use the Len() built-in function to determine how many characters the string contains. The *i* variable is the position in the string of the character you are currently processing.

    For each character, use the Mid$() function to isolate the current character from the string. Use the InStr() function to determine if the previous character (*OldChar*) is one of the characters in our list of word separating characters (*Sep*) variable—if InStr() doesn't find the character in *Sep*, it returns a zero. If the character is in *Sep*, capitalize the current character using the UCase$() built-in function. If not, leave it lowercase. Finally, copy the current character to *OldChar* to get ready to process the next character.

5. When all the characters have been processed, copy the *Temp* variable to the *ProperCase* variable so that the function returns this value. Also copy it to the *Text* variable to replace the original value of the argument.

To make a version of this function that doesn't change the value of its argument, remove the statement that assigns a value to *Text* in section 5. If you don't want the function to return a value, remove the statements that assign a value to *ProperCase* in sections 2 and 5.

Calculating the First and Last Day of the Quarter

If you create a quarterly report and need to select all the records in a quarter, you can create functions to calculate the first and last days of the quarter.

For example, in the church membership database is based on the Donations for One Quarter query selects the donation records for one quarter by prompting for any date in the quarter. The FirstOfQtr() and LastOfQtr() functions listed below calculate the beginning and ending dates of the query. In the query grid, the Criteria row for the donation date column contains this expression:

```
Between FirstOfQtr([Enter date in quarter]) And LastOfQtr([Enter date
  in quarter])
```

Because the two parameters have the same name, Access asks only once and uses the same value for both parameters.

Here is the FirstOfQtr() function:

```
Function FirstOfQtr (Dt)
   '1. Declarations
   Dim Q As Integer
   Dim Y As Integer

   '2. Convert argument to date
   If IsDate(Dt) Then
     Dt = CVDate(Dt)
   Else
     FirstOfQtr = Null
     Exit Function
   End If

   '3. Calculate the date
   Q = DatePart("q", Dt)
   Y = DatePart("yyyy", Dt)
   Dt = DateSerial(Y, (Q * 3) - 2, 1)

   '4. Return the result
   FirstOfQtr = Dt
End Function
```

Here's how Access interprets each section of the function:

1. The *Q* variable will hold the quarter (1 through 4) of the date; *Y* will hold the year.

2. Return null if the argument can't be converted to a date.

3. Use the DatePart() function to find the quarter and year of the date. Multiply the quarter by three and subtract two to calculate the first month of the quarter. Use the DateSerial() function to create the date.

4. Return the date and change the value of the argument.

To calculate the last day of the quarter that contains a date, use this LastOfQtr() function:

```
Function LastOfQtr (Dt)
  '1. Declarations
  Dim Q As Integer
  Dim Y As Integer
  Dim M As Integer

  '2. Convert argument to date
  If IsDate(Dt) Then
   Dt = CVDate(Dt)
  Else
   LastOfQtr = Null
   Exit Function
  End If

  '3. Calculate the date
  Q = DatePart("q", Dt) 'quarter number 1-4
  Y = DatePart("yyyy", Dt) 'year
  M = (Q * 3) + 1 ' first month of next quarter
  If M = 13 Then 'adjust for January
   M = 1
   Y = Y + 1
  End If
  Dt = DateSerial(Y, M, 1) - 1

  '4. Return the result
  LastOfQtr = Dt
End Function
```

Here's how the function works:

1. The variables Y, Q, and M will hold the year, quarter, and month numbers of the calculated date.

2. Return null if the argument can't be converted to a date.

3. Use the DatePart() function to calculate the year (Y) and quarter (Q) of the date. Then calculate the first month of the following quarter (M). If M is 13, change it to 1 and add 1 to the year. Use the DateSerial() function to create a date using Y as the year, M as the month, and 1 as the day—the first day of the following quarter. Then subtract 1 from this date to create the last day of the quarter containing the argument.

   For example, if the date is 12/4/94, Q is 4 (the fourth quarter), Y is 1994, and M starts out as (Q*3)+1, or 13. Because M is 13, Access changes M to 1 and adds 1 to Y, so Y is 1995. The DateSerial() function creates the date 1/1/95. After subtracting one (day) from this date, the result is 12/31/94.

4. Return the date as well as changing the value of the argument.

Check the Data Type of Arguments

As I mentioned earlier, it is important to make sure that arguments contain the correct type of data. One way to check the type of data a variable contains is to use the VarType() function, which returns these codes:

0 Empty, that is, has never been assigned a value
1 Null
2 Integer
3 Long
4 Single
5 Double
6 Currency
7 Date
8 String

By requiring that your argument contains the right type of data, you avoid errors later in the function.

The other method you can use is to check whether the data could be *converted* to the type you want. Use these functions to find out if the value of a variable can be converted to a date or a number:

```
IsDate(variablename)
IsNumeric(variablename)
```

There is no function to check whether a value can be converted into a string, because any value can be converted into text. Once you have checked that the information can be converted to the type you want, use these functions to convert the values:

CVDate(*variablename*)   converts to Variant containing a date
CCur(*variablename*)   converts to Currency
CDbl(*variablename*)   converts to Double (number)
CInt(*variablename*)   converts to Integer (number), rounding off decimal places
CLng(*variablename*)   converts to Long (number)
CSng(*variablename*)   converts to Single (number)
CStr(*variablename*)   converts to String

Section 2 of the previous example shows how to make sure that your argument contains a date. *Rounding Off Numbers* later in this chapter shows how to make sure an argument is numeric.

Rounding Off Numbers

When reports contain calculated currency values, it is important to round them off before totaling them.

Earlier in this chapter, I described the Dollars() function to round a number off to two decimal places.

Here is a modified Dollars() function, which checks that its argument is a Currency value:

```
Function Dollars (Amount) As Currency
   '1. Convert argument to Currency
   If IsNumeric(Amount) Then
     Amount = CCur(Amount)
   Else
     Amount = Null
     Dollars = Null
     Exit Function
   End If

   '2. Round off number
   Amount = CInt(Amount * 100) / 100
   Dollars = Amount
End Function
```

Here's what the sections in this function do:

1. Use the IsNumeric() built-in function to determine if the argument is either a number or could be converted to a numeric value. If so, the function converts the argument to a Currency value using the CCur() function. If not, it returns a null and changes its argument to a null.

2. Round off the number to two decimal places using the CInt() function. The function returns a Currency value because of the As Currency declaration in its Function statement.

You can easily change this function to round to any number of decimal places. Replace 100 in the expression with 10 to the *n*th, where *n* is the number of decimal places you want. 100 is 10 to the second power, so it rounds to two places.

Converting Nulls to Zeros

When a table contains null (blank) values, your calculations can be wrong or missing.

Consider this situation: You might use an expression in a query to create a calculated field named Donation Due based on a field named Amount in your table. If the Amount field is null in a record, the Donation Due field is null, too. In many tables, especially those containing mainly financial information, it is more convenient for all fields to contain a value, that is, never to be null.

Here is a function that checks whether its argument is null—if so, it converts it to 0:

```
Function NullToZero (N)
  If IsNull(N) Then
    N = 0
  End If
  NullToZero = N
End Function
```

You can use this function on forms in the After Update property of fields that you do not want to contain null values.

Other Procedures

So far, all the functions I have described accept input values and transform them in some way, returning a result. You can use Access Basic procedures for a vast array of applications, from functions that print multiple copies of your mailing label report to entire menu-driven applications.

Writing complex functions and entire applications using Access Basic is beyond the scope of this book, but this section describes a few functions you may find useful.

Printing Sheets of Mailing Labels

If you use sheets of labels and print only a few labels at a time, you may want to tell Access to start printing on a label other than the first label on the page.

You can write an Access Basic function that asks for the number of labels to skip before beginning to print. You can even ask for the number of times to print each label. Before going to the trouble, though, make sure that after you have peeled off and used the first few labels on the page, the page will feed properly through the printer!

To skip used labels and print multiple copies of labels, you need three functions (based on functions written by Kim Abercrombie of Microsoft):

- LabelSetup(): Attached to the On Open property of your mailing label report, this function asks for the number of blank labels to skip and the number of copies of each label to print

- LabelInitialize(): Attached to the On Format property of the Report Header section of your mailing label report, this function sets two variables, *BlankCount* and *CopyCount*, to 0 at the beginning of the report

- LabelLayout(): Attached to the On Format property of the Detail section of your mailing label report, this function either prints the Detail section or skips the label, and determines which record to print

The LabelLayout() uses two properties of report sections:

- NextRecord tells Access whether to advance to the next record: If the property is set to true (the default), Access moves to the next record in the record source; if you set the property to false, Access processes the same record again

- PrintSection tells Access whether to print the section: If the property is set to true (the default), Access prints the section on the page; if you set the property to false, Access doesn't print the section

These properties, along with the MoveLayout property (which tells Access whether to move to the next print location on the page), do not appear on the property sheet for report sections in Design view. Instead, you can set the values of these properties using a macro or Access Basic function attached to the On Format property of the report section.

To modify an existing mailing label report so that you can choose how many labels to skip and how many of each label to print:

1. Create a new module. Enter these statements in the Declarations section:

```
Option Explicit
Dim LabelBlanks&
Dim LabelCopies&
Dim BlankCount&
Dim CopyCount&
```

The Option statement tells Access that you will declare all the variables you use, and the four Dim statements declare four variables to be used in your functions. (All four variables are numbers of type Long since their names end with the special character ampersand—see the *Indicate Variable Types Automatically* Hot Tip earlier in this chapter.) Here's how the variables are used:

- LabelBlanks&: Number of labels that the user wants to skip at the top of the first page of the report
- LabelCopies&: Number of copies of each label that the user wants to print
- BlankCount&: Number of labels skipped so far; it is set to 0 at the beginning of the report
- CopyCount&: Number of copies of the current label printed so far; it is set to 0 at the beginning of the report and when printing the last copy of each label

2. In the same module, enter this LabelSetup() function, to be run when the mailing label report is opened:

```
Function LabelSetup ()
    'when report is opened, prompt for numbers
    LabelBlanks& = Val(InputBox$("Enter number of _
            blank labels to skip:"))
    LabelCopies& = Val(InputBox$("Enter number of _
            copies of each label to print:"))

    'make sure they are reasonable numbers
    If LabelBlanks& < 0 Then
      LabelBlanks& = 0
    End If
    If LabelCopies& < 1 Then
      LabelCopies& = 1
    End If
End Function
```

First the LabelSetup() function uses the InputBox$() built-in function to display boxes asking for the number of labels to skip (LabelBlanks&) and the number of copies to print (LabelCopies&). The function then uses the Val() function to convert the responses to numbers. Finally, the function checks that the user didn't enter an impossible value for either variable.

3. Enter this LabelInitialize() function, to be run when Access begins to format the report:

```
Function LabelInitialize ()
    'set counts to 0 at beginning of report
    BlankCount& = 0
    CopyCount& = 0
End Function
```

This function sets both counter variables to zero at the beginning of the report.

4. Enter this LabelLayout() function to be run each time that Access formats the Detail section of the report:

```
Function LabelLayout (R As Report)
  'a. Skip blank labels
  If BlankCount& < LabelBlanks& Then
    'skip this label
    R.NextRecord = False
    R.PrintSection = False
    BlankCount& = BlankCount& + 1

  'b. Print copies of labels
  Else
    If CopyCount& < (LabelCopies& - 1) Then
      'print the same label again
      R.NextRecord = False
      CopyCount& = CopyCount& + 1
    Else
      'printing last label for this record,
      'and setting count to zero for next record
      CopyCount& = 0
    End If
  End If
End Function
```

The LabelLayout() function accepts one argument, the name of the mailing label report. The function needs this information so that it can change the Next Record and Print Section properties of the report. Here's how the function works (I've used letters for each section of the function so as not to be confused with the steps you are following.):

a. Determine whether enough blank labels have already been skipped. If not, skip printing on the current label by setting the Print Section property of the report to False. In order not to skip printing the label for the current record, the Next Record property of the report must also be set to False.

b. Determine whether this is the last copy of this label, or if more copies will be needed. If more copies are needed, set the Next Record property to False and increment the *CopyCount&* variable. If this is the last copy of this label, reset the *CopyCount&* variable to 0 for the next record.

5. Save your new module.

6. Open your mailing label report in Design view. For the On Open property of the report, enter:

```
=LabelSetup()
```

7. The LabelInitialize() function must be called when Access starts to format the report. If your report doesn't have a Report Header section (and it probably doesn't), choose Layout Report Hdr/Ftr to add one. Set the Height property of both sections to 0 so that they don't print—otherwise, the length of your mailing label report will be wrong. For the On Format property of the Report Header section, enter:

```
=LabelInitialize()
```

8. For the On Format property of the Detail section, enter:

```
=LabelLayout(Reports![reportname])
```

replacing *reportname* with the name of the mailing label report.

When you view the mailing label report in Print Preview, it prompts for the number of labels to strip and the number of copies to print, then displays the report.

You can use the functions you just created for printing more than one mailing label report. Since the name of the report isn't specified within any of the functions, just follow steps 6 through 8 for another report.

Creating a Multi-User Custom Counter

To make your own counter variable for a shared database, you must use a table to store the next value of the counter.

In Chapter 16, I described how to make your own custom counter field for applications in which an Access Counter field wouldn't work. For example, if you need to be able to skip numbers or reuse the numbers of deleted records, or if you want to number records by tens (for instnace, 10, 20, ...), you can't use a Counter field.

If more than one user will enter records into the table that contains the custom counter field, the macro shown in Chapter 16 won't work. While the form to which the macro is attached is open, a hidden control on the form holds the next available value of the counter. If you and other users are entering records at the same time, the counter values that other people use won't be reflected in the counter value on your form.

Instead, you must store the next available counter value in a table. Access' record-locking can make sure that only one user at a time can use the current value of the counter. This table will have one field and one record, which will contain the next available counter value. You can then write an Access Basic function that opens the table, retrieves the current value stored there, adds one to the value (or ten, if you want to number records by tens), and returns the current value.

The Access Basic function can use an *error-handling routine* to handle the error you will get if another user is updating the table that contains the counter when you want to open it. At the beginning of the function, you include an On Error statement that tells Access what to do when an error occurs.

To create the table and to write an Access Basic function that provides the next value of the counter:

1. Create a table named Counter, containing one Number field (size Long Integer) and named Next Available Counter. Make this field the primary key. In Datasheet view, add one record to the table containing the starting value of the counter, shown in Figure 17.9.

2. Create a module to contain the function that returns the next available counter value. Enter this function:

```
Function NextCounter ()
    'a. Declarations
    Const TABLE_LOCKED = 3000
    On Error GoTo NextCounterErr
    Dim MyDB As Database
    Dim MyTable As Table
    Dim NextC As Integer

    'b. Open table and get the next available number
    Set MyDB = CurrentDB()
    Set MyTable = MyDB.OpenTable("Counter")
    MyTable.Edit
    NextC = MyTable("Next Available Counter")

    'c. Increment the counter and save it
    MyTable("Next Available Counter") = NextC + 10
    MyTable.Update
```

Figure 17.9 Table containing the next available value of a multi-user custom counter.

```
    'd. Return the counter value
    NextCounter = NextC
    Exit Function

    'e. If error, display a message
NextCounterErr:
    If Err = TABLE_LOCKED Then Resume
    MsgBox "An unexpected error has occurred:" & Err
    End
End Function
```

Here is how the NextCounter() function works:

- Declare a constant called TABLE_LOCKED and set it to the error number that Access returns when a table is locked. This value is used in the error-handling routine in section e. Also use an On Error statement to tell Access to execute an error-handling routine if an error occurs. Declare variables for referring to the current database (MyDB) and the Counter table (MyTable), and a variable to contain the next available counter value (NextC).

- Open the Counter table and copy the value of the Next Available Counter field into the variable *NextC*.

- Increment the Next Available Counter field in the Counter table. In this example, the function adds 10 to the Next Available Counter value, so that records are numbered by tens.

- Return the value of *NextC*.

- If an error occurs while this function is executing, Access runs this error-handling routine. If the error occurred because the Counter table was locked, return to the statement that caused the error and try again. Otherwise, display a message box and exit from the function.

3. In Design view, open the form you want to use for adding records that contain the custom counter.

4. Create a text box control that is bound to the field you want to contain the counter value. For example, Figure 17.10 shows the Families form in the church membership database. If you want to assign numbers to each family using a custom counter, you can add a field called FamNum to the Families table and add a text box to the Families form to contain the new field.

5. Create the macro, shown in Table 17.1, to set the FamNum field by running the NextCounter() function.

6. For the On Exit property of the text box, enter the name of the macro you created in step 5.

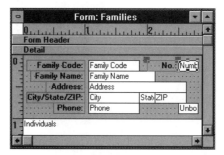

Figure 17.10 Form to display the counter value.

Now when you edit records using the Families form and you move the cursor out of the FamNum text box, if the FamNum is 0 or null the macro calls the NextCounter() function to get the next available counter value. If you need to look at or change the value of the next available counter, you can open the Counter table at any time.

Creating Library Databases

If you are interested in creating more ambitious Access Basic programs, you can create procedures that are useful in many databases. Libraries allow you to load procedures for use in all your Access databases without duplicating the modules in each one. This section describes how to create a library database and how to call a function in your library database by choosing a command you have added to the Access Help menu.

Creating a Library Database

Libraries let you use macros and procedures in any open database.

A *library* is a database that is loaded into memory using the [Libraries] section of you Access configuration file, MSACCESS.INI.

Table 17.1 Macro to Set a Field Using a Custom Counter

Macro Name	Condition	Action	Arguments
Counter	IsNull([FamNum]) Or [FamNum]=0	SetValue	Item: Forms![Families]![FamNum] Expression: =NextCounter()

For example, the ReportWizards and FormWizards that are included with Access are stored in the WIZARD.MDA database. Although they are stored in their own database, you can run them in any database you open. If WIZARD.MDA weren't loaded as a library, you could run Wizards only when you open WIZARD.MDA, which would not be very useful. By loading WIZARD.MDA as a library, rather than opening it with the File Open Database command, its objects remain available while Access is running. You can use its objects, although they do not appear in the Database window.

This book describes several library databases:

- The Database Analyzer contained in ANALYZER.MDA (Chapter 3)
- The OutputAs library contained in OUTPUTAS.MDA (Chapter 12)

The good news is that you can make your own library databases. If you have objects, especially modules, that you want to use in all your databases, turn the database into a library by including its name in the [Libraries] section of your MSACCESS.INI file (see *Adding Libraries to Access* in Chapter 15). You don't have to do anything special to the database itself to turn it into a library database.

Here are some design tips:

- Keep library databases small, since they occupy memory while you use other databases. Delete all extra objects.

- Macros can't be run from a library database, only modules. If your library includes forms or reports that call macros from properties, rewrite the macros as modules and delete the macros.

- Test out all the objects you want to include in the library. Make sure that the modules work perfectly. If the library database contains an error that occurs while it is loaded as a library, it can be very difficult to locate. You can't view a module in the Module window while it is loaded as a library. Include as many error checks as possible in library modules. You may want to display message boxes (using the MsgBox statement) to indicate what procedures are running, so you can tell where errors occur.

- When naming objects in a library database, avoid using names that may be used in your other databases. For example, precede the name of every table, query, form, report, and module in your library database with the characters *Lib*.

While a database is loaded as a library, you can't open it using the File Open Database command. To make changes to the library database, remove the reference to it from the [Libraries] section of MSACCESS.INI, exit from Access, and reload Access. Now Access is running without your library database loaded, and you can open it normally.

Adding Commands to the Help Menu

You can add your own commands to the Help menu, including commands that have nothing to do with online Help.

The MSACCESS.INI file can contain a section called [Menu Add-ins]. By adding a line to this section, you can create a choice on the Help menu that runs a macro or an Access Basic procedure. (See *Changing MSACCESS.INI Settings* in Chapter 15 for how to add lines to this file.) If your MSACCESS.INI file doesn't contain a [Menu Add-Ins] section, add one to the end of the file.

To add a Help command that runs a macro or procedure, add a line in one of these formats:

```
menutext=macroname
menutext==functionname
```

Menutext is the command you want to appear on the Help menu, for example, Add Families. If you want the command to have an access key, that is, an Alt+key combination so that it can be chosen using the keyboard, add an ampersand (&) before the letter you want to use as the access key. For example, if you enter *&Add Families* as the command, you will be able to press **Alt+A** to choose it from the Help menu.

Macroname is the name of a macro. Because library databases can't contain macros, the macro must be in the database that is open, so this is not usually useful.

Functionname is the name of an Access Basic function either in a library database or in the open database. Notice that when you enter the name of a function, you must type *two* equal signs before it.

For example, if you have written an Access Basic function called AddFams() and you want to add a command to the Help menu to call it, enter this command in the [Menu Add-ins] section of MSACCESS.INI:

```
&Add Families==AddFams()
```

After you make the changes to your MSACCESS.INI file, restart Access. When you choose Help from the menu, you will see your added command(s).

Appendix: Access Insider Companion Disk

The Access Insider Companion Disk contains all the databases mentioned in this book, as well as Microsoft's Access Knowledge Base. This appendix describes each file on the disk.

BOOKORD Database

The BOOKORD database, described in Chapter 9, contains an order entry system for a mail-order bookseller. The database includes reports, including a snaking-column report that prints camera-ready copy for a brochure, as well as the invoices, packing slips, and order confirmation reports described in Chapter 14.

CHECKBK Database

The CHECKBK database, described in Chapter 14, contains a checkbook for an individual or small business. To create a report with a running balance, see *Check Registers* in Chapter 14.

CHURCH Database

The CHURCH database, described in Chapter 14, contains information about the families and individuals who are members of a church. The database can be adapted for use with any membership organization, and includes pledge and donation information. To print a membership list for a church or similar organization, see *Membership Rosters* in Chapter 14.

MAILLIST Database

The MAILLIST database, described in Chapter 1, contains a mailing list and a table of the states and provinces in the U.S. and Canada. The

Mailing List table has validation rules to require that each part of the address confirm to standard addressing rules. You may want to import the States table into your own databases for validating two-letter state and province codes.

MEMBERS Database

The MEMBERS database, described in Chapter 1, contains information about a membership organization, including donation records and committee affiliation. The Committee Assignments table is a good example of using a table to store a many-to-many relationship, in this case between the Members and Committees tables.

Microsoft Knowledge Base on Access

Microsoft has created a Knowledge Base of articles on all Microsoft products, including technical bulletins, bug reports, and reports of fixed bugs. This version of the Knowledge Base contains only articles on Access, and has been formatted for use with the Windows Help program.

To use the Knowledge Base, which is in a file called ACC-KB.HLP, follow these steps:

1. Copy ACC-KB.HLP into any directory—you may want to store it in your Access program directory.
2. In the Windows Program Manager, create an icon for the Knowledge Base file. Choose File New from the Program Manager menu, and choose Program Item on the New Program Object dialog box. In the Program Item Properties dialog box, enter a description like *MSKB Access.* In the Command Line text box enter:

```
winhelp.exe c:\access\acc-kb.hlp
```

substituting the path where you stored the ACC-KB.HLP file. Click on OK.

Now you can click on the icon to run Windows Help to view the Knowledge Base.

Microsoft updates the Knowledge Base file every few months. You can get a more up-to-date version of the file—and many other useful files—on the MSACCESS forum on CompuServe.

Index